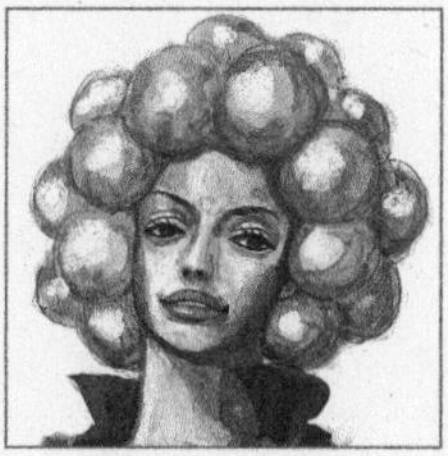

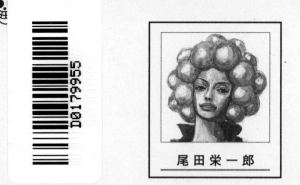

尾田栄一郎

There's a type of seedless grape that you can eat whole, skin and all. There's nothing that can make me happier than this. I love them. I love seedless watermelons and seedless persimmons. Let's keep this up and make shell-less crabs or shell-less shrimp! I can eat them whole! Boneless fish sounds good too. Those tiny bones jab the insides of my mouth from time to time, so boneless eels might be nice. But there is one thing I don't want. A manga-less life! Okay, volume 56 is starting now!

-Eiichiro Oda, 2009

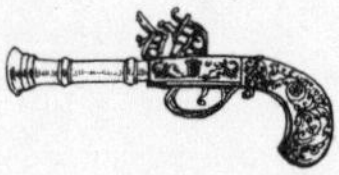

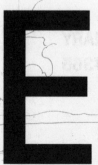

Eiichiro Oda began his manga career at the age of 17, when his one-shot cowboy manga **Wanted!** won second place in the coveted Tezuka manga awards. Oda went on to work as an assistant to some of the biggest manga artists in the industry, including Nobuhiro Watsuki, before winning the Hop Step Award for new artists. His pirate adventure **One Piece**, which debuted in **Weekly Shonen Jump** in 1997, quickly became one of the most popular manga in Japan.

ONE PIECE VOL. 56
IMPEL DOWN PART 3

SHONEN JUMP Manga Edition

This graphic novel contains material that was originally published in English in SHONEN JUMP #89–91. Artwork in the magazine may have been slightly altered from that presented here.

STORY AND ART BY EIICHIRO ODA

English Adaptation/Lance Caselman
Translation/Laabaman, HC Language Solutions, Inc.
Touch-up Art & Lettering/Vanessa Satone
Design/Sean Lee, Fawn Lau
Editor/Alexis Kirsch

ONE PIECE © 1997 by Eiichiro Oda. All rights reserved.
First published in Japan in 1997 by SHUEISHA Inc., Tokyo.
English translation rights arranged by SHUEISHA Inc.

Printed in the U.S.A.

Published by VIZ Media, LLC
P.O. Box 77010
San Francisco, CA 94107

10 9 8 7
First printing, February 2011
Seventh printing, December 2016

www.viz.com

THE WORLD'S MOST POPULAR MANGA
www.shonenjump.com

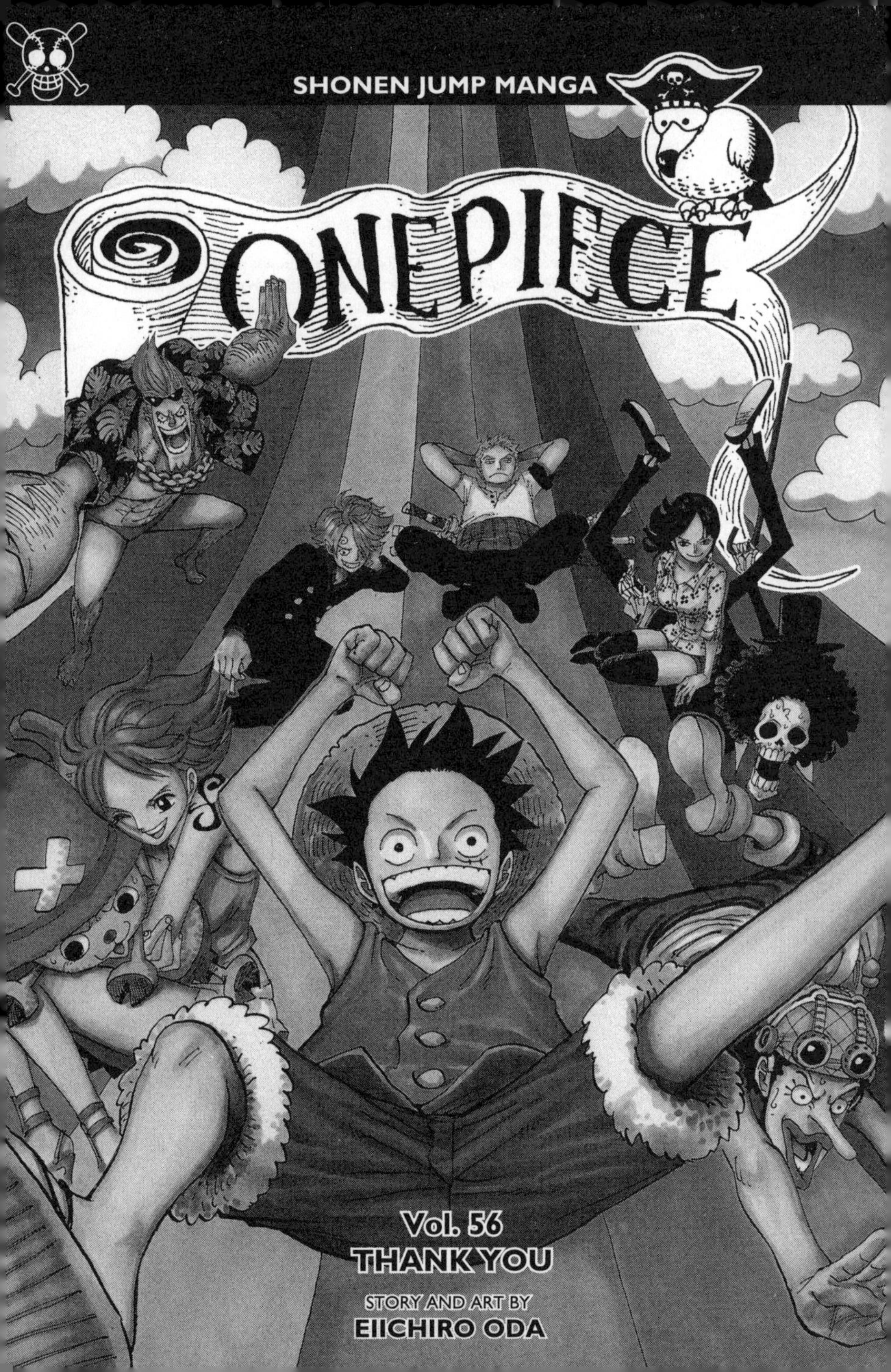

SHONEN JUMP MANGA

ONE PIECE

Vol. 56
THANK YOU

STORY AND ART BY
EIICHIRO ODA

Underwater Prison Impel Down

LEVEL 1 Crimson Hell
LEVEL 2 Beast Hell
LEVEL 3 Starvation Hell
LEVEL 4 Inferno Hell
LEVEL 5 Frozen Hell
LEVEL 5.5 New Kama Land
LEVEL 6 Infinite Hell

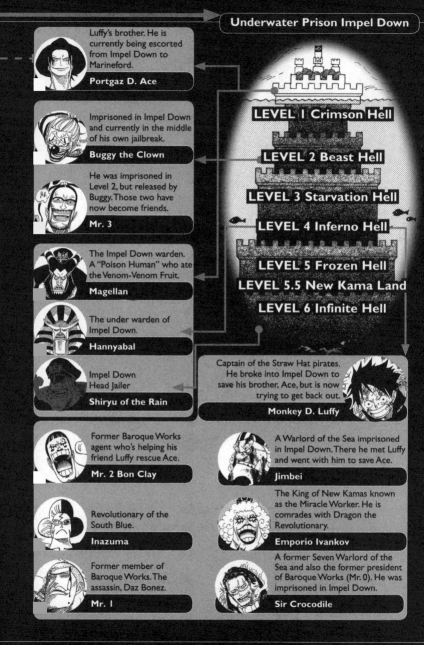

Luffy's brother. He is currently being escorted from Impel Down to Marineford.

Portgaz D. Ace

Imprisoned in Impel Down and currently in the middle of his own jailbreak.

Buggy the Clown

He was imprisoned in Level 2, but released by Buggy. Those two have now become friends.

Mr. 3

The Impel Down warden. A "Poison Human" who ate the Venom-Venom Fruit.

Magellan

The under warden of Impel Down.

Hannyabal

Impel Down Head Jailer

Shiryu of the Rain

Captain of the Straw Hat pirates. He broke into Impel Down to save his brother, Ace, but is now trying to get back out.

Monkey D. Luffy

Former Baroque Works agent who's helping his friend Luffy rescue Ace.

Mr. 2 Bon Clay

A Warlord of the Sea imprisoned in Impel Down. There he met Luffy and went with him to save Ace.

Jimbei

Revolutionary of the South Blue.

Inazuma

The King of New Kamas known as the Miracle Worker. He is comrades with Dragon the Revolutionary.

Emporio Ivankov

Former member of Baroque Works. The assassin, Daz Bonez.

Mr. 1

A former Seven Warlord of the Sea and also the former president of Baroque Works (Mr. 0). He was imprisoned in Impel Down.

Sir Crocodile

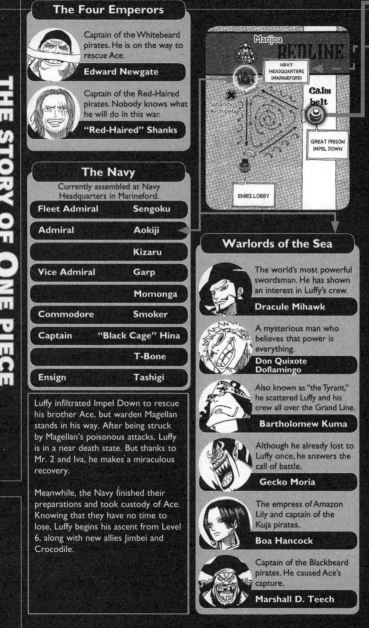

THE STORY OF ONE PIECE

Volume 56

The Four Emperors

Captain of the Whitebeard pirates. He is on the way to rescue Ace.

Edward Newgate

Captain of the Red-Haired pirates. Nobody knows what he will do in this war.

"Red-Haired" Shanks

Marijoa
REDLINE
NAVY HEADQUARTERS (MARINEFORD)
Calm belt
Sabaody Archipelago
GREAT PRISON IMPEL DOWN
ENIES LOBBY

The Navy

Currently assembled at Navy Headquarters in Marineford.

Fleet Admiral	Sengoku
Admiral	Aokiji
	Kizaru
Vice Admiral	Garp
	Momonga
Commodore	Smoker
Captain	"Black Cage" Hina
	T-Bone
Ensign	Tashigi

Warlords of the Sea

The world's most powerful swordsman. He has shown an interest in Luffy's crew.

Dracule Mihawk

A mysterious man who believes that power is everything.

Don Quixote Doflamingo

Also known as "the Tyrant," he scattered Luffy and his crew all over the Grand Line.

Bartholomew Kuma

Although he already lost to Luffy once, he answers the call of battle.

Gecko Moria

The empress of Amazon Lily and captain of the Kuja pirates.

Boa Hancock

Captain of the Blackbeard pirates. He caused Ace's capture.

Marshall D. Teech

Luffy infiltrated Impel Down to rescue his brother Ace, but warden Magellan stands in his way. After being struck by Magellan's poisonous attacks, Luffy is in a near death state. But thanks to Mr. 2 and Iva, he makes a miraculous recovery.

Meanwhile, the Navy finished their preparations and took custody of Ace. Knowing that they have no time to lose, Luffy begins his ascent from Level 6, along with new allies Jimbei and Crocodile.

IMPEL DOWN

ONE PIECE

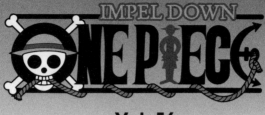

Vol. 56
Thank You

CONTENTS

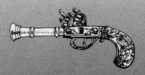

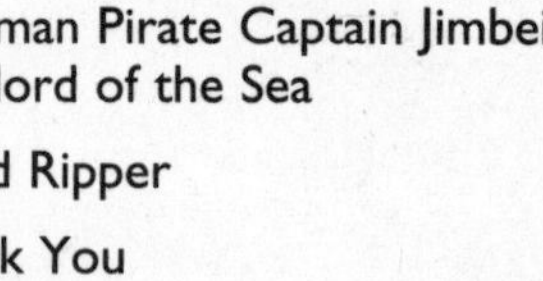

Chapter 542:
YET ANOTHER EPIC INCIDENT

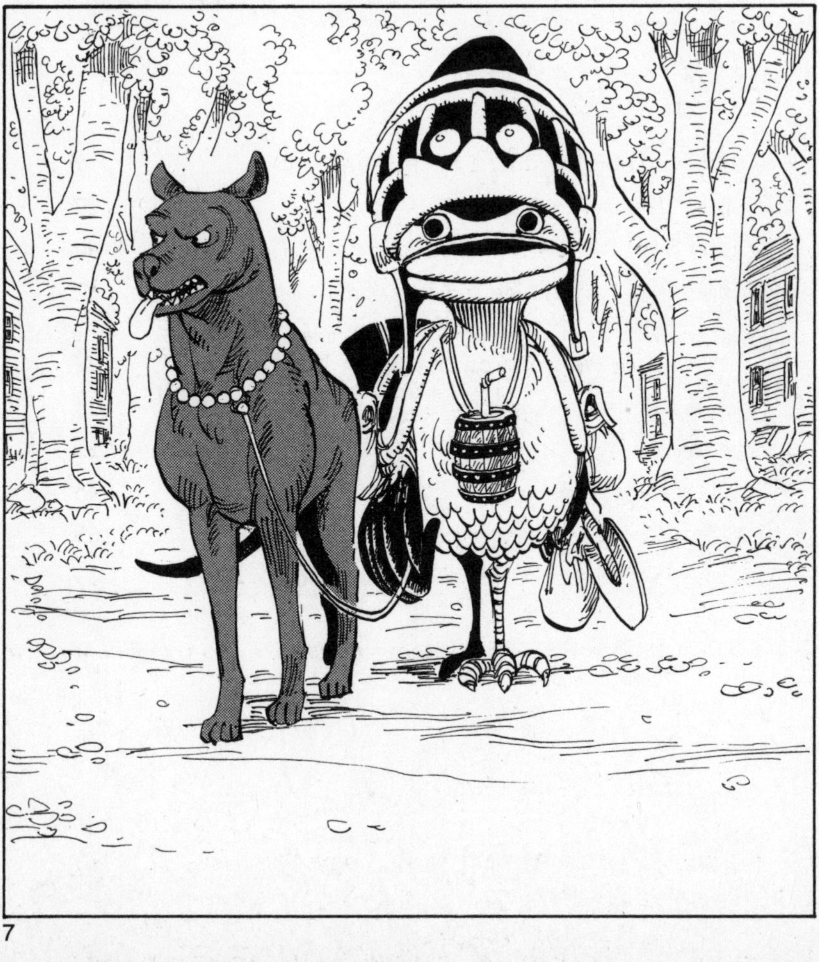

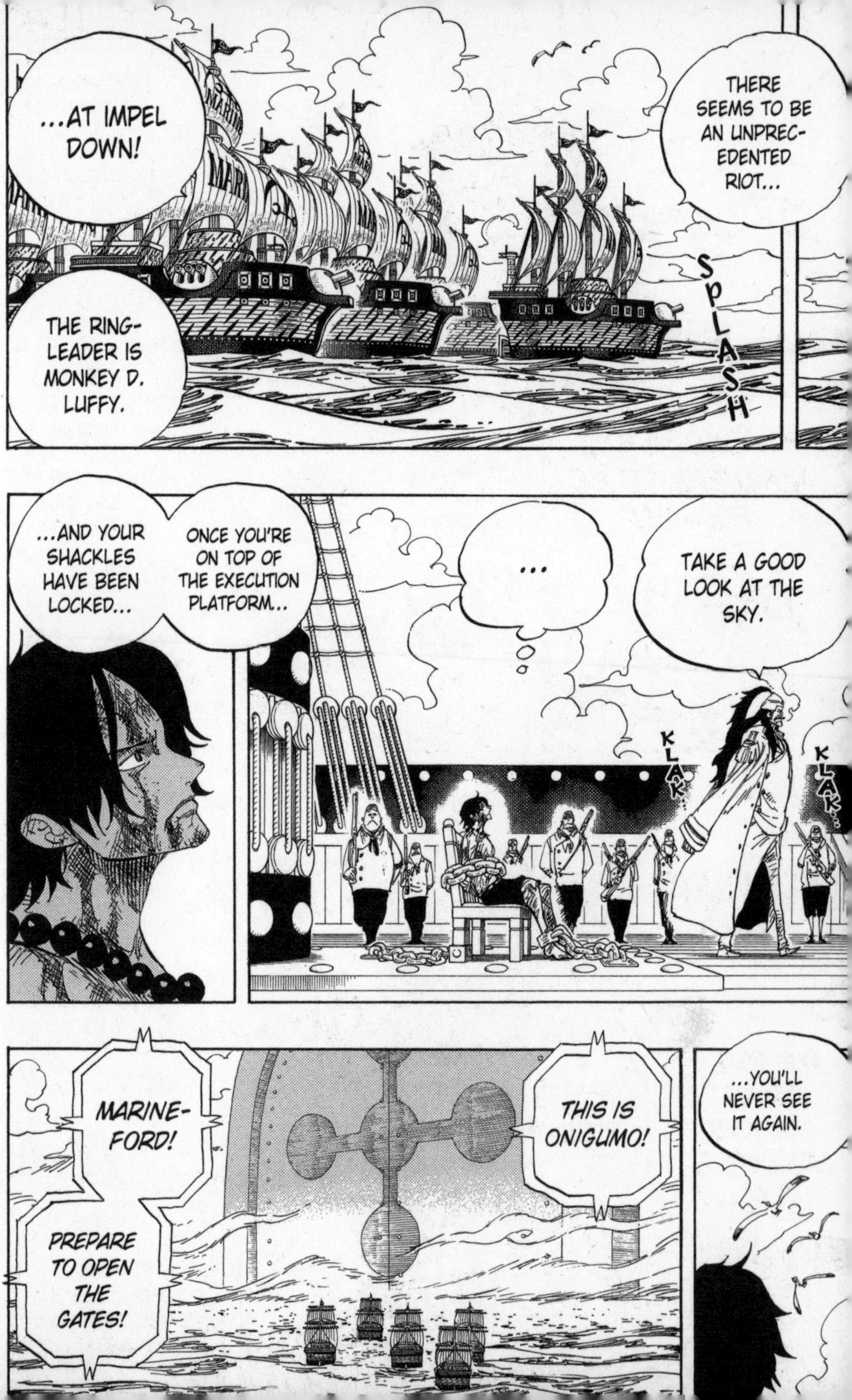
THERE SEEMS TO BE AN UNPREC-EDENTED RIOT...
SPLASH
...AT IMPEL DOWN!
THE RING-LEADER IS MONKEY D. LUFFY.
TAKE A GOOD LOOK AT THE SKY.
KLAK...
KLAK...
...
ONCE YOU'RE ON TOP OF THE EXECUTION PLATFORM...
...AND YOUR SHACKLES HAVE BEEN LOCKED...
...YOU'LL NEVER SEE IT AGAIN.
THIS IS ONIGUMO!
MARINE-FORD!
PREPARE TO OPEN THE GATES!

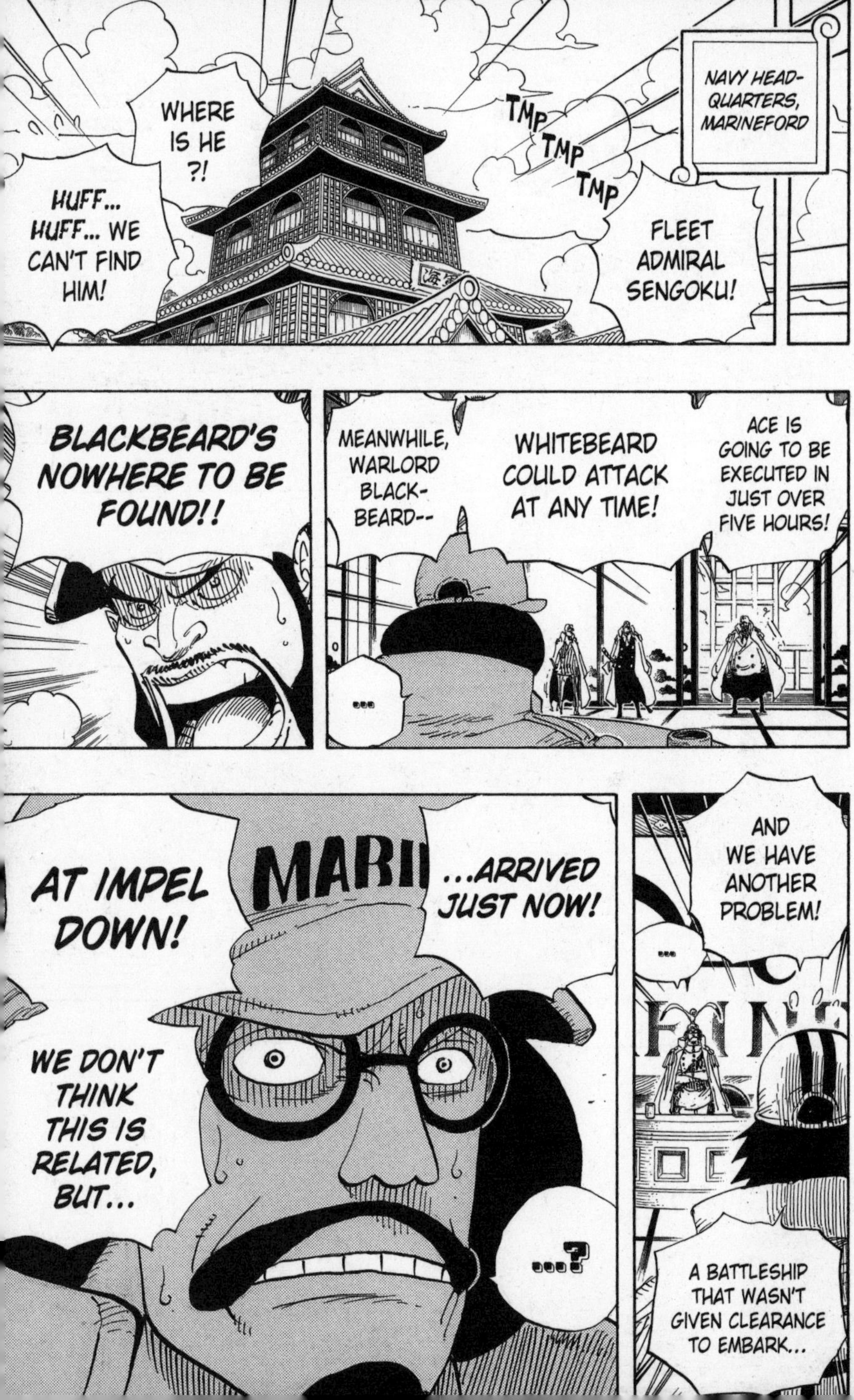
NAVY HEADQUARTERS, MARINEFORD
TMP TMP TMP
FLEET ADMIRAL SENGOKU!
WHERE IS HE ?!
HUFF... HUFF... WE CAN'T FIND HIM!
ACE IS GOING TO BE EXECUTED IN JUST OVER FIVE HOURS!
WHITEBEARD COULD ATTACK AT ANY TIME!
MEANWHILE, WARLORD BLACKBEARD--
...
BLACKBEARD'S NOWHERE TO BE FOUND!!
AND WE HAVE ANOTHER PROBLEM!
...
A BATTLESHIP THAT WASN'T GIVEN CLEARANCE TO EMBARK...
...ARRIVED JUST NOW!
AT IMPEL DOWN!
WE DON'T THINK THIS IS RELATED, BUT...
...?

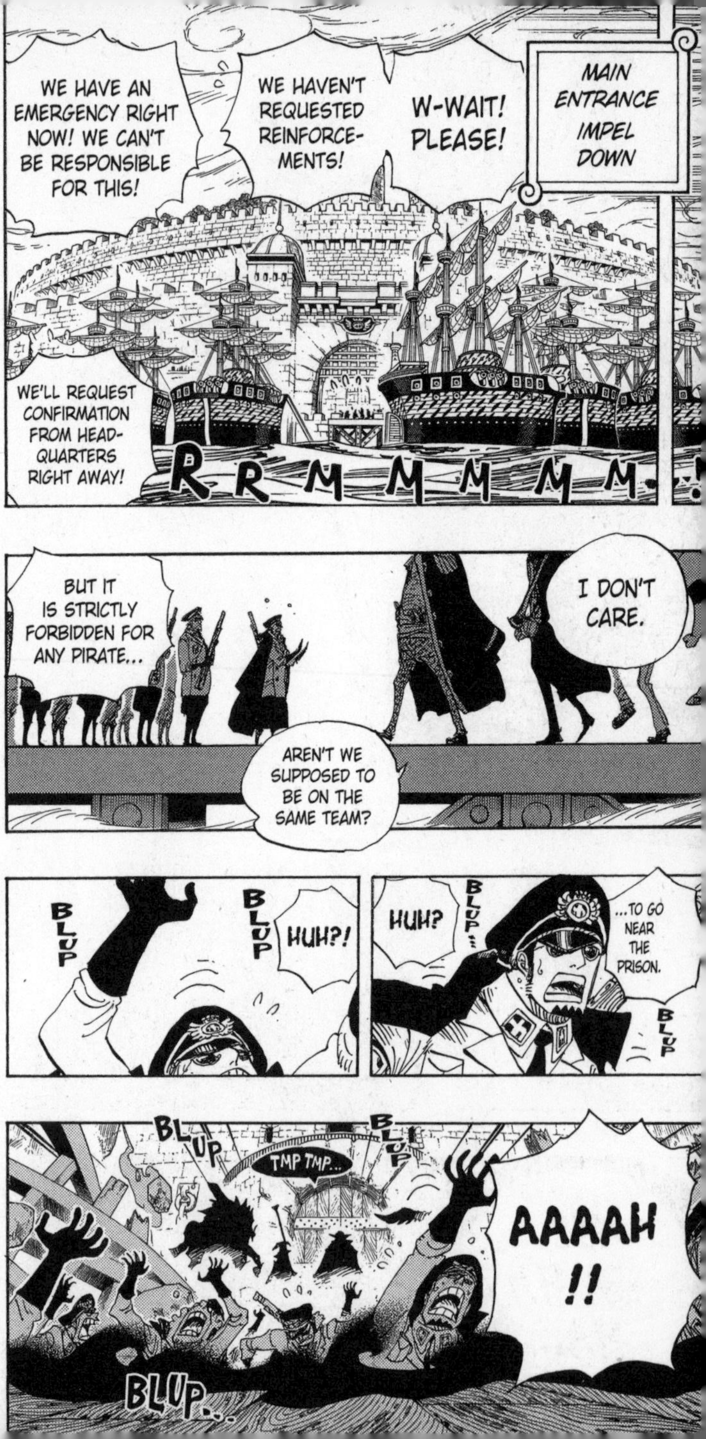
MAIN ENTRANCE IMPEL DOWN
W-WAIT! PLEASE!
WE HAVEN'T REQUESTED REINFORCEMENTS!
WE HAVE AN EMERGENCY RIGHT NOW! WE CAN'T BE RESPONSIBLE FOR THIS!
WE'LL REQUEST CONFIRMATION FROM HEADQUARTERS RIGHT AWAY!
RRMMMMM..!
I DON'T CARE.
BUT IT IS STRICTLY FORBIDDEN FOR ANY PIRATE...
AREN'T WE SUPPOSED TO BE ON THE SAME TEAM?
...TO GO NEAR THE PRISON.
BLUP
BLUP...
HUH?
HUH?!
BLUP
BLUP
AAAAH!!
BLUP
TMP TMP...
BLUP
BLUP...
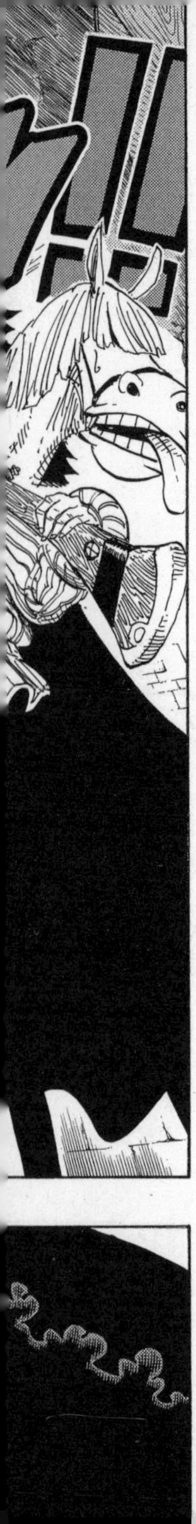

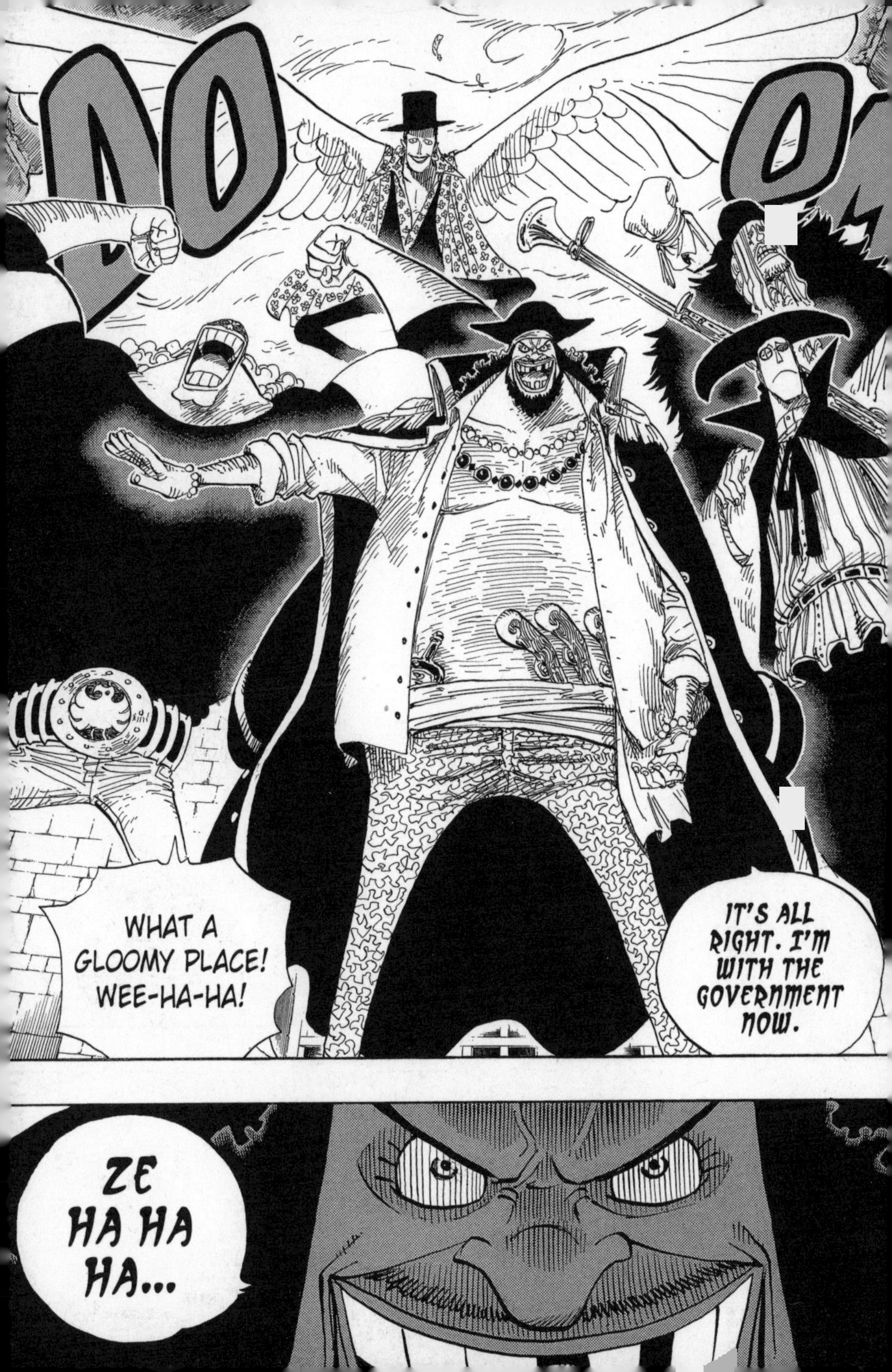
IT'S ALL RIGHT. I'M WITH THE GOVERNMENT NOW.
WHAT A GLOOMY PLACE! WEE-HA-HA!
ZE HA HA HA...

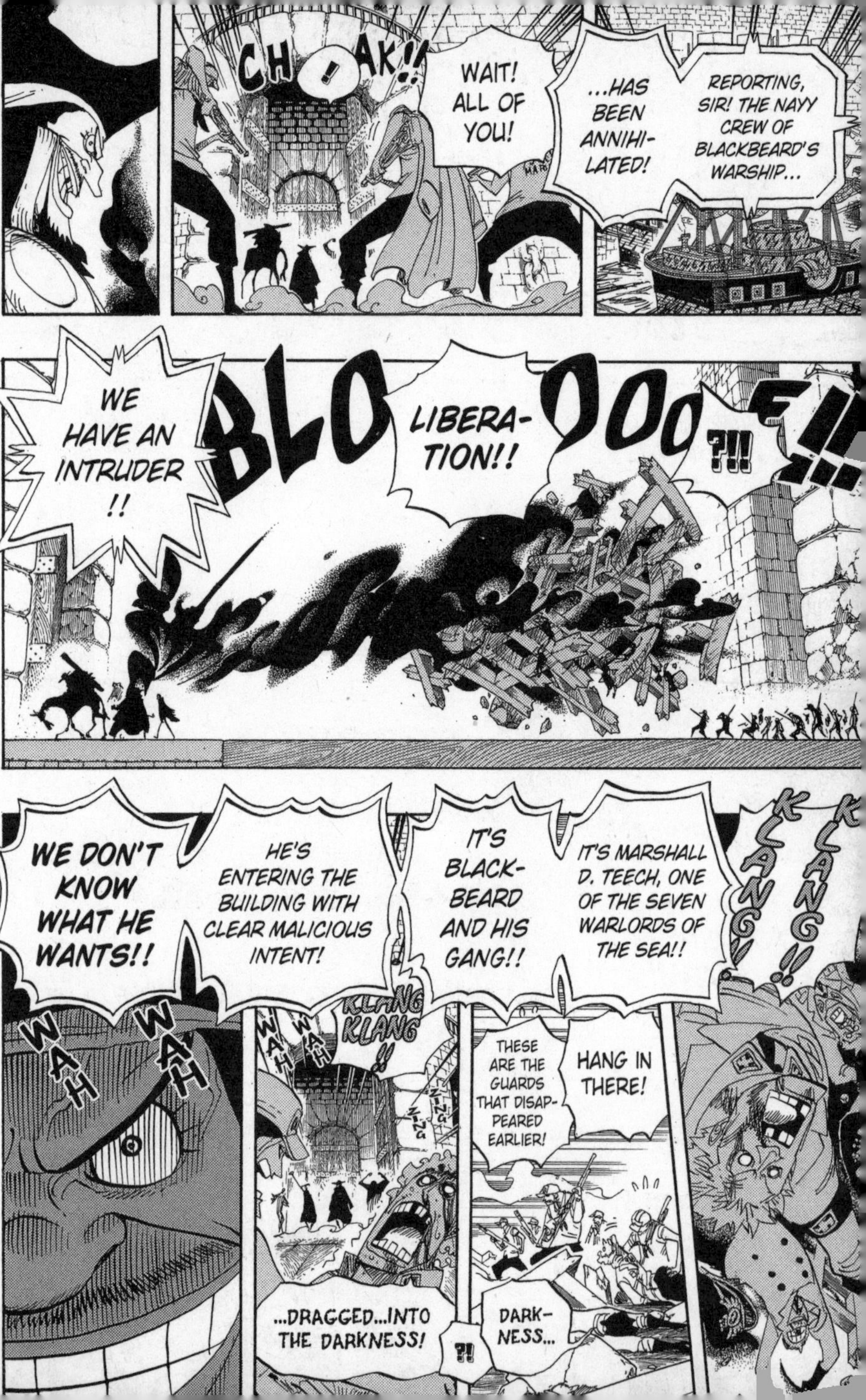
REPORTING, SIR! THE NAVY CREW OF BLACKBEARD'S WARSHIP...
...HAS BEEN ANNIHI-LATED!
WAIT! ALL OF YOU!
CH!AK!!
BLOOOOF!!
?!!
LIBERA-TION!!
WE HAVE AN INTRUDER !!
KLANG KLANG!!
KLANG KLANG!!
IT'S MARSHALL D. TEECH, ONE OF THE SEVEN WARLORDS OF THE SEA!!
IT'S BLACK-BEARD AND HIS GANG!!
HE'S ENTERING THE BUILDING WITH CLEAR MALICIOUS INTENT!
WE DON'T KNOW WHAT HE WANTS!!
HANG IN THERE!
THESE ARE THE GUARDS THAT DISAP-PEARED EARLIER!
DARK-NESS...
?!
ZING ZING
KLANG KLANG !!
WAH WAH
...DRAGGED...INTO THE DARKNESS!
WAH WAH

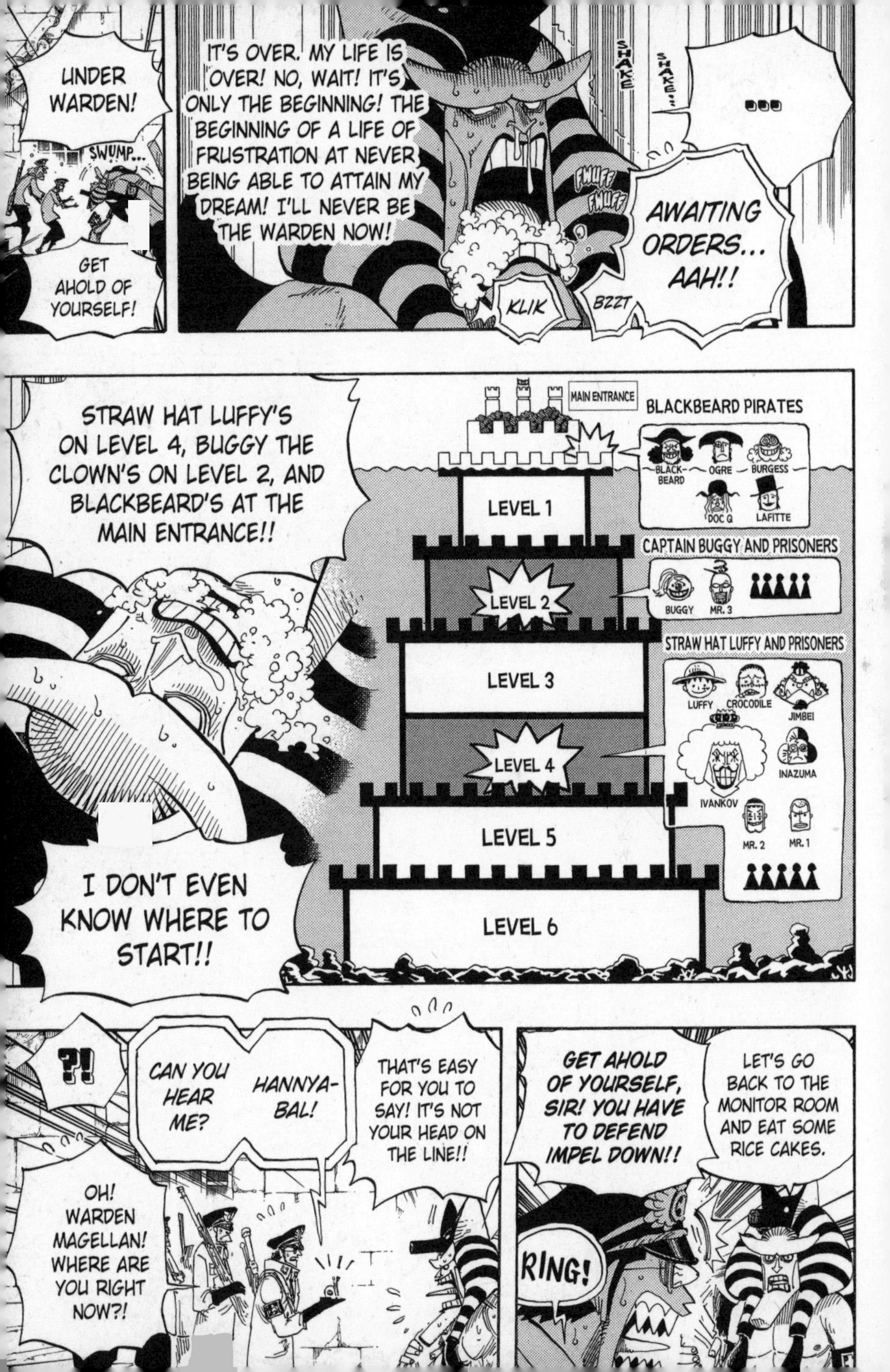

...
SHAKE
SHAKE...
AWAITING ORDERS... AAH!!
FMUFF
FMUFF
BZZT
KLIK
IT'S OVER. MY LIFE IS OVER! NO, WAIT! IT'S ONLY THE BEGINNING! THE BEGINNING OF A LIFE OF FRUSTRATION AT NEVER BEING ABLE TO ATTAIN MY DREAM! I'LL NEVER BE THE WARDEN NOW!
UNDER WARDEN!
SWUMP...
GET AHOLD OF YOURSELF!
MAIN ENTRANCE
BLACKBEARD PIRATES
BLACK-BEARD
OGRE
BURGESS
DOC Q
LAFITTE
LEVEL 1
CAPTAIN BUGGY AND PRISONERS
LEVEL 2
BUGGY
MR. 3
STRAW HAT LUFFY AND PRISONERS
LEVEL 3
LUFFY
CROCODILE
JIMBEI
LEVEL 4
IVANKOV
INAZUMA
LEVEL 5
MR. 2
MR. 1
LEVEL 6
STRAW HAT LUFFY'S ON LEVEL 4, BUGGY THE CLOWN'S ON LEVEL 2, AND BLACKBEARD'S AT THE MAIN ENTRANCE!!
I DON'T EVEN KNOW WHERE TO START!!
LET'S GO BACK TO THE MONITOR ROOM AND EAT SOME RICE CAKES.
GET AHOLD OF YOURSELF, SIR! YOU HAVE TO DEFEND IMPEL DOWN!!
RING!
THAT'S EASY FOR YOU TO SAY! IT'S NOT YOUR HEAD ON THE LINE!!
HANNYA-BAL!
CAN YOU HEAR ME?
?!
OH! WARDEN MAGELLAN! WHERE ARE YOU RIGHT NOW?!

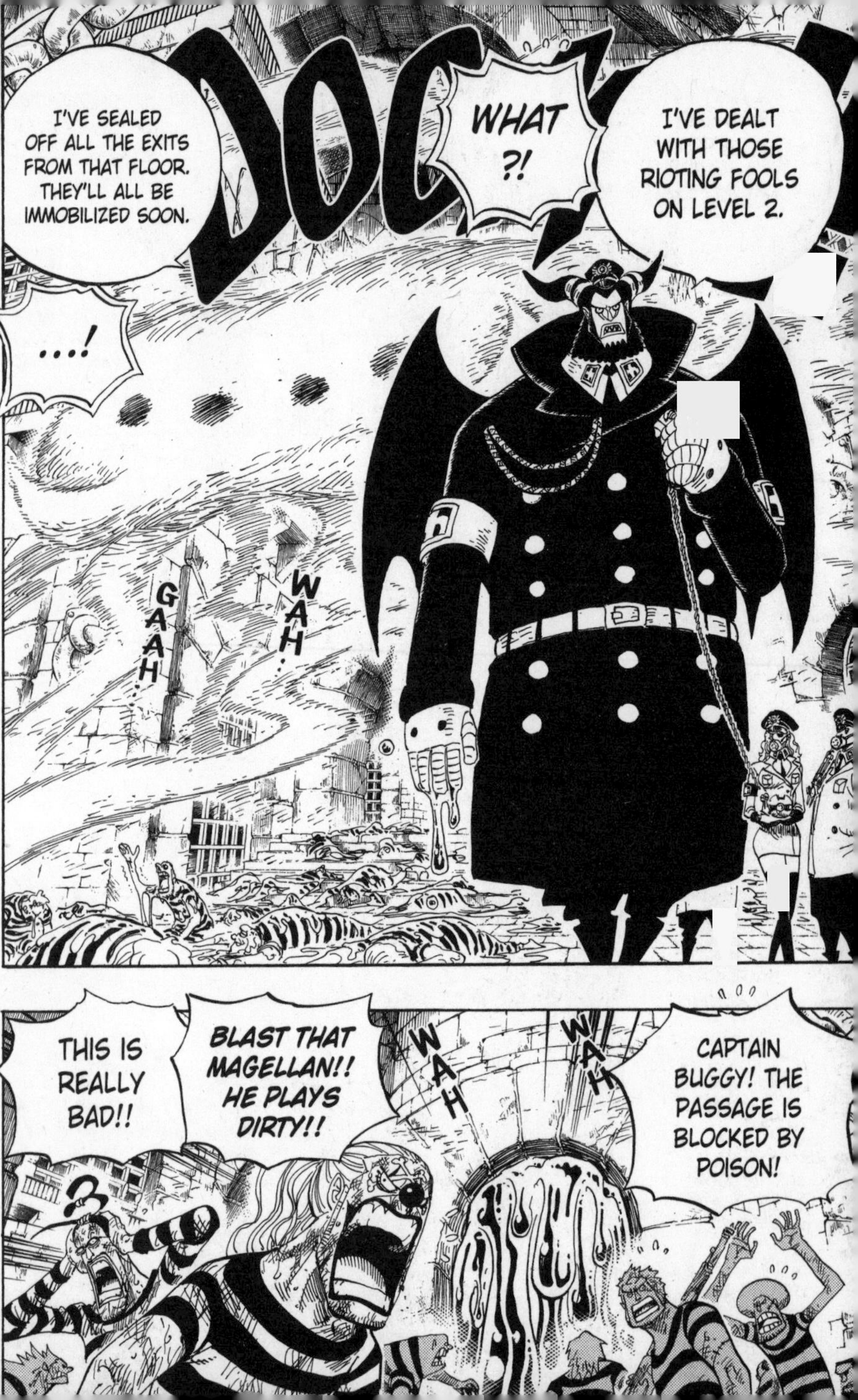
I'VE DEALT WITH THOSE RIOTING FOOLS ON LEVEL 2.
WHAT?!
I'VE SEALED OFF ALL THE EXITS FROM THAT FLOOR. THEY'LL ALL BE IMMOBILIZED SOON.
...!
WAH...
GAAH...
CAPTAIN BUGGY! THE PASSAGE IS BLOCKED BY POISON!
WAH
WAH
BLAST THAT MAGELLAN!! HE PLAYS DIRTY!!
THIS IS REALLY BAD!!

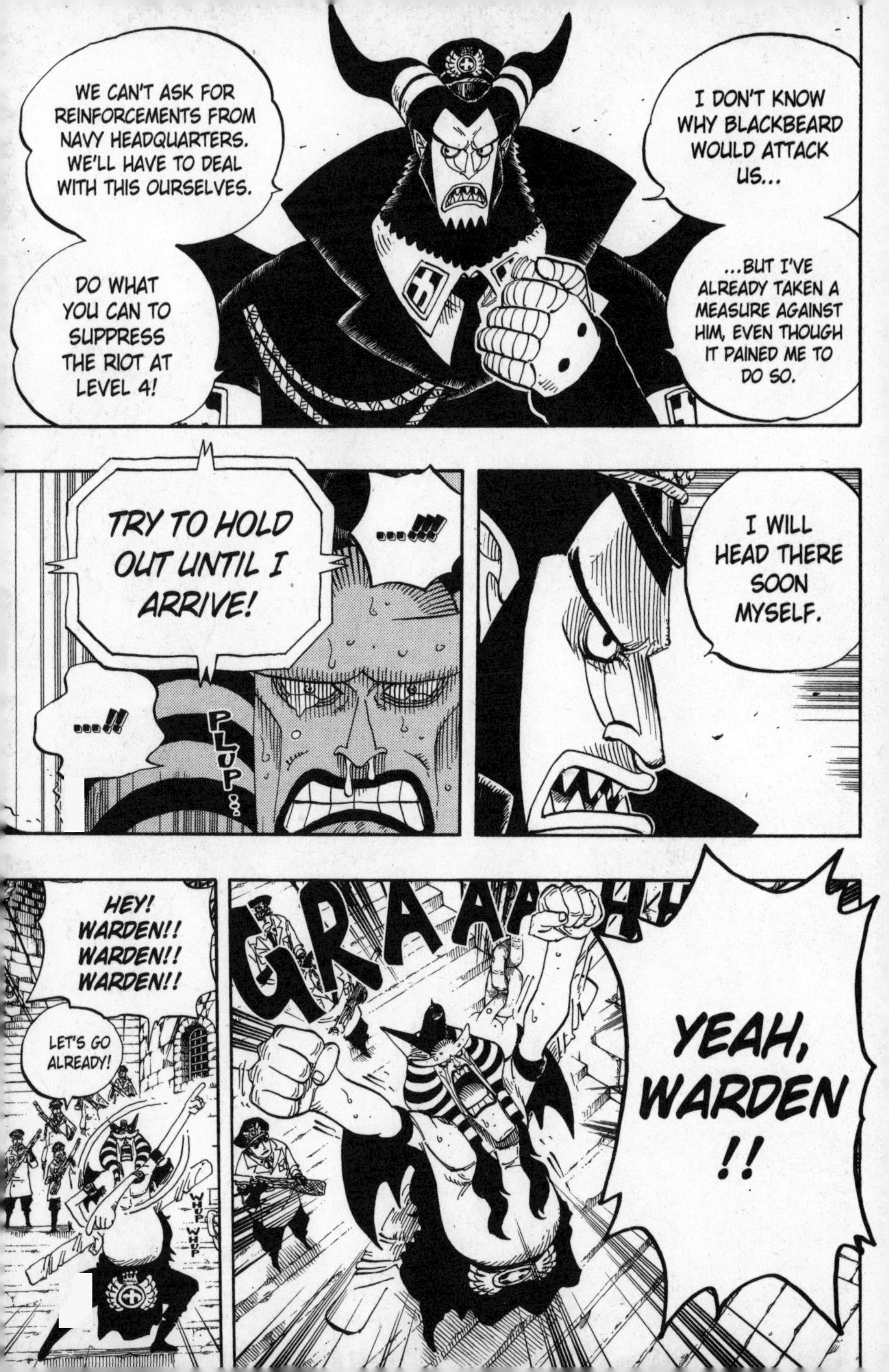
I DON'T KNOW WHY BLACKBEARD WOULD ATTACK US...
...BUT I'VE ALREADY TAKEN A MEASURE AGAINST HIM, EVEN THOUGH IT PAINED ME TO DO SO.
WE CAN'T ASK FOR REINFORCEMENTS FROM NAVY HEADQUARTERS. WE'LL HAVE TO DEAL WITH THIS OURSELVES.
DO WHAT YOU CAN TO SUPPRESS THE RIOT AT LEVEL 4!
I WILL HEAD THERE SOON MYSELF.
TRY TO HOLD OUT UNTIL I ARRIVE!
...!!!
...!!
PLUP..
GRAAAAH
YEAH, WARDEN!!
HEY! WARDEN!! WARDEN!! WARDEN!!
LET'S GO ALREADY!
WHUP WHUP

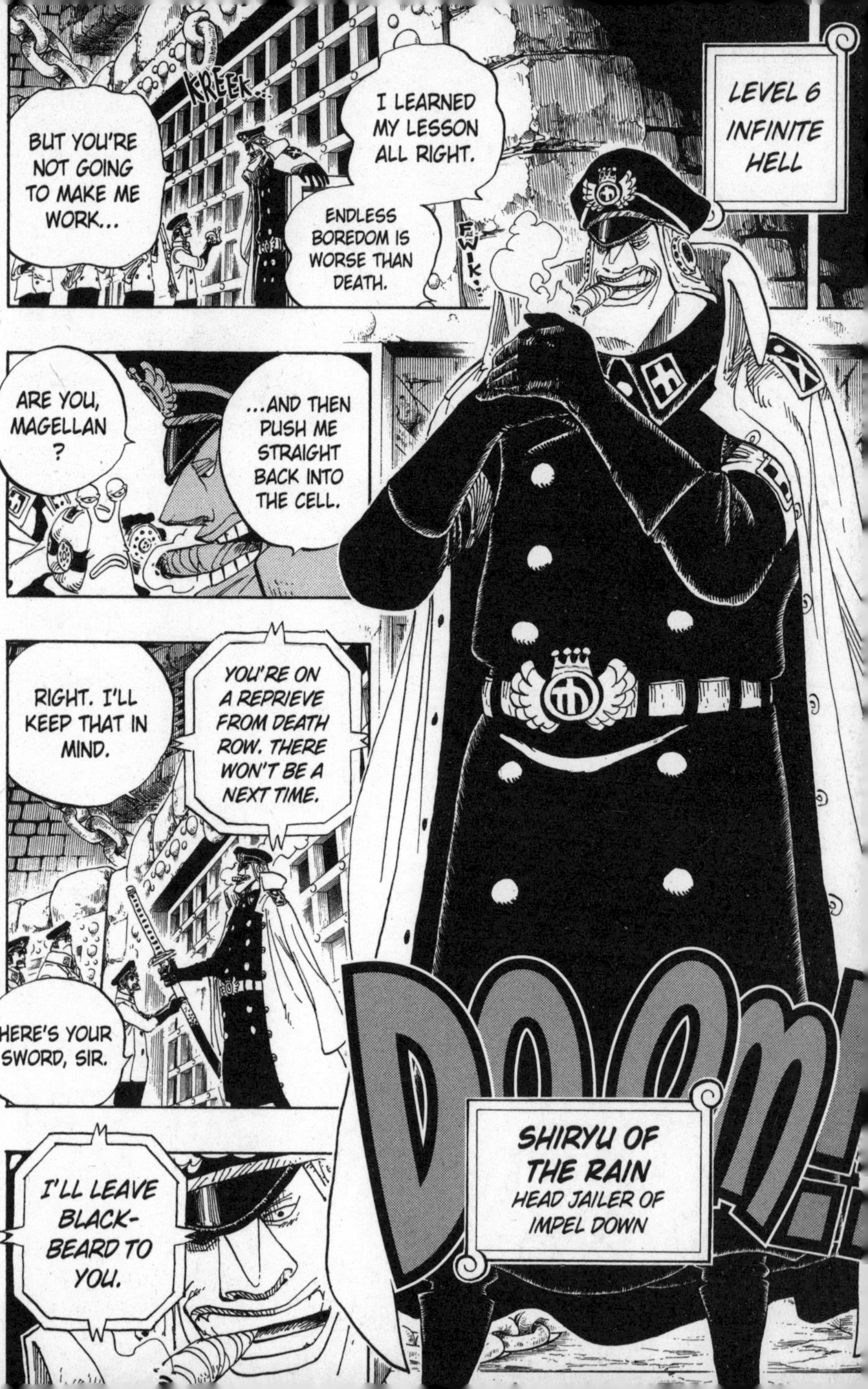
LEVEL 6
INFINITE
HELL
KREEK..
I LEARNED MY LESSON ALL RIGHT.
ENDLESS BOREDOM IS WORSE THAN DEATH.
FWIK..
BUT YOU'RE NOT GOING TO MAKE ME WORK...
DOOM!!
SHIRYU OF THE RAIN
HEAD JAILER OF IMPEL DOWN
...AND THEN PUSH ME STRAIGHT BACK INTO THE CELL.
ARE YOU, MAGELLAN ?
YOU'RE ON A REPRIEVE FROM DEATH ROW. THERE WON'T BE A NEXT TIME.
RIGHT. I'LL KEEP THAT IN MIND.
HERE'S YOUR SWORD, SIR.
I'LL LEAVE BLACK-BEARD TO YOU.

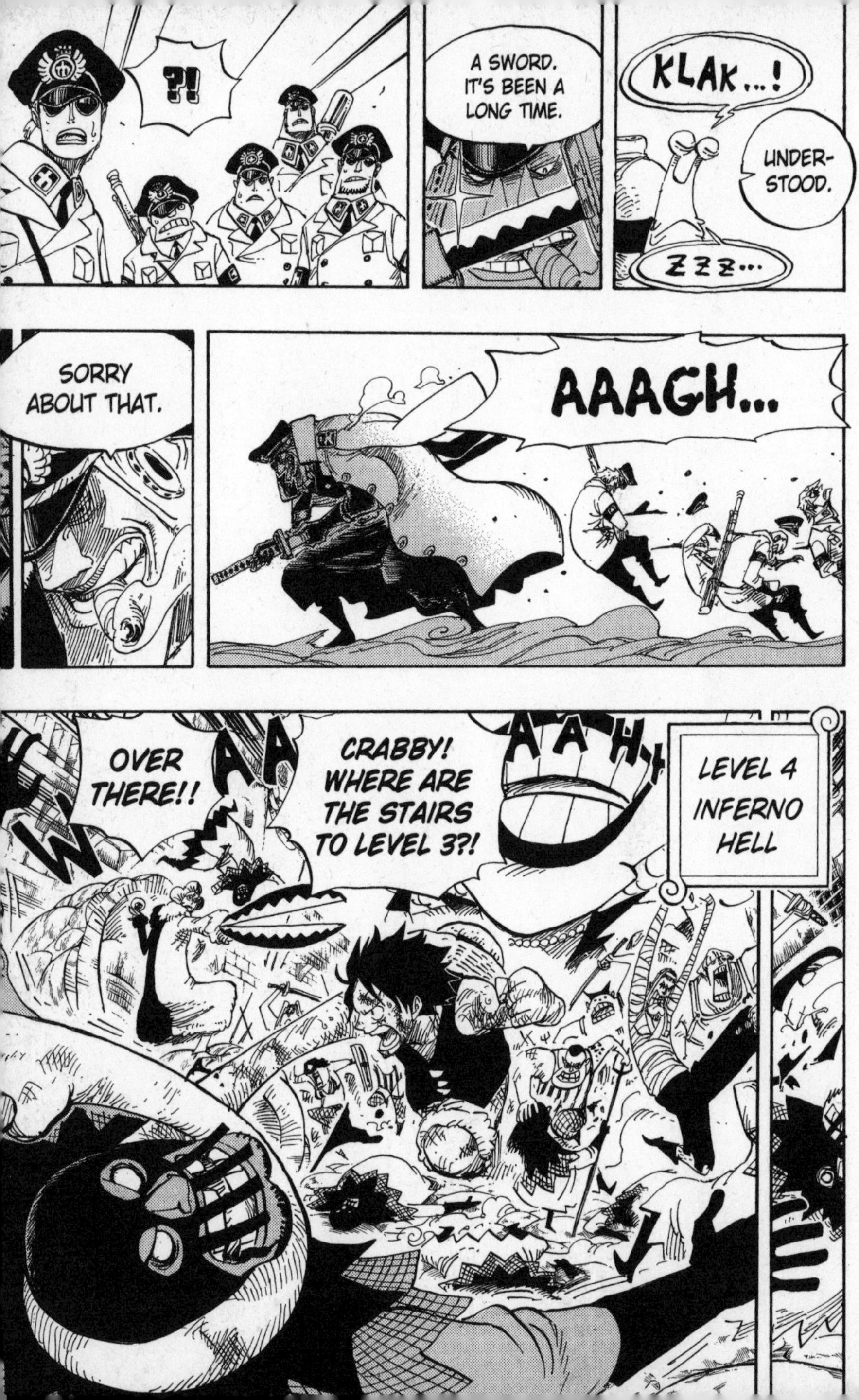
KLAK...!
UNDER-STOOD.
ZZZ...
A SWORD. IT'S BEEN A LONG TIME.
?!
AAAGH...
SORRY ABOUT THAT.
LEVEL 4 INFERNO HELL
CRABBY! WHERE ARE THE STAIRS TO LEVEL 3?!
OVER THERE!!

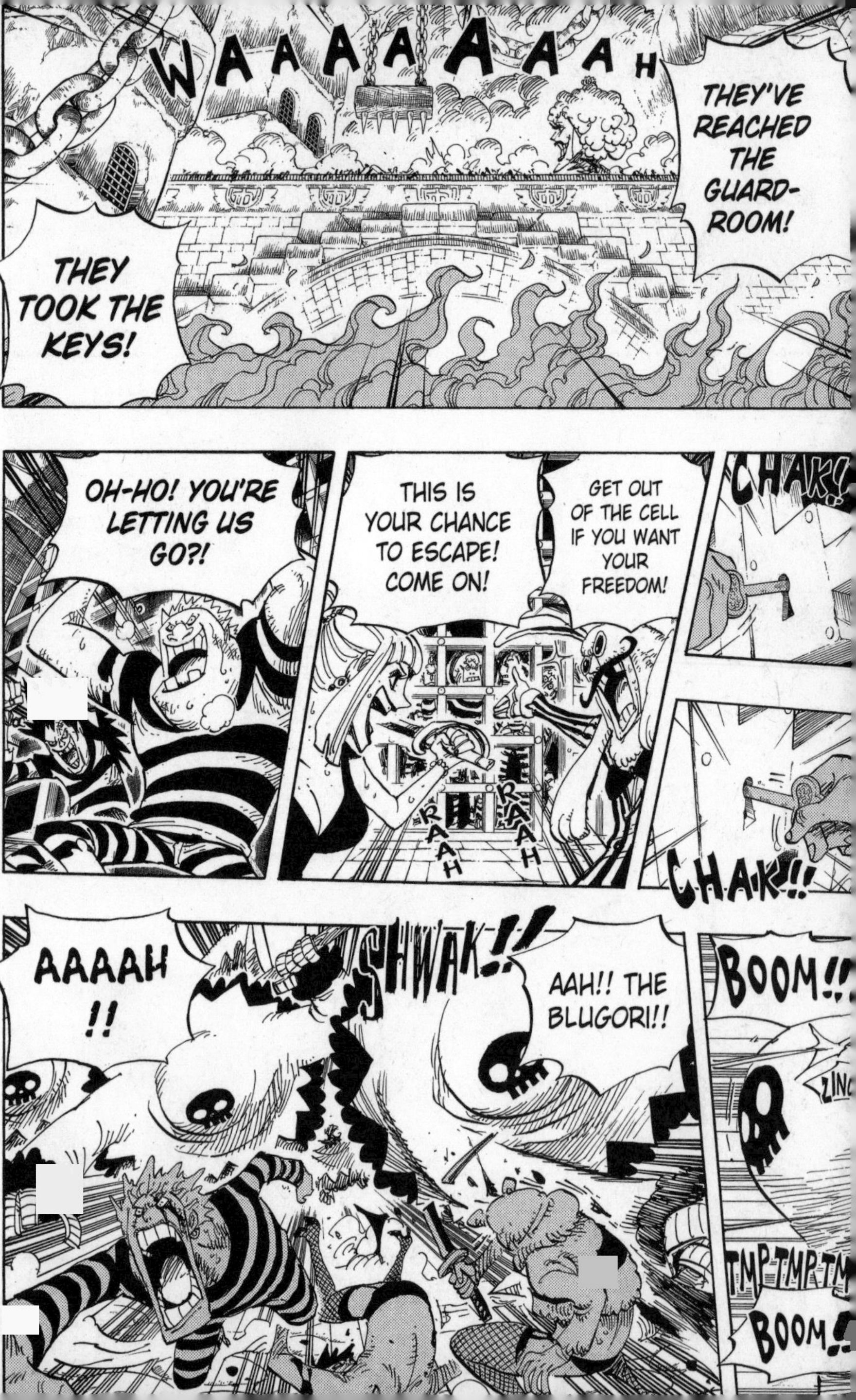
THEY'VE REACHED THE GUARD-ROOM!
WAAAAAAAH
THEY TOOK THE KEYS!
CHAK!
CHAK!!
GET OUT OF THE CELL IF YOU WANT YOUR FREEDOM!
THIS IS YOUR CHANCE TO ESCAPE! COME ON!
RAAH
RAAH
OH-HO! YOU'RE LETTING US GO?!
BOOM!!
TMP TMP TM
BOOM!
AAH!! THE BLUGORI!!
SHWAK!!
AAAAH !!

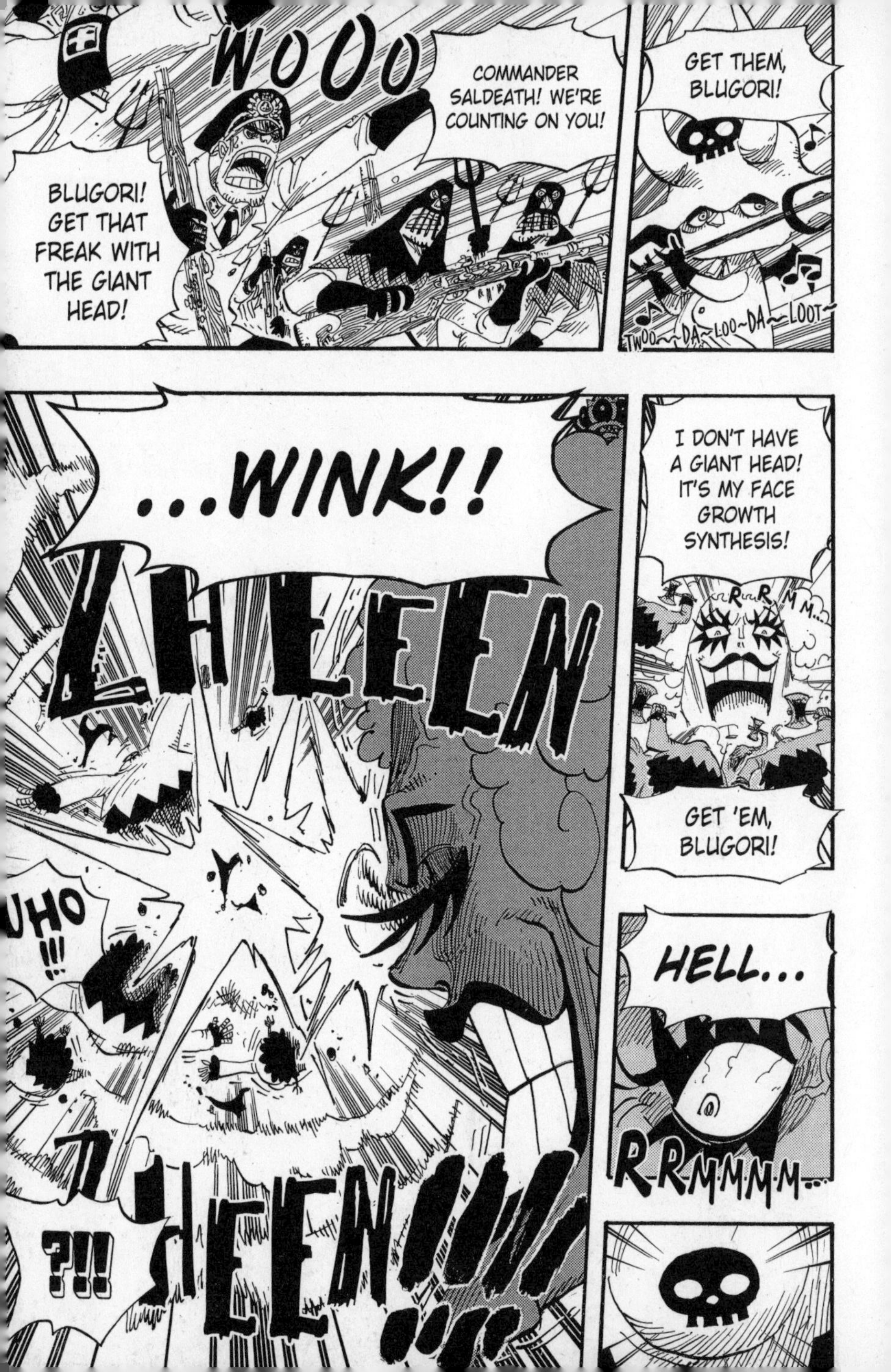
GET THEM, BLUGORI!
TWOO~~DA~LOO~DA~LOOT~
WOOO
COMMANDER SALDEATH! WE'RE COUNTING ON YOU!
BLUGORI! GET THAT FREAK WITH THE GIANT HEAD!
I DON'T HAVE A GIANT HEAD! IT'S MY FACE GROWTH SYNTHESIS!
RRRMMM...
GET 'EM, BLUGORI!
HELL...
R-R-MMMMM...
...WINK!!
ZHEEEN
UHO!!!
?!!
SHEEN!!!!

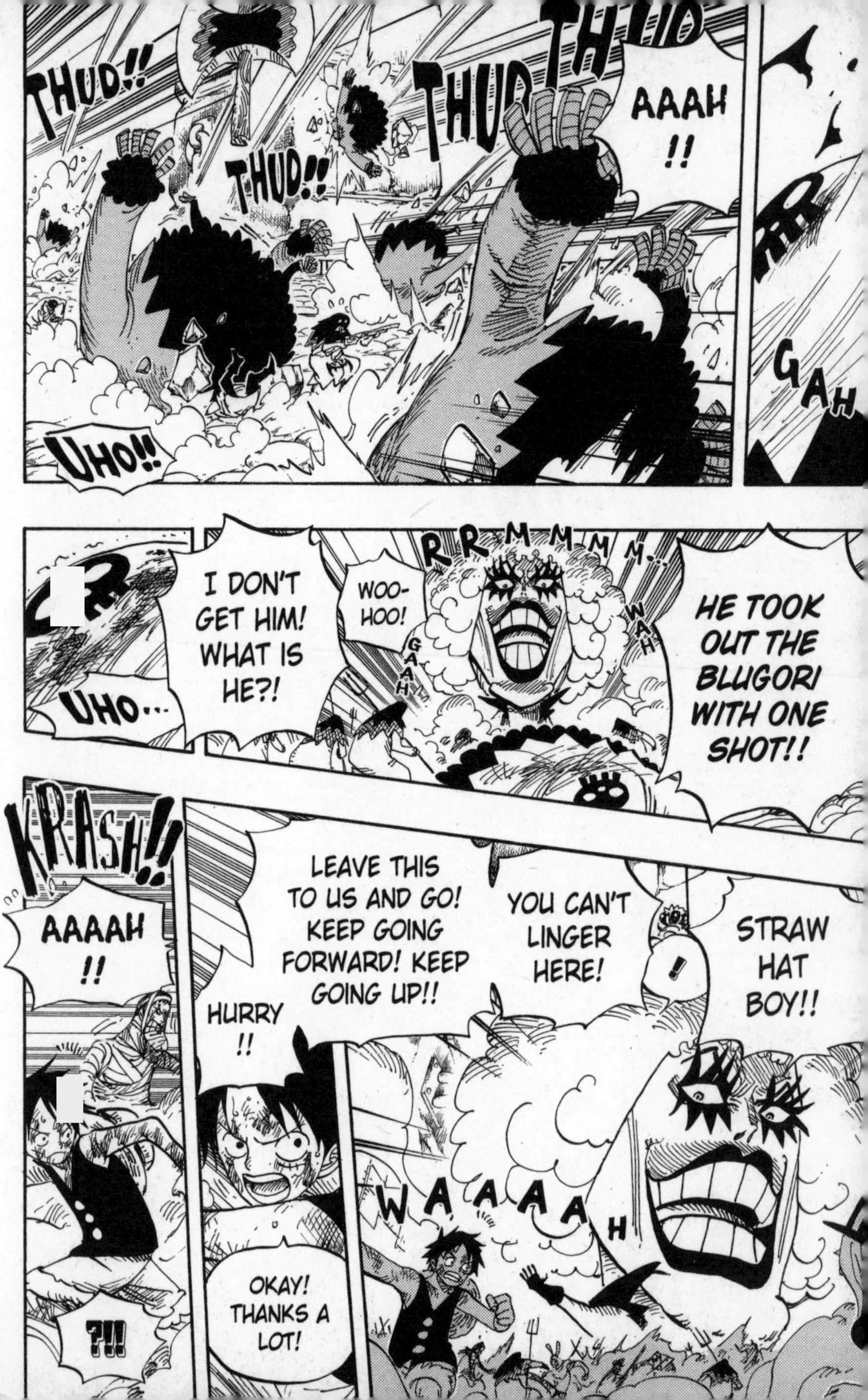
RRR
GAH
AAAH!!
THUD
THUD
THUD!!
THUD!!
UHO!!
HE TOOK OUT THE BLUGORI WITH ONE SHOT!!
RRMMMMM...
WAH
GAAH
WOO-HOO!
I DON'T GET HIM! WHAT IS HE?!
UHO...
STRAW HAT BOY!!
!
YOU CAN'T LINGER HERE!
LEAVE THIS TO US AND GO! KEEP GOING FORWARD! KEEP GOING UP!!
HURRY!!
WAAAAAH
OKAY! THANKS A LOT!
KRASH!!
AAAAH!!
?!!

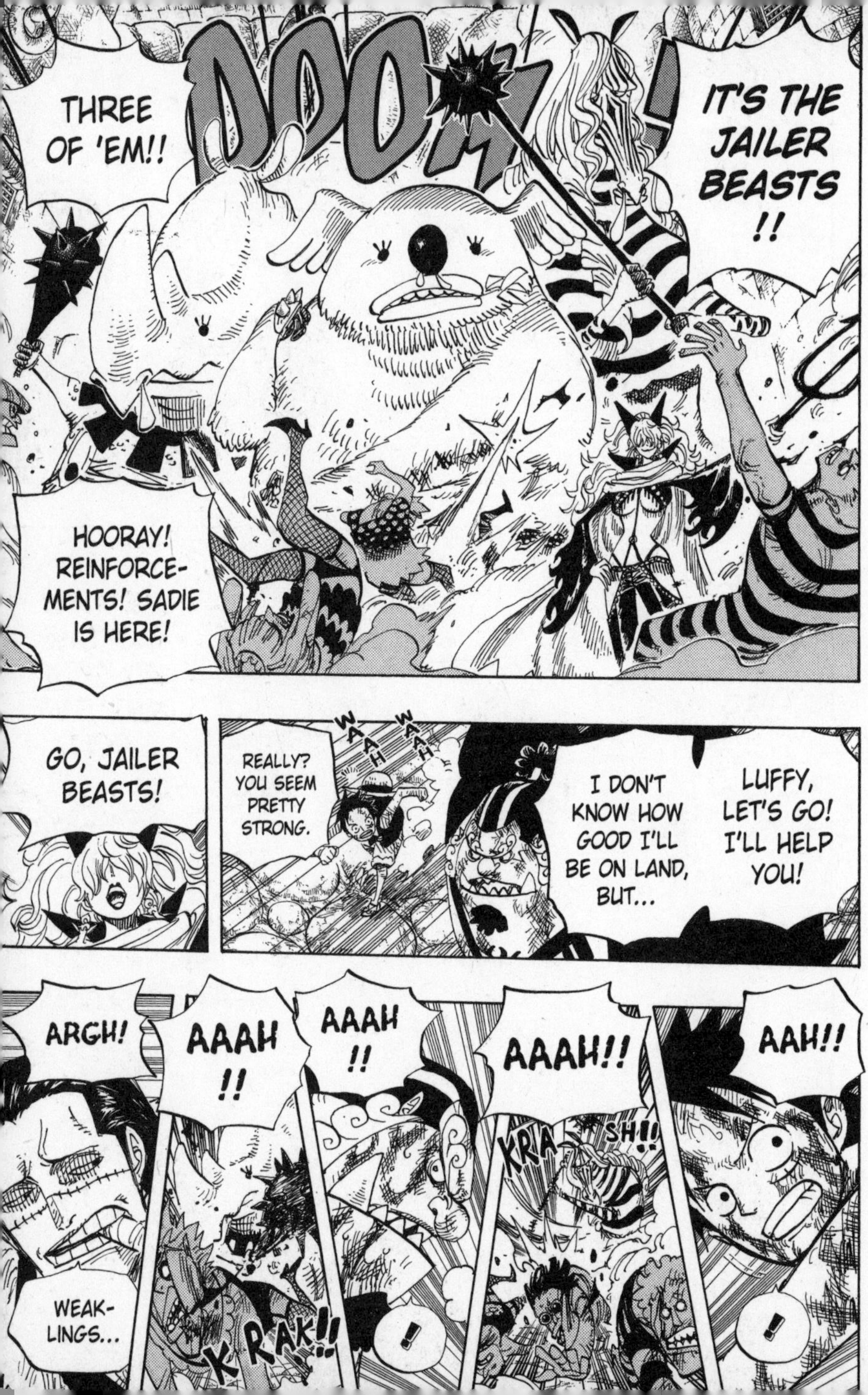

DOOM!
IT'S THE JAILER BEASTS!!
THREE OF 'EM!!
HOORAY! REINFORCEMENTS! SADIE IS HERE!
LUFFY, LET'S GO! I'LL HELP YOU!
I DON'T KNOW HOW GOOD I'LL BE ON LAND, BUT...
REALLY? YOU SEEM PRETTY STRONG.
WAAH WAAH
GO, JAILER BEASTS!
AAH!!
!
AAAH!!
KRASH!!
AAAH !!
!
AAAH !!
KRAK!!
ARGH!
WEAK-LINGS...

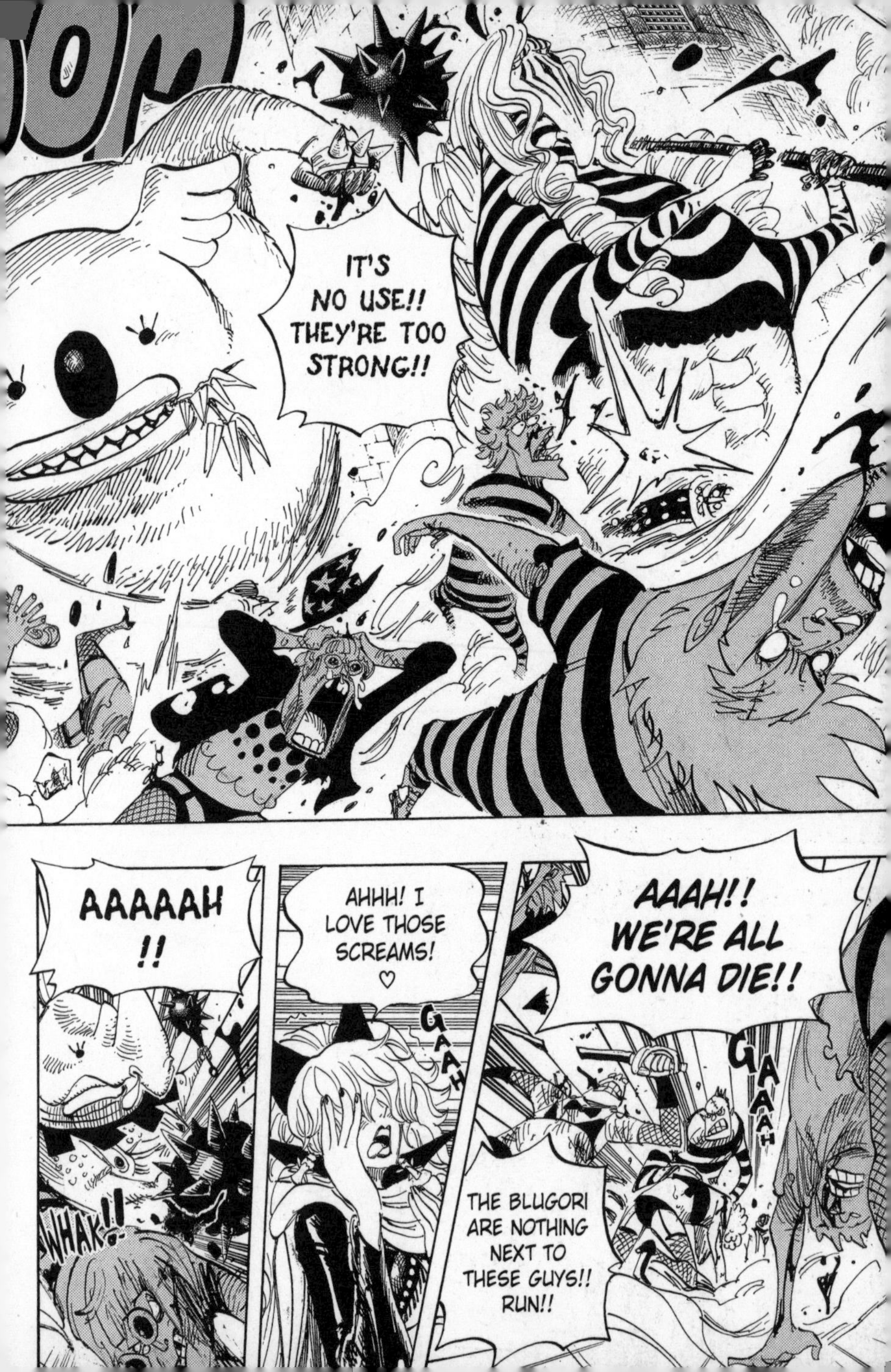

IT'S NO USE!! THEY'RE TOO STRONG!!
AAAH!! WE'RE ALL GONNA DIE!!
GAAAAH
THE BLUGORI ARE NOTHING NEXT TO THESE GUYS!! RUN!!
AHHH! I LOVE THOSE SCREAMS! ♡
GAAH
AAAAAH !!
WHAK!!

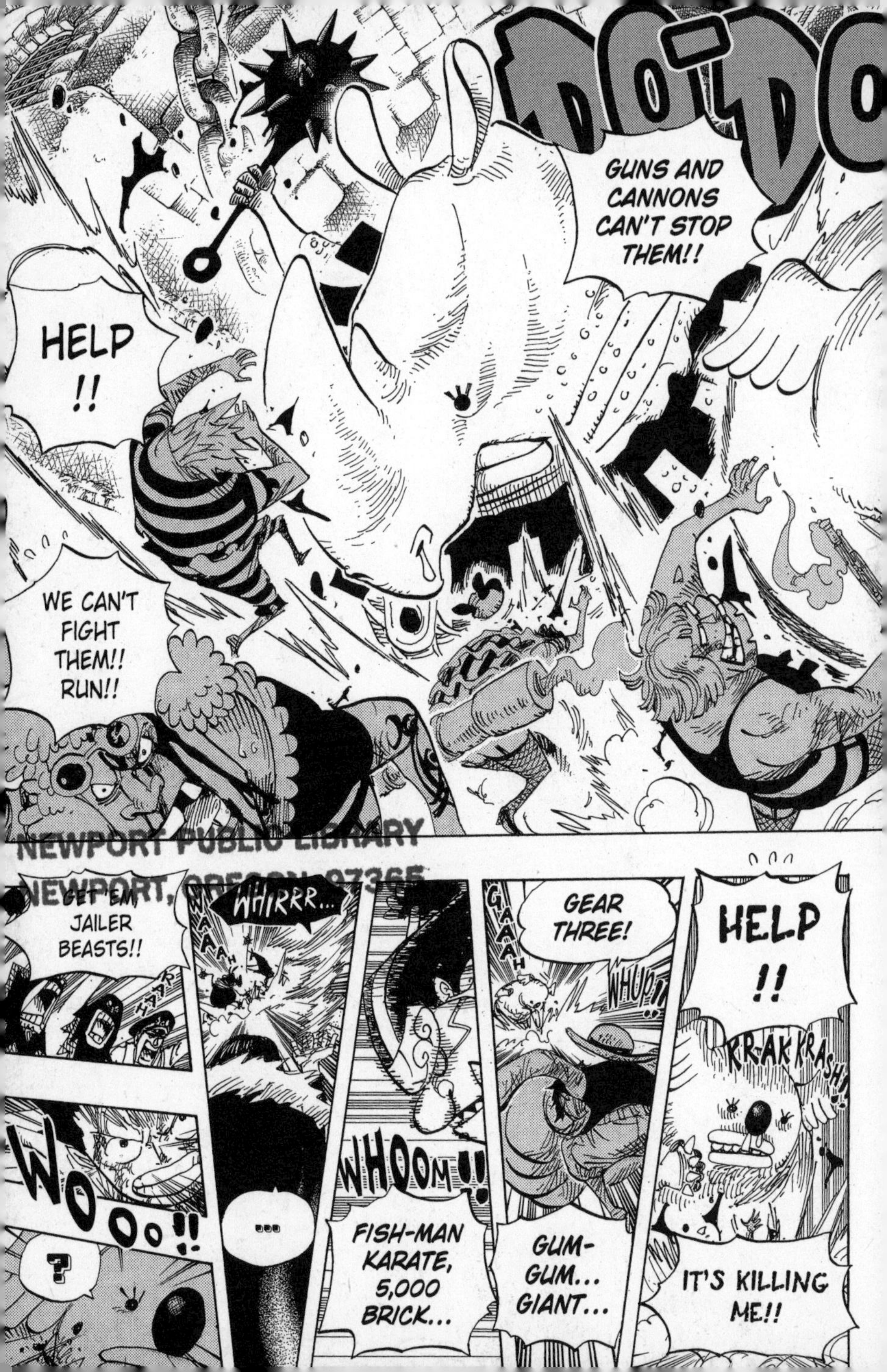
DO-DO
GUNS AND CANNONS CAN'T STOP THEM!!
HELP !!
WE CAN'T FIGHT THEM!! RUN!!
HELP !!
KRAKKRASH!!
IT'S KILLING ME!!
GEAR THREE!
GAAAAH
WHUP!!
GUM-GUM... GIANT...
WHOOM!!
FISH-MAN KARATE, 5,000 BRICK...
WHIRRR...
WAAAAH
...
GET 'EM JAILER BEASTS!!
WOOOO!!
?

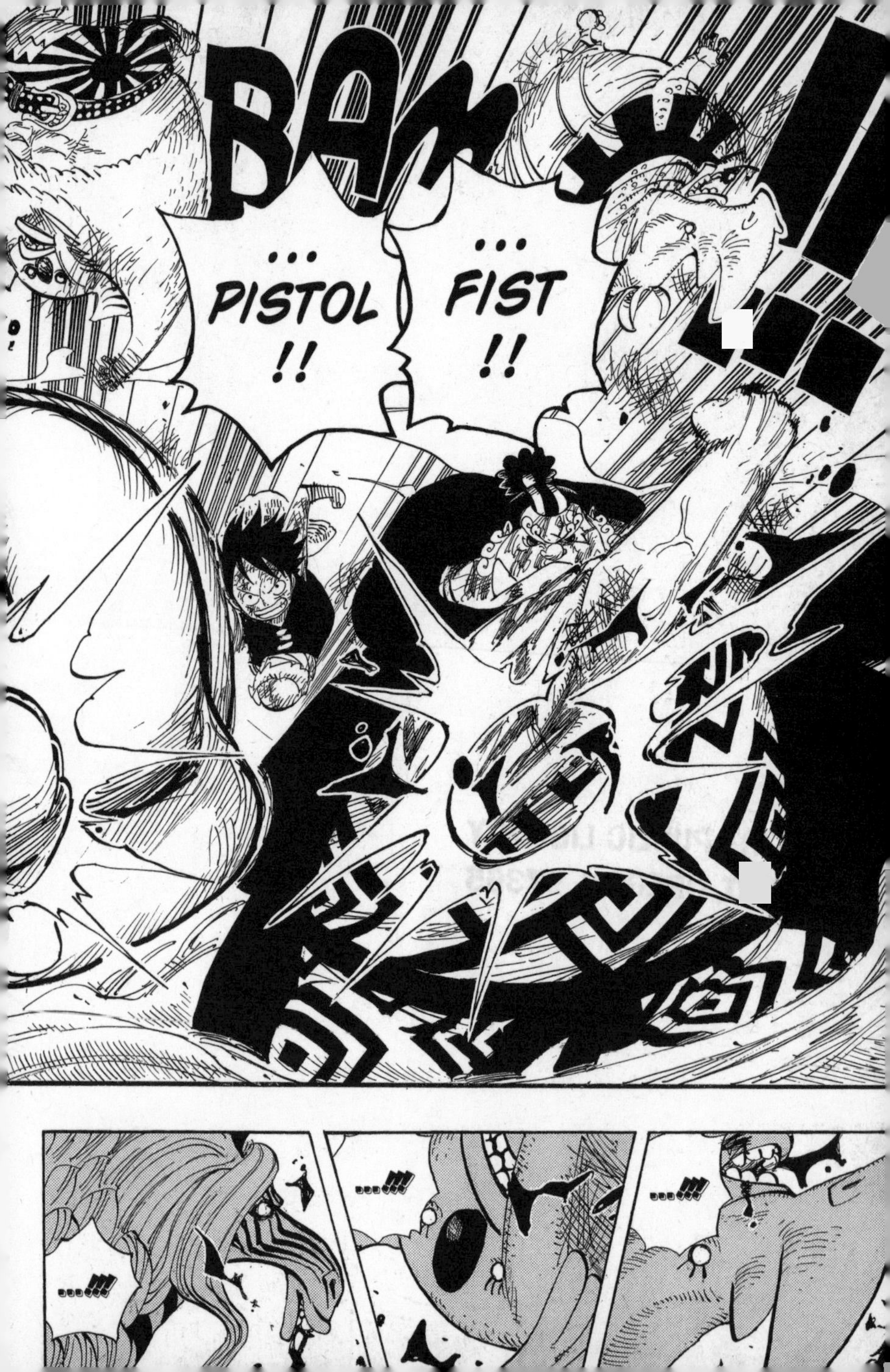
BAM!!!
...FIST!!
...PISTOL!!
...!!!
...!!!
...!!!

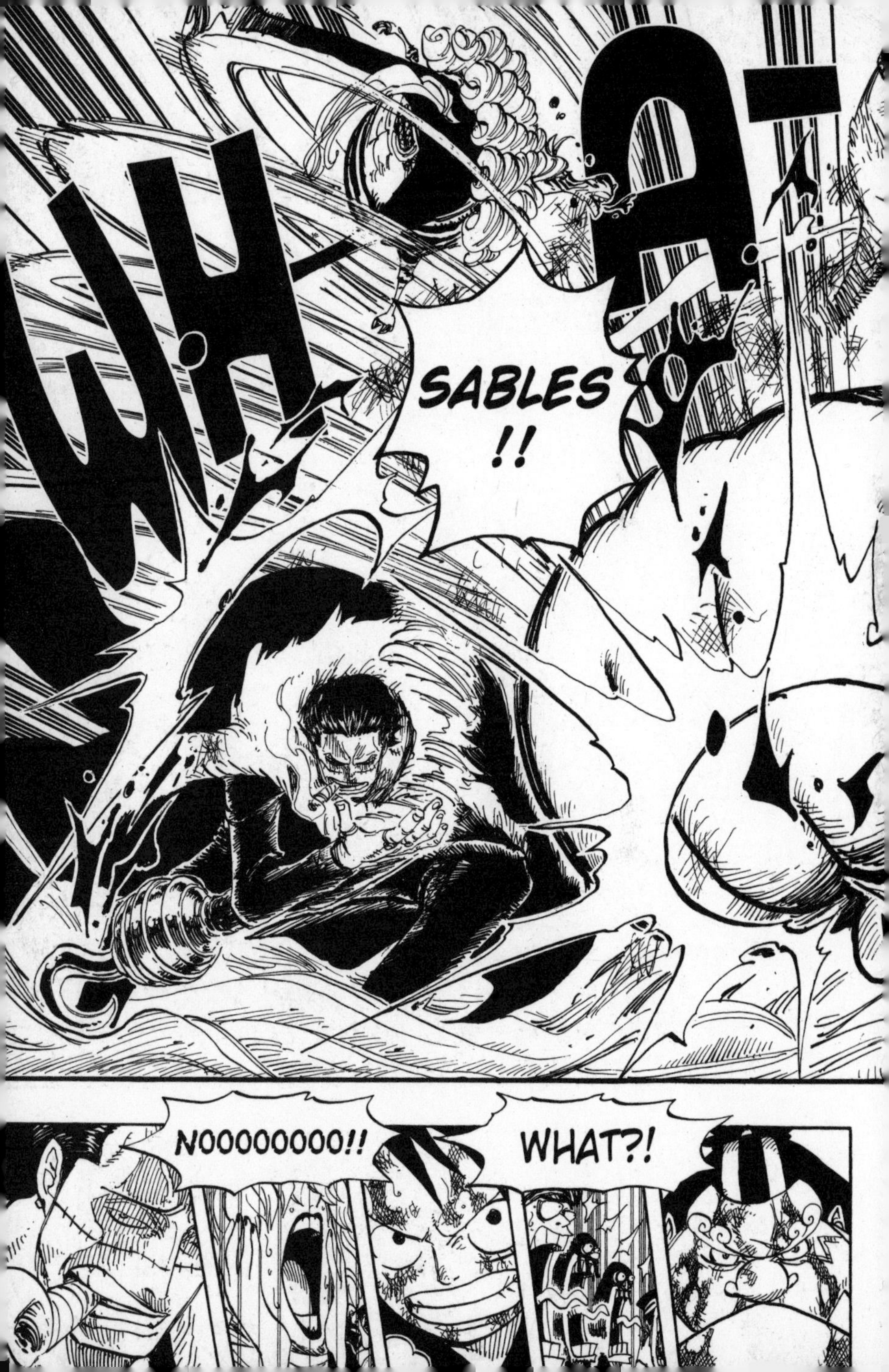
SABLES !!
WHAT?!
NOOOOOOOO!!

質問コーナー
エスビーエス

(A★S, Kanagawa)

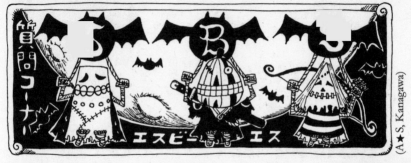

Reader(Q): Time to start SBS...NOT! --[Sun]

Oda(A): You're not going to start it?! You got me there!

WUZ

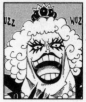

Q: Mr. Oda! **Emporio "Female" Hormone!** Now bring on the par-tay!

--Some New Kama

A: SBS ♡ is about to start! ♡ Teehee! ♡

Q: This is about the miracle worker of the drag queen world, Emporio Ivankov. Are those eyelashes his own, or are they attachments? Since he does Death Winks, does he put on three layers of mascara? (By the way, even if I put on two layers and use attached eyelashes, I still can't make my winks that strong.3)

--I ♡ Odacchi *ε*

A: Those eyelashes are 100% home-grown. I get letters asking if Death Wink uses Haki, but no. It's simply a blast of wind that occurs when he blinks.

ARE YOU READY?
LEVEL 5 FROZEN HELL
DOOM!

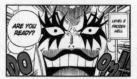

Q: Help me, Odacchi! I'm studying for my entrance exams, but I just can't concentrate! Say something to get me motivated! Seriously! Say something to all students around the country! I guess this isn't a question.

--Potechin

A: Let's read some manga! Let's watch some movies (*Strong World*)! And then study a lot! You know what they say about people who chase after two rabbits? But I say, catch them both!

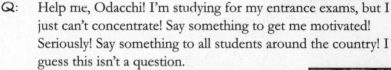

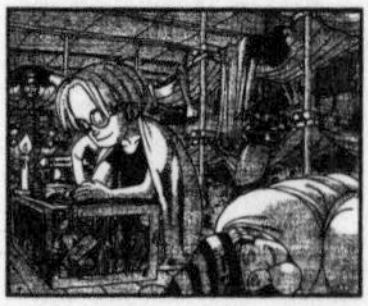

Chapter 543:
STRAW HAT AND BLACKBEARD

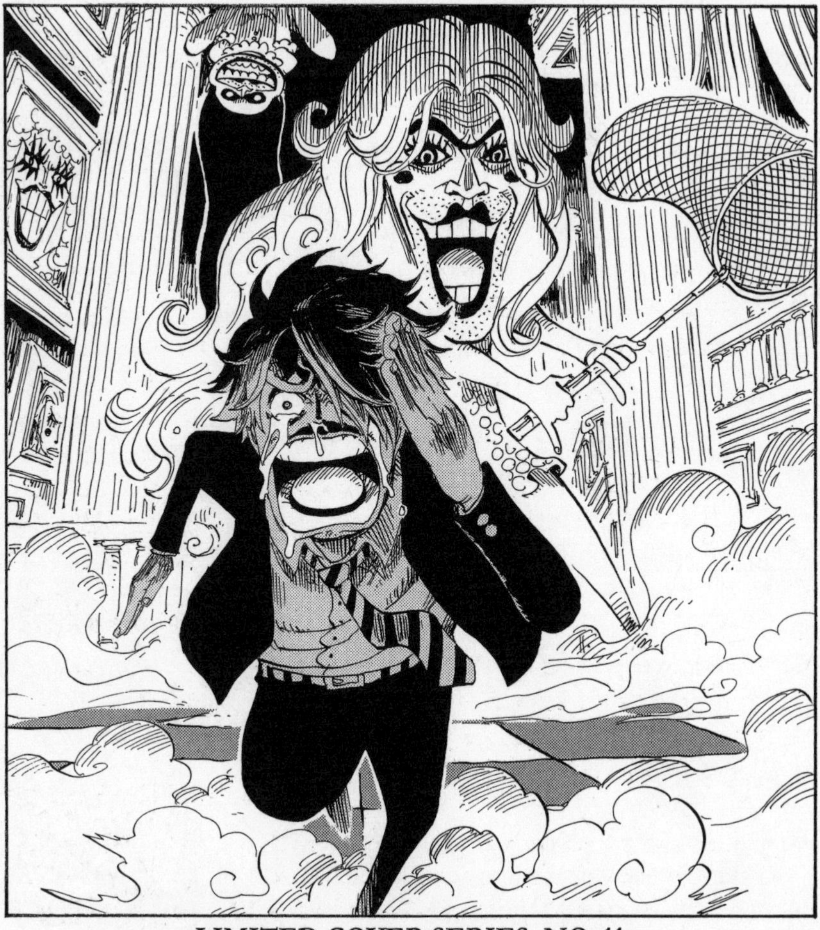

LIMITED COVER SERIES, NO. 11:
SANJI'S KAMABAKKA HELL INSANITY
VOL. 1: "ADVENTURE ON THE ISLAND OF NO WAY OUT"

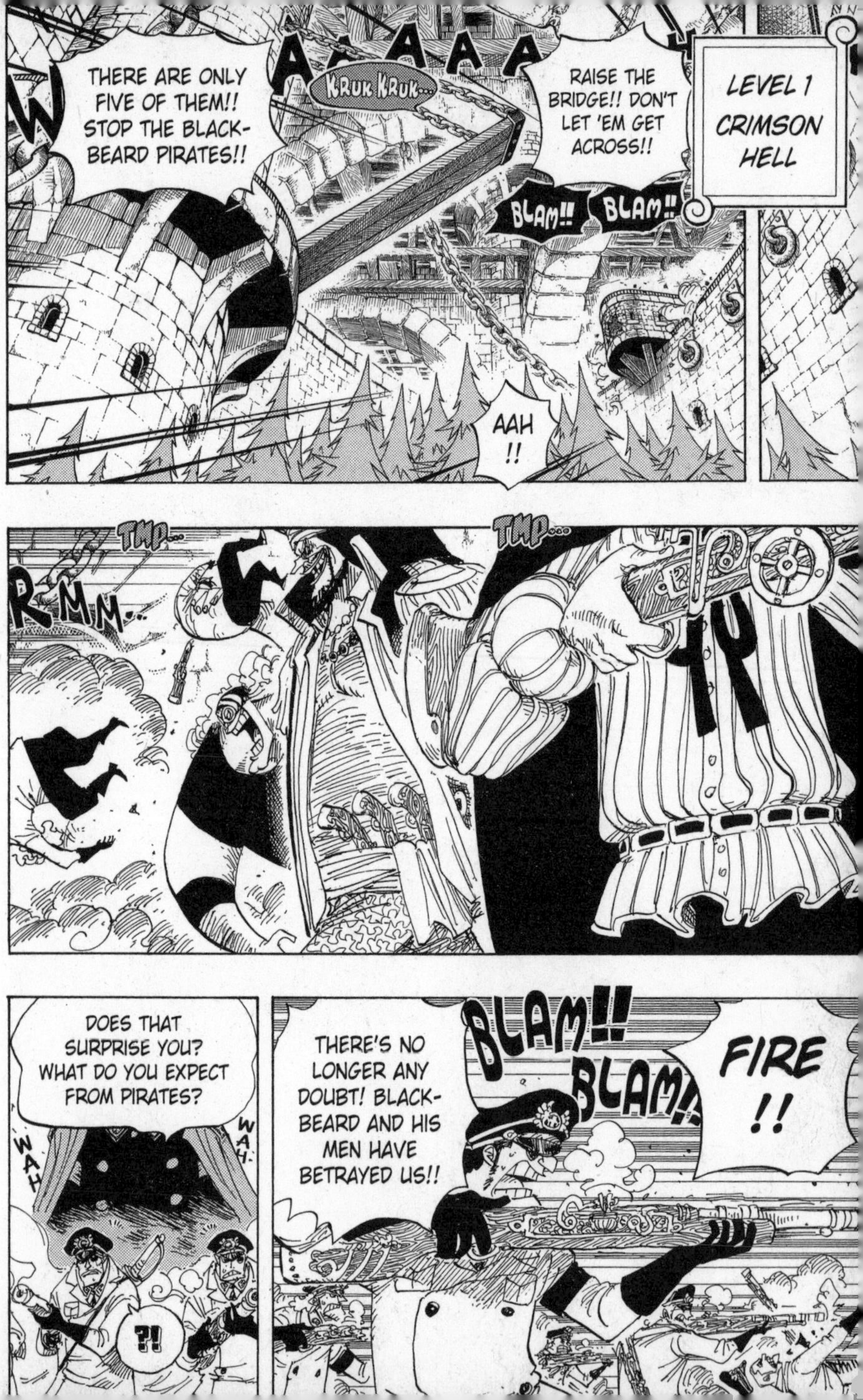
LEVEL 1 CRIMSON HELL
RAISE THE BRIDGE!! DON'T LET 'EM GET ACROSS!!
BLAM!! BLAM!!
KRUK KRUK...
AAAAA
THERE ARE ONLY FIVE OF THEM!! STOP THE BLACK-BEARD PIRATES!!
W
AAH !!
TMP...
TMP...
RMM...
FIRE !!
BLAM!! BLAM!!
THERE'S NO LONGER ANY DOUBT! BLACK-BEARD AND HIS MEN HAVE BETRAYED US!!
DOES THAT SURPRISE YOU? WHAT DO YOU EXPECT FROM PIRATES?
WAH-
WAH
?!

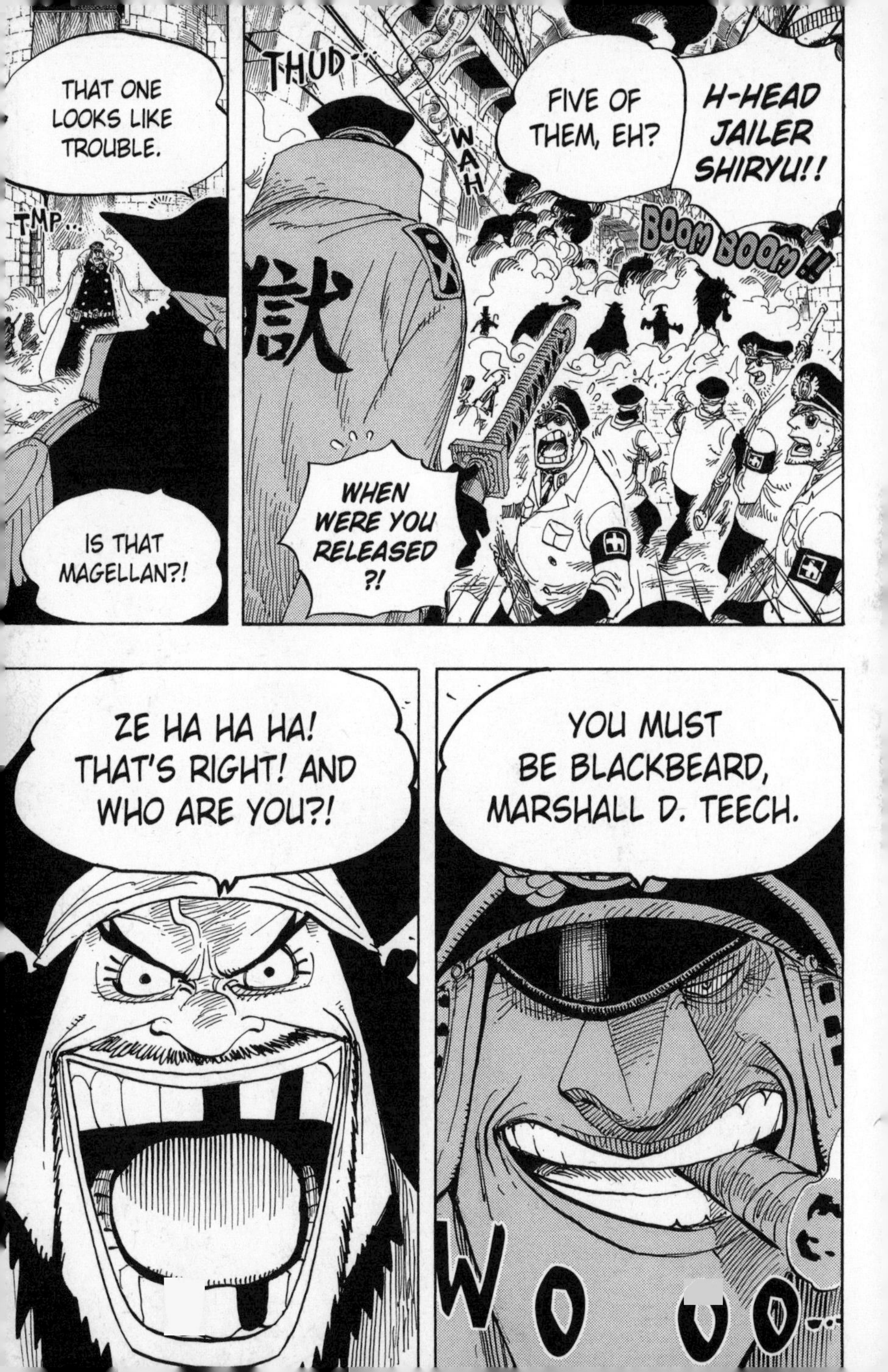
H-HEAD JAILER SHIRYU!!
FIVE OF THEM, EH?
BOOM BOOM!!
THUD...
WAH
WHEN WERE YOU RELEASED?!
THAT ONE LOOKS LIKE TROUBLE.
TMP...
IS THAT MAGELLAN?!
YOU MUST BE BLACKBEARD, MARSHALL D. TEECH.
WO OO...
ZE HA HA HA! THAT'S RIGHT! AND WHO ARE YOU?!

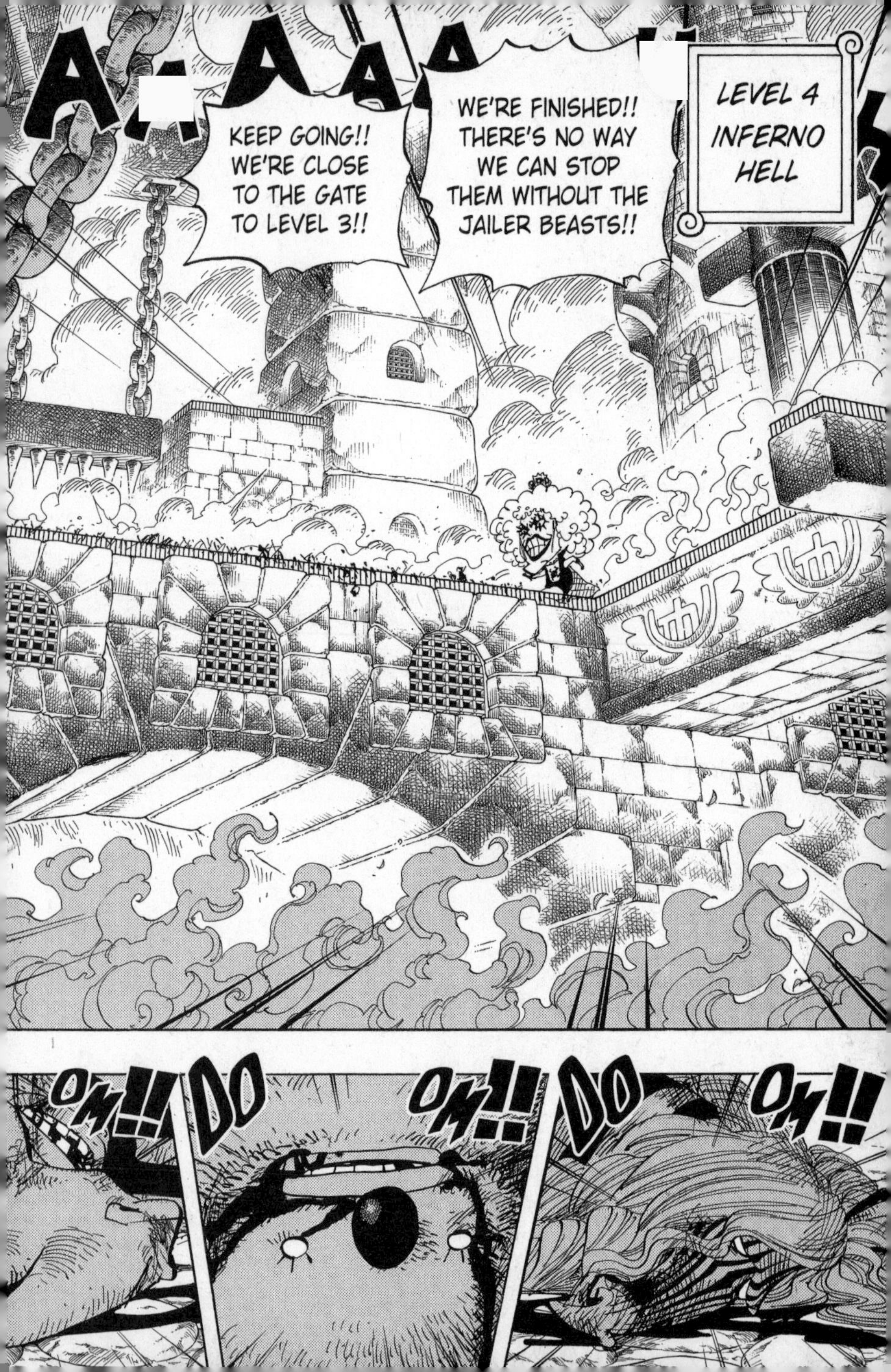

LEVEL 4 INFERNO HELL
WE'RE FINISHED!! THERE'S NO WAY WE CAN STOP THEM WITHOUT THE JAILER BEASTS!!
KEEP GOING!! WE'RE CLOSE TO THE GATE TO LEVEL 3!!
DO OM!!
DO OM!!
OM!!

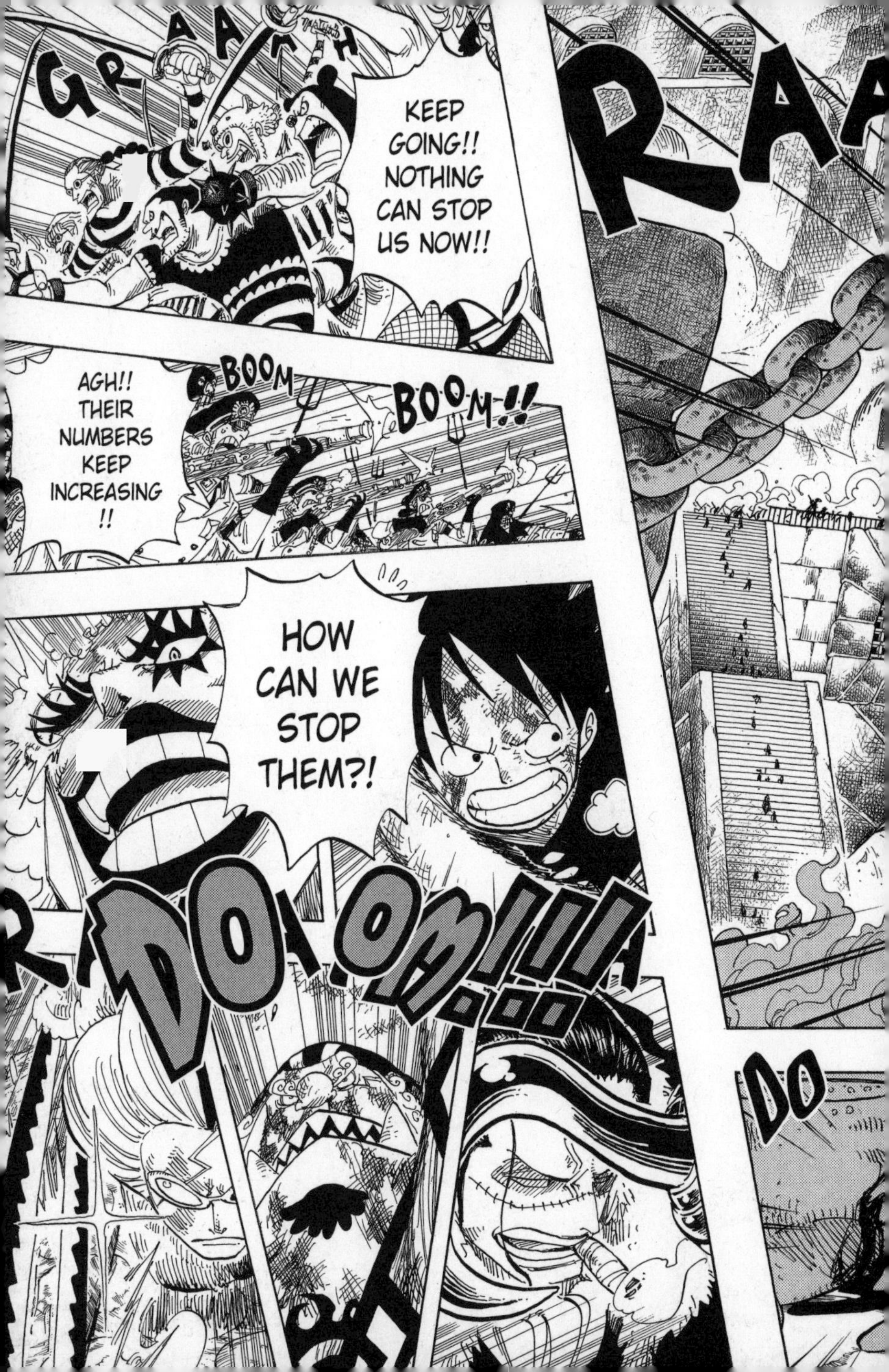
RAA
DO
GRAAH
KEEP GOING!! NOTHING CAN STOP US NOW!!
BOOM
BOOM!!
AGH!! THEIR NUMBERS KEEP INCREASING!!
HOW CAN WE STOP THEM?!
DOOM!!!

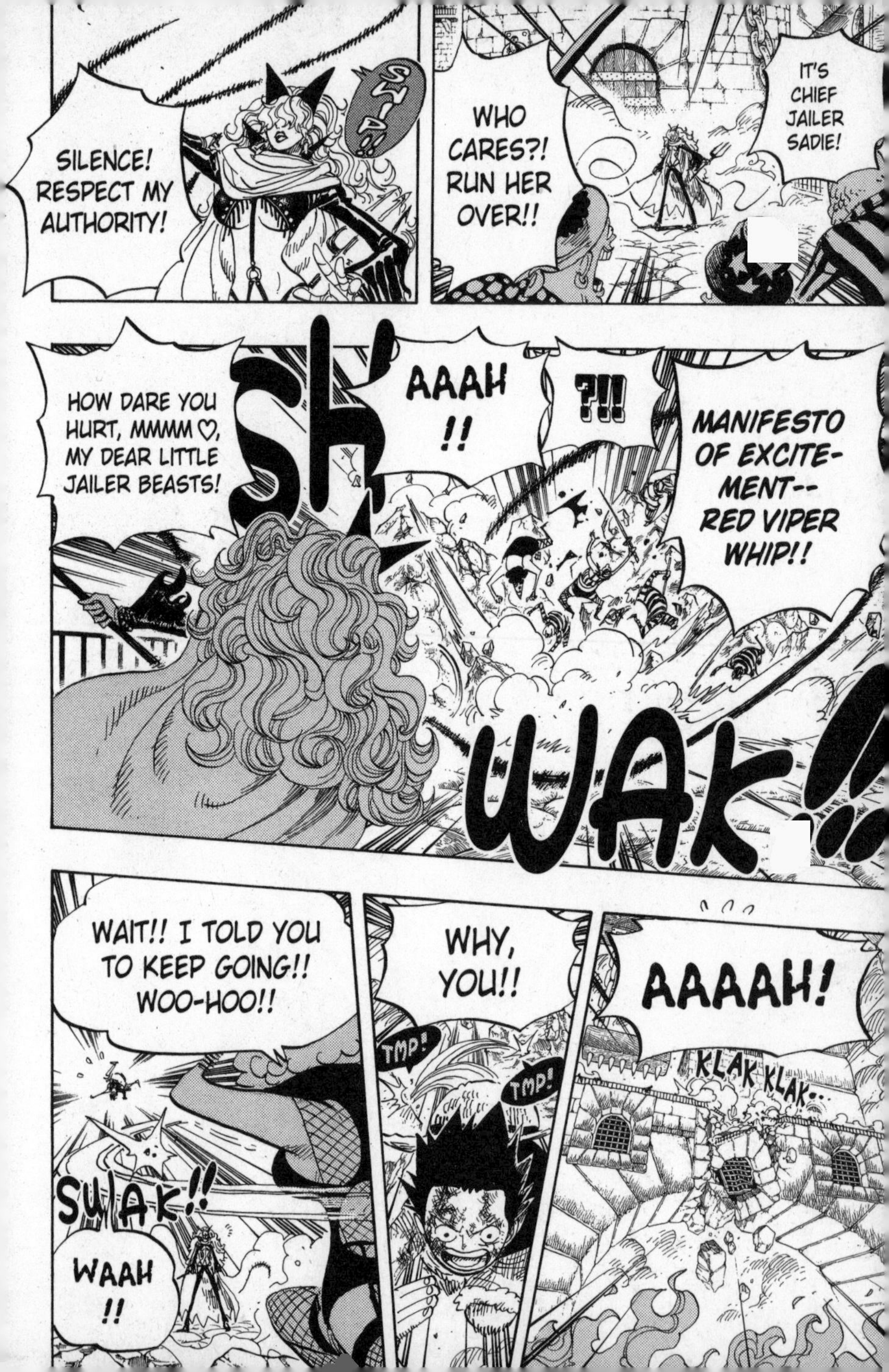
IT'S CHIEF JAILER SADIE!
WHO CARES?! RUN HER OVER!!
SWIP!!
SILENCE! RESPECT MY AUTHORITY!
MANIFESTO OF EXCITEMENT-- RED VIPER WHIP!!
?!!
AAAH !!
SH'
HOW DARE YOU HURT, MMMM ♡, MY DEAR LITTLE JAILER BEASTS!
WAK!!
AAAAH!
KLAK KLAK...
WHY, YOU!!
TMP!
TMP!
WAIT!! I TOLD YOU TO KEEP GOING!! WOO-HOO!!
SWAK!!
WAAH !!

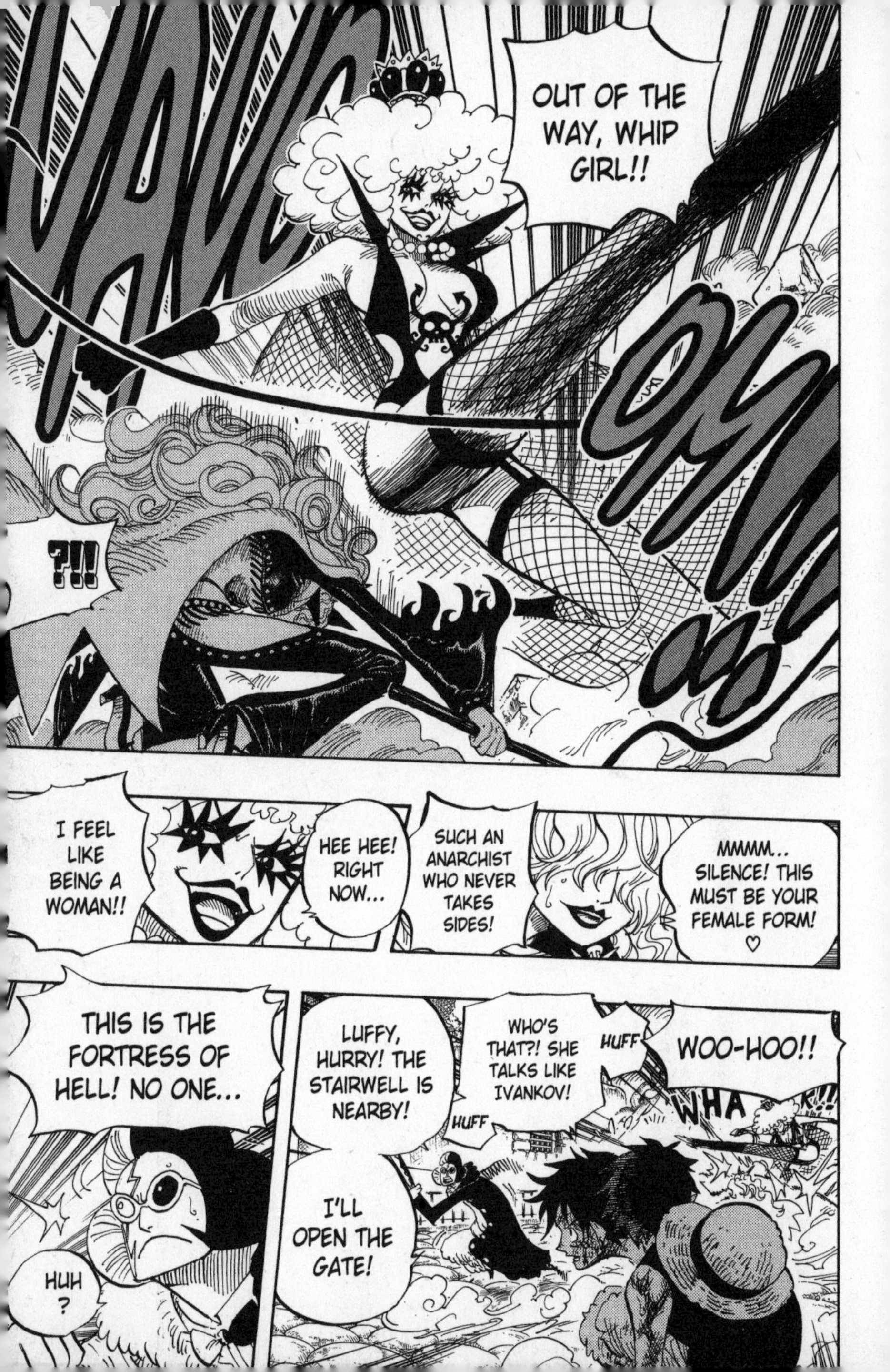
OUT OF THE WAY, WHIP GIRL!!
?!!
MMMM... SILENCE! THIS MUST BE YOUR FEMALE FORM! ♡
SUCH AN ANARCHIST WHO NEVER TAKES SIDES!
HEE HEE! RIGHT NOW...
I FEEL LIKE BEING A WOMAN!!
WOO-HOO!!
HUFF
WHO'S THAT?! SHE TALKS LIKE IVANKOV!
HUFF
LUFFY, HURRY! THE STAIRWELL IS NEARBY!
WHAK!!
I'LL OPEN THE GATE!
THIS IS THE FORTRESS OF HELL! NO ONE...
HUH ?

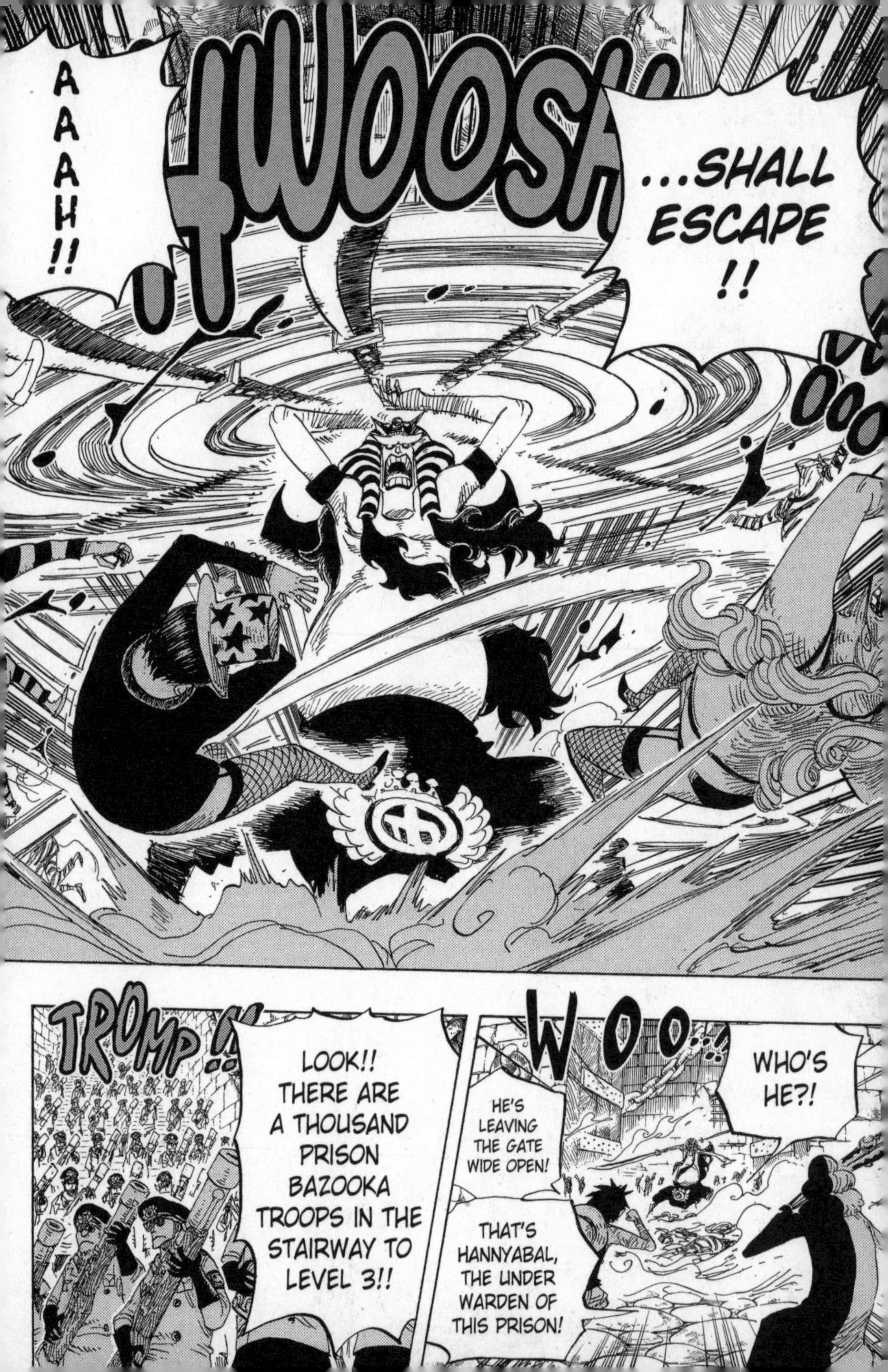
...SHALL ESCAPE !!
WOOSH
AAAAH!!
WHO'S HE?!
WOO..!!
HE'S LEAVING THE GATE WIDE OPEN!
THAT'S HANNYABAL, THE UNDER WARDEN OF THIS PRISON!
TROMP!!
LOOK!! THERE ARE A THOUSAND PRISON BAZOOKA TROOPS IN THE STAIRWAY TO LEVEL 3!!

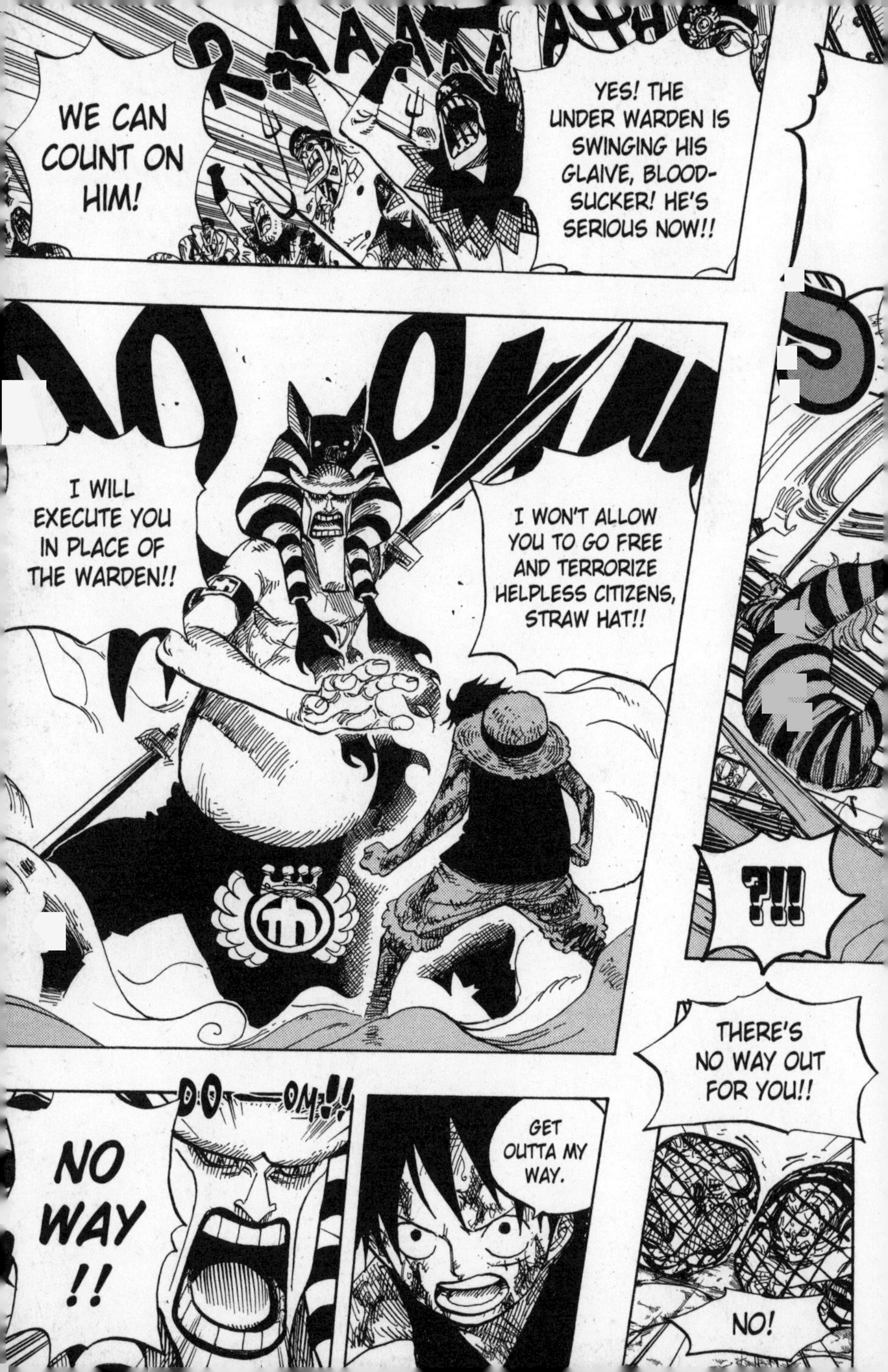
YES! THE UNDER WARDEN IS SWINGING HIS GLAIVE, BLOOD-SUCKER! HE'S SERIOUS NOW!!
WE CAN COUNT ON HIM!
I WON'T ALLOW YOU TO GO FREE AND TERRORIZE HELPLESS CITIZENS, STRAW HAT!!
I WILL EXECUTE YOU IN PLACE OF THE WARDEN!!
?!!
THERE'S NO WAY OUT FOR YOU!!
NO!
GET OUTTA MY WAY.
D-O-OM!!
NO WAY !!

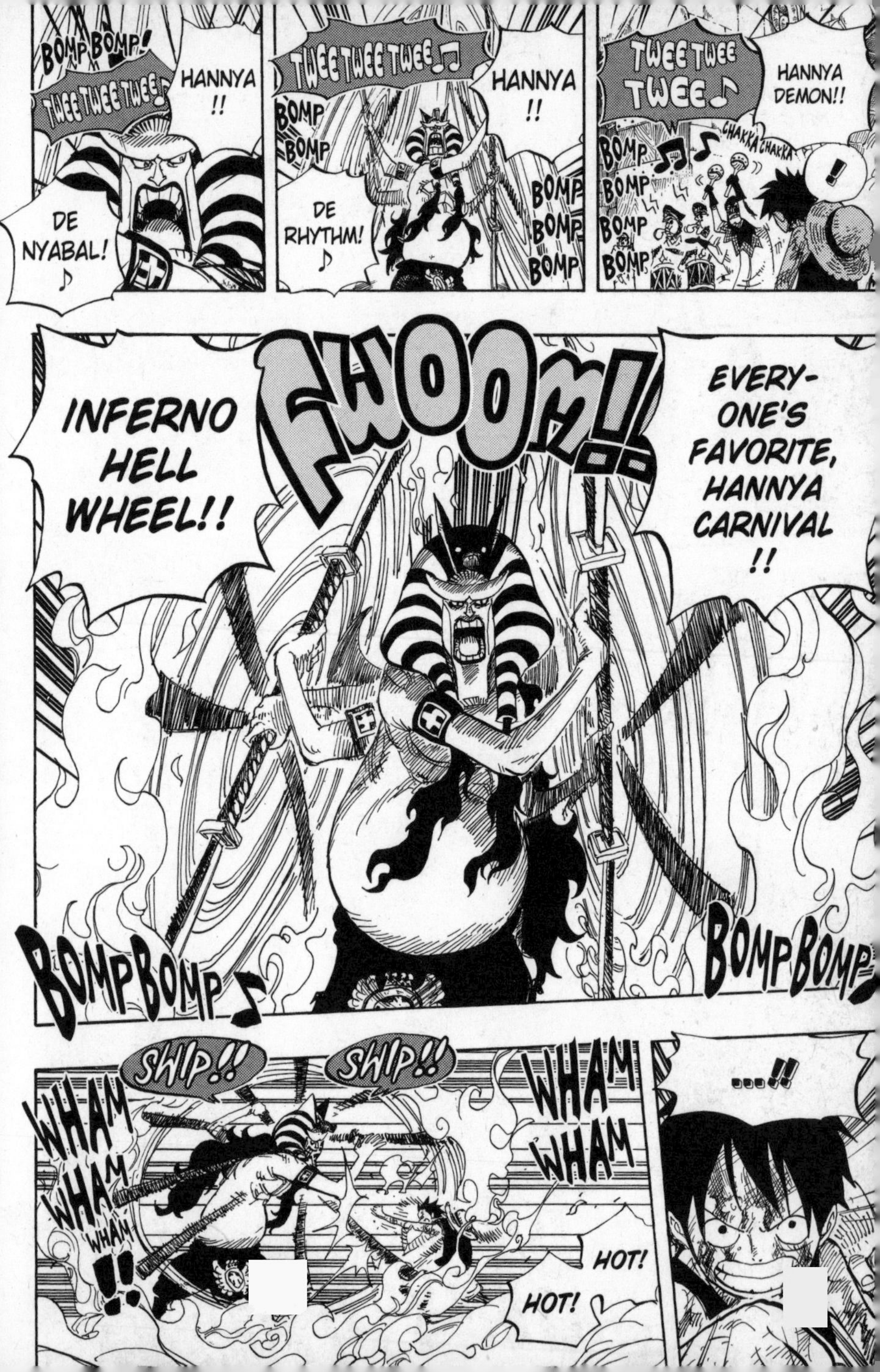
TWEE TWEE TWEE ♪
HANNYA DEMON!!
BOMP BOMP BOMP BOMP
CHAKKA CHAKKA
!
TWEE TWEE TWEE ♫
HANNYA !!
BOMP BOMP BOMP
DE RHYTHM! ♪
BOMP BOMP BOMP
BOMP BOMP!
TWEE TWEE TWEE ♪
HANNYA !!
DE NYABAL! ♪
EVERY-ONE'S FAVORITE, HANNYA CARNIVAL !!
FWOOM!!
INFERNO HELL WHEEL!!
BOMP BOMP
BOMP BOMP ♪
...!!
WHAM WHAM
SWIP!!
SWIP!!
WHAM WHAM WHAM!!
HOT!
HOT!

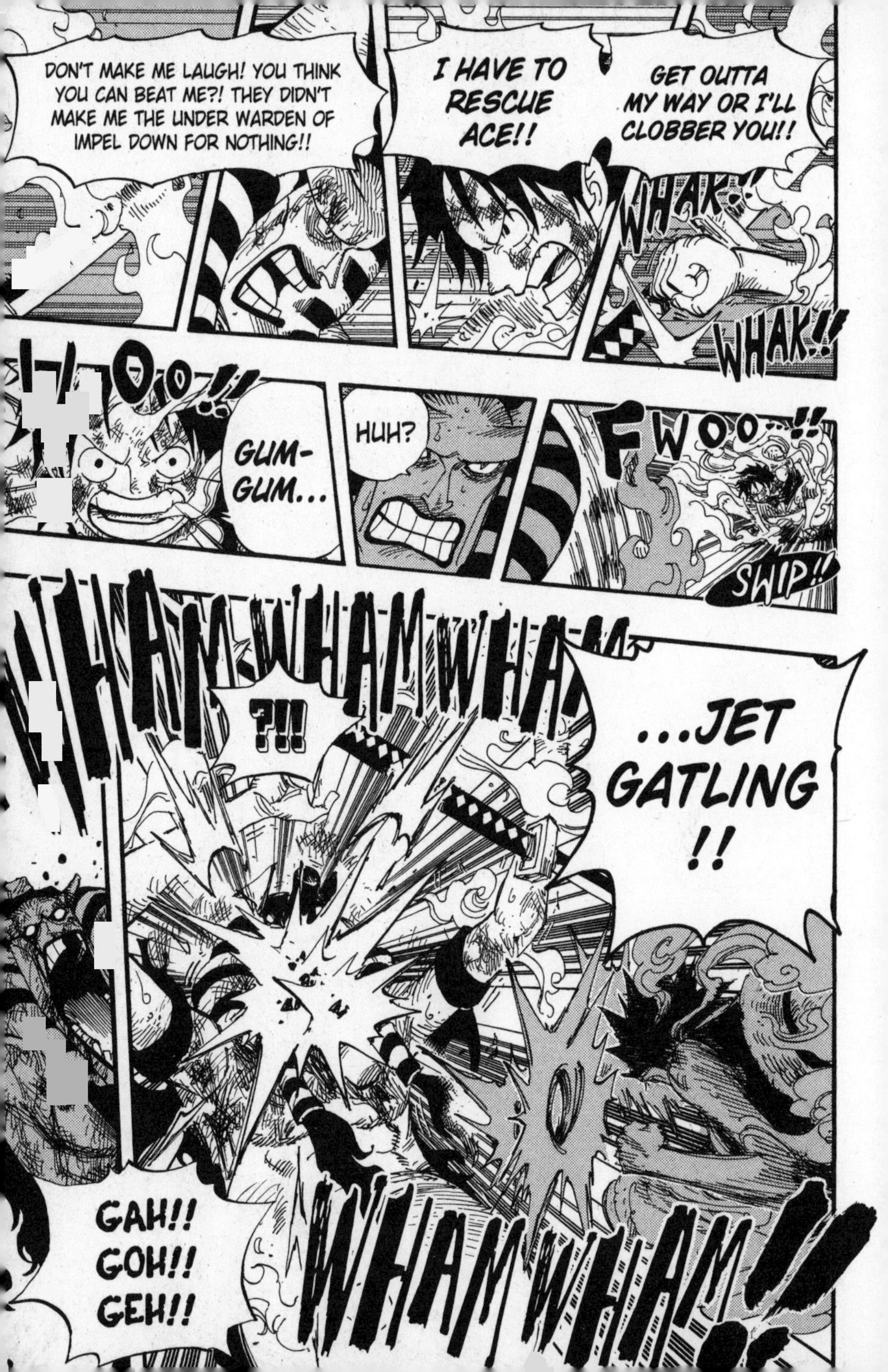
GET OUTTA MY WAY OR I'LL CLOBBER YOU!!
WHAK!!
WHAK!!
I HAVE TO RESCUE ACE!!
DON'T MAKE ME LAUGH! YOU THINK YOU CAN BEAT ME?! THEY DIDN'T MAKE ME THE UNDER WARDEN OF IMPEL DOWN FOR NOTHING!!
FWOO!!
SWIP!!
HUH?
GUM-GUM...
...JET GATLING!!
WHAM WHAM WHAM
?!!
GAH!! GOH!! GEH!!
WHAM WHAM!!

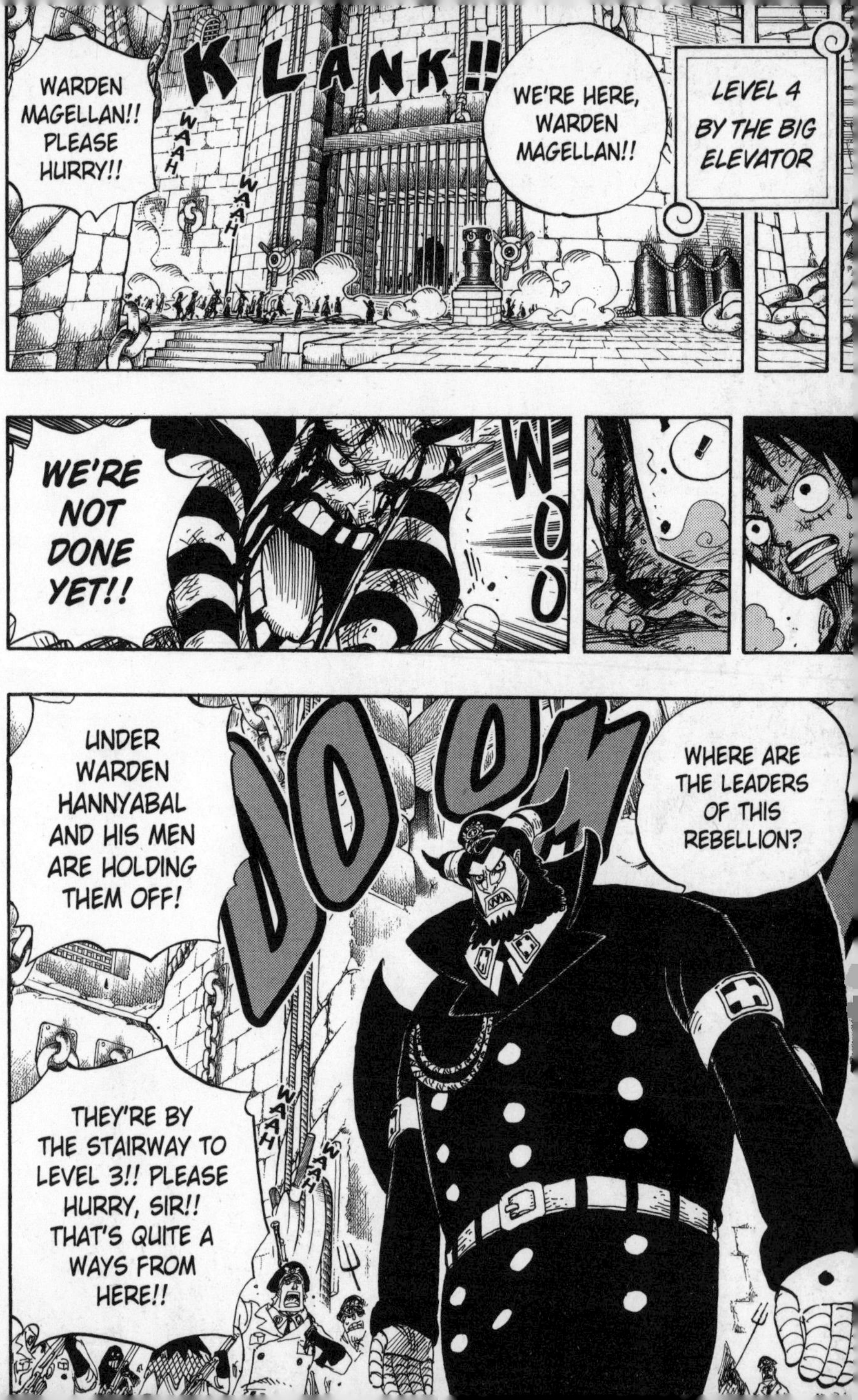
LEVEL 4 BY THE BIG ELEVATOR
WE'RE HERE, WARDEN MAGELLAN!!
KLANK!!
WAAH
WAAH
WARDEN MAGELLAN!! PLEASE HURRY!!
!
WOOO
WE'RE NOT DONE YET!!
WHERE ARE THE LEADERS OF THIS REBELLION?
DOOM
UNDER WARDEN HANNYABAL AND HIS MEN ARE HOLDING THEM OFF!
WAAH
WAAH
THEY'RE BY THE STAIRWAY TO LEVEL 3!! PLEASE HURRY, SIR!! THAT'S QUITE A WAYS FROM HERE!!

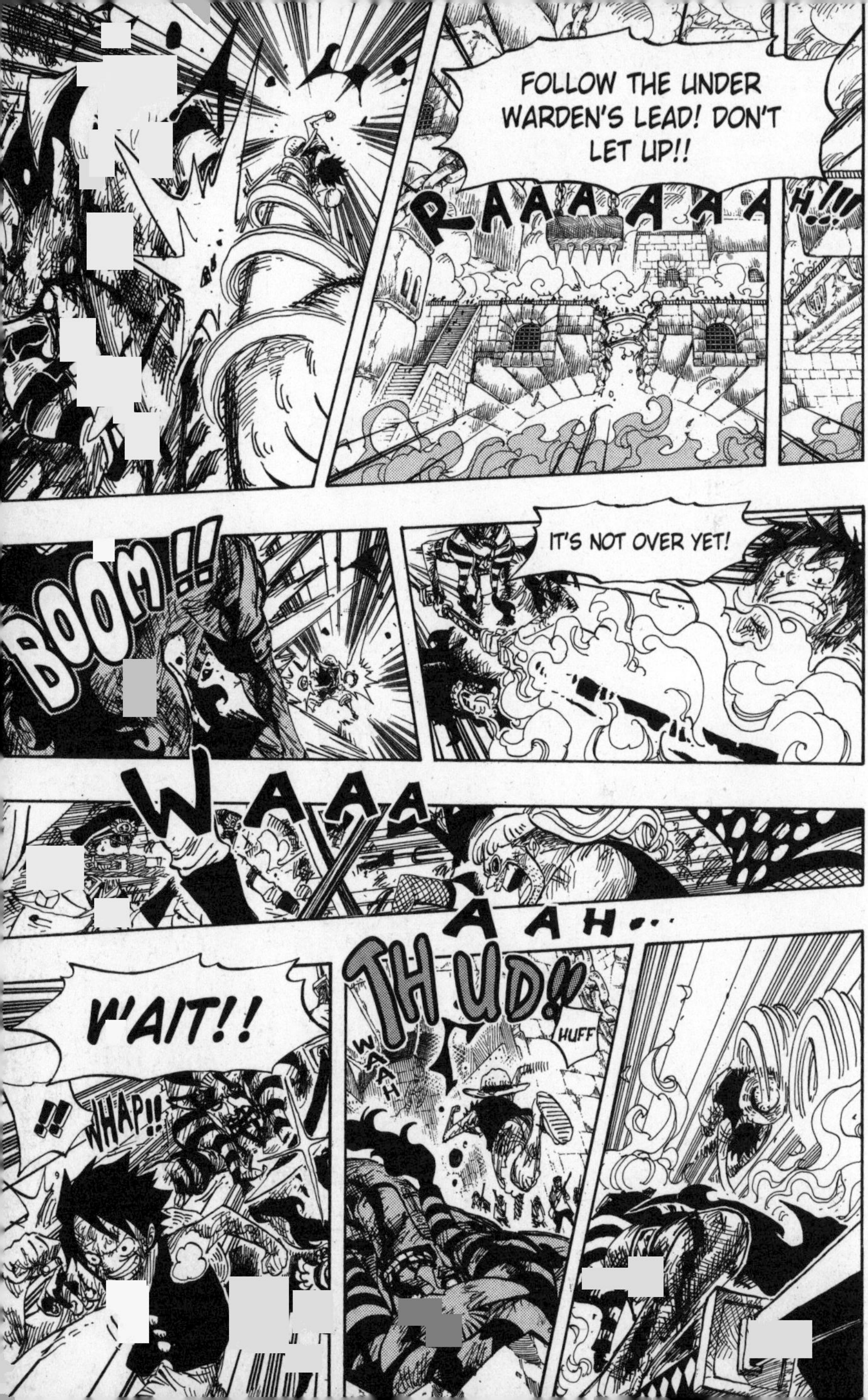
FOLLOW THE UNDER WARDEN'S LEAD! DON'T LET UP!!
RAAAAAAH!!!
IT'S NOT OVER YET!
BOOM!!
WAAAAAAH...
HUFF
THUD!!
WAAAH
WAIT!!
!!
WHAP!!

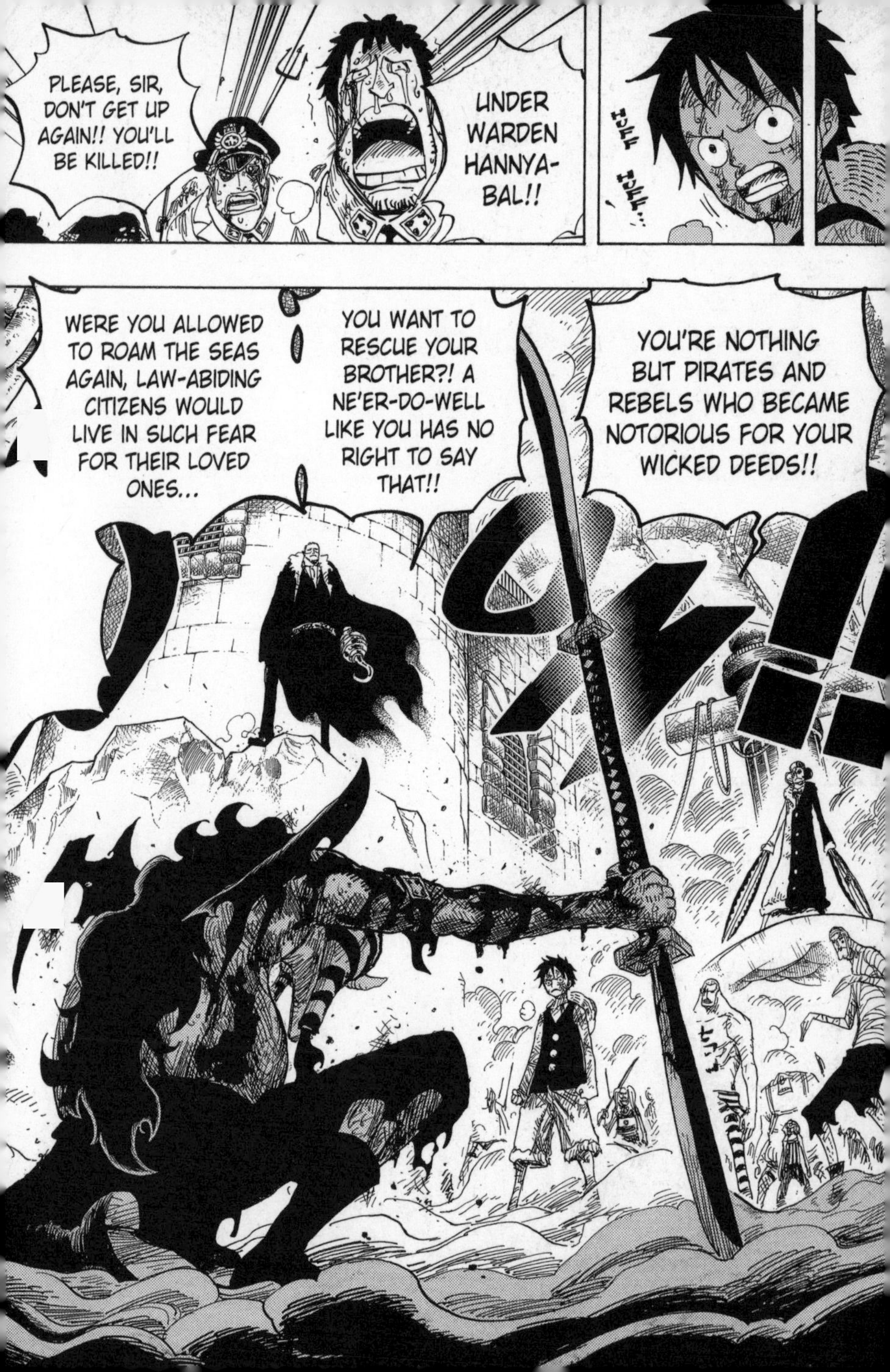
HUFF HUFF...
UNDER WARDEN HANNYA-BAL!!
PLEASE, SIR, DON'T GET UP AGAIN!! YOU'LL BE KILLED!!
YOU'RE NOTHING BUT PIRATES AND REBELS WHO BECAME NOTORIOUS FOR YOUR WICKED DEEDS!!
YOU WANT TO RESCUE YOUR BROTHER?! A NE'ER-DO-WELL LIKE YOU HAS NO RIGHT TO SAY THAT!!
WERE YOU ALLOWED TO ROAM THE SEAS AGAIN, LAW-ABIDING CITIZENS WOULD LIVE IN SUCH FEAR FOR THEIR LOVED ONES...

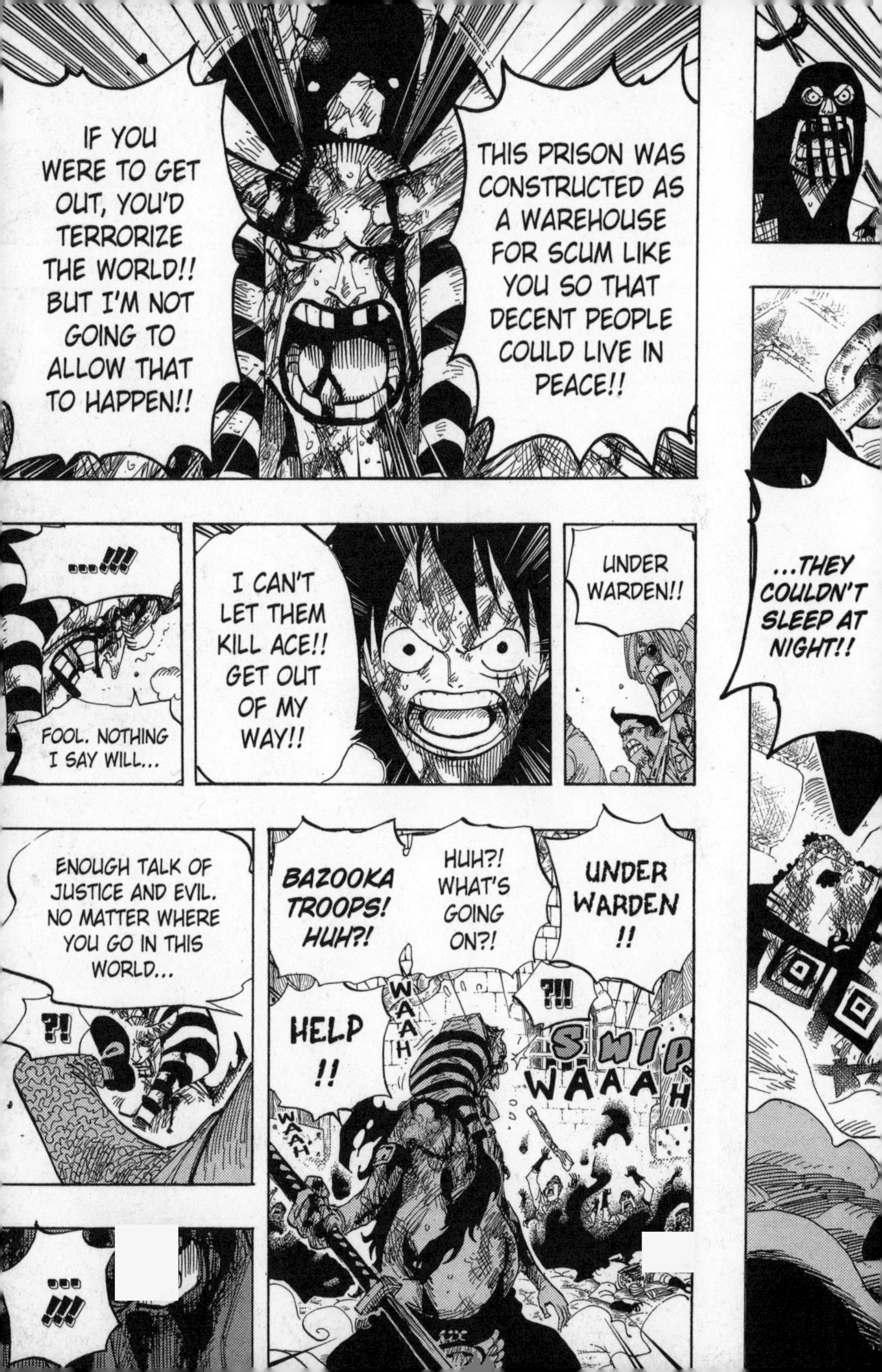
THIS PRISON WAS CONSTRUCTED AS A WAREHOUSE FOR SCUM LIKE YOU SO THAT DECENT PEOPLE COULD LIVE IN PEACE!!
IF YOU WERE TO GET OUT, YOU'D TERRORIZE THE WORLD!! BUT I'M NOT GOING TO ALLOW THAT TO HAPPEN!!
...THEY COULDN'T SLEEP AT NIGHT!!
UNDER WARDEN!!
I CAN'T LET THEM KILL ACE!! GET OUT OF MY WAY!!
...!!!
FOOL. NOTHING I SAY WILL...
UNDER WARDEN !!
HUH?! WHAT'S GOING ON?!
BAZOOKA TROOPS! HUH?!
?!!
SWIP
WAAAH
WAAAH
HELP !!
WAAH
ENOUGH TALK OF JUSTICE AND EVIL. NO MATTER WHERE YOU GO IN THIS WORLD...
?!
...!!!

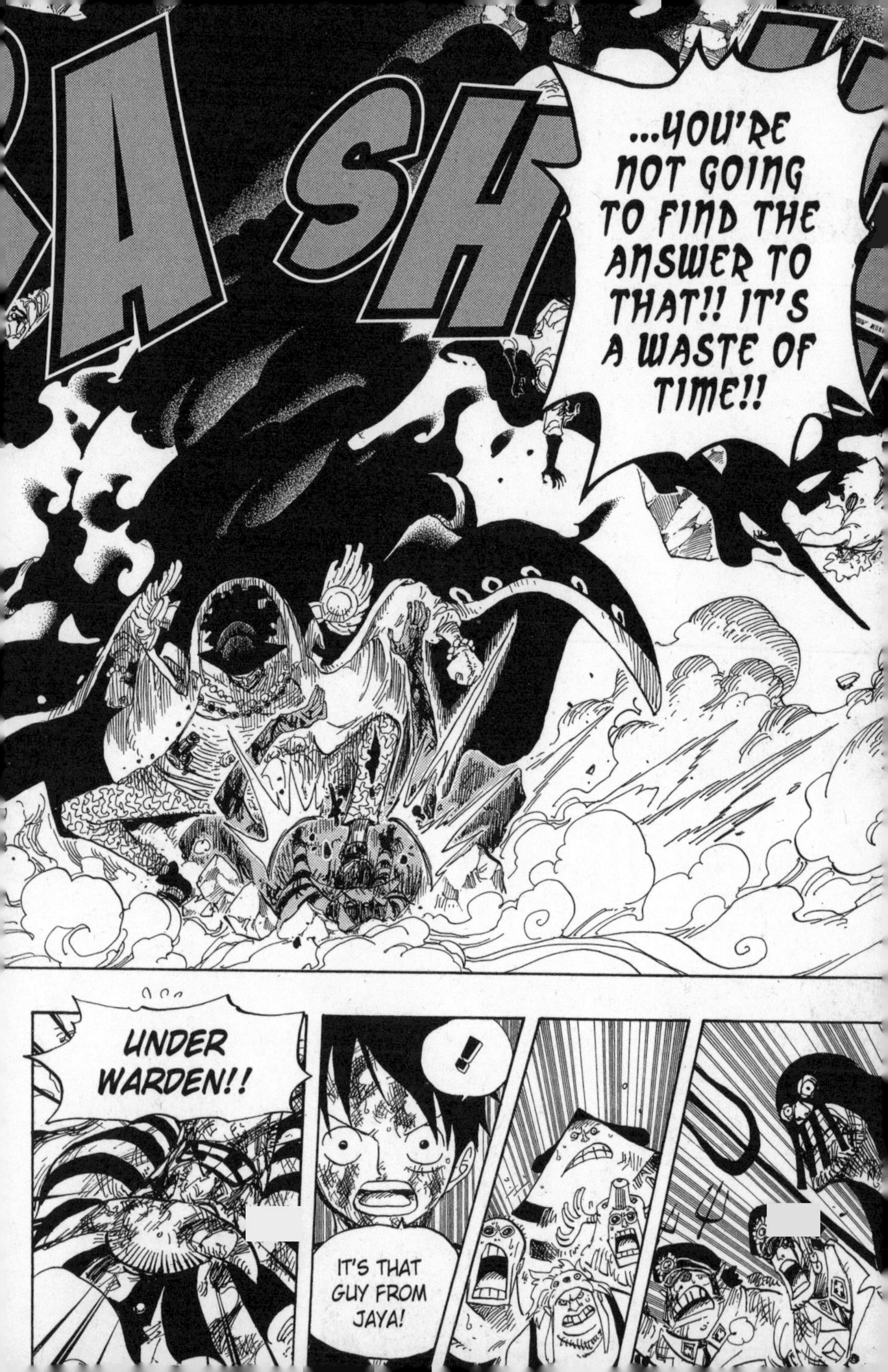
...YOU'RE NOT GOING TO FIND THE ANSWER TO THAT!! IT'S A WASTE OF TIME!!
!
IT'S THAT GUY FROM JAYA!
UNDER WARDEN!!

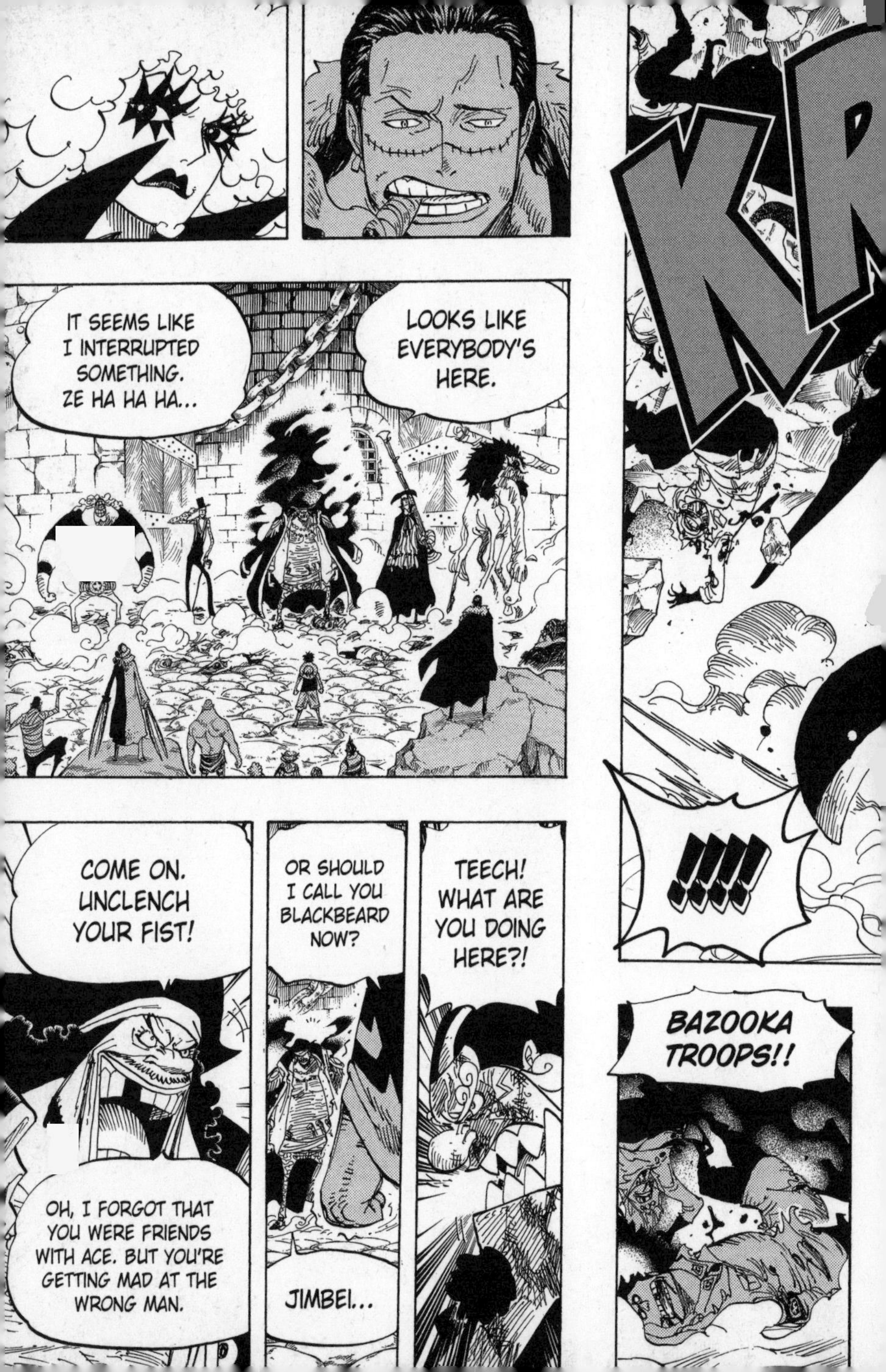
!!!!
BAZOOKA TROOPS!!
LOOKS LIKE EVERYBODY'S HERE.
IT SEEMS LIKE I INTERRUPTED SOMETHING. ZE HA HA HA...
TEECH! WHAT ARE YOU DOING HERE?!
OR SHOULD I CALL YOU BLACKBEARD NOW?
JIMBEI...
COME ON. UNCLENCH YOUR FIST!
OH, I FORGOT THAT YOU WERE FRIENDS WITH ACE. BUT YOU'RE GETTING MAD AT THE WRONG MAN.

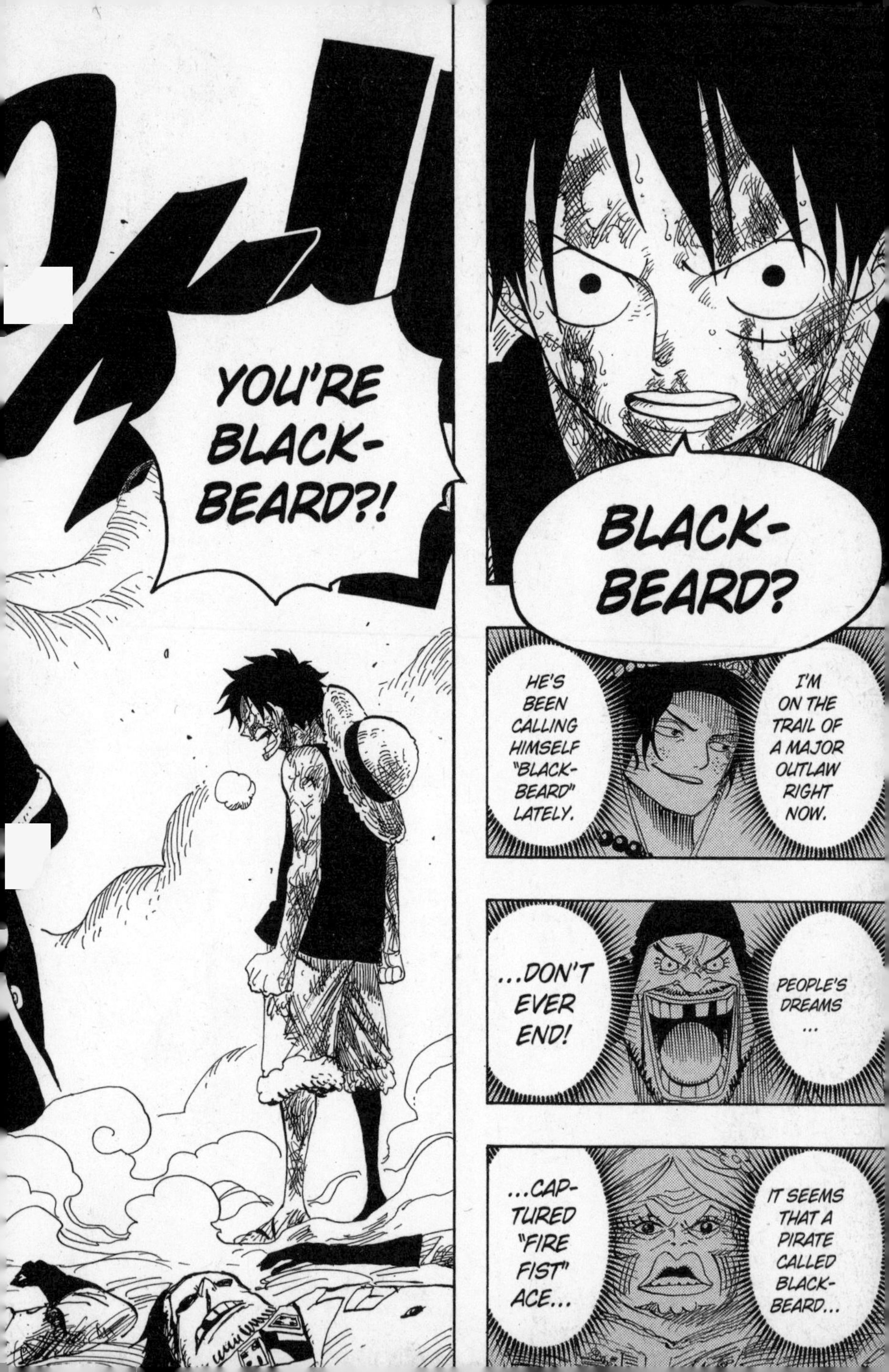
BLACK-BEARD?
I'M ON THE TRAIL OF A MAJOR OUTLAW RIGHT NOW.
HE'S BEEN CALLING HIMSELF "BLACK-BEARD" LATELY.
PEOPLE'S DREAMS ...
...DON'T EVER END!
IT SEEMS THAT A PIRATE CALLED BLACK-BEARD...
...CAPTURED "FIRE FIST" ACE...
YOU'RE BLACK-BEARD?!

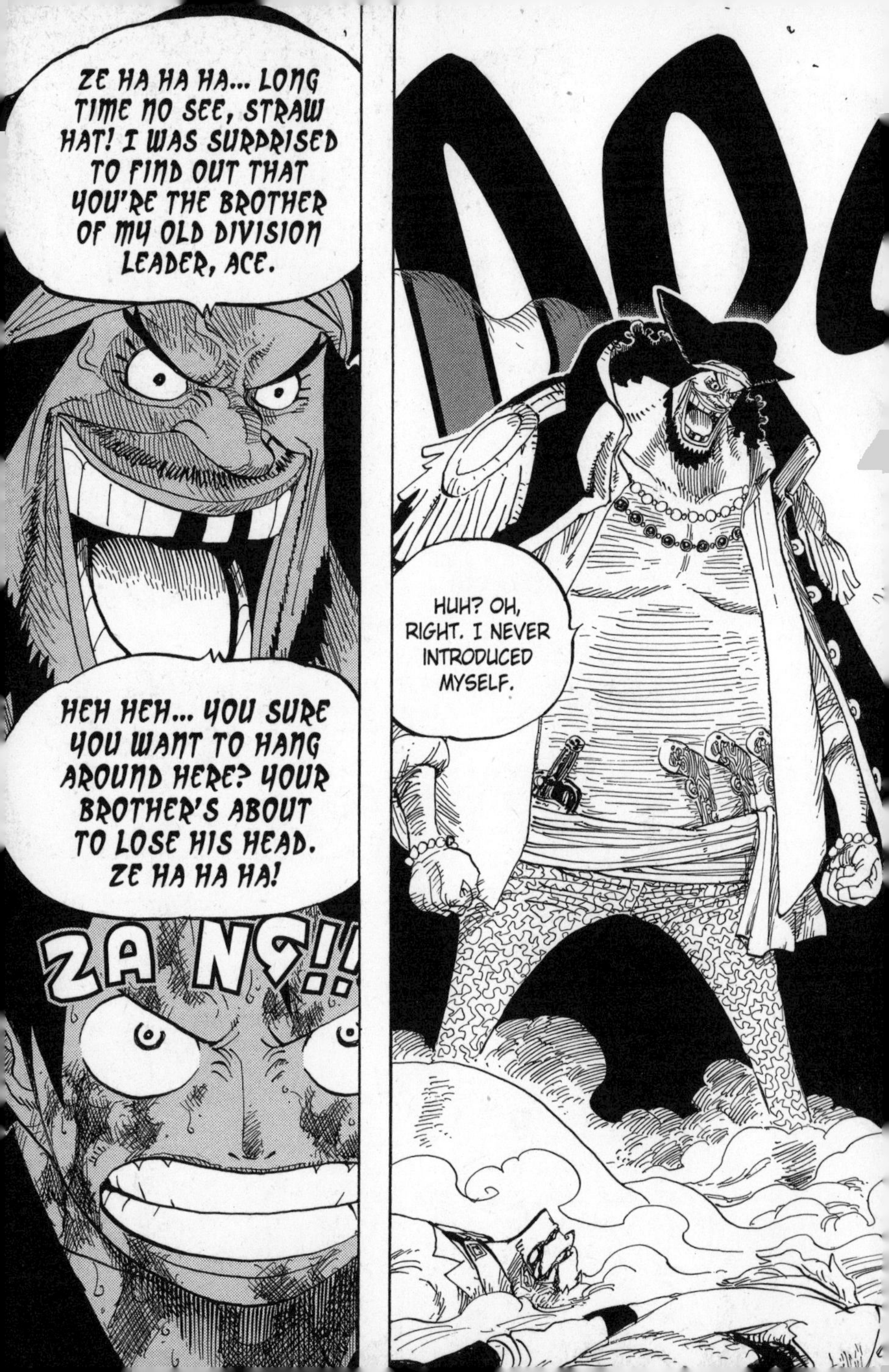
HUH? OH, RIGHT. I NEVER INTRODUCED MYSELF.
ZE HA HA HA... LONG TIME NO SEE, STRAW HAT! I WAS SURPRISED TO FIND OUT THAT YOU'RE THE BROTHER OF MY OLD DIVISION LEADER, ACE.
HEH HEH... YOU SURE YOU WANT TO HANG AROUND HERE? YOUR BROTHER'S ABOUT TO LOSE HIS HEAD. ZE HA HA HA!
ZANG!!

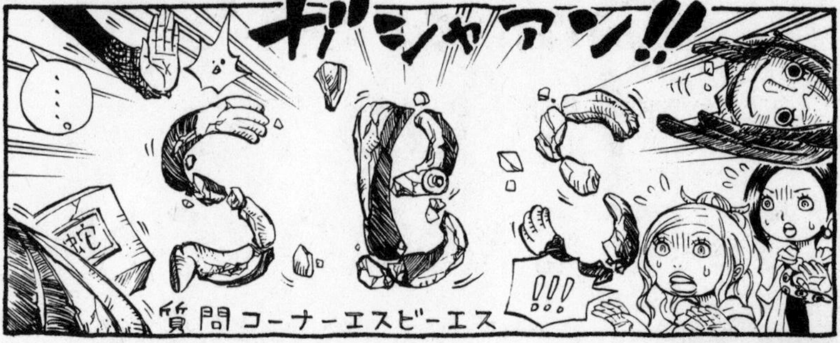
ガシャアン!!
!!!
質問コーナーエスビーエス

(Fool Junk, Tokyo)

Q: I want to go to Disneyland! (`◦3・´)⇚
--Take me there, Odacchi♡

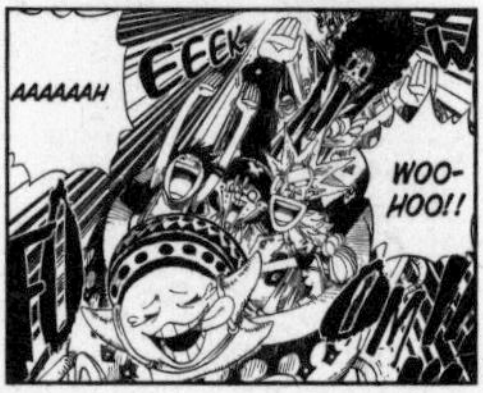
WOO-HOO!!
EEEK
AAAAAAH

A: All right! Let's go ride the Blue Mountain! (Wait, that's the name of the coffee.)

Q: Hello, Mr. Oda! I discovered something about Saldeath! In the scene when he first appears in volume 54, the spear that he carries has black holes set apart in regular intervals! And when we read on, in the panel below the part where it explains Mr. 2's powers, it shows Saldeath holding his spear to his mouth! That means that Saldeath's spear is also some kind of flute and he uses it to play tunes when controlling the Blugoris!

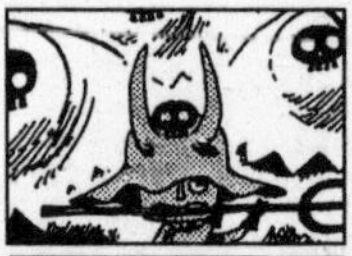

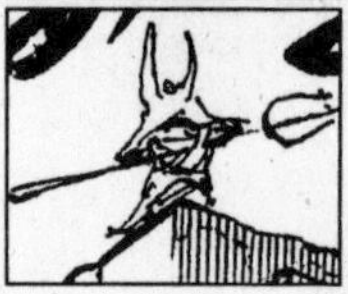

-- "Morning Musume are the Cutest Ever"

A: Yup. I'm surprised you found this out. I didn't want to spend too much time in the battle or else the story would be at a standstill. So those kinds of details end up being pushed into the corner! That's right! Saldeath's spear is also a flute that controls the Blugoris!

Q: I have a question for you, Odacchi. Why do all the inhabitants of New Kama Land wear fishnet stockings? Do you like fishnet stockings, Odacchi? Please tell me.
--Mosako

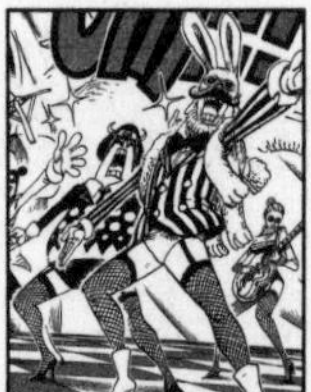

A: Do I like them? I wear fishnet stockings with a fur coat and nothing else when I draw my manga. As for the reason why the people of New Kama Land wear them, it's because the fishnet stockings were there. It's kind of like how a mountain climber climbs because the mountain is there.

Chapter 544: THE LID TO THE CAULDRON OF HELL OPENS

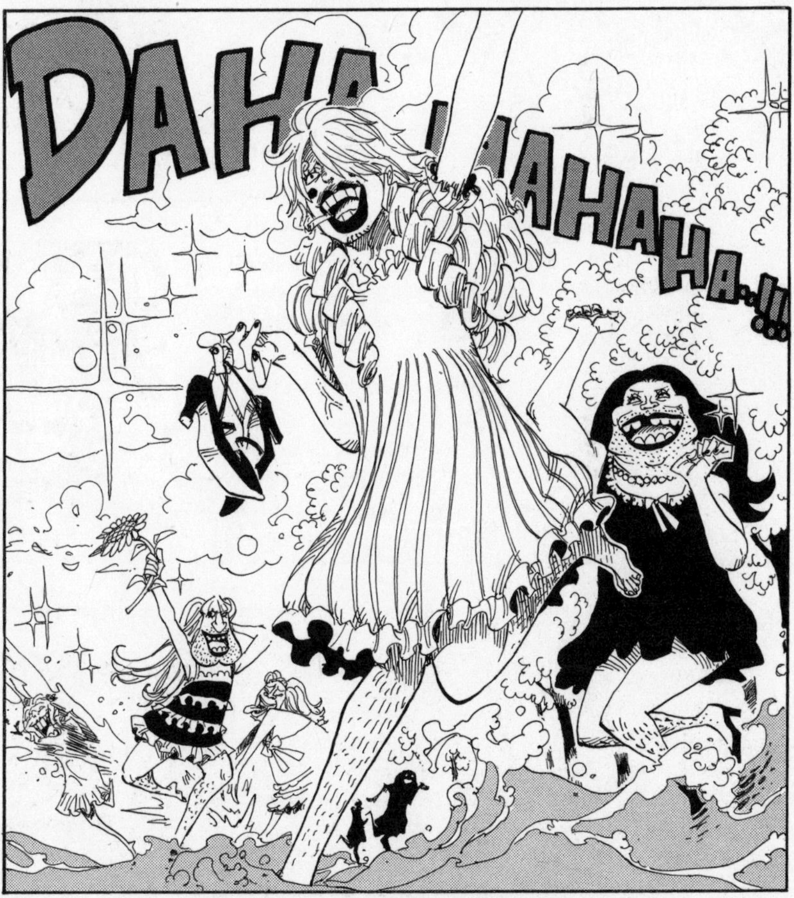
DAHAHAHAHAHAHA..!!!

LIMITED COVER SERIES, NO. 11:
SANJI'S KAMABAKKA HELL INSANITY
FINAL VOLUME: "ONE OF THE GIRLS"

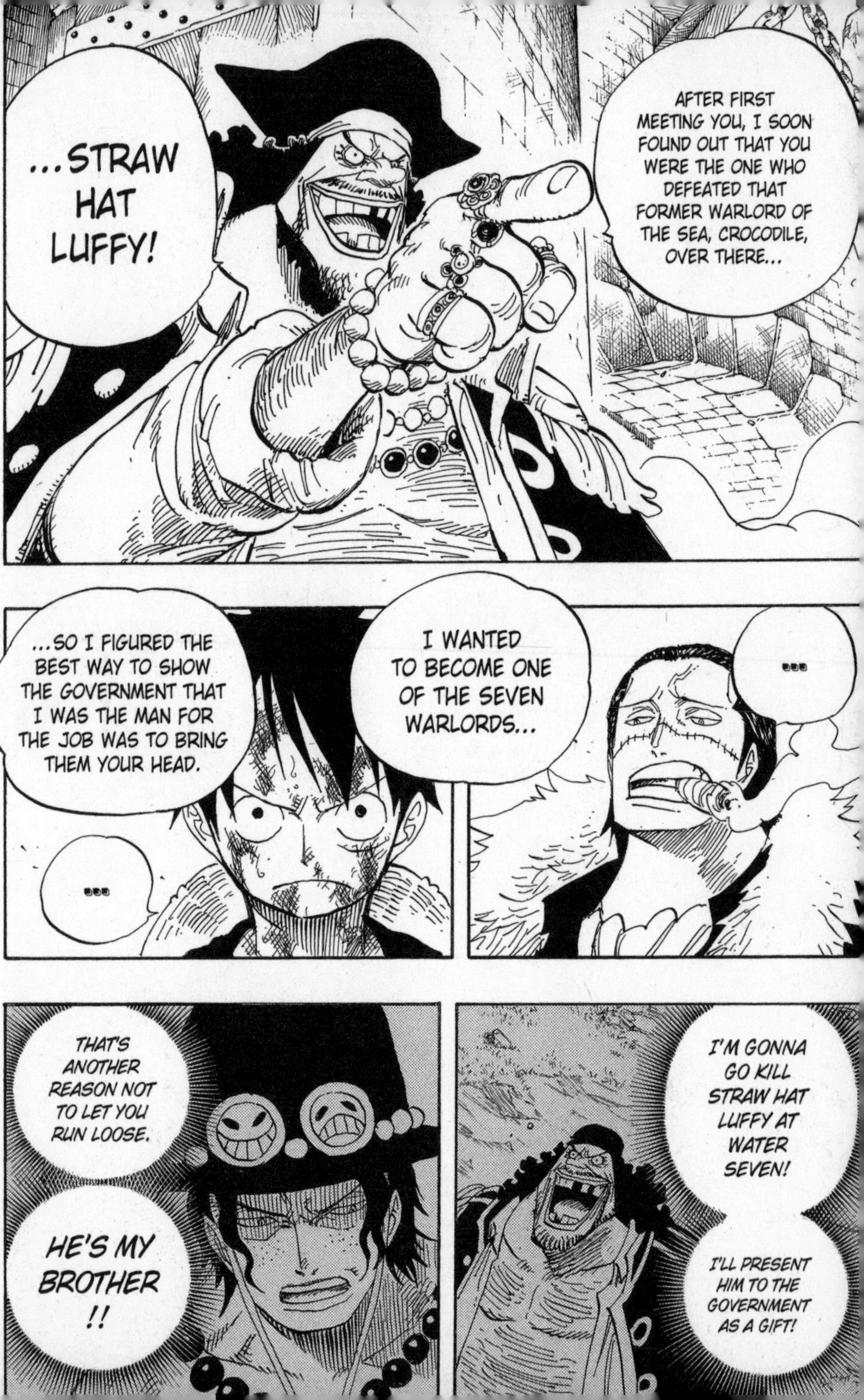
AFTER FIRST MEETING YOU, I SOON FOUND OUT THAT YOU WERE THE ONE WHO DEFEATED THAT FORMER WARLORD OF THE SEA, CROCODILE, OVER THERE...
...STRAW HAT LUFFY!
...
I WANTED TO BECOME ONE OF THE SEVEN WARLORDS...
...SO I FIGURED THE BEST WAY TO SHOW THE GOVERNMENT THAT I WAS THE MAN FOR THE JOB WAS TO BRING THEM YOUR HEAD.
...
I'M GONNA GO KILL STRAW HAT LUFFY AT WATER SEVEN!
I'LL PRESENT HIM TO THE GOVERNMENT AS A GIFT!
THAT'S ANOTHER REASON NOT TO LET YOU RUN LOOSE.
HE'S MY BROTHER !!

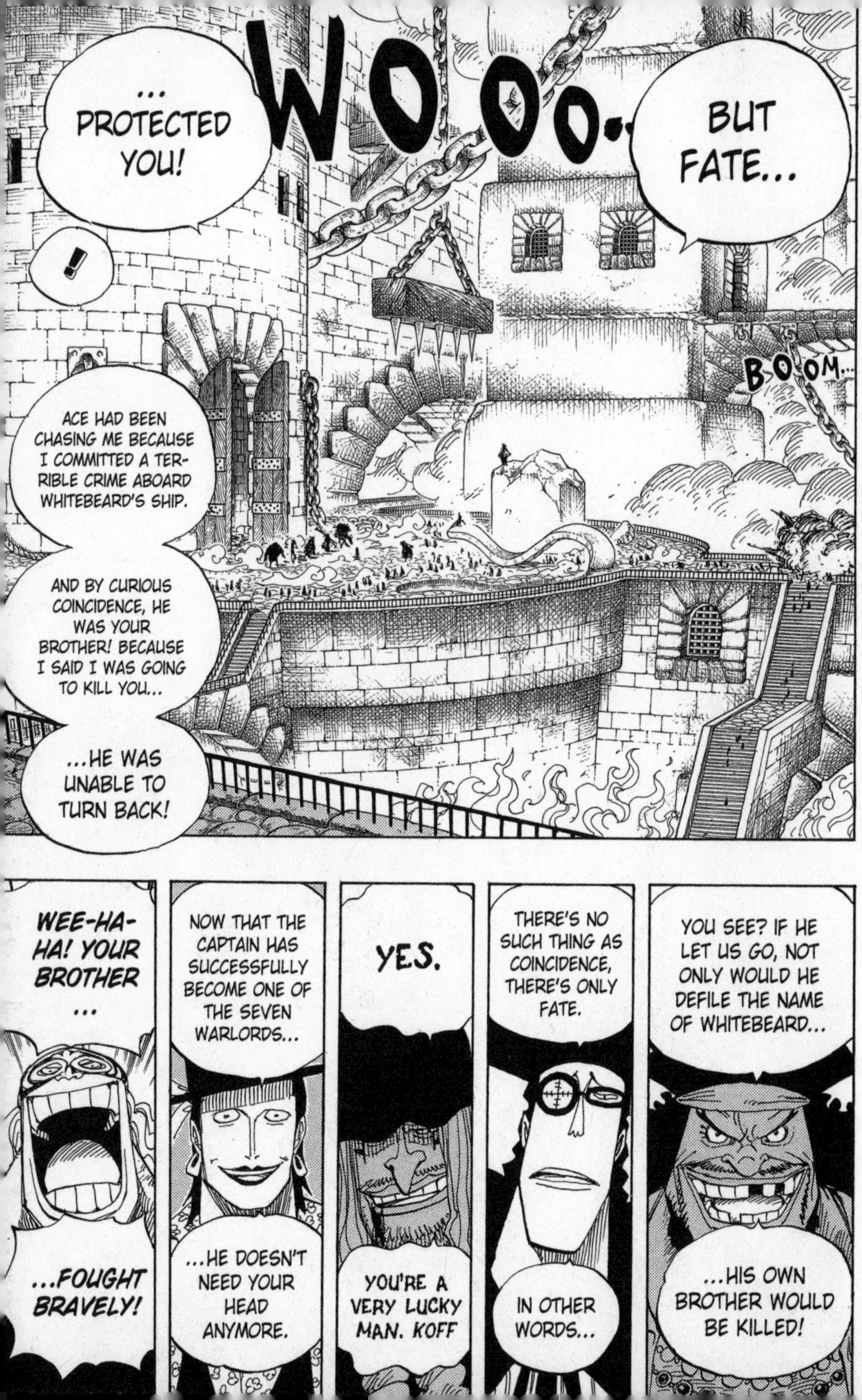
BUT FATE...
WOOO...
... PROTECTED YOU!
!
BOOM...
ACE HAD BEEN CHASING ME BECAUSE I COMMITTED A TERRIBLE CRIME ABOARD WHITEBEARD'S SHIP.
AND BY CURIOUS COINCIDENCE, HE WAS YOUR BROTHER! BECAUSE I SAID I WAS GOING TO KILL YOU...
...HE WAS UNABLE TO TURN BACK!
YOU SEE? IF HE LET US GO, NOT ONLY WOULD HE DEFILE THE NAME OF WHITEBEARD...
...HIS OWN BROTHER WOULD BE KILLED!
THERE'S NO SUCH THING AS COINCIDENCE, THERE'S ONLY FATE.
IN OTHER WORDS...
YES.
YOU'RE A VERY LUCKY MAN. KOFF
NOW THAT THE CAPTAIN HAS SUCCESSFULLY BECOME ONE OF THE SEVEN WARLORDS...
...HE DOESN'T NEED YOUR HEAD ANYMORE.
WEE-HA-HA! YOUR BROTHER...
...FOUGHT BRAVELY!

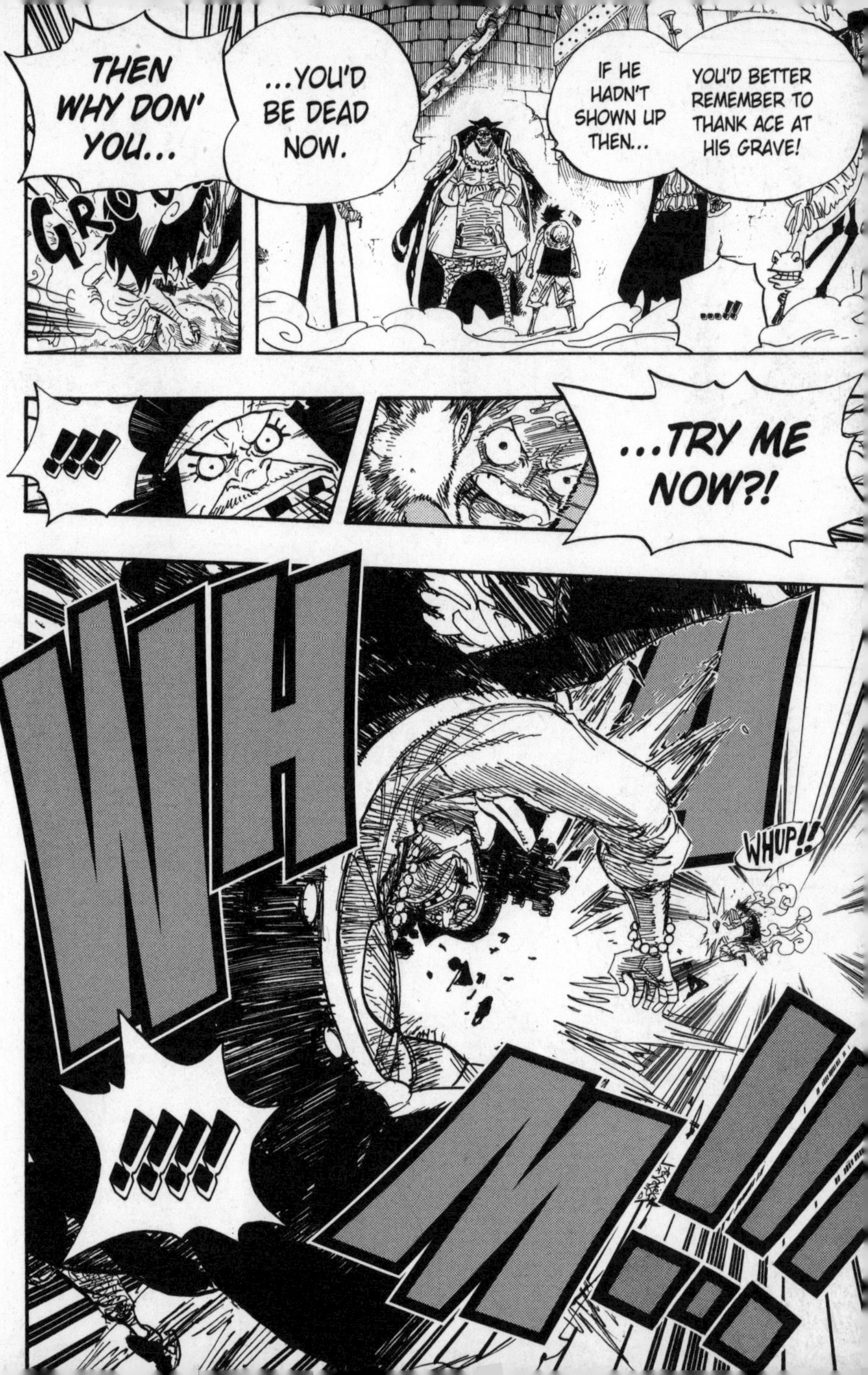
YOU'D BETTER REMEMBER TO THANK ACE AT HIS GRAVE!
IF HE HADN'T SHOWN UP THEN...
...YOU'D BE DEAD NOW.
...!!
THEN WHY DON' YOU...
GRO
...TRY ME NOW?!
!!!
WHUP!!
WHAM!!...
!!!!

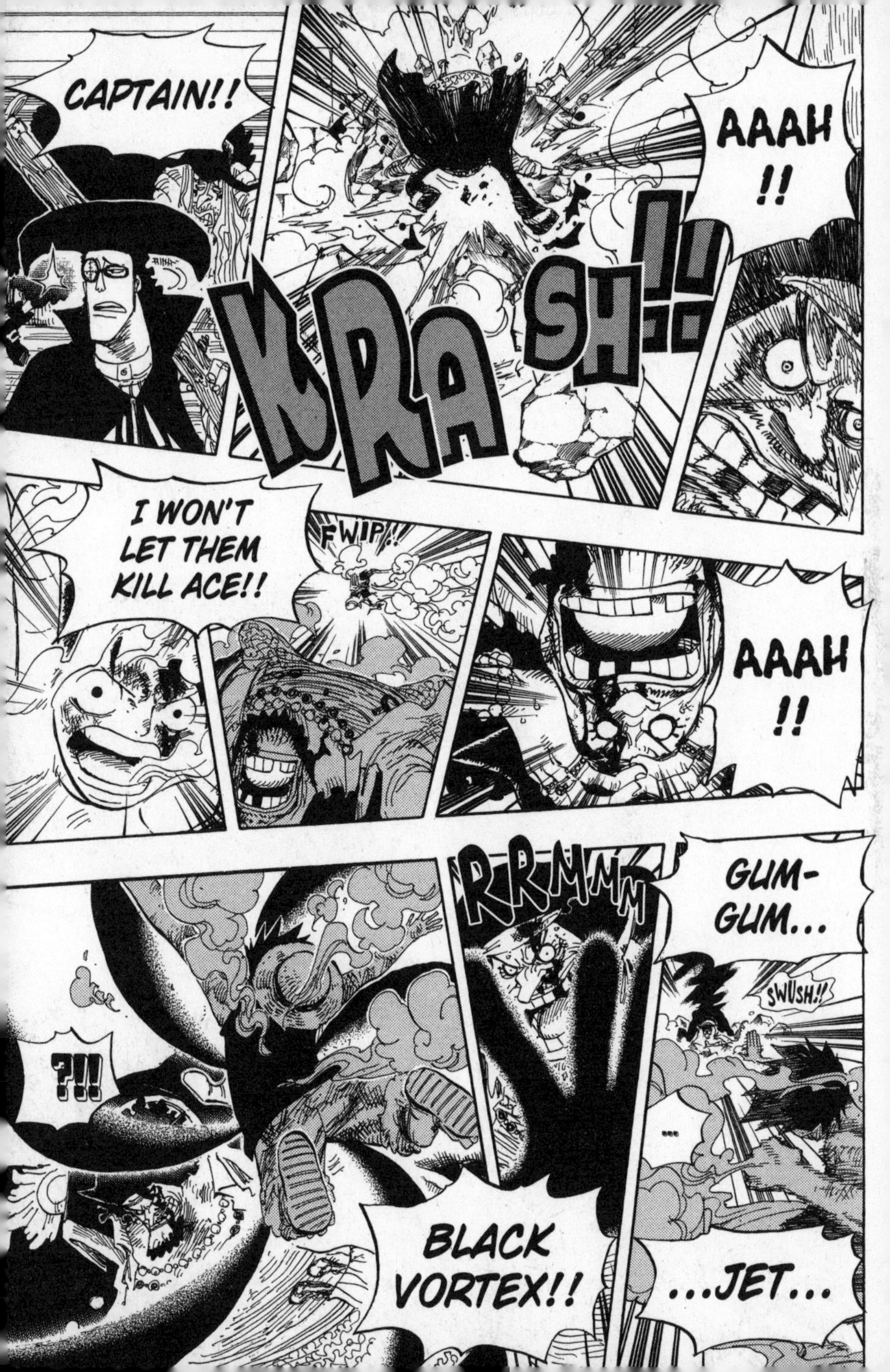
AAAH !!
KRASH!!
CAPTAIN!!
AAAH !!
FWIP!!
I WON'T LET THEM KILL ACE!!
GUM-GUM...
SWUSH!!
...
...JET...
RRMMMM
BLACK VORTEX!!
?!!

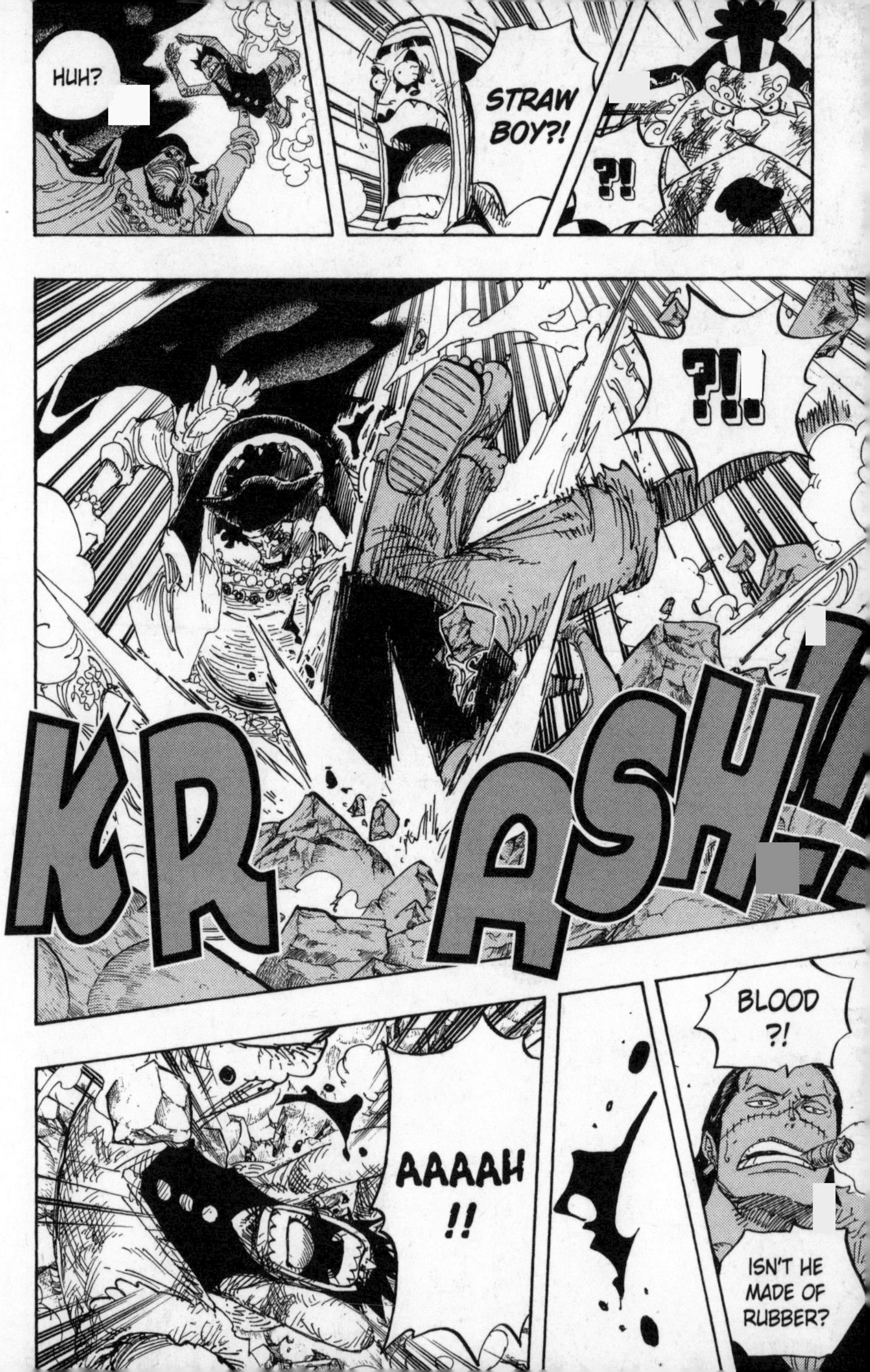
?!
STRAW BOY?!
HUH?
?!!
KRASH!!
BLOOD ?!
ISN'T HE MADE OF RUBBER?
AAAAH !!

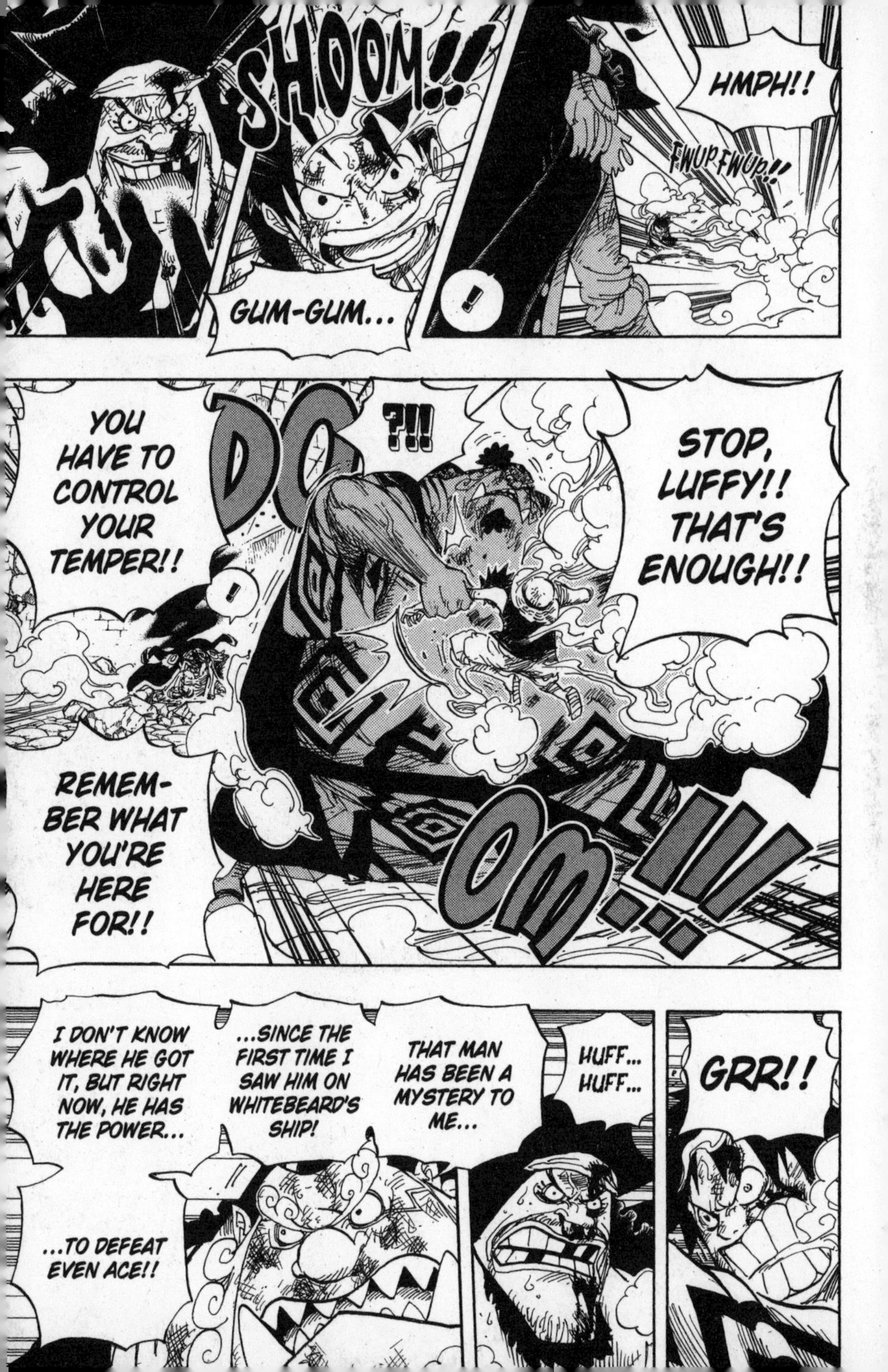
HMPH!!
FWUP FWUP!!
!
SHOOM!!
GUM-GUM...
STOP, LUFFY!! THAT'S ENOUGH!!
?!!
DO
OM!!!
!
YOU HAVE TO CONTROL YOUR TEMPER!!
REMEM-BER WHAT YOU'RE HERE FOR!!
GRR!!
HUFF... HUFF...
THAT MAN HAS BEEN A MYSTERY TO ME...
...SINCE THE FIRST TIME I SAW HIM ON WHITEBEARD'S SHIP!
I DON'T KNOW WHERE HE GOT IT, BUT RIGHT NOW, HE HAS THE POWER...
...TO DEFEAT EVEN ACE!!

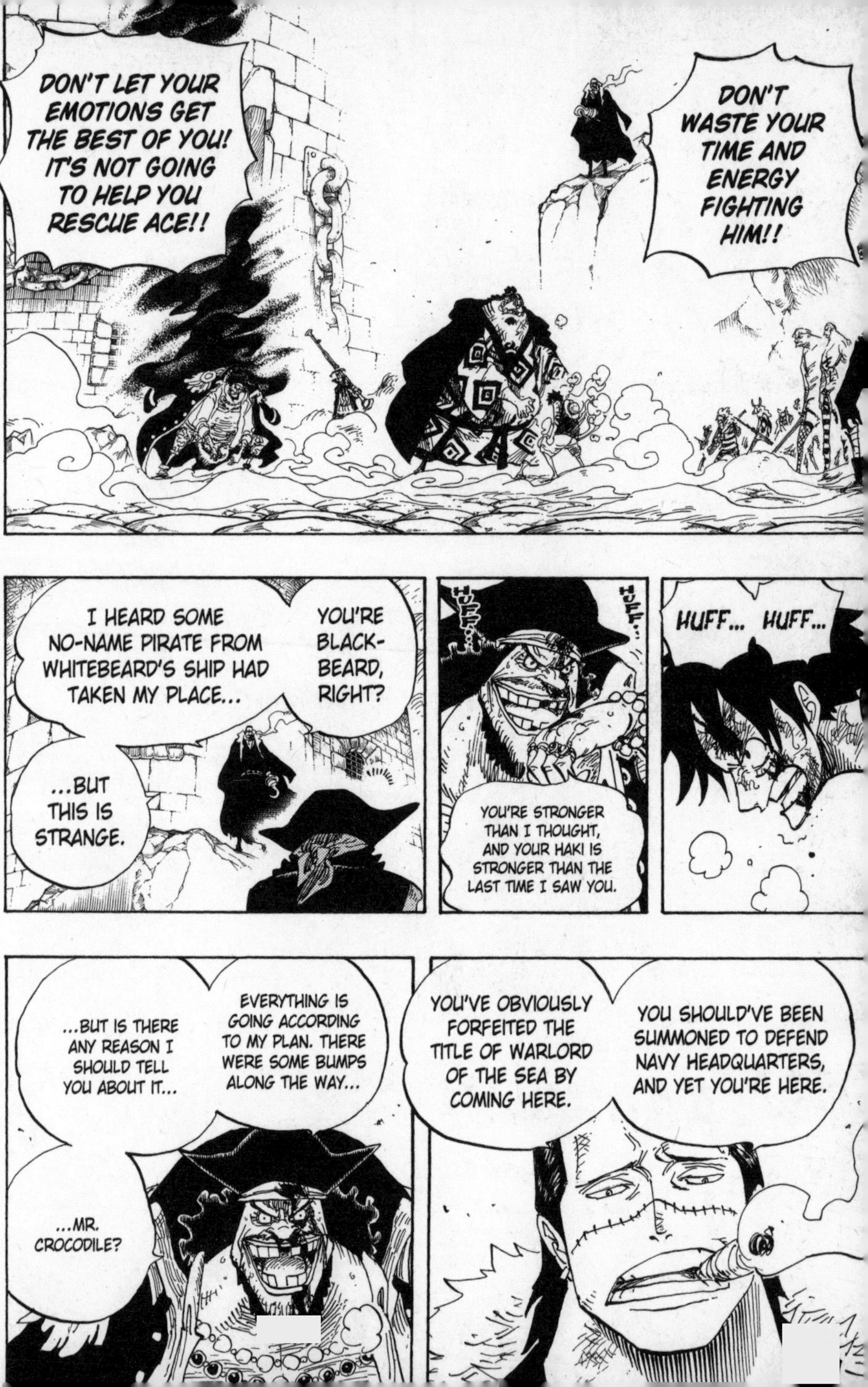
DON'T WASTE YOUR TIME AND ENERGY FIGHTING HIM!!
DON'T LET YOUR EMOTIONS GET THE BEST OF YOU! IT'S NOT GOING TO HELP YOU RESCUE ACE!!
HUFF... HUFF...
HUFF...
HUFF...
YOU'RE STRONGER THAN I THOUGHT, AND YOUR HAKI IS STRONGER THAN THE LAST TIME I SAW YOU.
YOU'RE BLACK-BEARD, RIGHT?
I HEARD SOME NO-NAME PIRATE FROM WHITEBEARD'S SHIP HAD TAKEN MY PLACE...
...BUT THIS IS STRANGE.
YOU SHOULD'VE BEEN SUMMONED TO DEFEND NAVY HEADQUARTERS, AND YET YOU'RE HERE.
YOU'VE OBVIOUSLY FORFEITED THE TITLE OF WARLORD OF THE SEA BY COMING HERE.
EVERYTHING IS GOING ACCORDING TO MY PLAN. THERE WERE SOME BUMPS ALONG THE WAY...
...BUT IS THERE ANY REASON I SHOULD TELL YOU ABOUT IT...
...MR. CROCODILE?

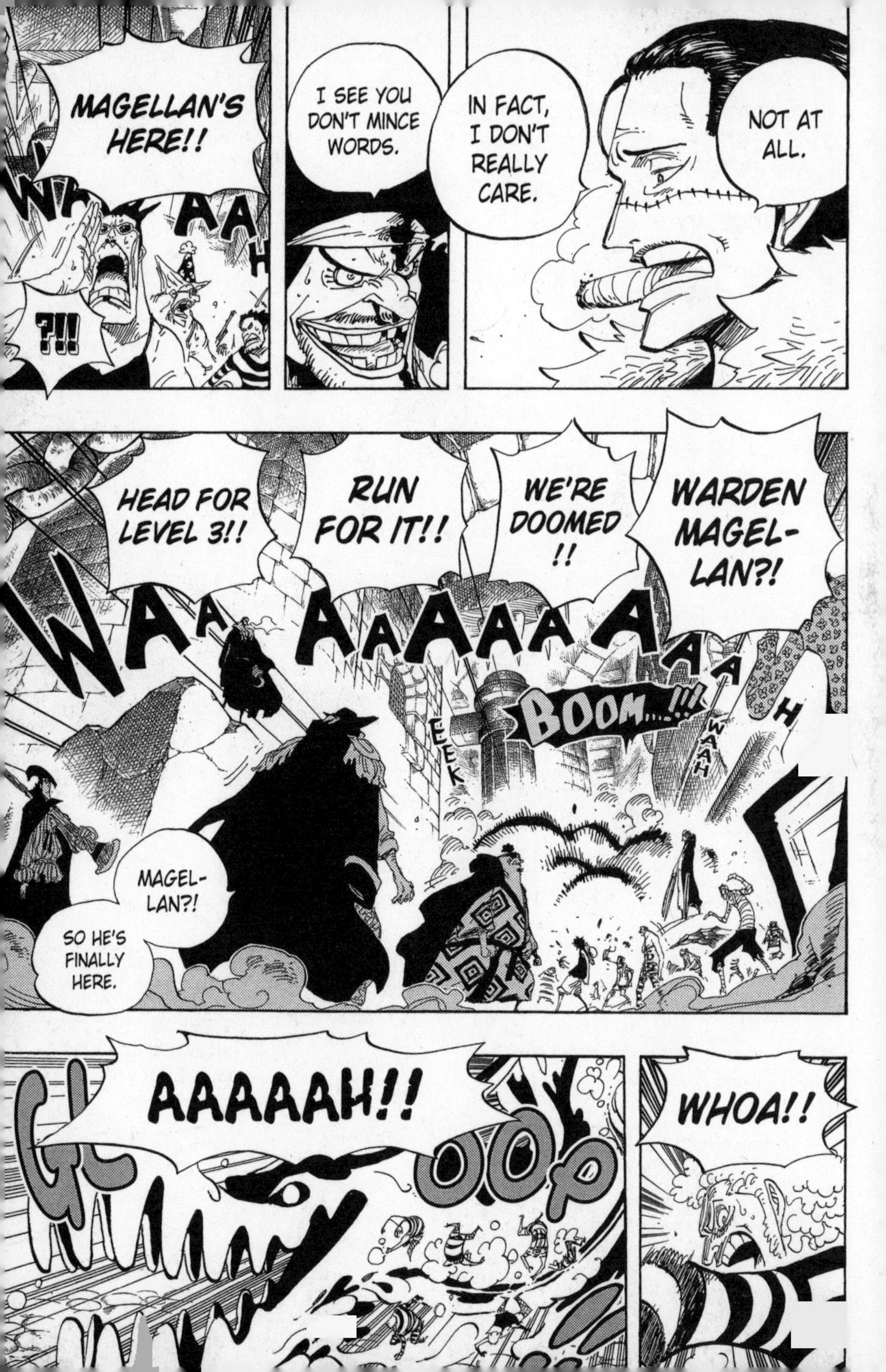
NOT AT ALL.
IN FACT, I DON'T REALLY CARE.
I SEE YOU DON'T MINCE WORDS.
MAGELLAN'S HERE!!
WHAAAAH
?!!
WARDEN MAGEL-LAN?!
WE'RE DOOMED!!
RUN FOR IT!!
HEAD FOR LEVEL 3!!
WAAAAAAAAAAAH
BOOM...!!!
WAAH
EEEK
MAGEL-LAN?!
SO HE'S FINALLY HERE.
WHOA!!
AAAAAH!!
GLOOP

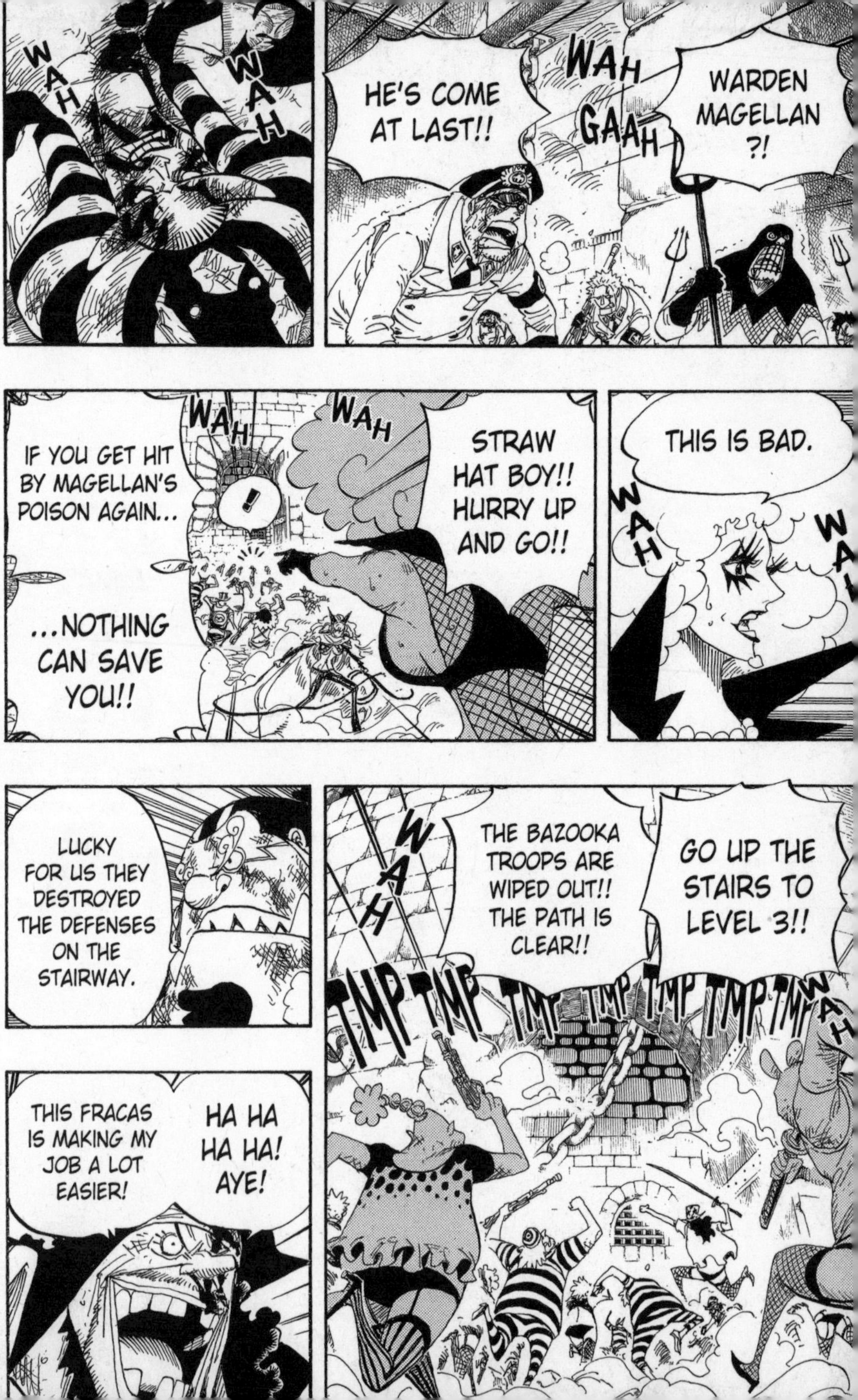
WARDEN MAGELLAN ?!
WAH GAAH
HE'S COME AT LAST!!
WAH
WAH
THIS IS BAD.
WAH
WAH
STRAW HAT BOY!! HURRY UP AND GO!!
WAH
WAH
IF YOU GET HIT BY MAGELLAN'S POISON AGAIN...
...NOTHING CAN SAVE YOU!!
GO UP THE STAIRS TO LEVEL 3!!
THE BAZOOKA TROOPS ARE WIPED OUT!! THE PATH IS CLEAR!!
WAH
WAH
TMP TMP TMP TMP TMP TMP TMP TMP
LUCKY FOR US THEY DESTROYED THE DEFENSES ON THE STAIRWAY.
HA HA HA HA! AYE!
THIS FRACAS IS MAKING MY JOB A LOT EASIER!

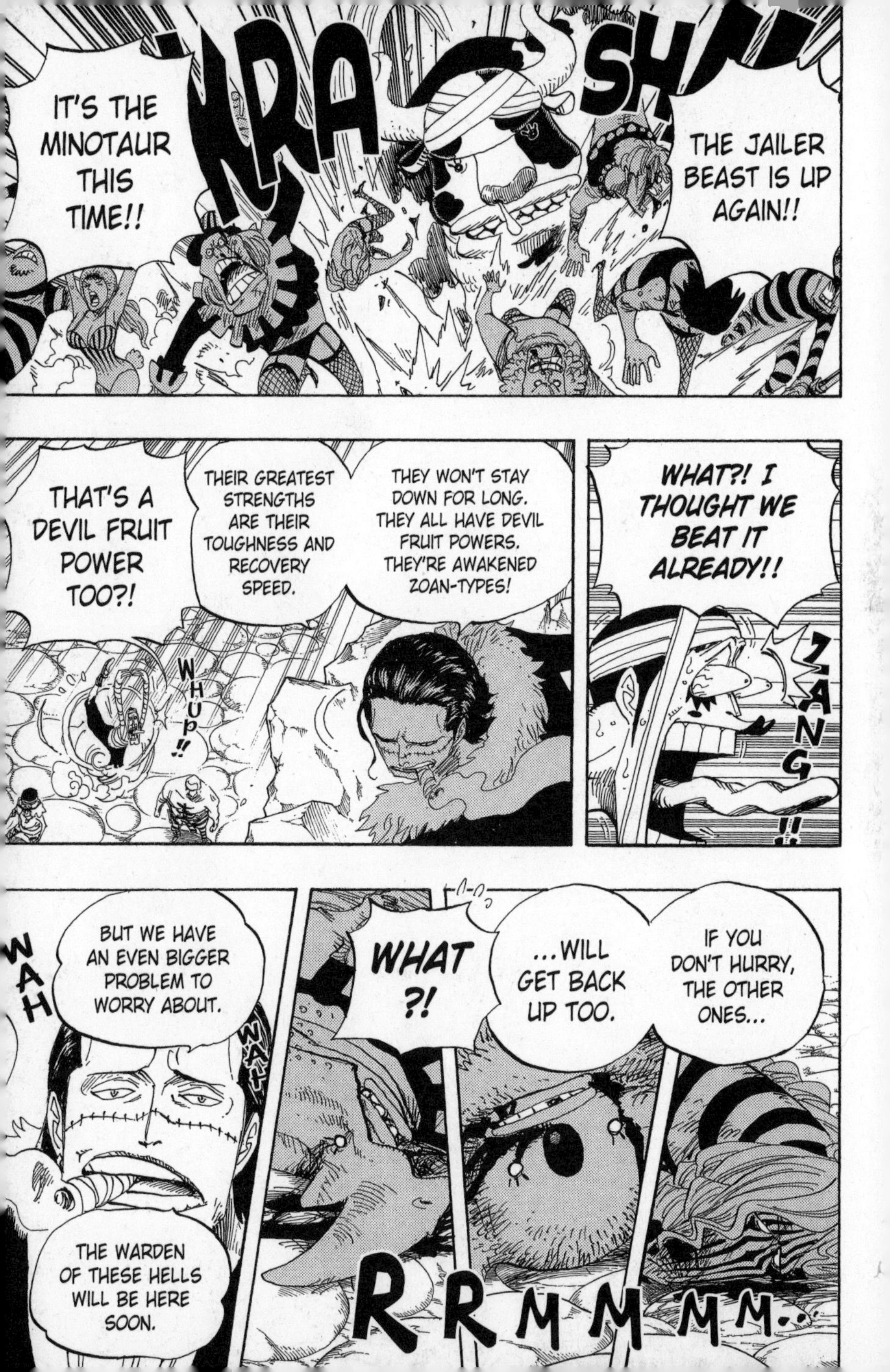
THE JAILER BEAST IS UP AGAIN!!
KRASH
IT'S THE MINOTAUR THIS TIME!!
WHAT?! I THOUGHT WE BEAT IT ALREADY!!
ZANG!!
THEY WON'T STAY DOWN FOR LONG. THEY ALL HAVE DEVIL FRUIT POWERS. THEY'RE AWAKENED ZOAN-TYPES!
THEIR GREATEST STRENGTHS ARE THEIR TOUGHNESS AND RECOVERY SPEED.
THAT'S A DEVIL FRUIT POWER TOO?!
WHUP!!
IF YOU DON'T HURRY, THE OTHER ONES...
...WILL GET BACK UP TOO.
WHAT ?!
RRMMMMM...
BUT WE HAVE AN EVEN BIGGER PROBLEM TO WORRY ABOUT.
WAH
WAH
THE WARDEN OF THESE HELLS WILL BE HERE SOON.

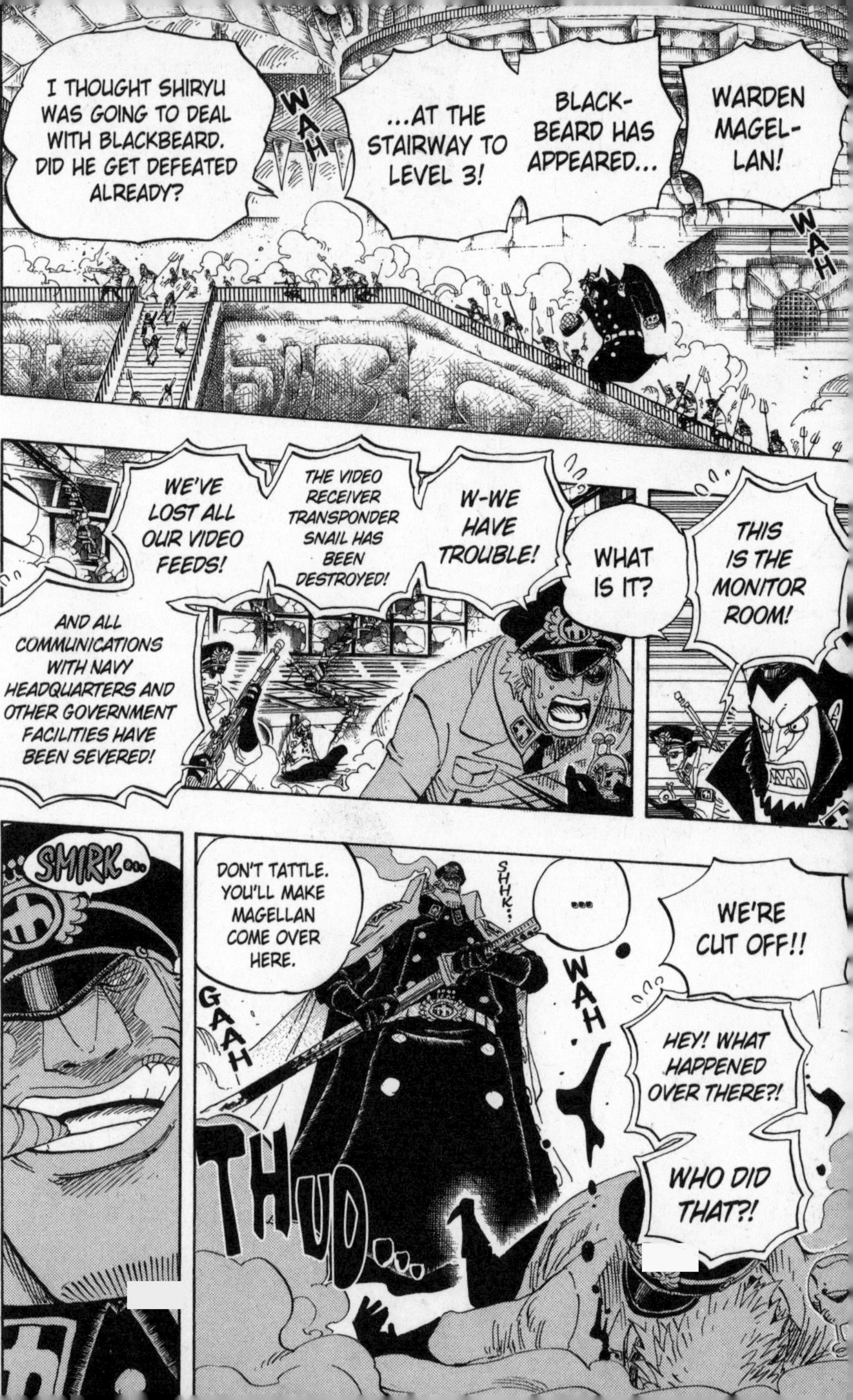
WARDEN MAGEL-LAN!
WAH
BLACK-BEARD HAS APPEARED...
...AT THE STAIRWAY TO LEVEL 3!
WAH
I THOUGHT SHIRYU WAS GOING TO DEAL WITH BLACKBEARD. DID HE GET DEFEATED ALREADY?
THIS IS THE MONITOR ROOM!
WHAT IS IT?
W-WE HAVE TROUBLE!
THE VIDEO RECEIVER TRANSPONDER SNAIL HAS BEEN DESTROYED!
WE'VE LOST ALL OUR VIDEO FEEDS!
AND ALL COMMUNICATIONS WITH NAVY HEADQUARTERS AND OTHER GOVERNMENT FACILITIES HAVE BEEN SEVERED!
WE'RE CUT OFF!!
...
SHHK...
WAH
DON'T TATTLE. YOU'LL MAKE MAGELLAN COME OVER HERE.
GAAH
HEY! WHAT HAPPENED OVER THERE?!
WHO DID THAT?!
THUD...
SMIRK...

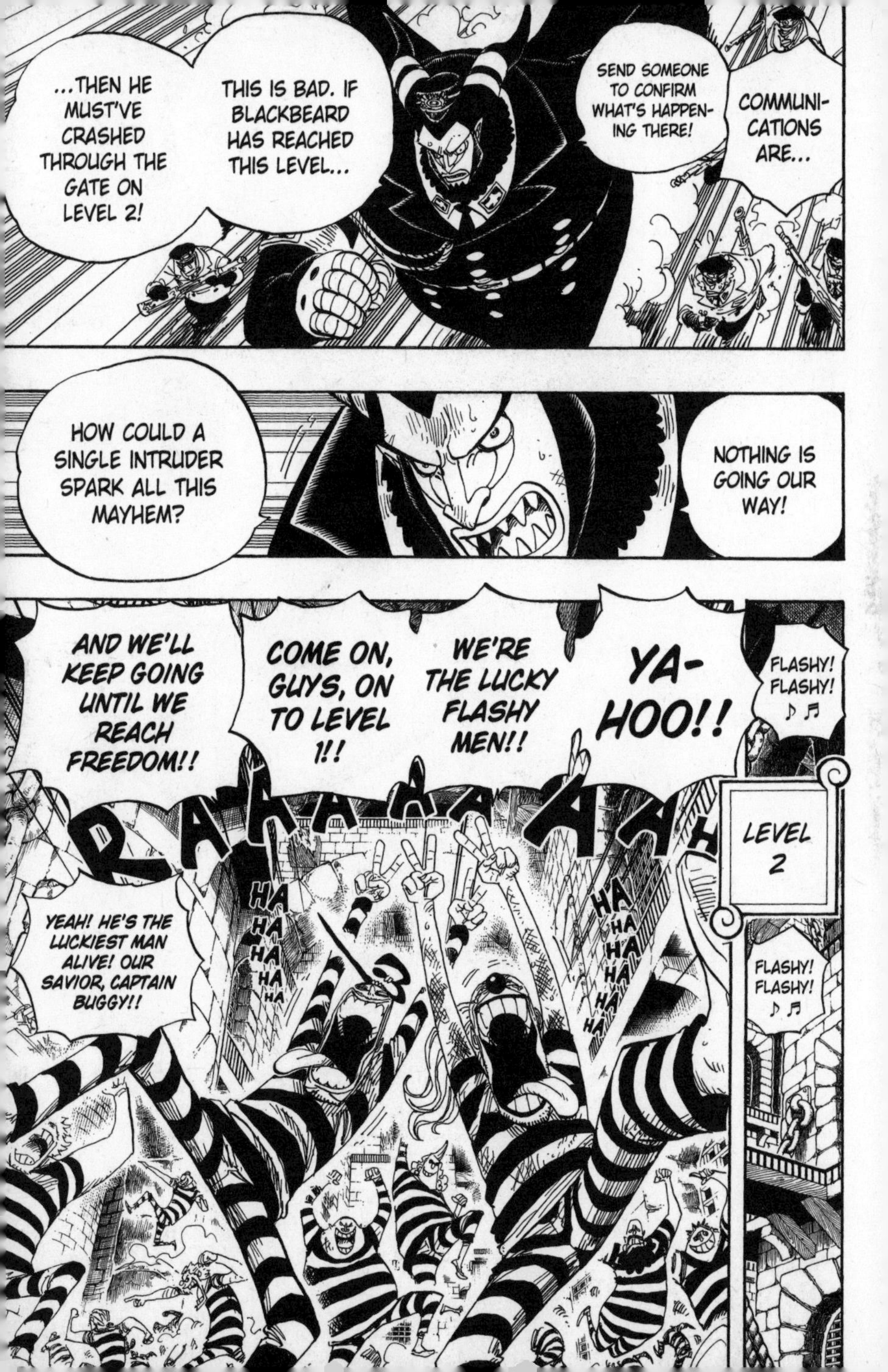
COMMUNICATIONS ARE...
SEND SOMEONE TO CONFIRM WHAT'S HAPPENING THERE!
THIS IS BAD. IF BLACKBEARD HAS REACHED THIS LEVEL...
...THEN HE MUST'VE CRASHED THROUGH THE GATE ON LEVEL 2!
NOTHING IS GOING OUR WAY!
HOW COULD A SINGLE INTRUDER SPARK ALL THIS MAYHEM?
FLASHY! FLASHY! ♪ ♬
YA-HOO!!
WE'RE THE LUCKY FLASHY MEN!!
COME ON, GUYS, ON TO LEVEL 1!!
AND WE'LL KEEP GOING UNTIL WE REACH FREEDOM!!
RAAAAAAAH
LEVEL 2
HA HA HA HA HA HA HA HA
HA HA HA HA HA HA HA
FLASHY! FLASHY! ♪ ♬
YEAH! HE'S THE LUCKIEST MAN ALIVE! OUR SAVIOR, CAPTAIN BUGGY!!

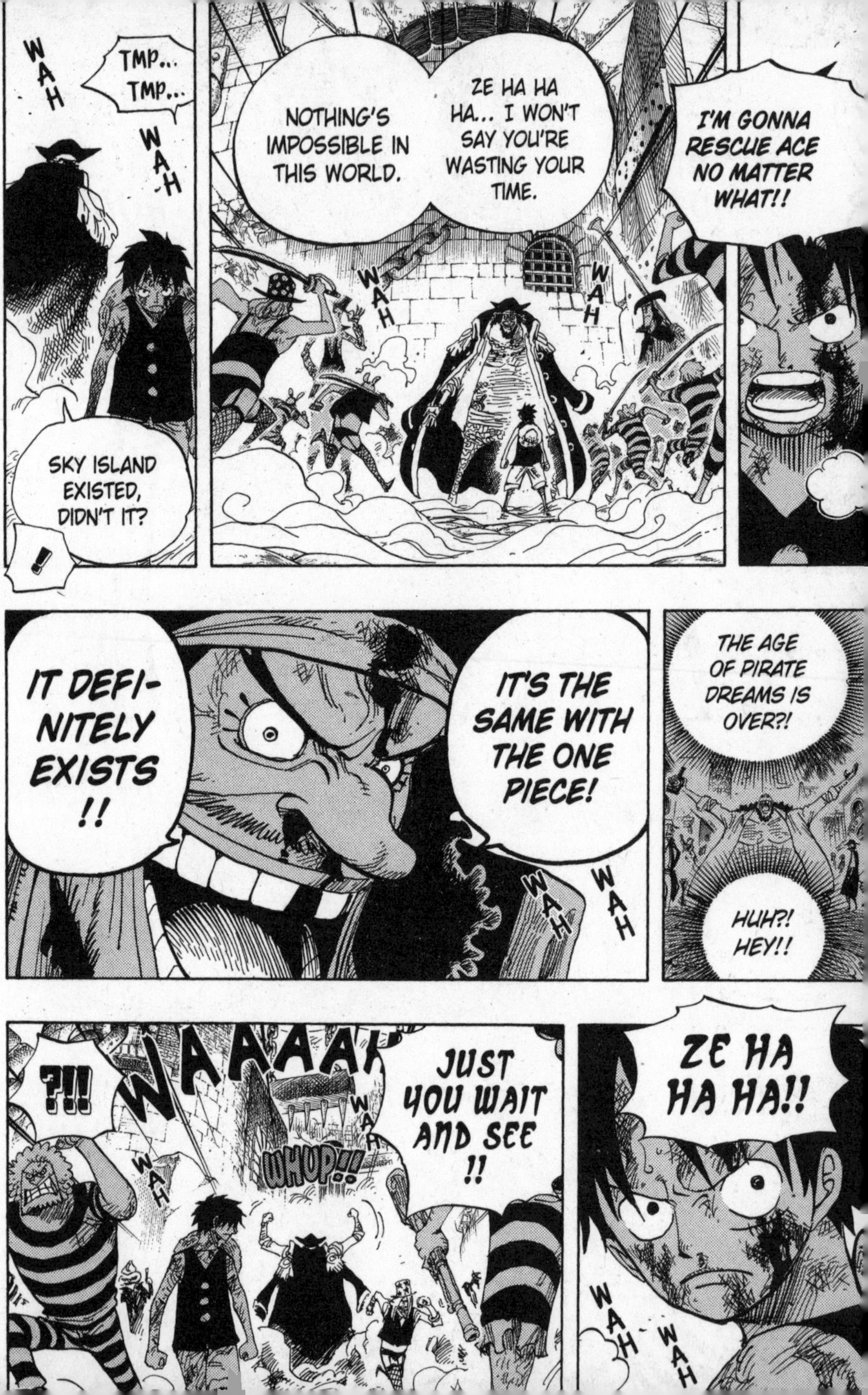
I'M GONNA RESCUE ACE NO MATTER WHAT!!
ZE HA HA HA... I WON'T SAY YOU'RE WASTING YOUR TIME.
NOTHING'S IMPOSSIBLE IN THIS WORLD.
WAH
WAH
TMP... TMP...
WAH
WAH
SKY ISLAND EXISTED, DIDN'T IT?
!
THE AGE OF PIRATE DREAMS IS OVER?!
HUH?! HEY!!
IT'S THE SAME WITH THE ONE PIECE!
IT DEFI-NITELY EXISTS!!
WAH
WAH
ZE HA HA HA!!
WAH
WAH
JUST YOU WAIT AND SEE!!
WAAAA!
WAH
WHUP!!
?!!
WAH

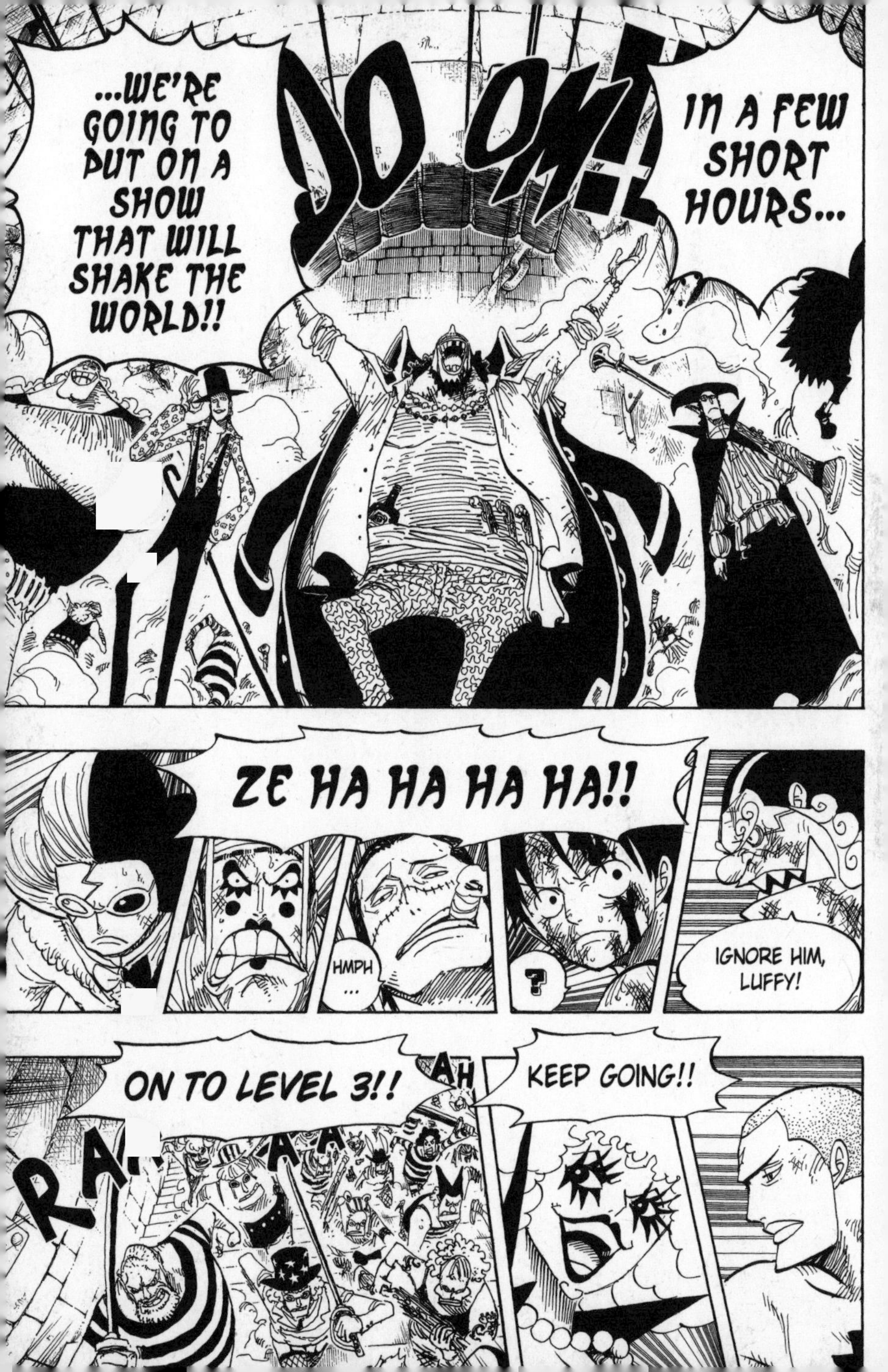
IN A FEW SHORT HOURS...
DO ON!
...WE'RE GOING TO PUT ON A SHOW THAT WILL SHAKE THE WORLD!!
ZE HA HA HA HA!!
IGNORE HIM, LUFFY!
?
HMPH ...
KEEP GOING!!
ON TO LEVEL 3!!
RA A A AH

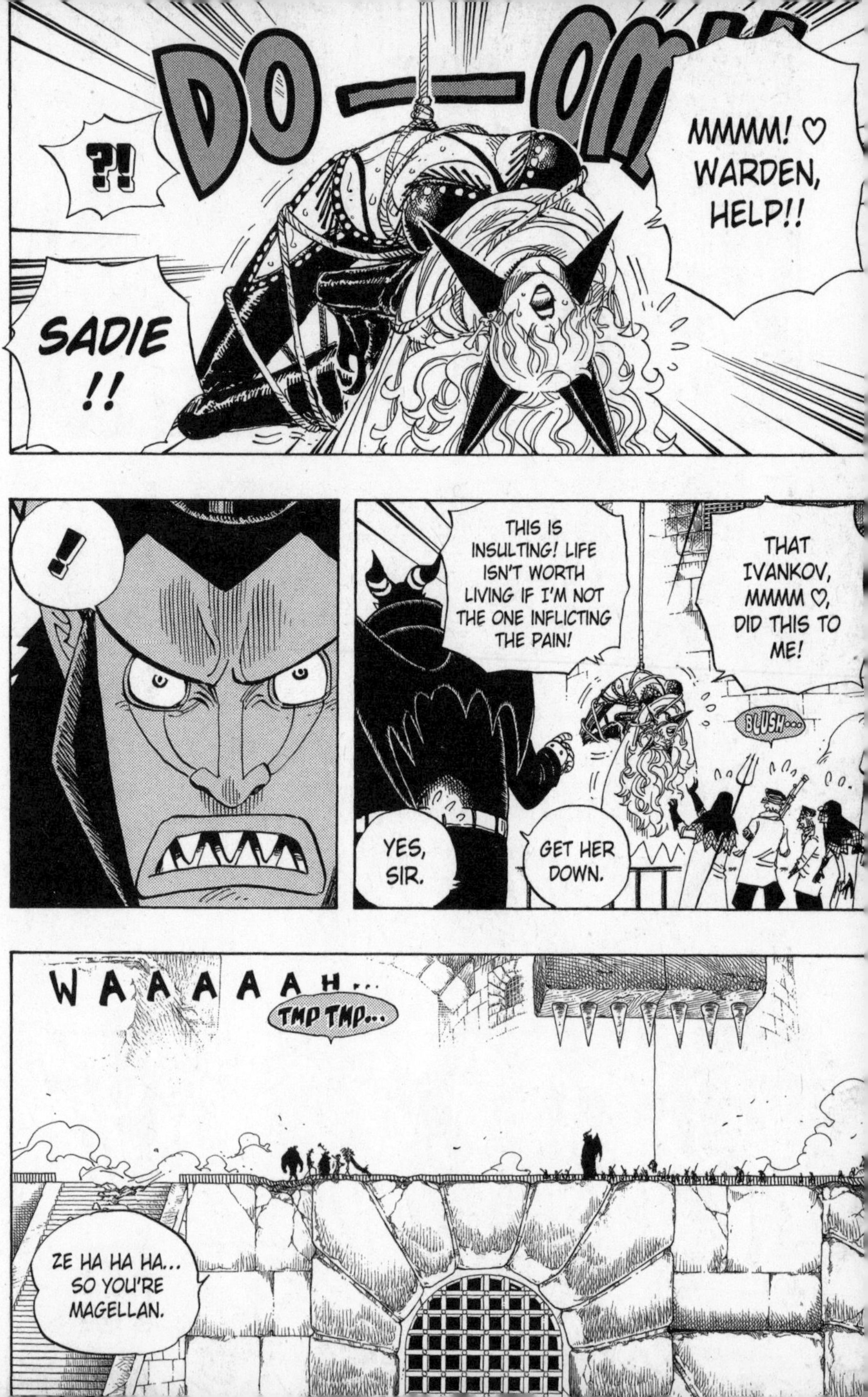
DO——OM
MMMM! ♡ WARDEN, HELP!!
?!
SADIE !!
THAT IVANKOV, MMMM ♡, DID THIS TO ME!
THIS IS INSULTING! LIFE ISN'T WORTH LIVING IF I'M NOT THE ONE INFLICTING THE PAIN!
BLUSH...
GET HER DOWN.
YES, SIR.
!
WAAAAAH...
TMP TMP...
ZE HA HA HA... SO YOU'RE MAGELLAN.

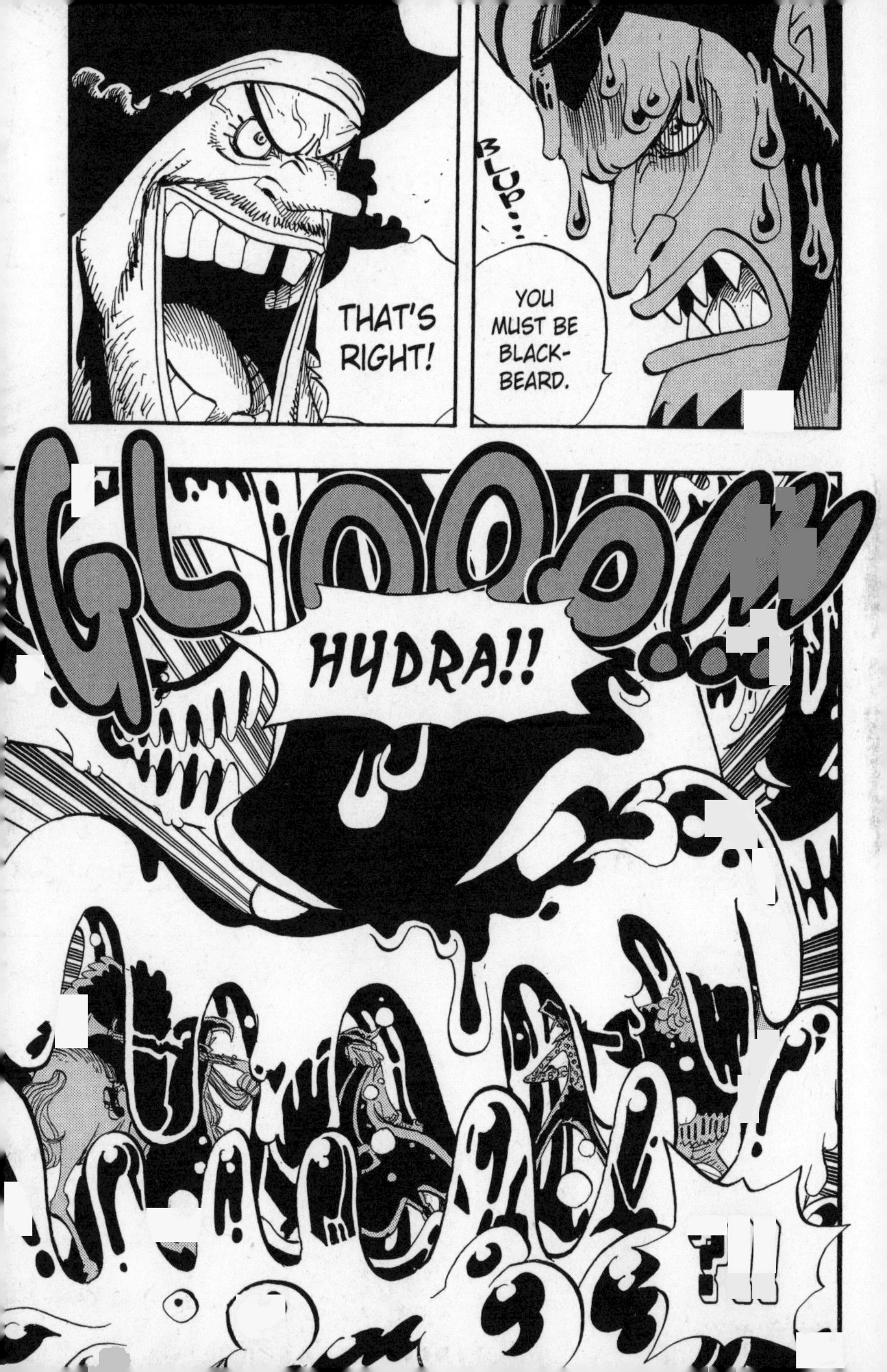
BLUP...
YOU MUST BE BLACK-BEARD.
THAT'S RIGHT!
HYDRA!!

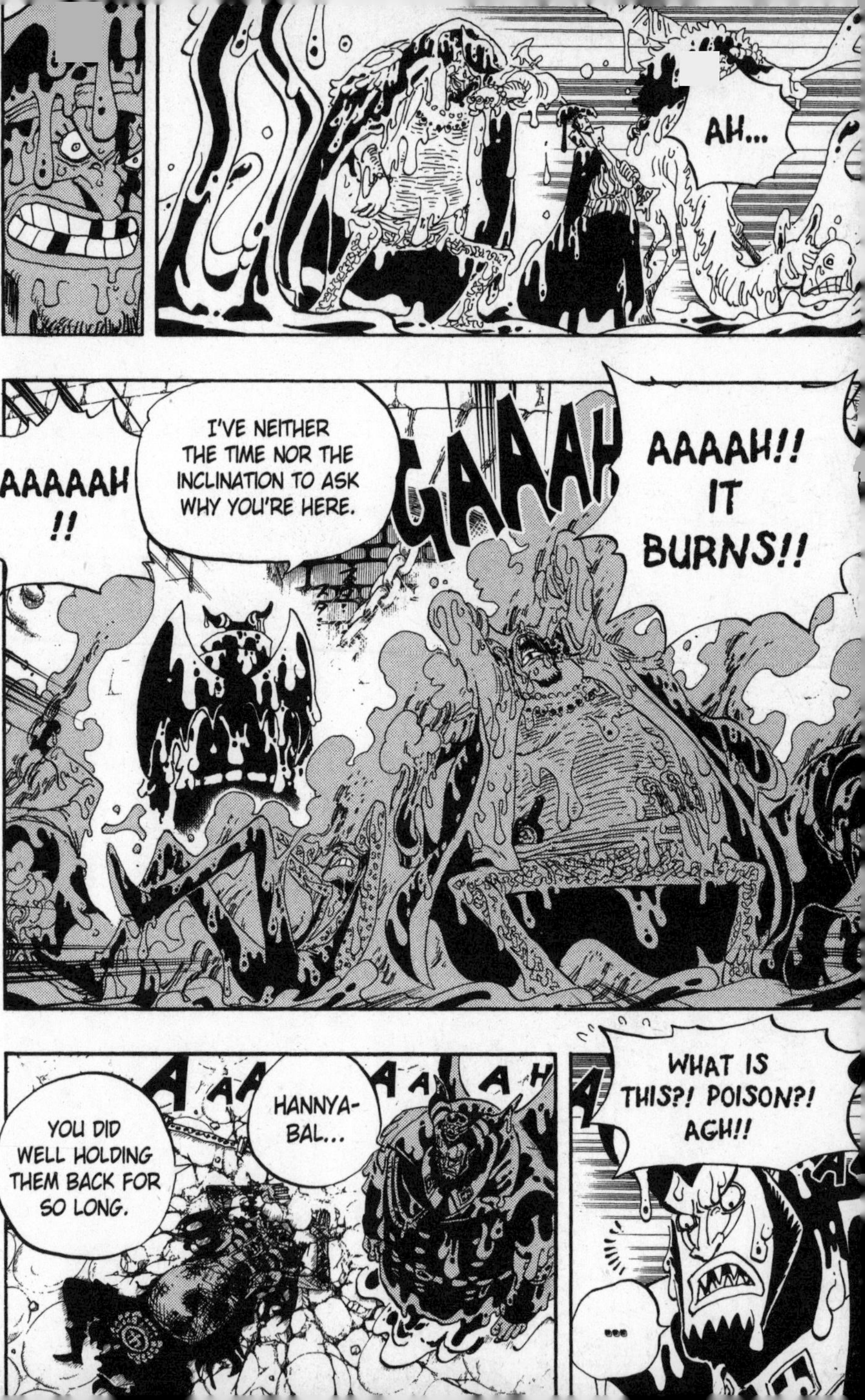
AH...
AAAAH!!
IT
BURNS!!
I'VE NEITHER THE TIME NOR THE INCLINATION TO ASK WHY YOU'RE HERE.
AAAAAH !!
WHAT IS THIS?! POISON?! AGH!!
...
HANNYA-BAL...
YOU DID WELL HOLDING THEM BACK FOR SO LONG.

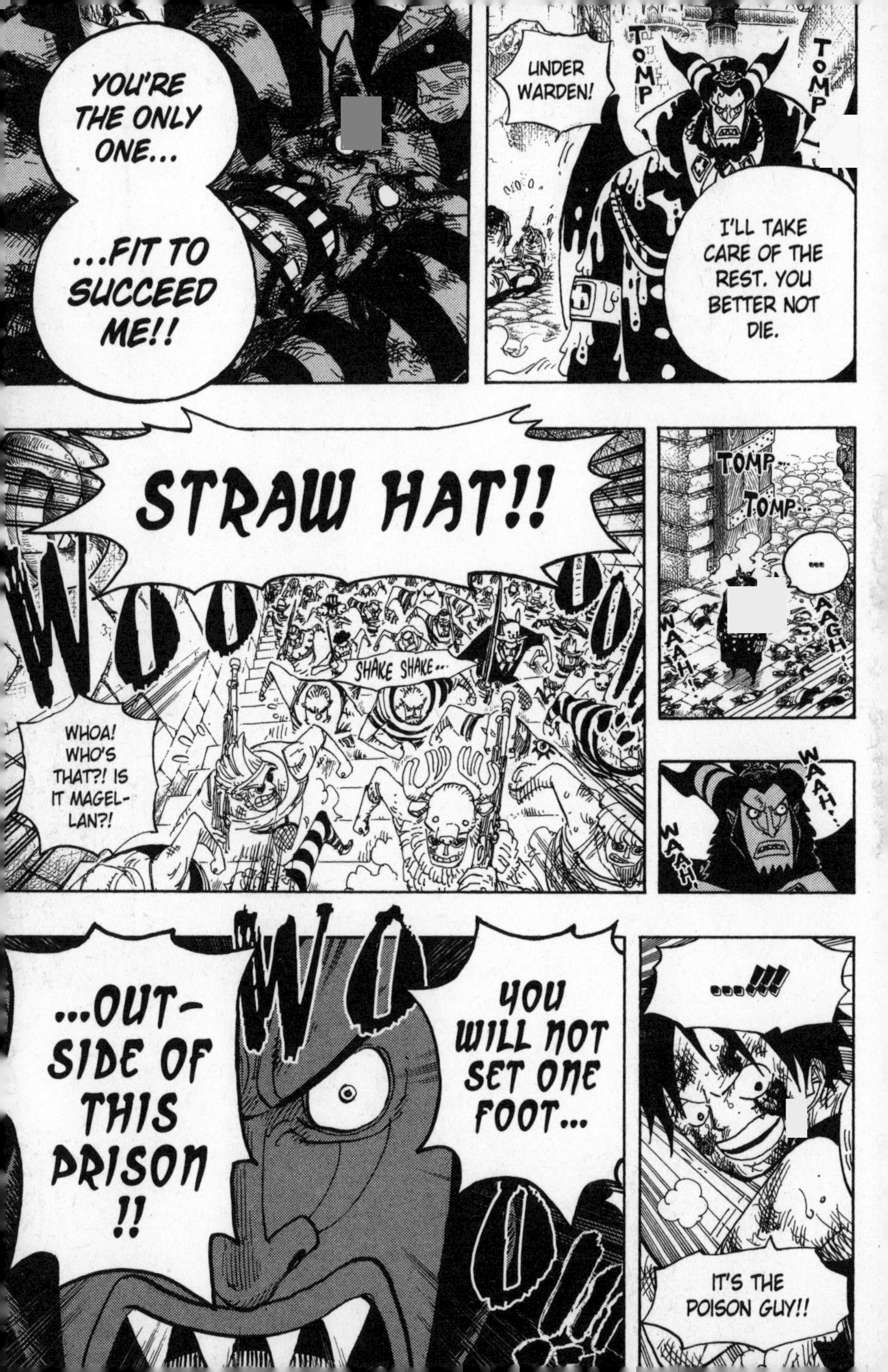
UNDER WARDEN!
TOMP
TOMP
I'LL TAKE CARE OF THE REST. YOU BETTER NOT DIE.
YOU'RE THE ONLY ONE...
...FIT TO SUCCEED ME!!
TOMP...
TOMP...
...
AAGH!!
WAAH!!
WAAH!!
WAAH!!
STRAW HAT!!
WOOO
SHAKE SHAKE...
WHOA! WHO'S THAT?! IS IT MAGEL-LAN?!
...!!!
IT'S THE POISON GUY!!
YOU WILL NOT SET ONE FOOT...
...OUT-SIDE OF THIS PRISON!!
WO

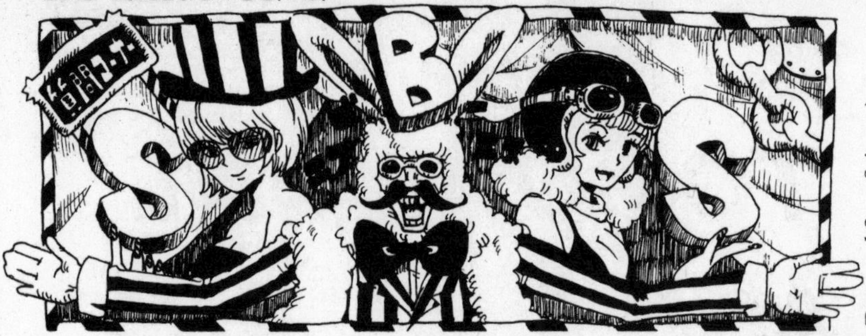
SBS

(Papa and Son, Saitama)

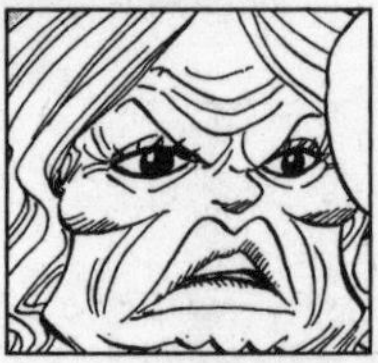

Q: Does Old Lady Nyon have a double butt chin?

--Gon-chan

A: You're right! It's a double chin just like Franky! I wonder if she can shoot out Coup de Vent!

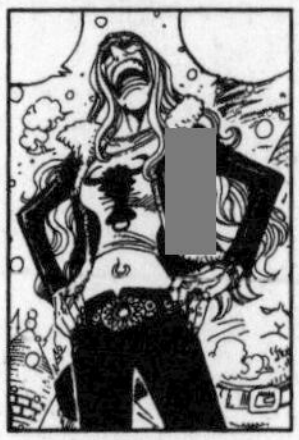

Q: Mr. Oda. On the cover of volume 54, you said that people can normally live up to 140 years. Is Dr. Kureha all right?

--Dummy

A: Well, hmm. Wasn't she 139 years old? Well, 140 is about the max for normal folk, but she's a "super-human." An elderly person that will die in a year usually doesn't walk around with her belly exposed in the middle of snow.

Q: I just noticed this, but you always listen to your readers, Odacchi. So how about a "New Character Design Contest" or a "The Devil Fruit that I came up with!" type of thing? As for me, well… How about a Diarrhea-Diarrhea Fruit or Poo-Poo Fruit? A person that will never be constipated thanks to the Poo-Poo Fruit!"

--Scorpion Woman

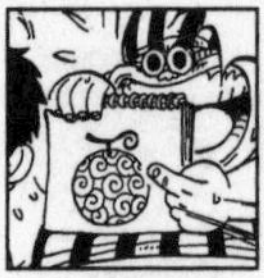

A: No! That's nothing but a normal healthy person! And about that contest, I probably won't be doing it. I don't need it. This might seem a bit cold on my part, but I don't want anybody else's ideas. My editor at Jump changes from time to time, but the first thing I always say to my new editor is "Do not give me any of your ideas." I want to say that all the characters and story are something that I came up with myself. If I started relying on one person, I would end up doing it again with another person. And if I messed up, I might end up blaming that person. If it goes well, it's thanks to me. If it flops, it's my fault. That's something I like. Oh, but there are ideas I want that aren't related to the main story. The cover art of members of the Straw Hat Pirates together with animals. I want ideas relating to that. If you send me letters with stuff like "Draw this character doing something with this animal" then I'll gladly draw it.

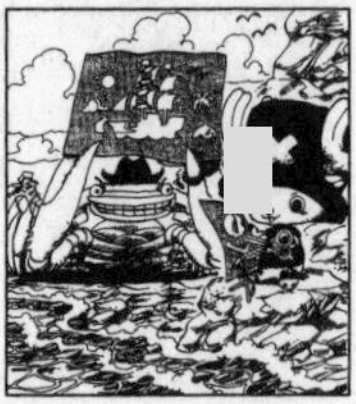

Chapter 545:
TO SUNSHINE AND FREEDOM

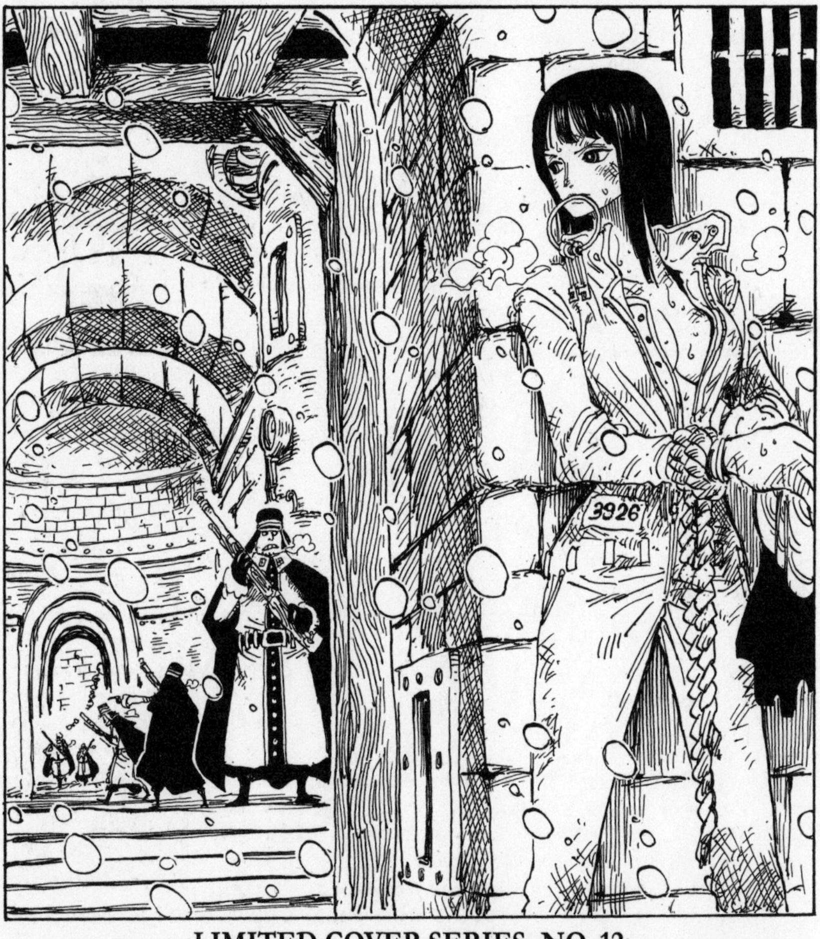
3926

LIMITED COVER SERIES, NO. 12:
ROBIN'S "THEY DO SUCH TERRIBLE THINGS"
VOL. 1: "ADVENTURE IN THE LAND OF THE SLAVES"

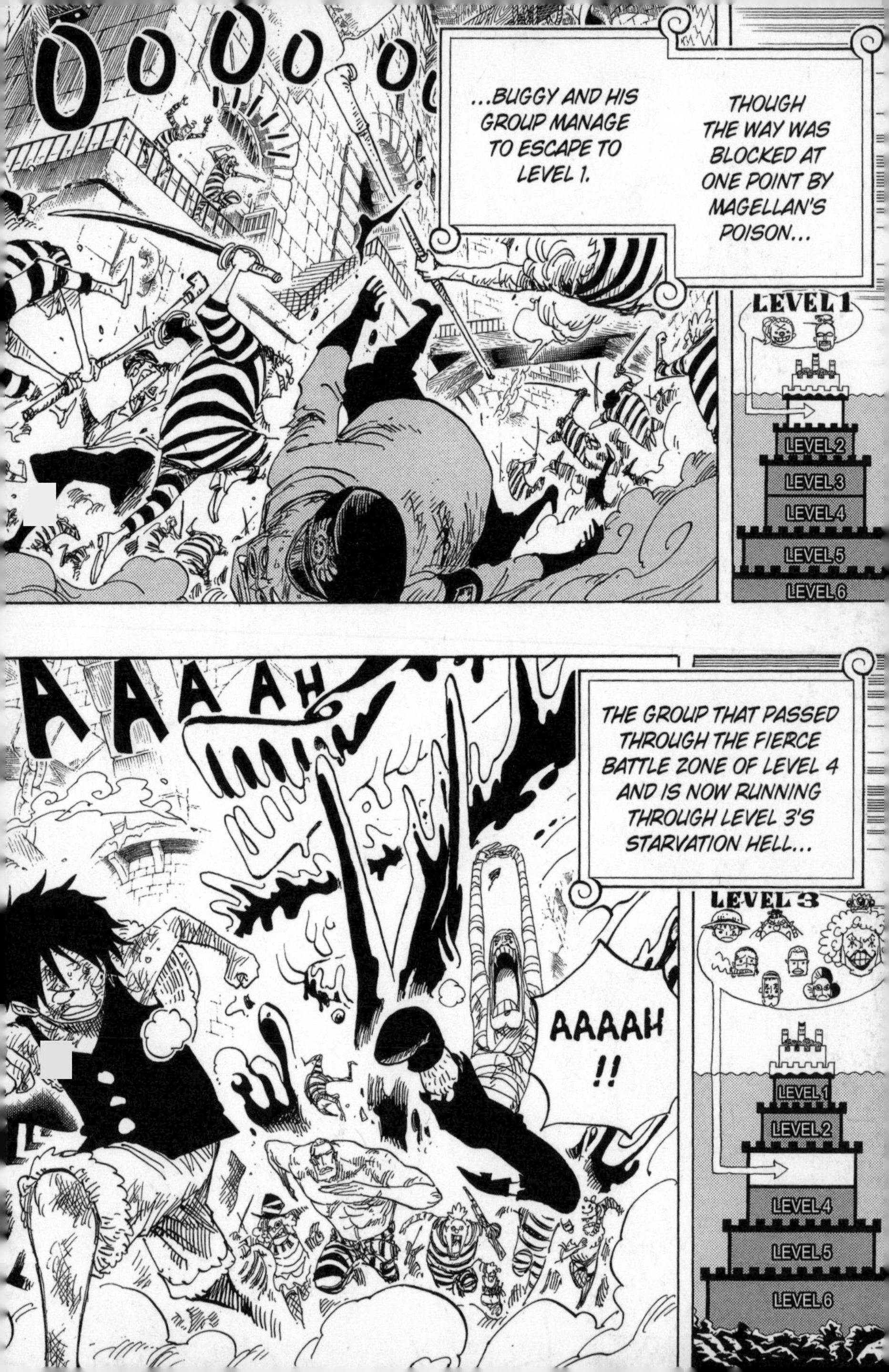
THOUGH THE WAY WAS BLOCKED AT ONE POINT BY MAGELLAN'S POISON...
...BUGGY AND HIS GROUP MANAGE TO ESCAPE TO LEVEL 1.
LEVEL 1
LEVEL 2
LEVEL 3
LEVEL 4
LEVEL 5
LEVEL 6
OOOOOO
THE GROUP THAT PASSED THROUGH THE FIERCE BATTLE ZONE OF LEVEL 4 AND IS NOW RUNNING THROUGH LEVEL 3'S STARVATION HELL...
LEVEL 3
LEVEL 1
LEVEL 2
LEVEL 4
LEVEL 5
LEVEL 6
AAAAH !!
AAAAH

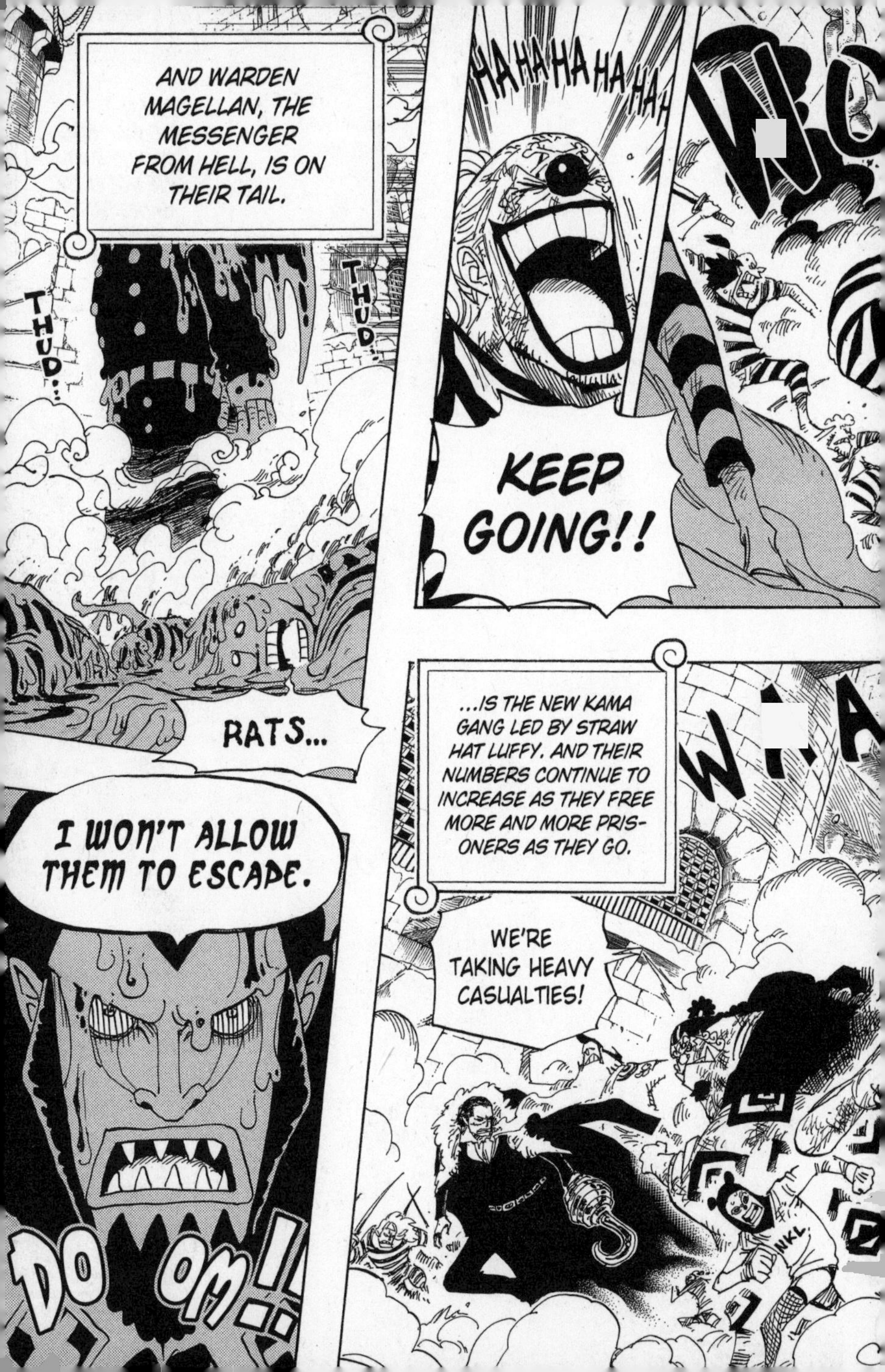
HAHAHAHAHAHAH
KEEP GOING!!
...IS THE NEW KAMA GANG LED BY STRAW HAT LUFFY. AND THEIR NUMBERS CONTINUE TO INCREASE AS THEY FREE MORE AND MORE PRISONERS AS THEY GO.
WE'RE TAKING HEAVY CASUALTIES!
NKL
AND WARDEN MAGELLAN, THE MESSENGER FROM HELL, IS ON THEIR TAIL.
THUD...
THUD...
RATS...
I WON'T ALLOW THEM TO ESCAPE.
DO OM!!

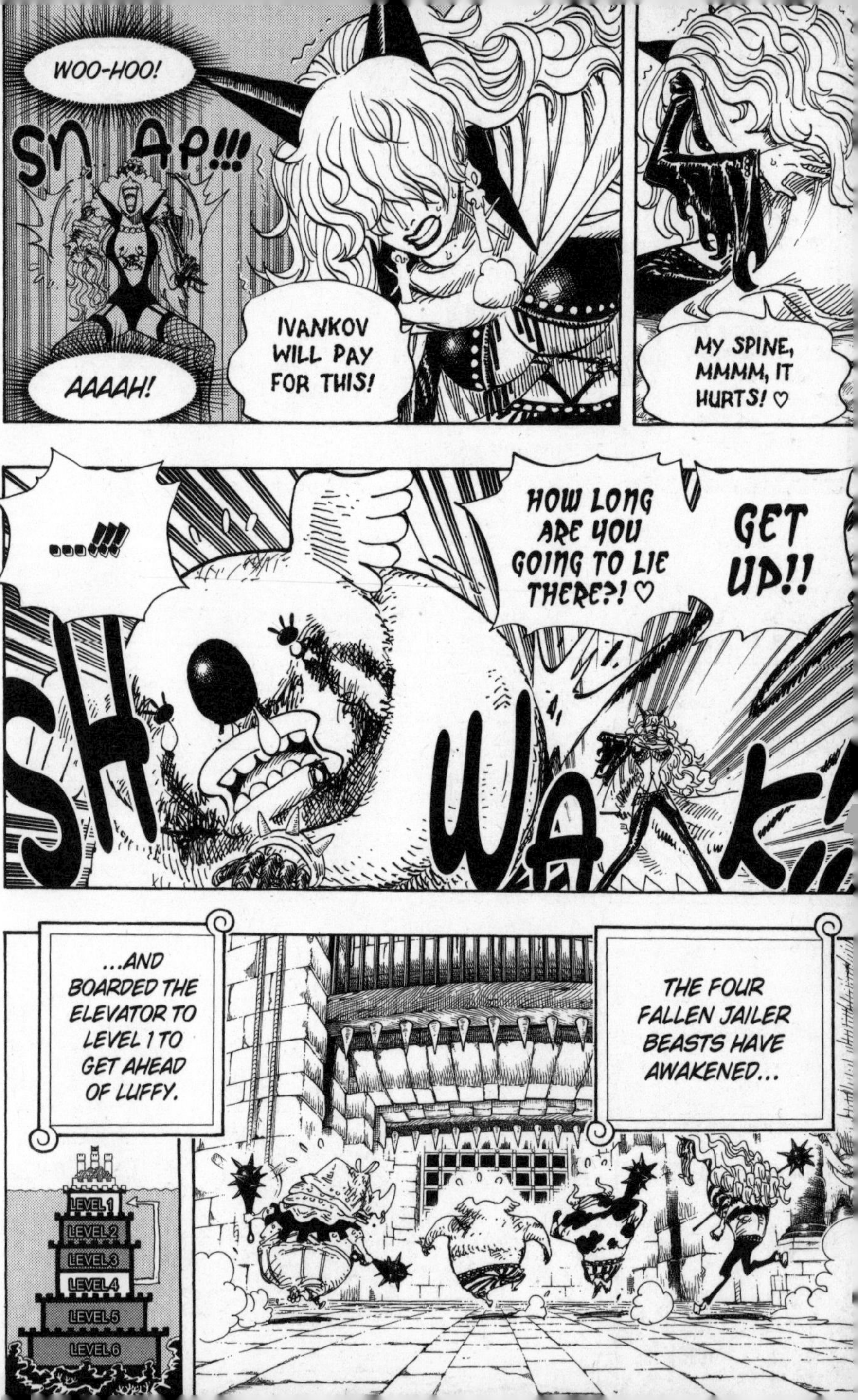
MY SPINE, MMMM, IT HURTS! ♡
IVANKOV WILL PAY FOR THIS!
WOO-HOO!
SNAP!!!
AAAAH!
GET UP!!
HOW LONG ARE YOU GOING TO LIE THERE?! ♡
...!!!
THE FOUR FALLEN JAILER BEASTS HAVE AWAKENED...
...AND BOARDED THE ELEVATOR TO LEVEL 1 TO GET AHEAD OF LUFFY.
LEVEL 1
LEVEL 2
LEVEL 3
LEVEL 4
LEVEL 5
LEVEL 6

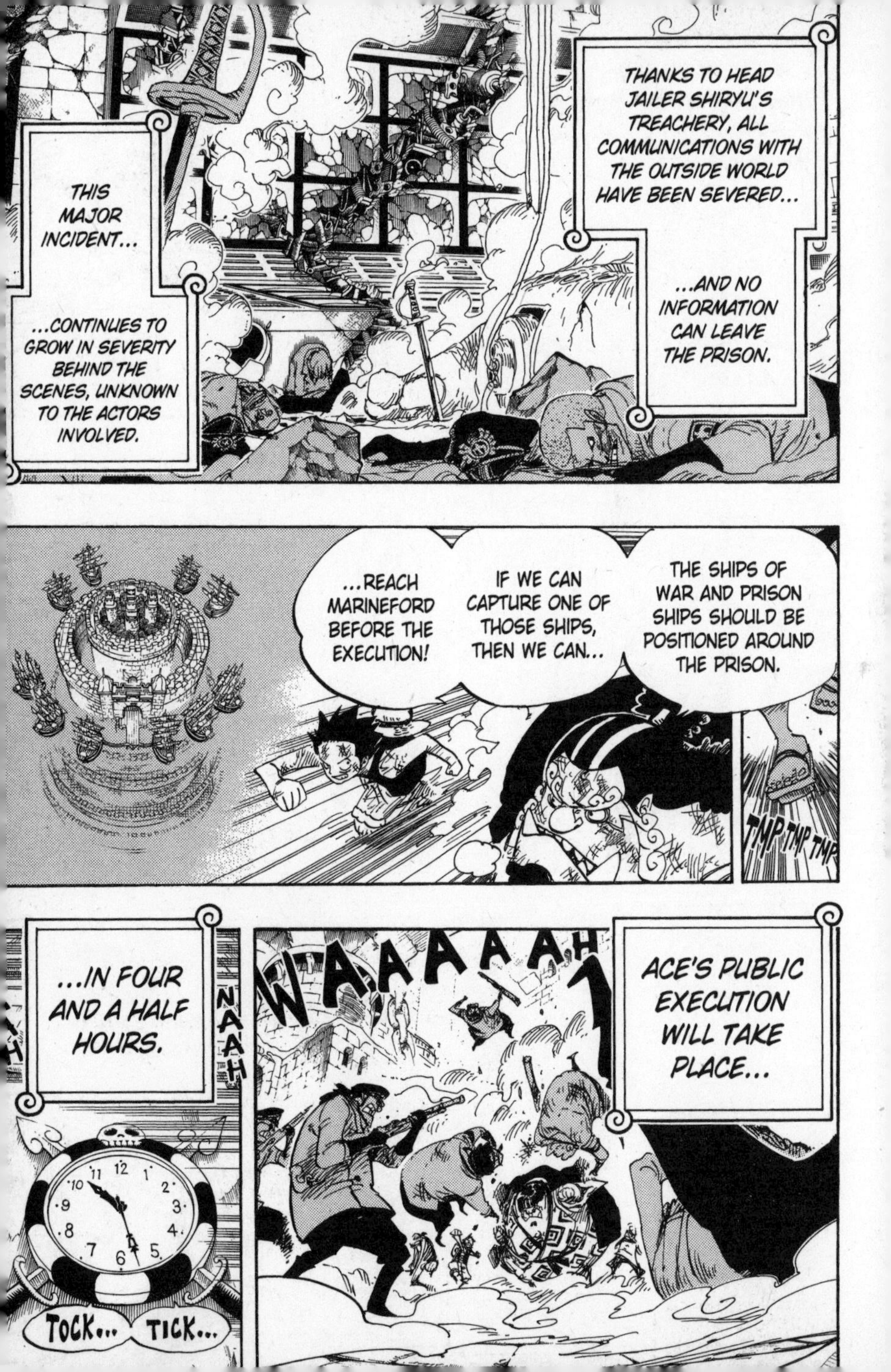
THANKS TO HEAD JAILER SHIRYU'S TREACHERY, ALL COMMUNICATIONS WITH THE OUTSIDE WORLD HAVE BEEN SEVERED...
...AND NO INFORMATION CAN LEAVE THE PRISON.
THIS MAJOR INCIDENT...
...CONTINUES TO GROW IN SEVERITY BEHIND THE SCENES, UNKNOWN TO THE ACTORS INVOLVED.
THE SHIPS OF WAR AND PRISON SHIPS SHOULD BE POSITIONED AROUND THE PRISON.
IF WE CAN CAPTURE ONE OF THOSE SHIPS, THEN WE CAN...
...REACH MARINEFORD BEFORE THE EXECUTION!
TMP TMP TMP
ACE'S PUBLIC EXECUTION WILL TAKE PLACE...
WAAAAAH
...IN FOUR AND A HALF HOURS.
NAAAH
TICK...
TOCK...

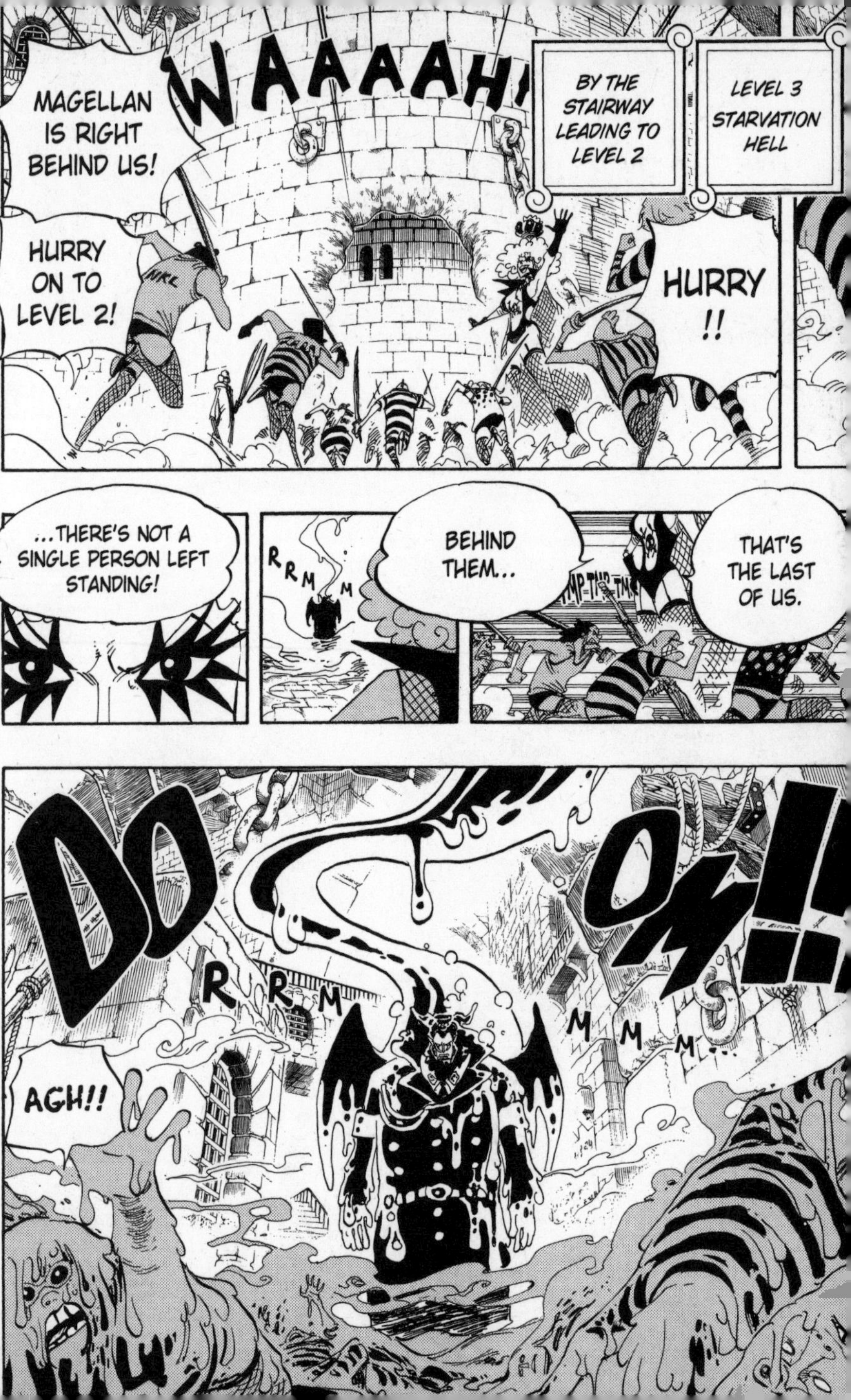
LEVEL 3 STARVATION HELL
BY THE STAIRWAY LEADING TO LEVEL 2
HURRY!!
WAAAAH!
MAGELLAN IS RIGHT BEHIND US!
HURRY ON TO LEVEL 2!
THAT'S THE LAST OF US.
BEHIND THEM...
RRMM
...THERE'S NOT A SINGLE PERSON LEFT STANDING!
DOOM!!
RRRMMMM
AGH!!

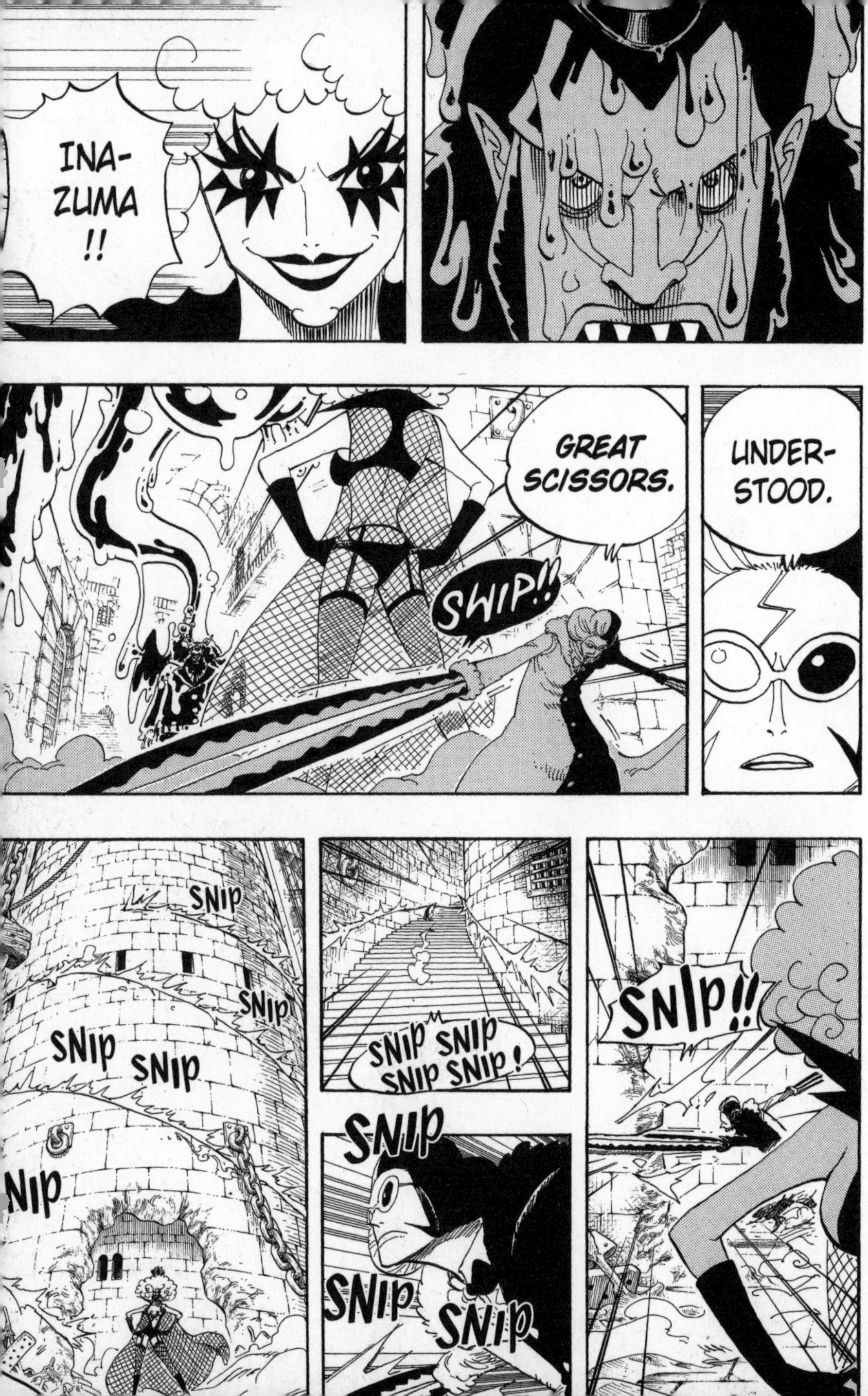
INA-ZUMA!!
UNDER-STOOD.
GREAT SCISSORS.
SWIP!!
SNIP!!
SNIP SNIP SNIP SNIP!
SNIP
SNIP
SNIP
SNIP
SNIP
SNIP
SNIP
NIP

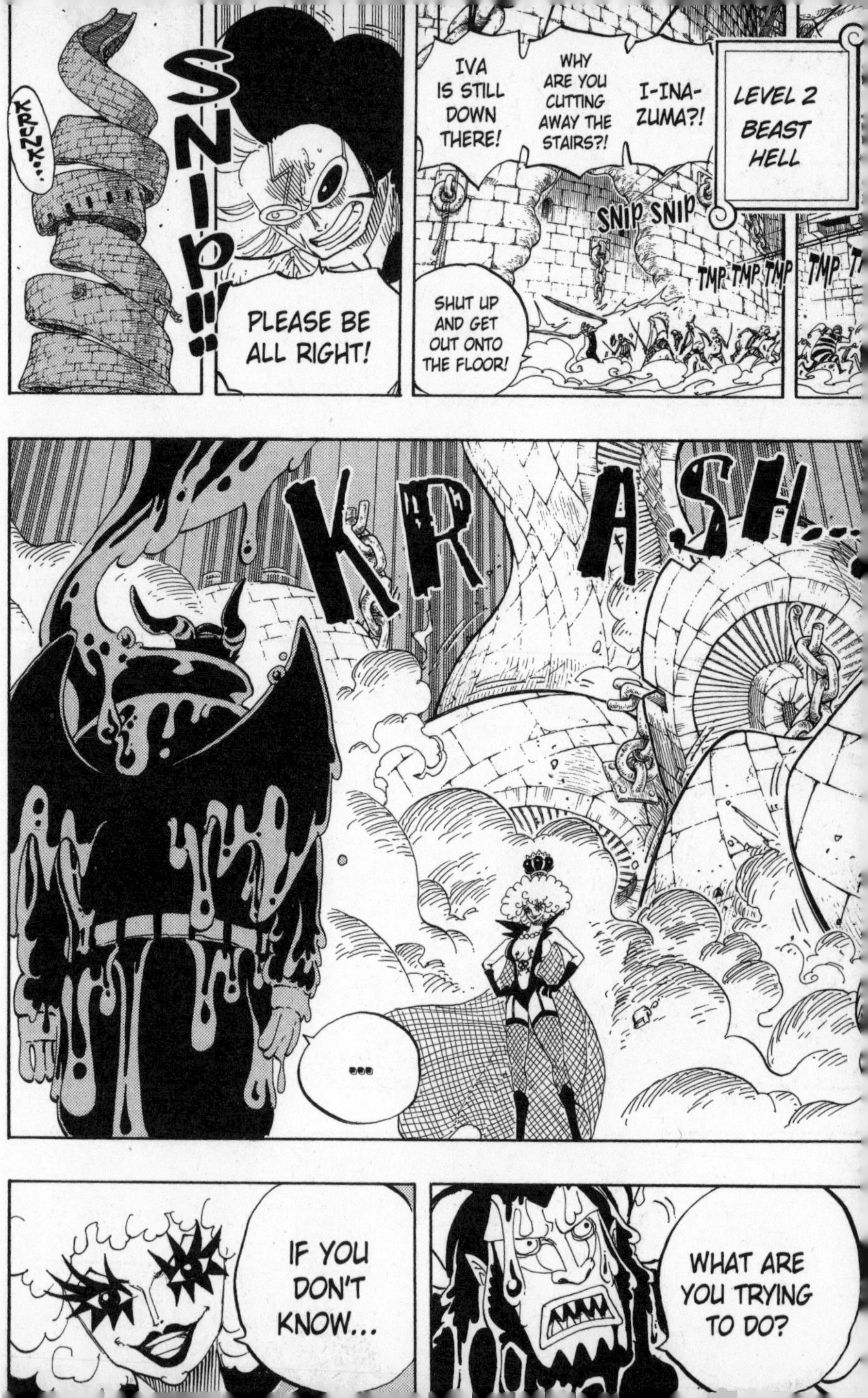
LEVEL 2
BEAST
HELL
TMP TMP TMP TMP
I-INA-
ZUMA?!
WHY
ARE YOU
CUTTING
AWAY THE
STAIRS?!
IVA
IS STILL
DOWN
THERE!
SNIP SNIP
SHUT UP
AND GET
OUT ONTO
THE FLOOR!
SNIP!!!
PLEASE BE
ALL RIGHT!
KRUNK...
KRASH...
...
WHAT ARE
YOU TRYING
TO DO?
IF YOU
DON'T
KNOW...

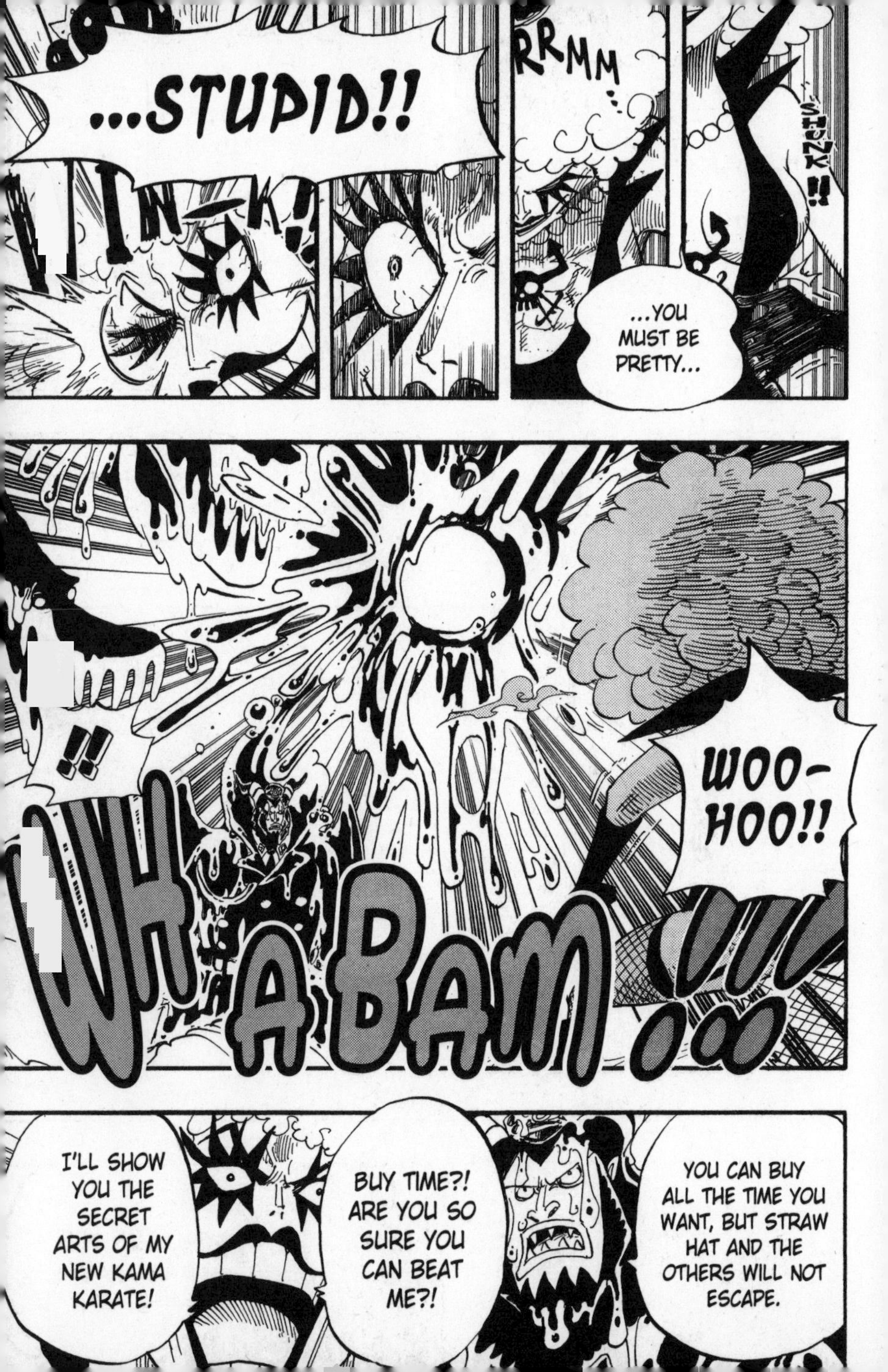
RRMM
SHUNK!!
...YOU MUST BE PRETTY...
...STUPID!!
WOO-HOO!!
!!
WHABAM!!
YOU CAN BUY ALL THE TIME YOU WANT, BUT STRAW HAT AND THE OTHERS WILL NOT ESCAPE.
BUY TIME?! ARE YOU SO SURE YOU CAN BEAT ME?!
I'LL SHOW YOU THE SECRET ARTS OF MY NEW KAMA KARATE!

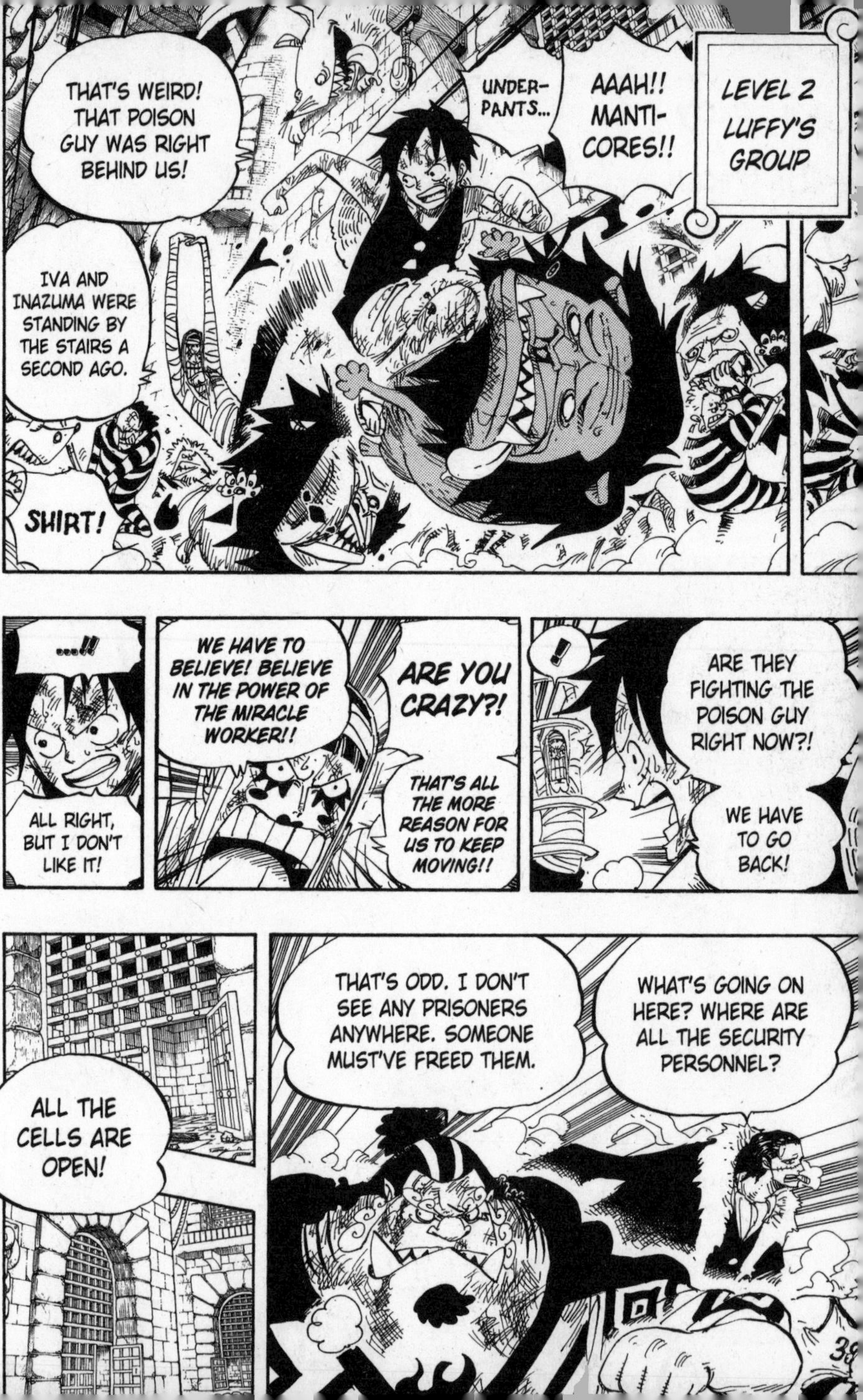
LEVEL 2 LUFFY'S GROUP
AAAH!! MANTICORES!!
UNDER-PANTS...
THAT'S WEIRD! THAT POISON GUY WAS RIGHT BEHIND US!
IVA AND INAZUMA WERE STANDING BY THE STAIRS A SECOND AGO.
SHIRT!
!
ARE THEY FIGHTING THE POISON GUY RIGHT NOW?!
WE HAVE TO GO BACK!
ARE YOU CRAZY?!
THAT'S ALL THE MORE REASON FOR US TO KEEP MOVING!!
WE HAVE TO BELIEVE! BELIEVE IN THE POWER OF THE MIRACLE WORKER!!
...!!
ALL RIGHT, BUT I DON'T LIKE IT!
WHAT'S GOING ON HERE? WHERE ARE ALL THE SECURITY PERSONNEL?
THAT'S ODD. I DON'T SEE ANY PRISONERS ANYWHERE. SOMEONE MUST'VE FREED THEM.
ALL THE CELLS ARE OPEN!

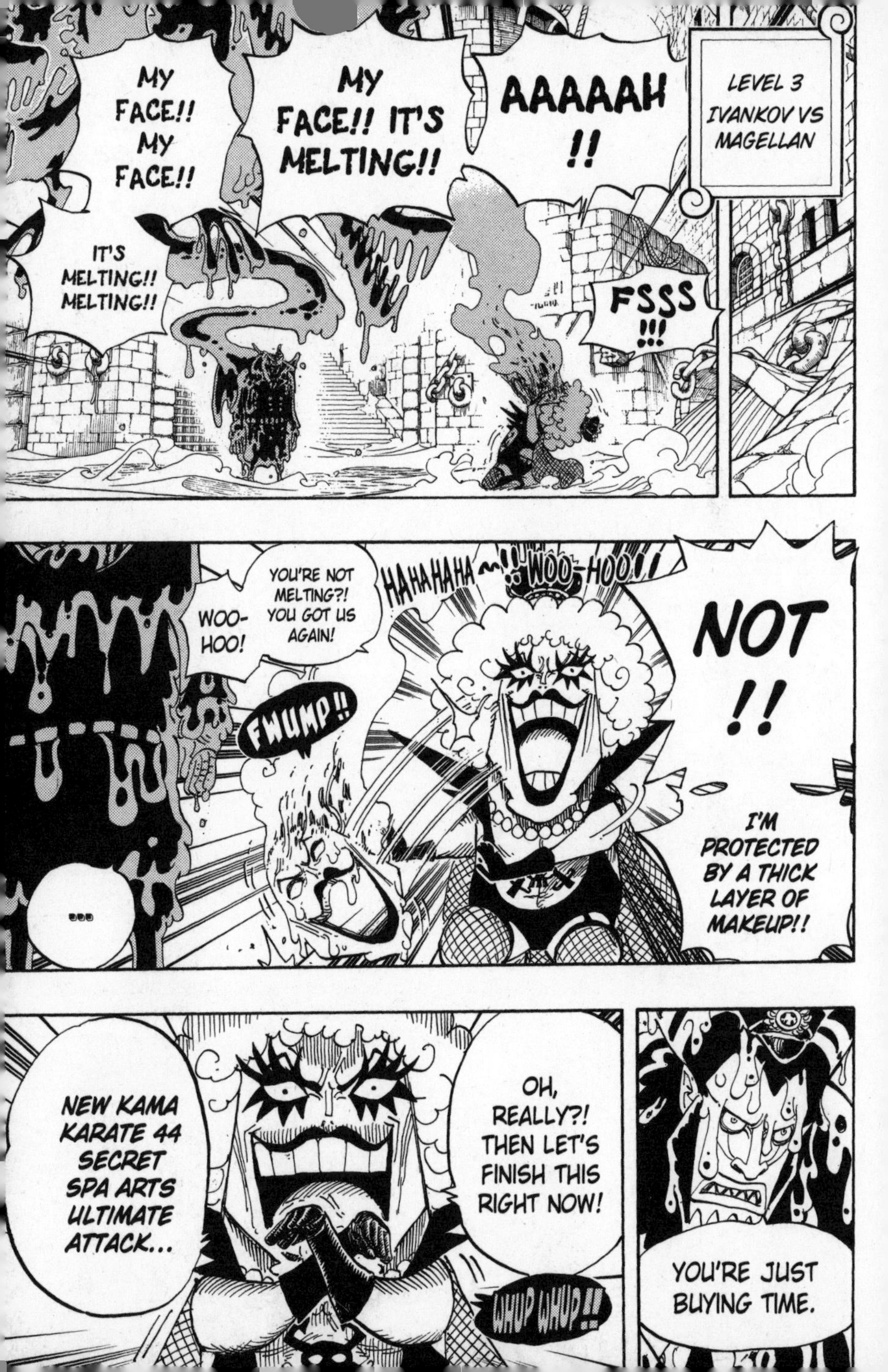
LEVEL 3 IVANKOV VS MAGELLAN
AAAAAH!!
FSSS!!!
MY FACE!! IT'S MELTING!!
MY FACE!! MY FACE!!
IT'S MELTING!! MELTING!!
NOT!!
HAHAHAHA~!! WOO-HOO!!
I'M PROTECTED BY A THICK LAYER OF MAKEUP!!
YOU'RE NOT MELTING?! YOU GOT US AGAIN!
WOO-HOO!
FWUMP!!
...
YOU'RE JUST BUYING TIME.
OH, REALLY?! THEN LET'S FINISH THIS RIGHT NOW!
WHUP WHUP!!
NEW KAMA KARATE 44 SECRET SPA ARTS ULTIMATE ATTACK...

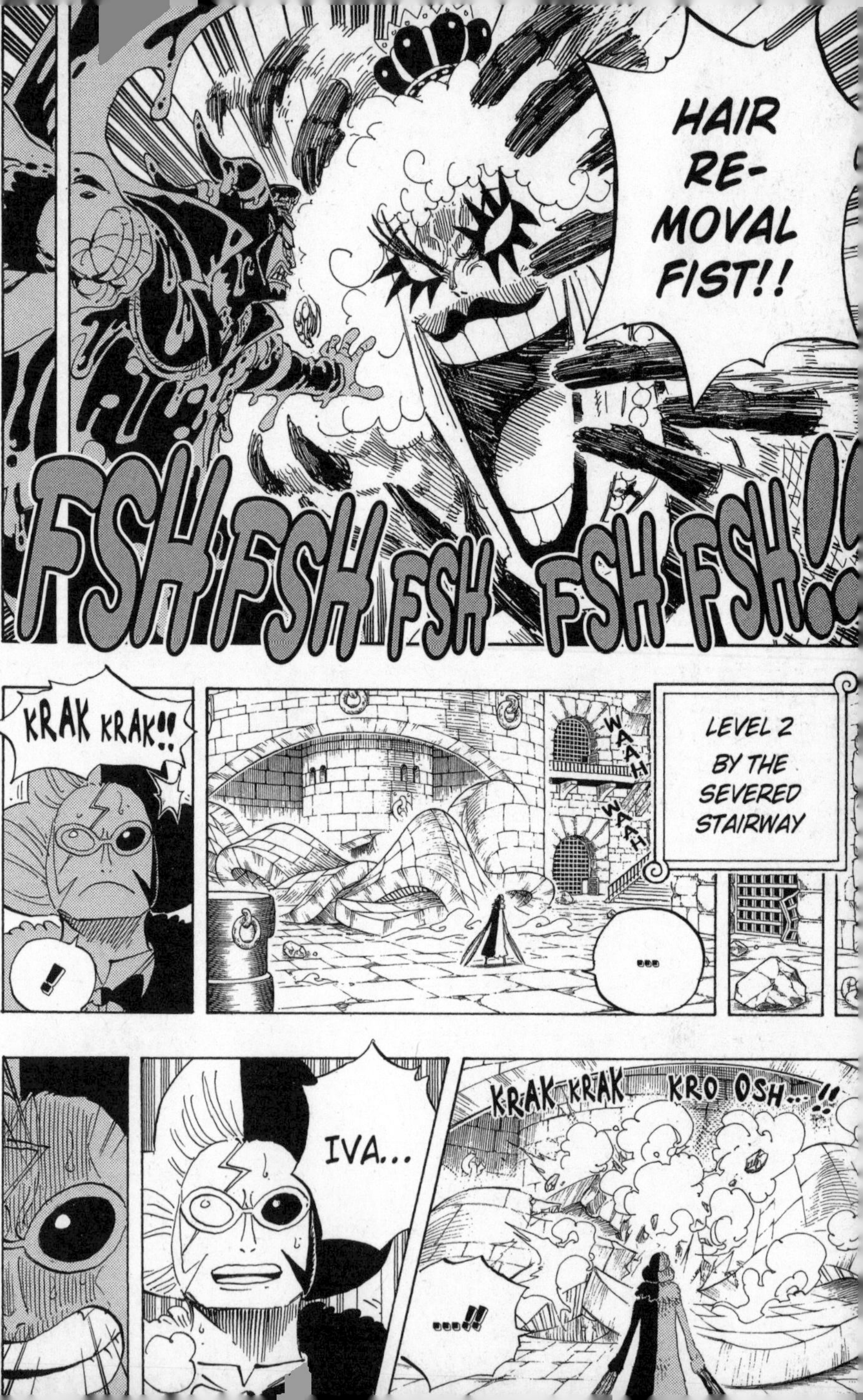
HAIR RE-MOVAL FIST!!
FSH FSH FSH FSH FSH!!
LEVEL 2 BY THE SEVERED STAIRWAY
WAAH WAAH
...
KRAK KRAK!!
!
KRAK KRAK KRO OSH...!!
...!!
IVA...

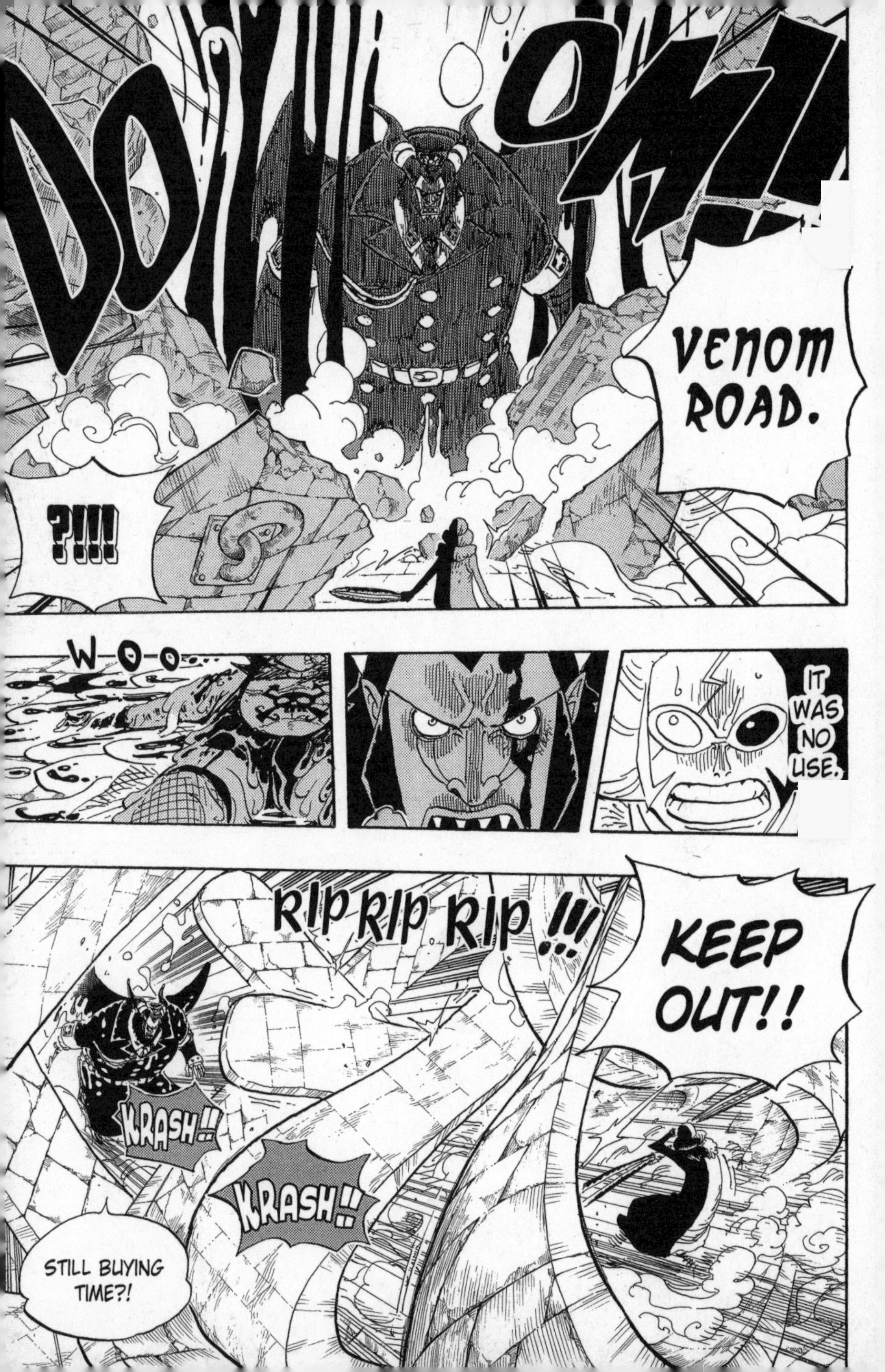
DOOM!!
VENOM ROAD.
?!!!
IT WAS NO USE.
W-O-O
KEEP OUT!!
RIP RIP RIP!!!
KRASH!!
KRASH!!
STILL BUYING TIME?!

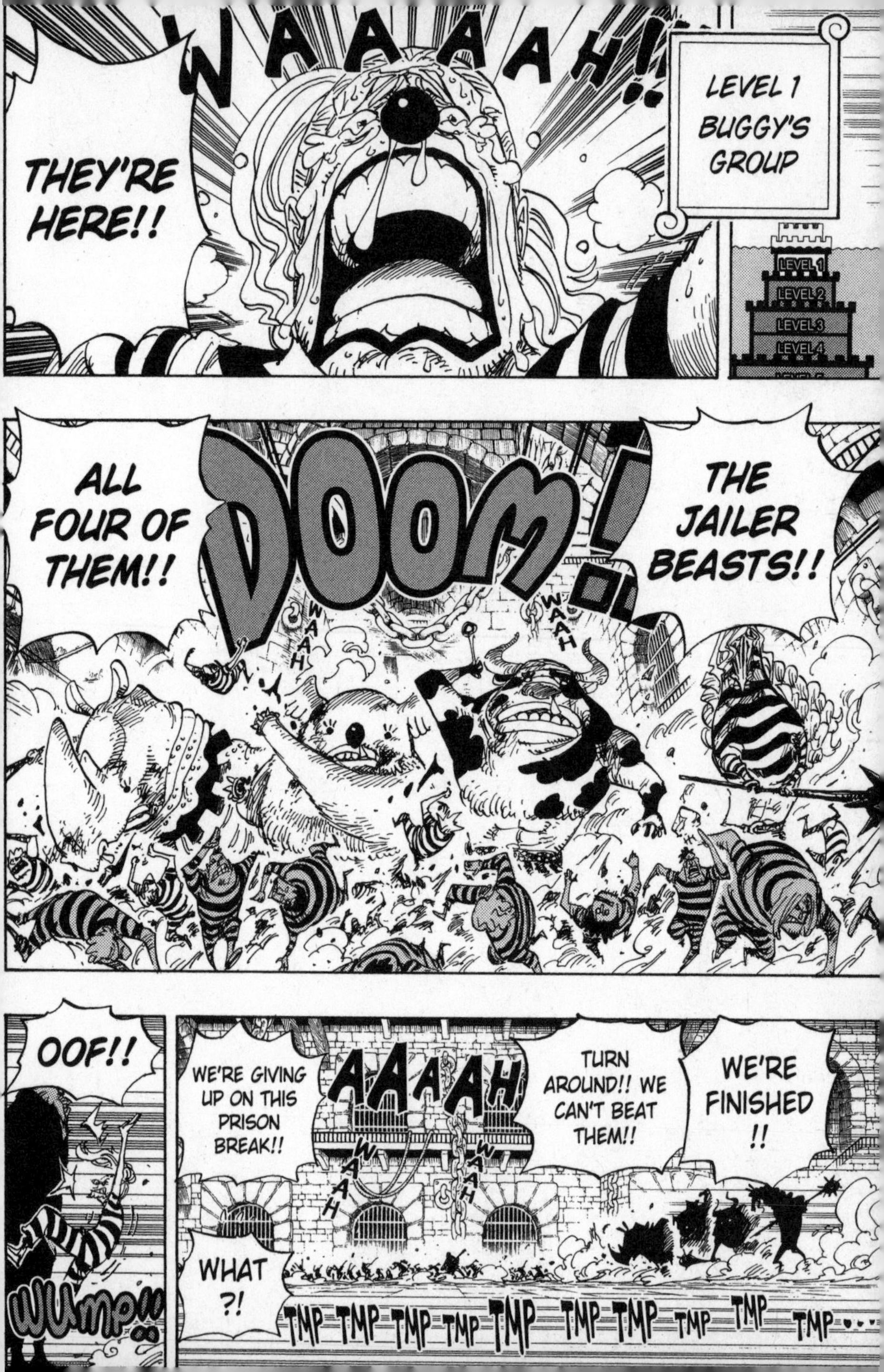
LEVEL 1
BUGGY'S GROUP
LEVEL 1
LEVEL 2
LEVEL 3
LEVEL 4
WAAAAAH!!
THEY'RE HERE!!
THE JAILER BEASTS!!
DOOM!!
ALL FOUR OF THEM!!
WAAH
WAAH
WE'RE FINISHED!!
TURN AROUND!! WE CAN'T BEAT THEM!!
AAAAH
WE'RE GIVING UP ON THIS PRISON BREAK!!
WAAH
WAAH
WHAT?!
TMP TMP TMP TMP TMP TMP TMP TMP TMP TMP...
OOF!!
WUMP!!

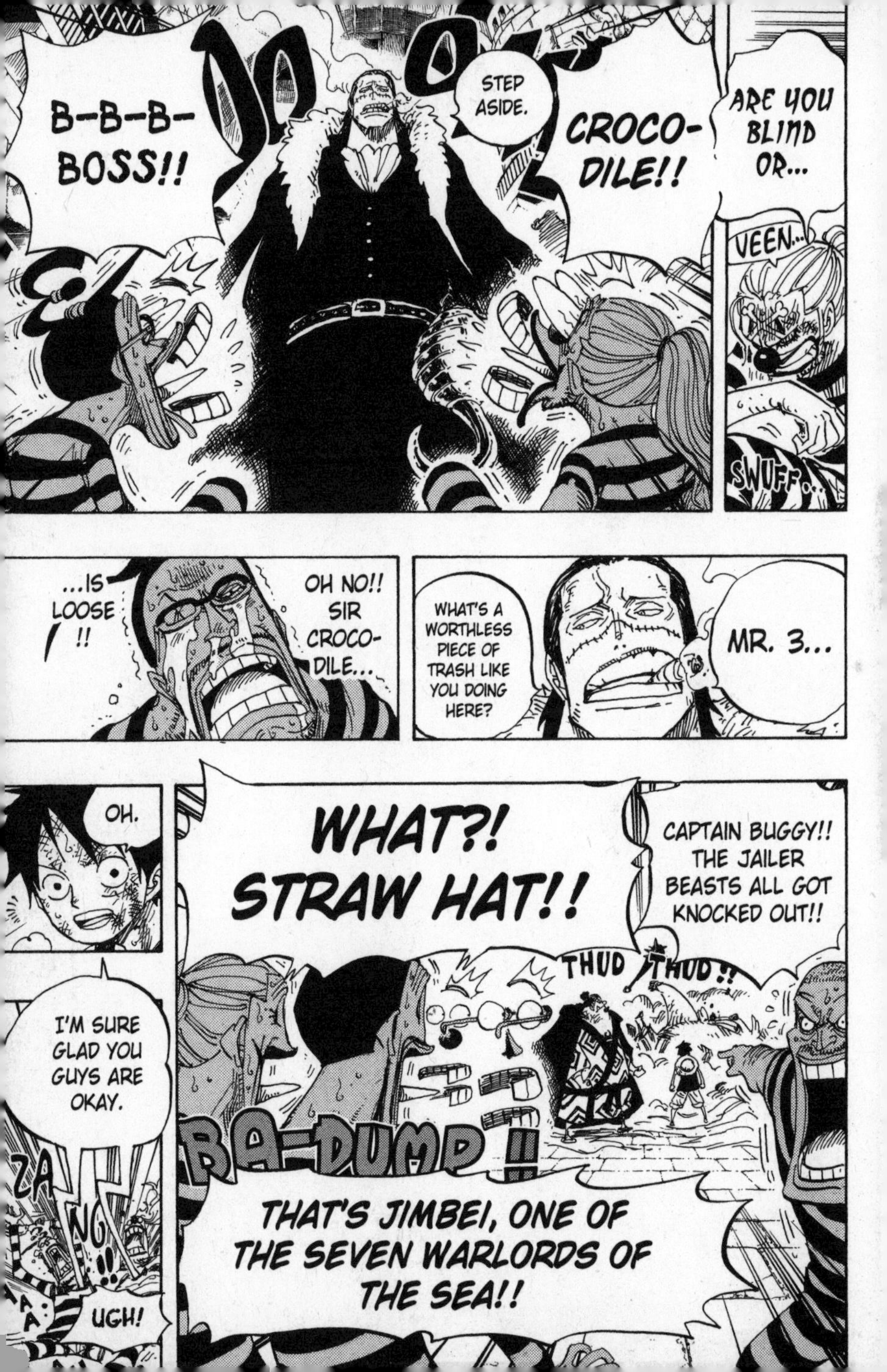
ARE YOU BLIND OR...
VEEN...
SWUFF...
CROCO-DILE!!
STEP ASIDE.
B-B-B-BOSS!!
MR. 3...
WHAT'S A WORTHLESS PIECE OF TRASH LIKE YOU DOING HERE?
OH NO!! SIR CROCO-DILE...
...IS LOOSE!!
CAPTAIN BUGGY!! THE JAILER BEASTS ALL GOT KNOCKED OUT!!
WHAT?! STRAW HAT!!
THUD THUD!!
BA-DUMP!!
THAT'S JIMBEI, ONE OF THE SEVEN WARLORDS OF THE SEA!!
OH.
I'M SURE GLAD YOU GUYS ARE OKAY.
ZANG!!
UGH!

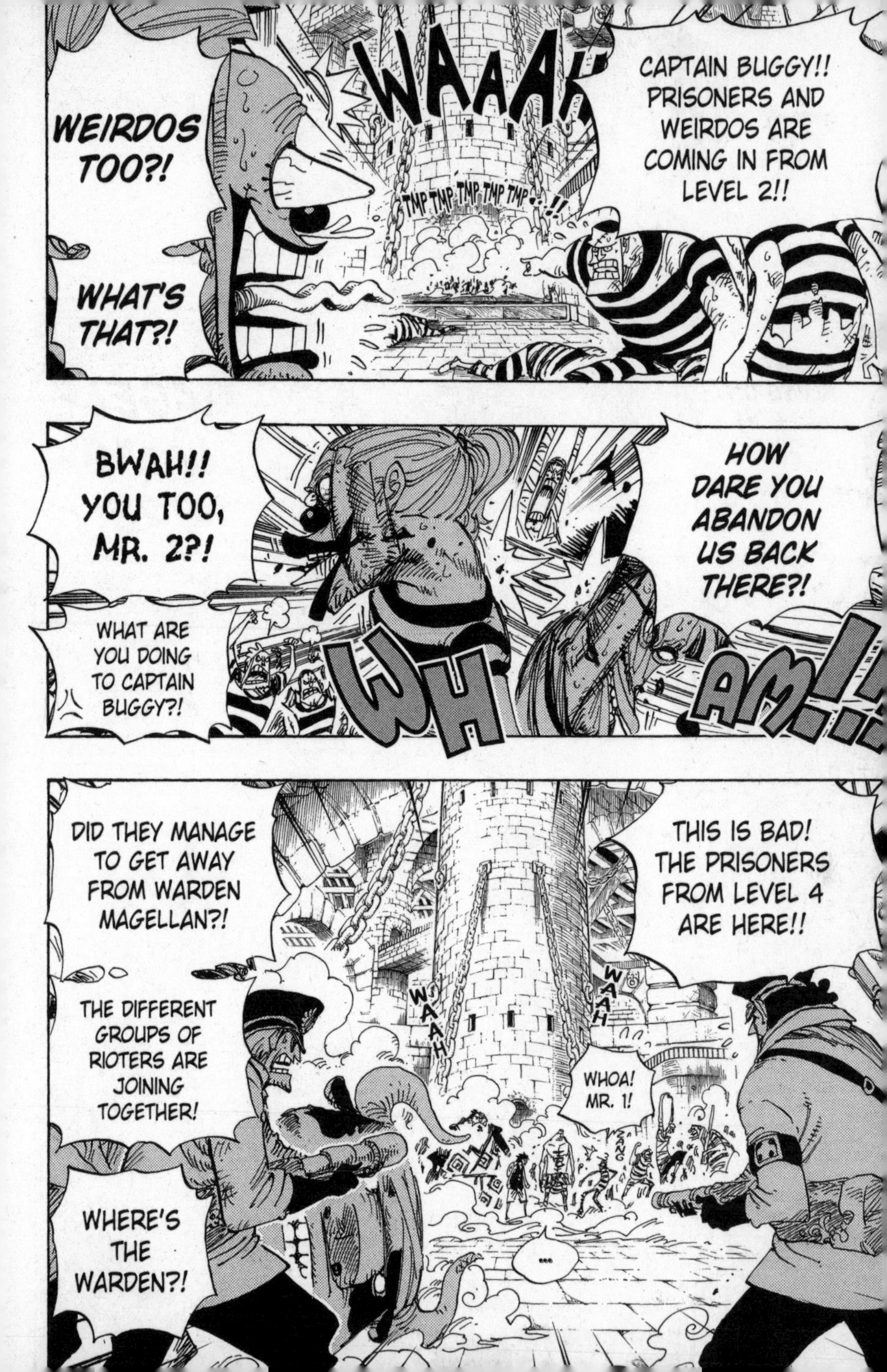
CAPTAIN BUGGY!! PRISONERS AND WEIRDOS ARE COMING IN FROM LEVEL 2!!
WAAAH
TMP TMP TMP TMP TMP...!!
WEIRDOS TOO?!
WHAT'S THAT?!
HOW DARE YOU ABANDON US BACK THERE?!
WHAM!!
BWAH!! YOU TOO, MR. 2?!
WHAT ARE YOU DOING TO CAPTAIN BUGGY?!
THIS IS BAD! THE PRISONERS FROM LEVEL 4 ARE HERE!!
WAAH
WAAH
WHOA! MR. 1!
...
DID THEY MANAGE TO GET AWAY FROM WARDEN MAGELLAN?!
THE DIFFERENT GROUPS OF RIOTERS ARE JOINING TOGETHER!
WHERE'S THE WARDEN?!

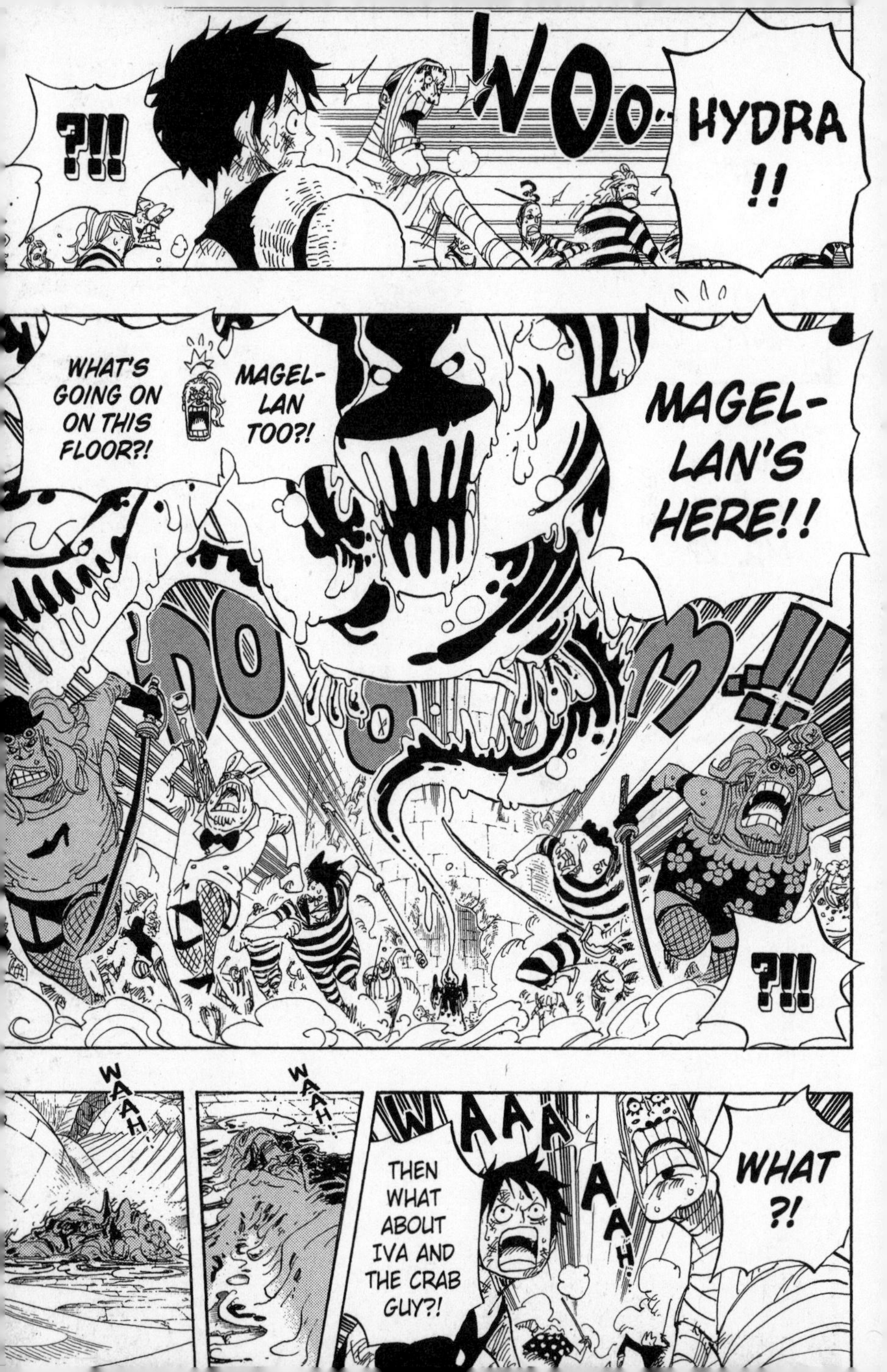
HYDRA !!
WOO-
?!!
MAGEL-LAN'S HERE!!
MAGEL-LAN TOO?!
WHAT'S GOING ON ON THIS FLOOR?!
DOOM!!
?!!
WHAT ?!
WAAAAAH
THEN WHAT ABOUT IVA AND THE CRAB GUY?!
WAAH!
WAAH!

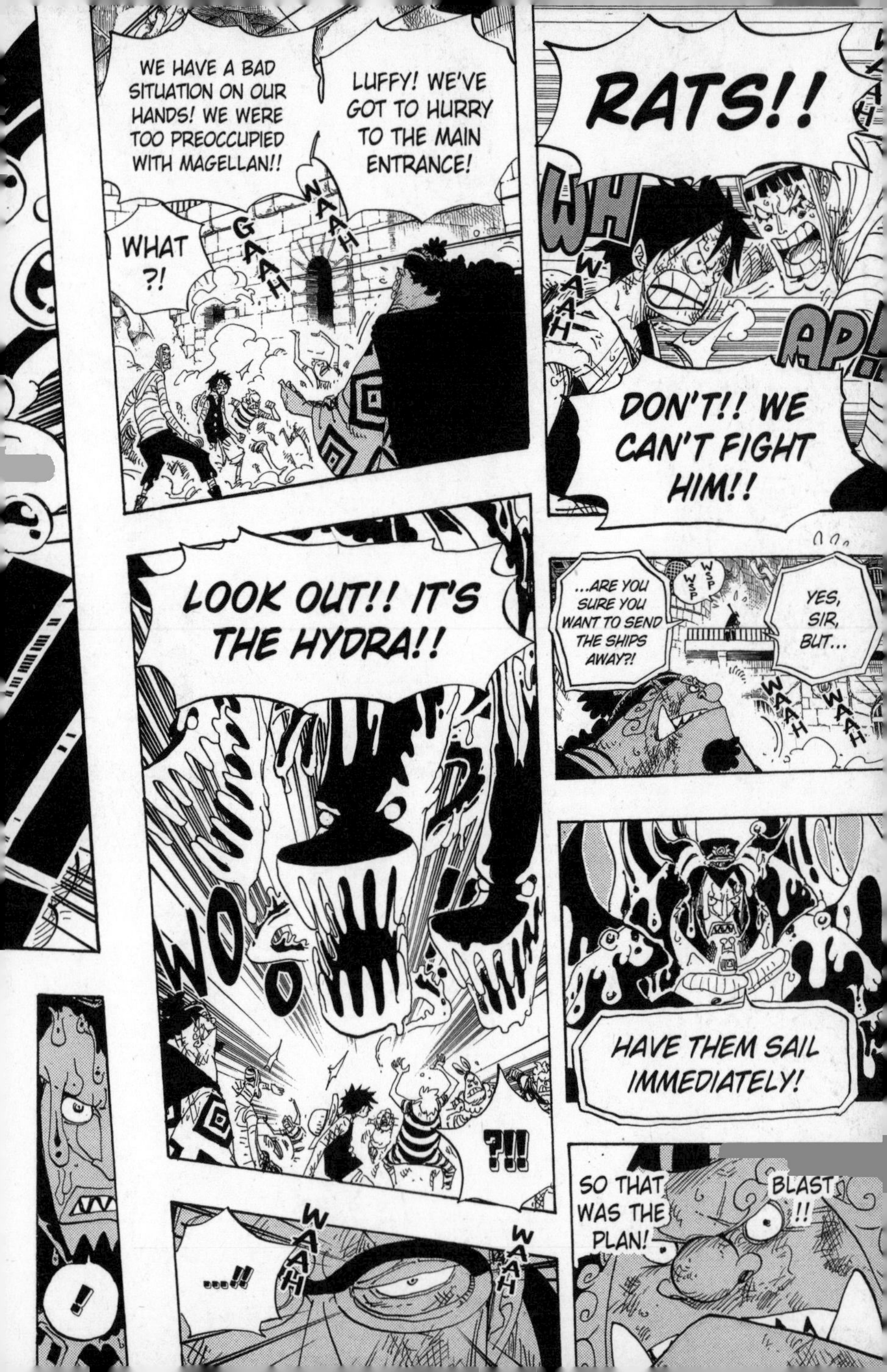
RATS!!
WH
AP!
WAAH
DON'T!! WE CAN'T FIGHT HIM!!
LUFFY! WE'VE GOT TO HURRY TO THE MAIN ENTRANCE!
WE HAVE A BAD SITUATION ON OUR HANDS! WE WERE TOO PREOCCUPIED WITH MAGELLAN!!
WAAH
GAAH
WHAT ?!
YES, SIR, BUT...
WSP WSP
...ARE YOU SURE YOU WANT TO SEND THE SHIPS AWAY?!
WAAH
WAAH
HAVE THEM SAIL IMMEDIATELY!
LOOK OUT!! IT'S THE HYDRA!!
WOO
?!!
BLAST!!
SO THAT WAS THE PLAN!
WAAH
WAAH
...!!
!

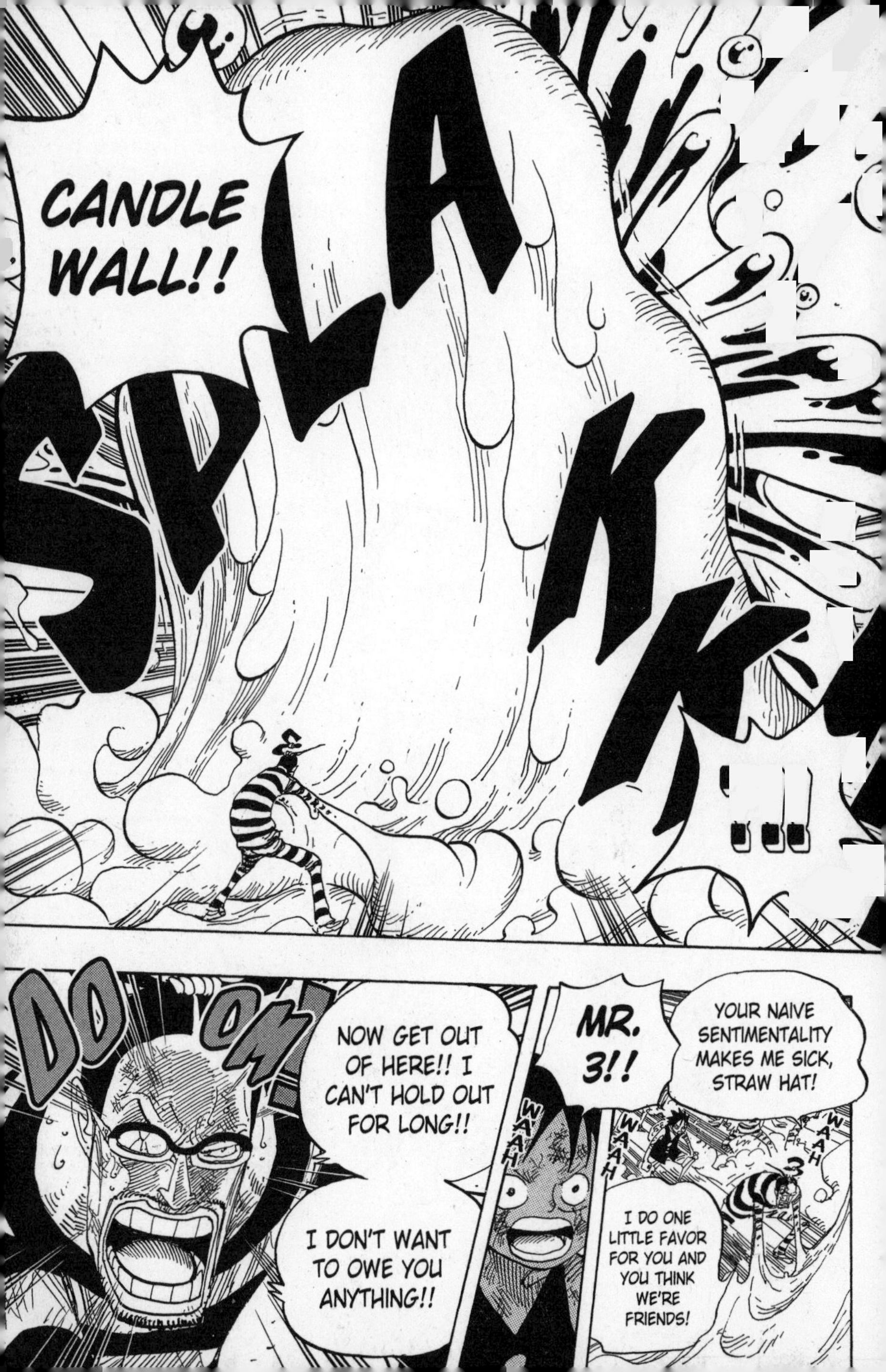
CANDLE WALL!!
SPLAKK!!!
MR. 3!!
YOUR NAIVE SENTIMENTALITY MAKES ME SICK, STRAW HAT!
WAAH
WAAH
WAAH
I DO ONE LITTLE FAVOR FOR YOU AND YOU THINK WE'RE FRIENDS!
DOOM
NOW GET OUT OF HERE!! I CAN'T HOLD OUT FOR LONG!!
I DON'T WANT TO OWE YOU ANYTHING!!

SBS Question Corner

(Toko Shizuki, Chiba)

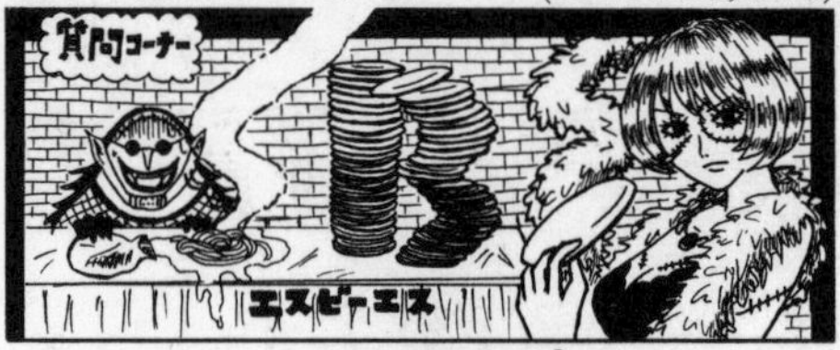

質問コーナー
エスビーエス

Q: I thought about this when I saw Iva, but I'd like to see a gender swap of the Straw Hat Pirates. Would you please draw it SERIOUSLY? I repeat, please draw it SERIOUSLY.

--TOMO-M

A: Sure. But it'll be something completely different.

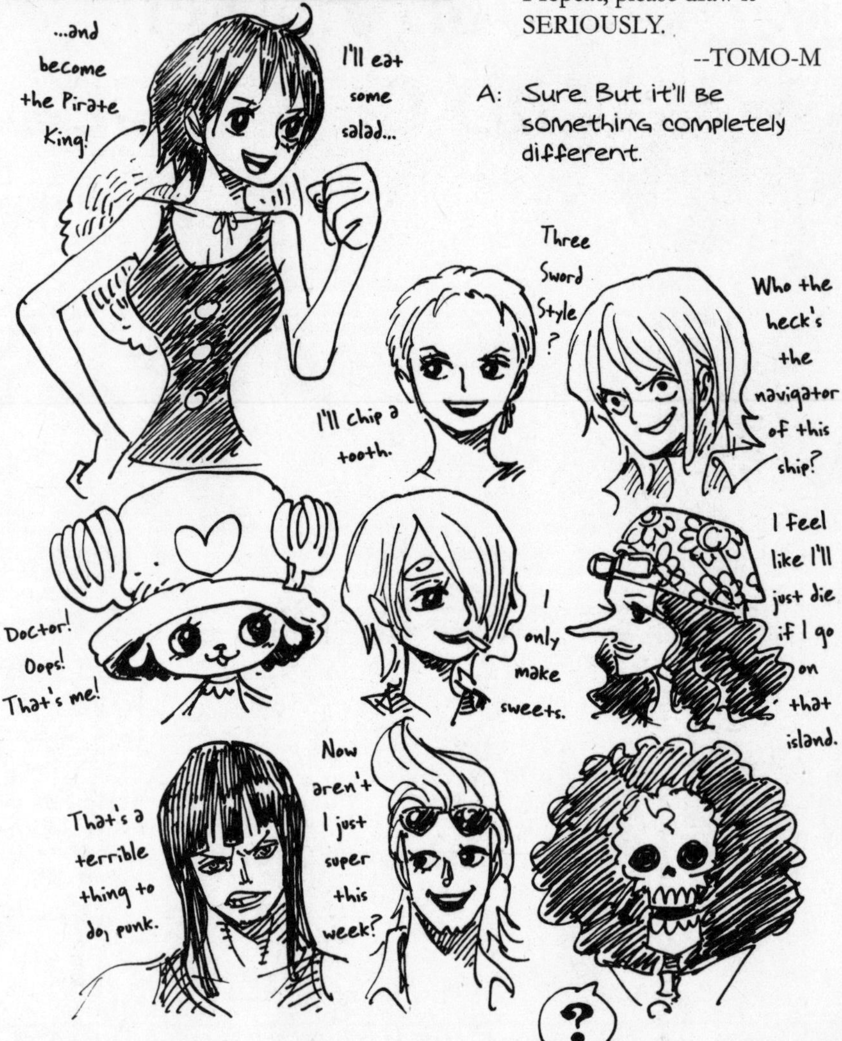

...and become the Pirate King!
I'll eat some salad...
Three Sword Style?
I'll chip a tooth.
Who the heck's the navigator of this ship?
I feel like I'll just die if I go on that island.
I only make sweets.
Doctor! Oops! That's me!
Now aren't I just super this week?
That's a terrible thing to do, punk.
?

Chapter 546:
FISH-MAN PIRATE CAPTAIN JIMBEI, WARLORD OF THE SEA

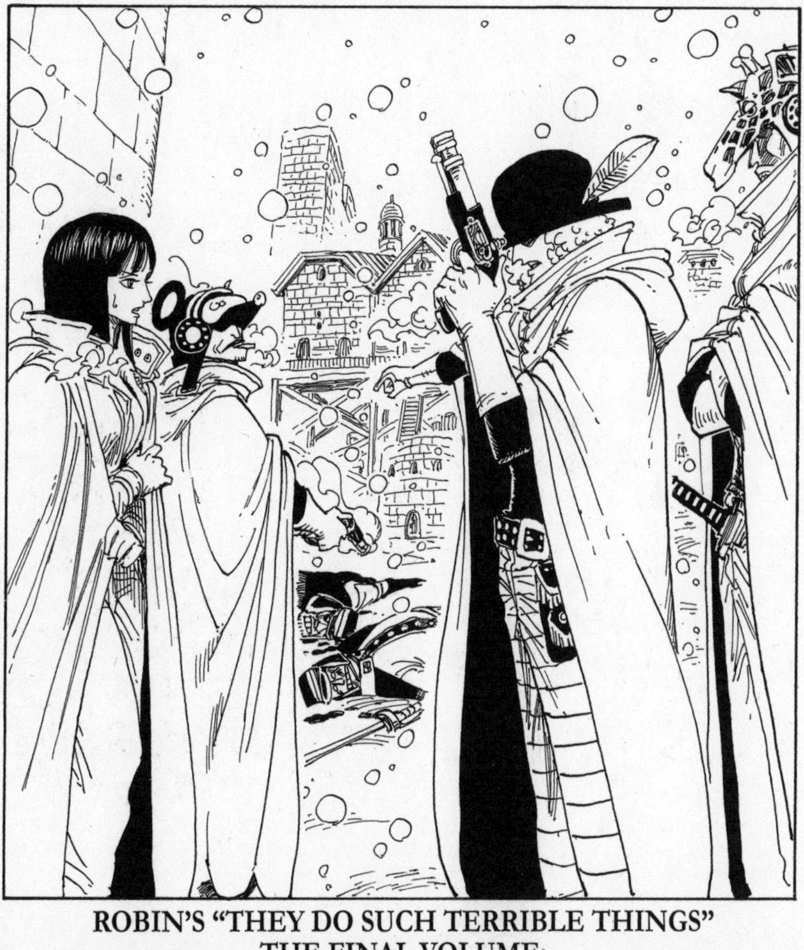

ROBIN'S "THEY DO SUCH TERRIBLE THINGS"
THE FINAL VOLUME:
"THE REBEL ARMY SAVES THE SLAVES"

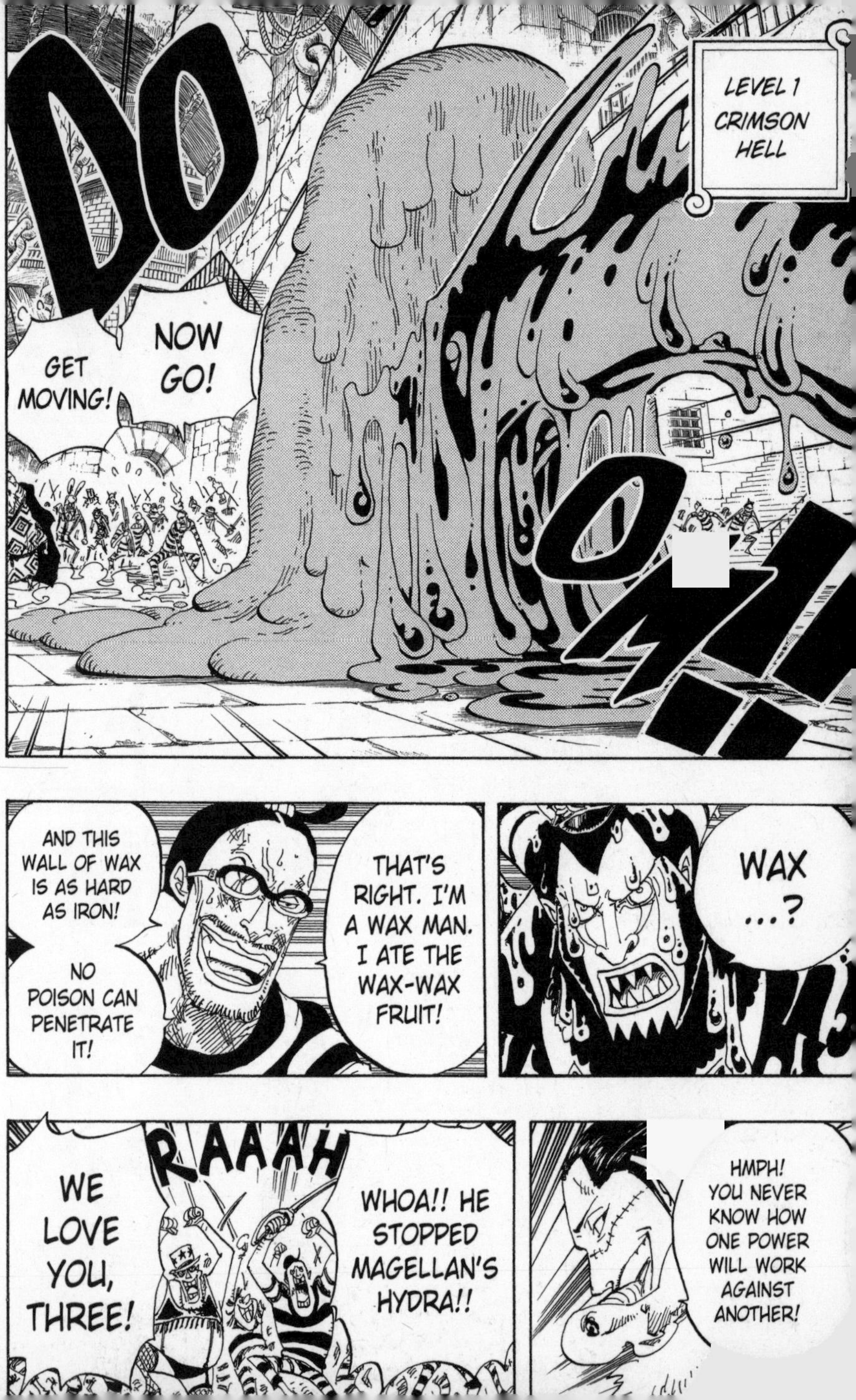
LEVEL 1 CRIMSON HELL
DO
NOW GO!
GET MOVING!
WAX ...?
THAT'S RIGHT. I'M A WAX MAN. I ATE THE WAX-WAX FRUIT!
AND THIS WALL OF WAX IS AS HARD AS IRON!
NO POISON CAN PENETRATE IT!
HMPH! YOU NEVER KNOW HOW ONE POWER WILL WORK AGAINST ANOTHER!
RAAAH
WHOA!! HE STOPPED MAGELLAN'S HYDRA!!
WE LOVE YOU, THREE!

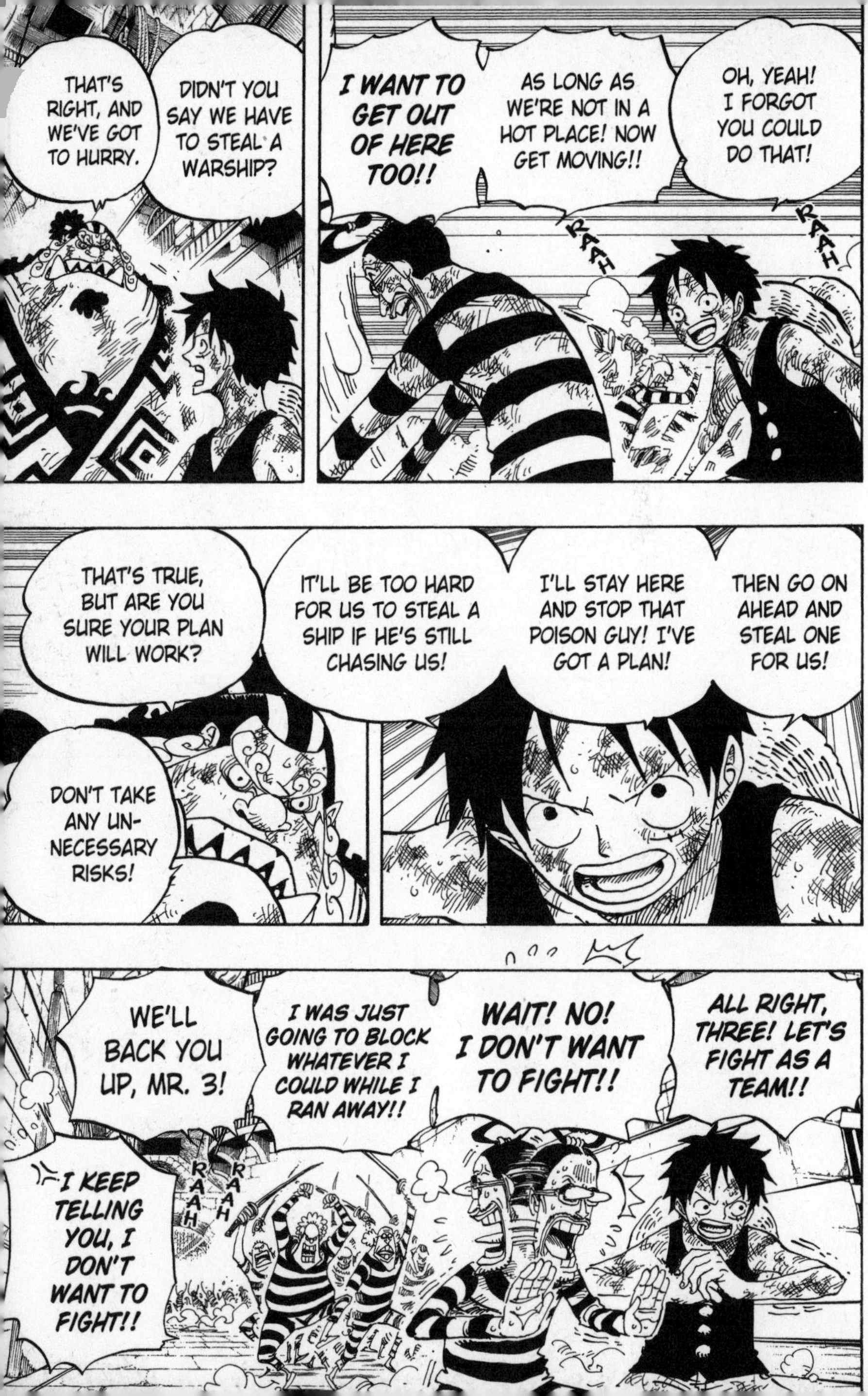
OH, YEAH! I FORGOT YOU COULD DO THAT!
RAAH
AS LONG AS WE'RE NOT IN A HOT PLACE! NOW GET MOVING!!
RAAH
I WANT TO GET OUT OF HERE TOO!!
DIDN'T YOU SAY WE HAVE TO STEAL A WARSHIP?
THAT'S RIGHT, AND WE'VE GOT TO HURRY.
THEN GO ON AHEAD AND STEAL ONE FOR US!
I'LL STAY HERE AND STOP THAT POISON GUY! I'VE GOT A PLAN!
IT'LL BE TOO HARD FOR US TO STEAL A SHIP IF HE'S STILL CHASING US!
THAT'S TRUE, BUT ARE YOU SURE YOUR PLAN WILL WORK?
DON'T TAKE ANY UN-NECESSARY RISKS!
ALL RIGHT, THREE! LET'S FIGHT AS A TEAM!!
WAIT! NO! I DON'T WANT TO FIGHT!!
I WAS JUST GOING TO BLOCK WHATEVER I COULD WHILE I RAN AWAY!!
WE'LL BACK YOU UP, MR. 3!
RAAH
RAAH
I KEEP TELLING YOU, I DON'T WANT TO FIGHT!!

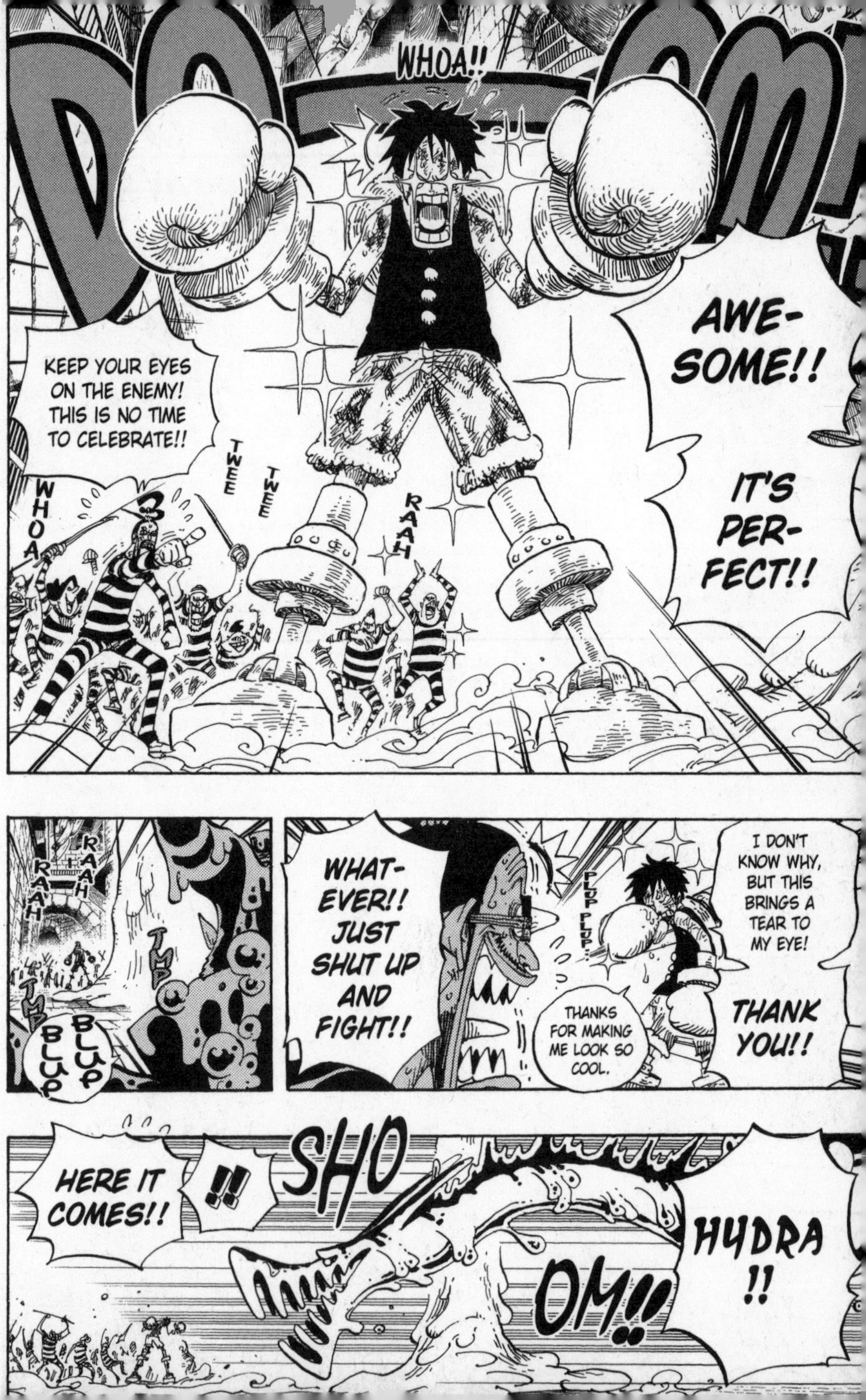
WHOA!!
AWE-SOME!!
IT'S PER-FECT!!
RAAH
TWEE TWEE
KEEP YOUR EYES ON THE ENEMY! THIS IS NO TIME TO CELEBRATE!!
WHOA
I DON'T KNOW WHY, BUT THIS BRINGS A TEAR TO MY EYE!
THANK YOU!!
PLUP PLUP
THANKS FOR MAKING ME LOOK SO COOL.
WHAT-EVER!! JUST SHUT UP AND FIGHT!!
RAAH RAAH
BLUP BLUP
HYDRA!!
SHO OM!!
!!
HERE IT COMES!!

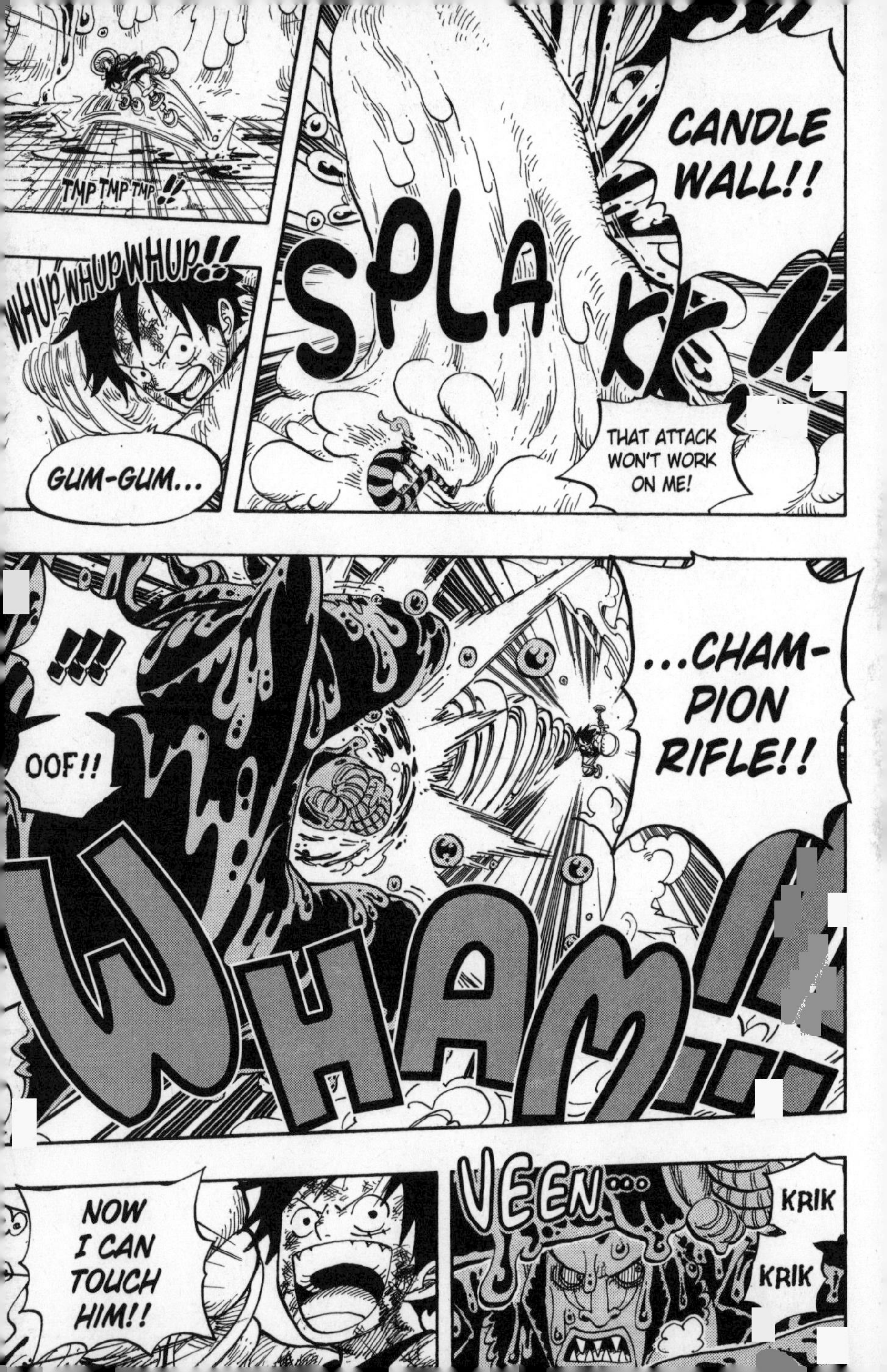
CANDLE WALL!!
SPLAKK!!
THAT ATTACK WON'T WORK ON ME!
TMP TMP TMP!!
WHUP WHUP WHUP!!
GUM-GUM...
...CHAMPION RIFLE!!
!!!
OOF!!
WHAM!!
VEEN...
KRIK
KRIK
NOW I CAN TOUCH HIM!!

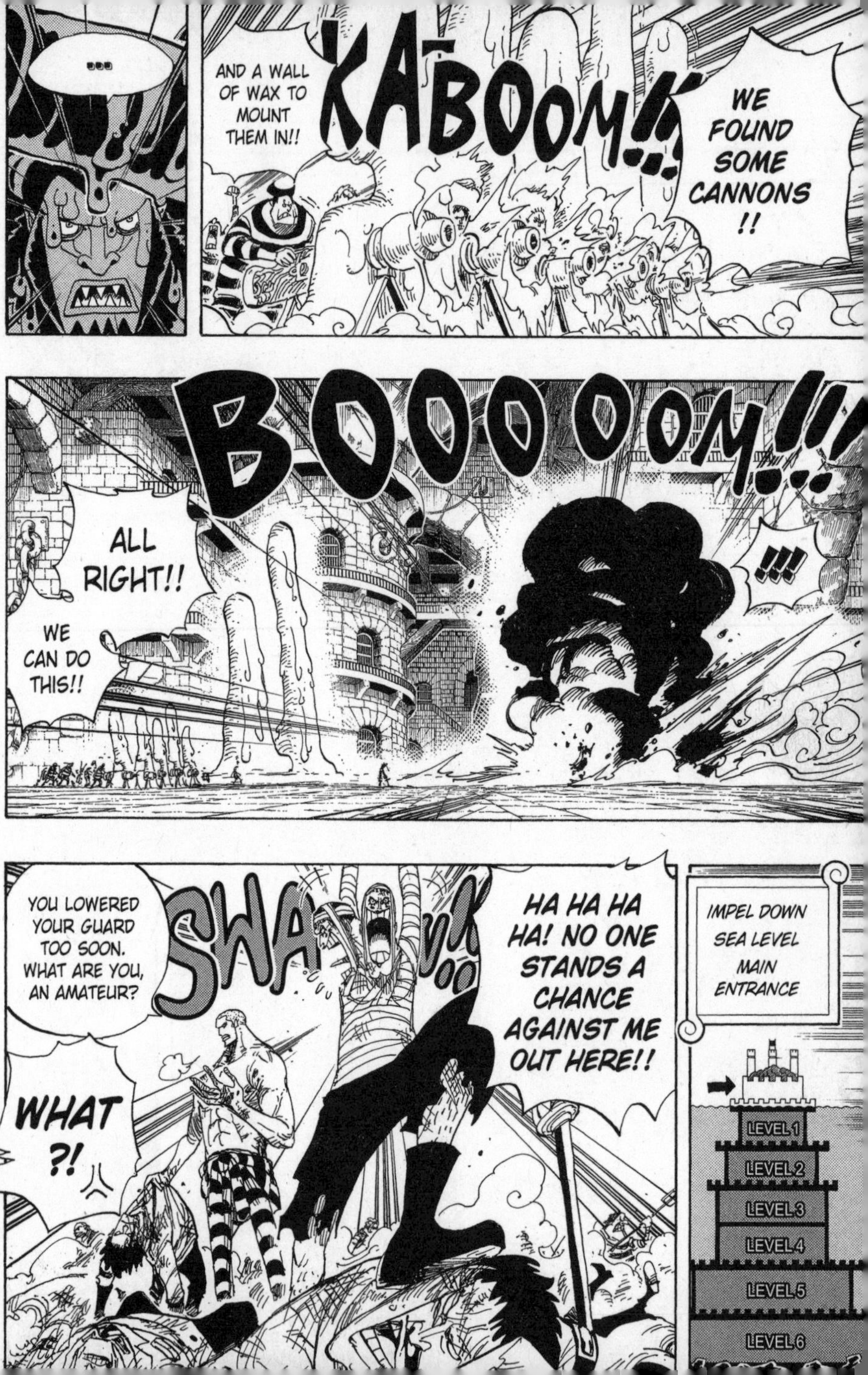
WE FOUND SOME CANNONS!!
KA-BOOM!!
AND A WALL OF WAX TO MOUNT THEM IN!!
...
BOOOOOM!!!
!!!
ALL RIGHT!!
WE CAN DO THIS!!
IMPEL DOWN SEA LEVEL MAIN ENTRANCE
LEVEL 1
LEVEL 2
LEVEL 3
LEVEL 4
LEVEL 5
LEVEL 6
HA HA HA HA! NO ONE STANDS A CHANCE AGAINST ME OUT HERE!!
SHA...
YOU LOWERED YOUR GUARD TOO SOON. WHAT ARE YOU, AN AMATEUR?
WHAT?!

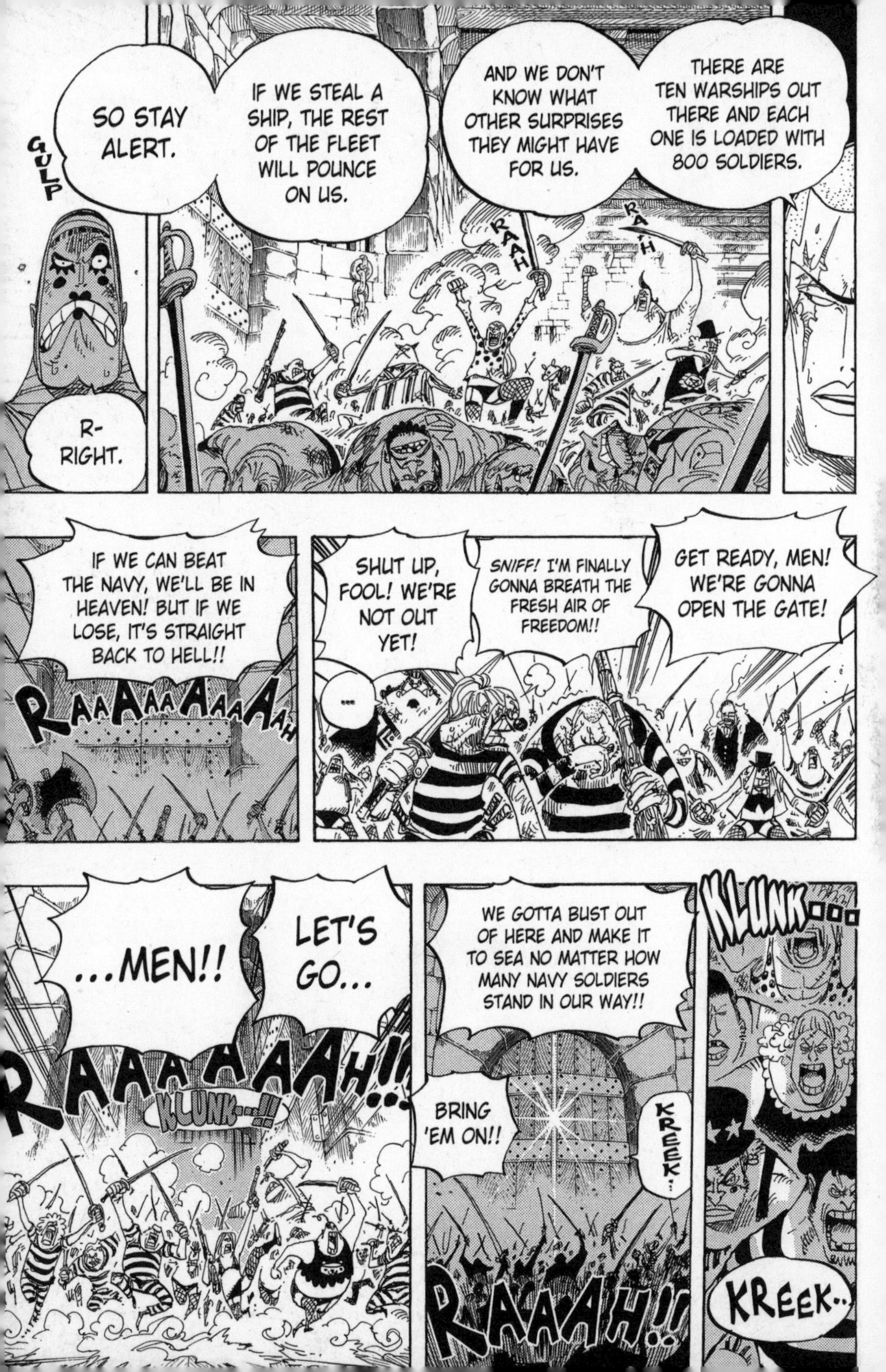

THERE ARE TEN WARSHIPS OUT THERE AND EACH ONE IS LOADED WITH 800 SOLDIERS.
AND WE DON'T KNOW WHAT OTHER SURPRISES THEY MIGHT HAVE FOR US.
IF WE STEAL A SHIP, THE REST OF THE FLEET WILL POUNCE ON US.
SO STAY ALERT.
RAAH
RAAH
GULP
R-RIGHT.
GET READY, MEN! WE'RE GONNA OPEN THE GATE!
SNIFF! I'M FINALLY GONNA BREATH THE FRESH AIR OF FREEDOM!!
SHUT UP, FOOL! WE'RE NOT OUT YET!
...
IF WE CAN BEAT THE NAVY, WE'LL BE IN HEAVEN! BUT IF WE LOSE, IT'S STRAIGHT BACK TO HELL!!
RAAAAAAAAAAH
KLUNK...
KREEK..
WE GOTTA BUST OUT OF HERE AND MAKE IT TO SEA NO MATTER HOW MANY NAVY SOLDIERS STAND IN OUR WAY!!
KREEK..
BRING 'EM ON!!
RAAAH!!
LET'S GO...
...MEN!!
RAAAAAAAH!!!
KLUNK--!!

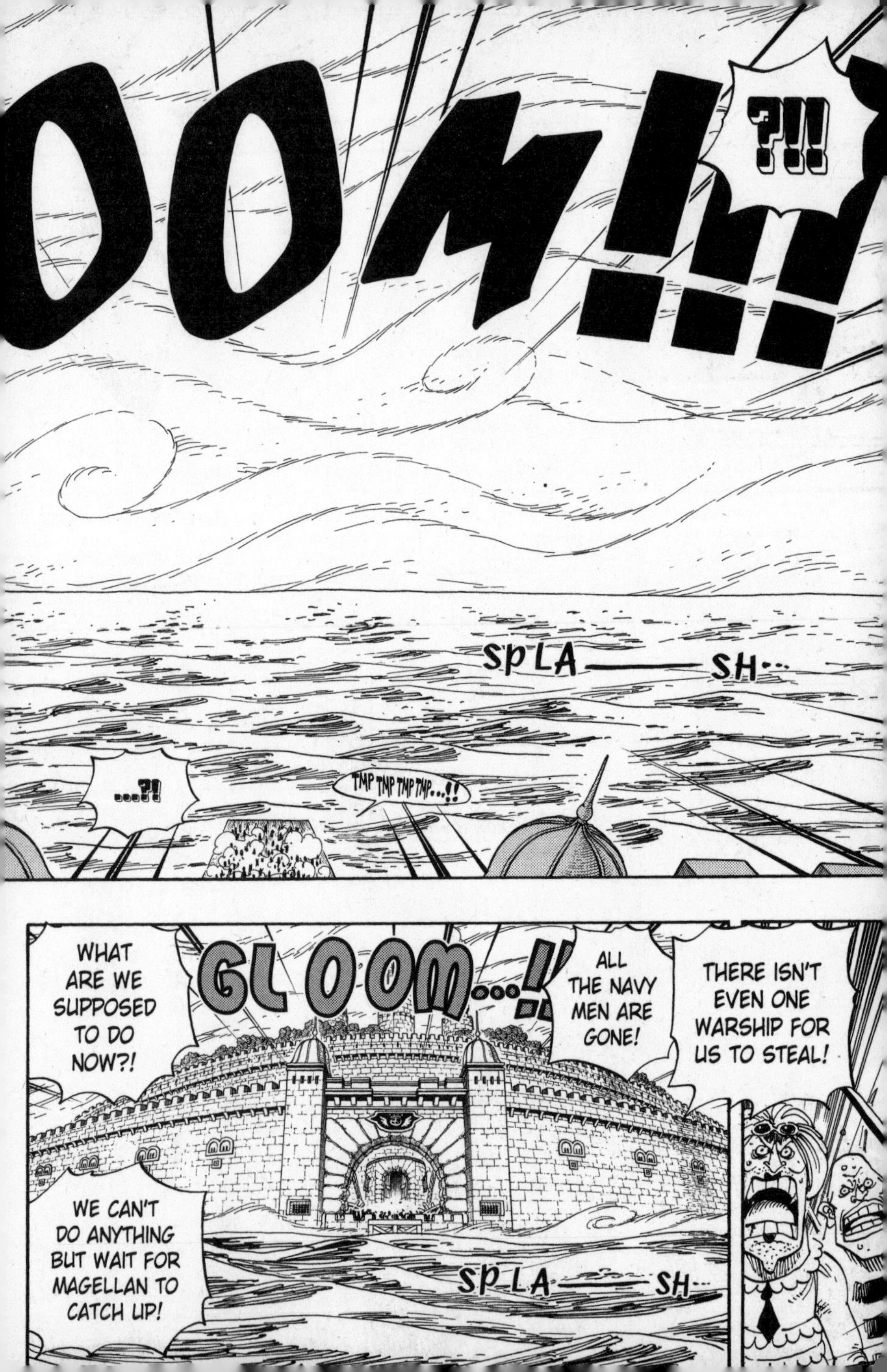
OOM!!!!
?!!
SPLA——SH...
TMP TMP TMP TMP...!!
...?!
GLOOM...!!
THERE ISN'T EVEN ONE WARSHIP FOR US TO STEAL!
ALL THE NAVY MEN ARE GONE!
WHAT ARE WE SUPPOSED TO DO NOW?!
WE CAN'T DO ANYTHING BUT WAIT FOR MAGELLAN TO CATCH UP!
SPLA——SH...

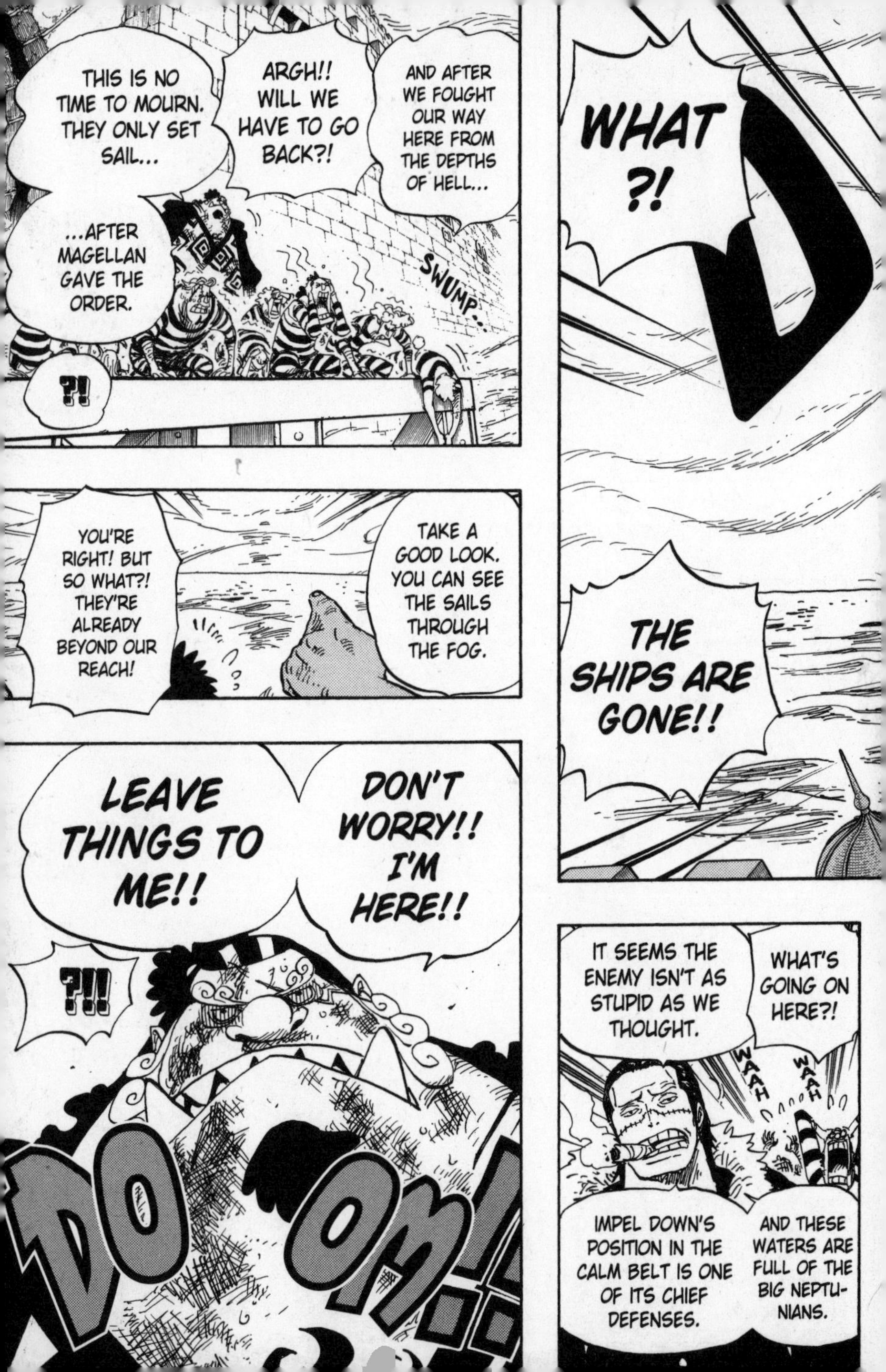
WHAT?!
THE SHIPS ARE GONE!!
AND AFTER WE FOUGHT OUR WAY HERE FROM THE DEPTHS OF HELL...
ARGH!! WILL WE HAVE TO GO BACK?!
THIS IS NO TIME TO MOURN. THEY ONLY SET SAIL...
...AFTER MAGELLAN GAVE THE ORDER.
SWUMP...
?!
TAKE A GOOD LOOK. YOU CAN SEE THE SAILS THROUGH THE FOG.
YOU'RE RIGHT! BUT SO WHAT?! THEY'RE ALREADY BEYOND OUR REACH!
WHAT'S GOING ON HERE?!
IT SEEMS THE ENEMY ISN'T AS STUPID AS WE THOUGHT.
WAAH
WAAH
IMPEL DOWN'S POSITION IN THE CALM BELT IS ONE OF ITS CHIEF DEFENSES.
AND THESE WATERS ARE FULL OF THE BIG NEPTU-NIANS.
DON'T WORRY!! I'M HERE!!
LEAVE THINGS TO ME!!
?!!
DO OM!!

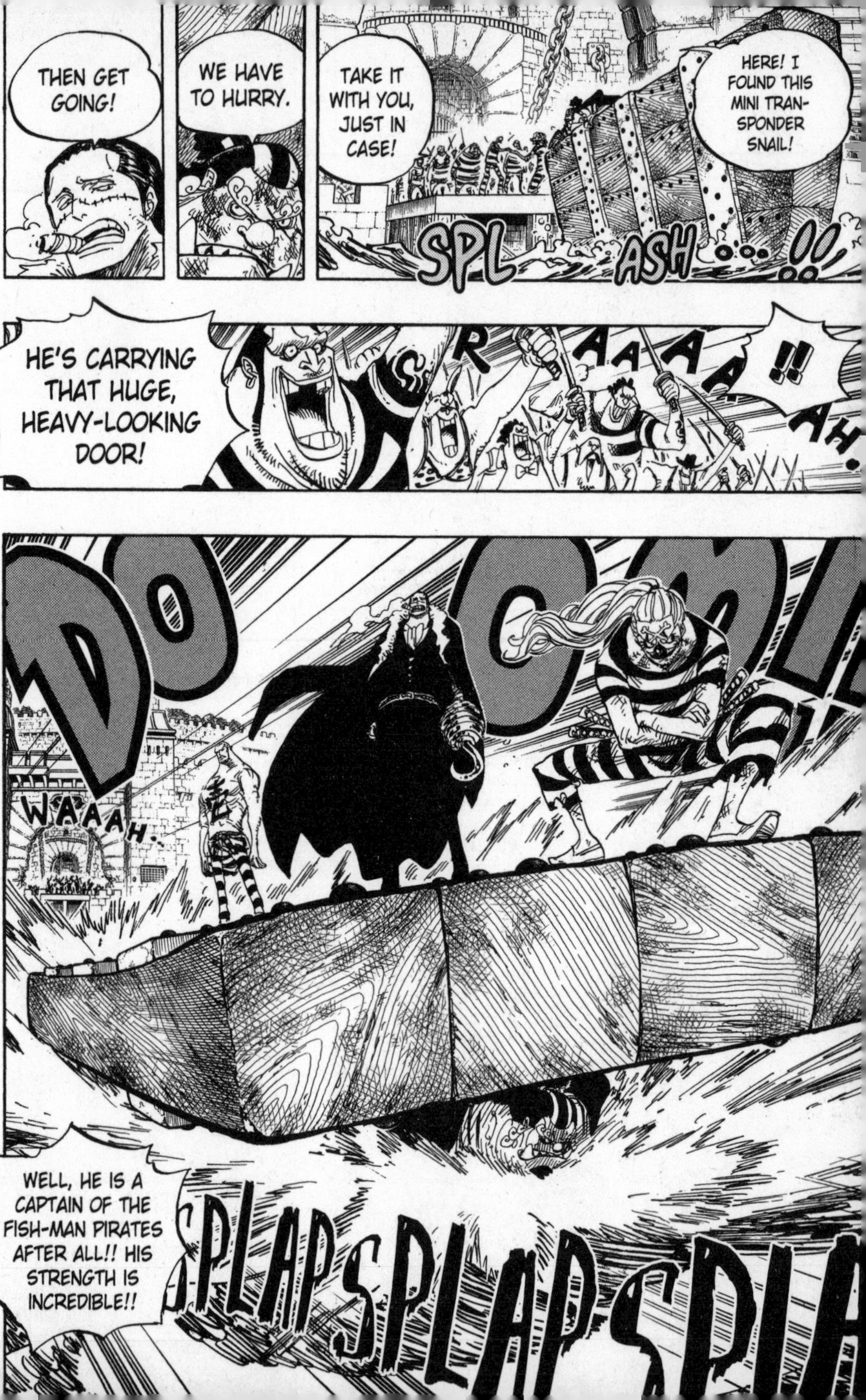

HERE! I FOUND THIS MINI TRAN-SPONDER SNAIL!
TAKE IT WITH YOU, JUST IN CASE!
SPLASH...!!
WE HAVE TO HURRY.
THEN GET GOING!
CRAAAA!!
AH...
HE'S CARRYING THAT HUGE, HEAVY-LOOKING DOOR!
DOOM
WAAAH..
WELL, HE IS A CAPTAIN OF THE FISH-MAN PIRATES AFTER ALL!! HIS STRENGTH IS INCREDIBLE!!
SPLAP SPLAP SPLA

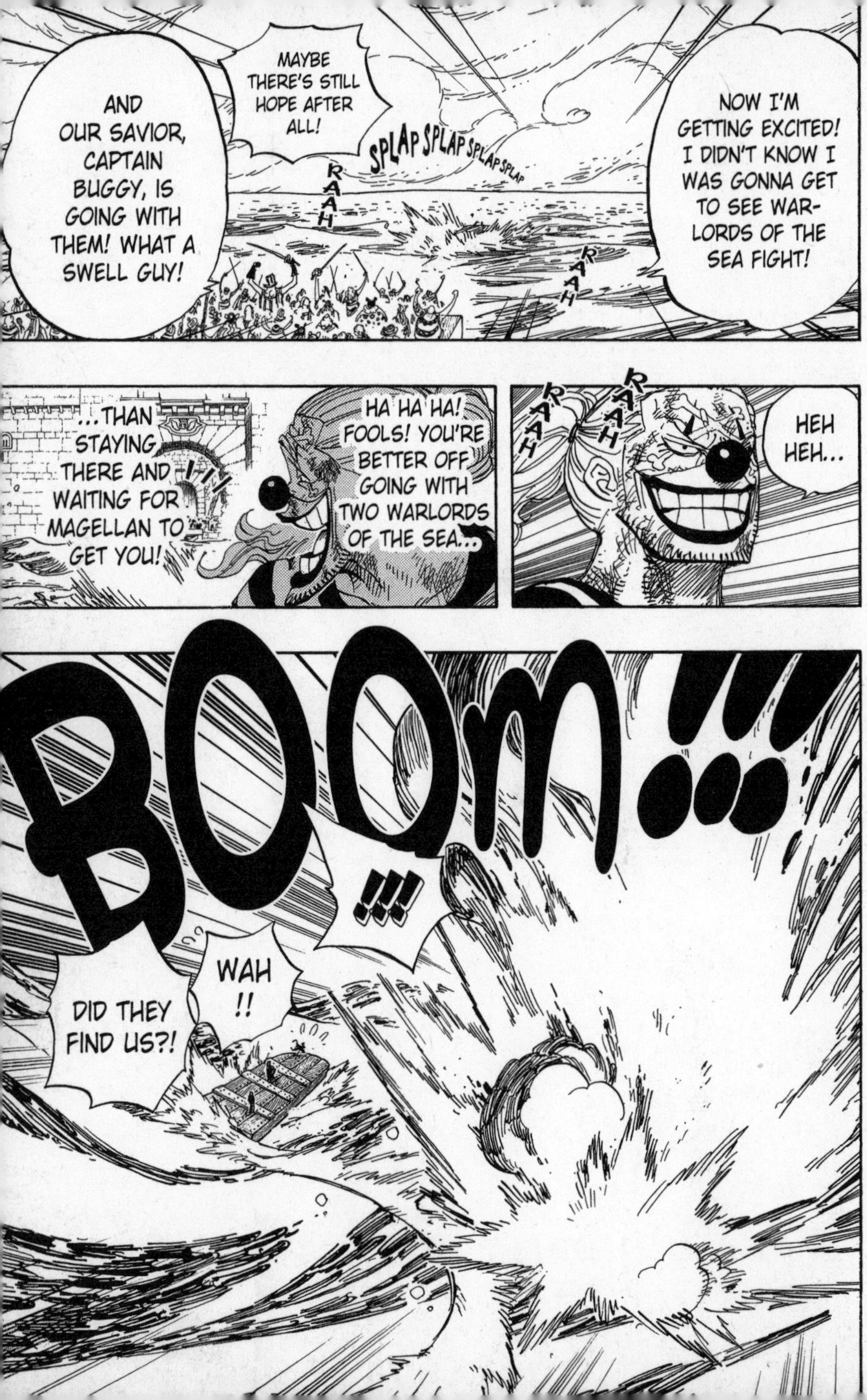
NOW I'M GETTING EXCITED! I DIDN'T KNOW I WAS GONNA GET TO SEE WAR-LORDS OF THE SEA FIGHT!
RAAH
MAYBE THERE'S STILL HOPE AFTER ALL!
SPLAP SPLAP SPLAP SPLAP
RAAH
AND OUR SAVIOR, CAPTAIN BUGGY, IS GOING WITH THEM! WHAT A SWELL GUY!
RAAH
RAAH
HEH HEH...
HA HA HA! FOOLS! YOU'RE BETTER OFF GOING WITH TWO WARLORDS OF THE SEA...
...THAN STAYING THERE AND WAITING FOR MAGELLAN TO GET YOU!
BOOM!!!...
!!!
WAH !!
DID THEY FIND US?!

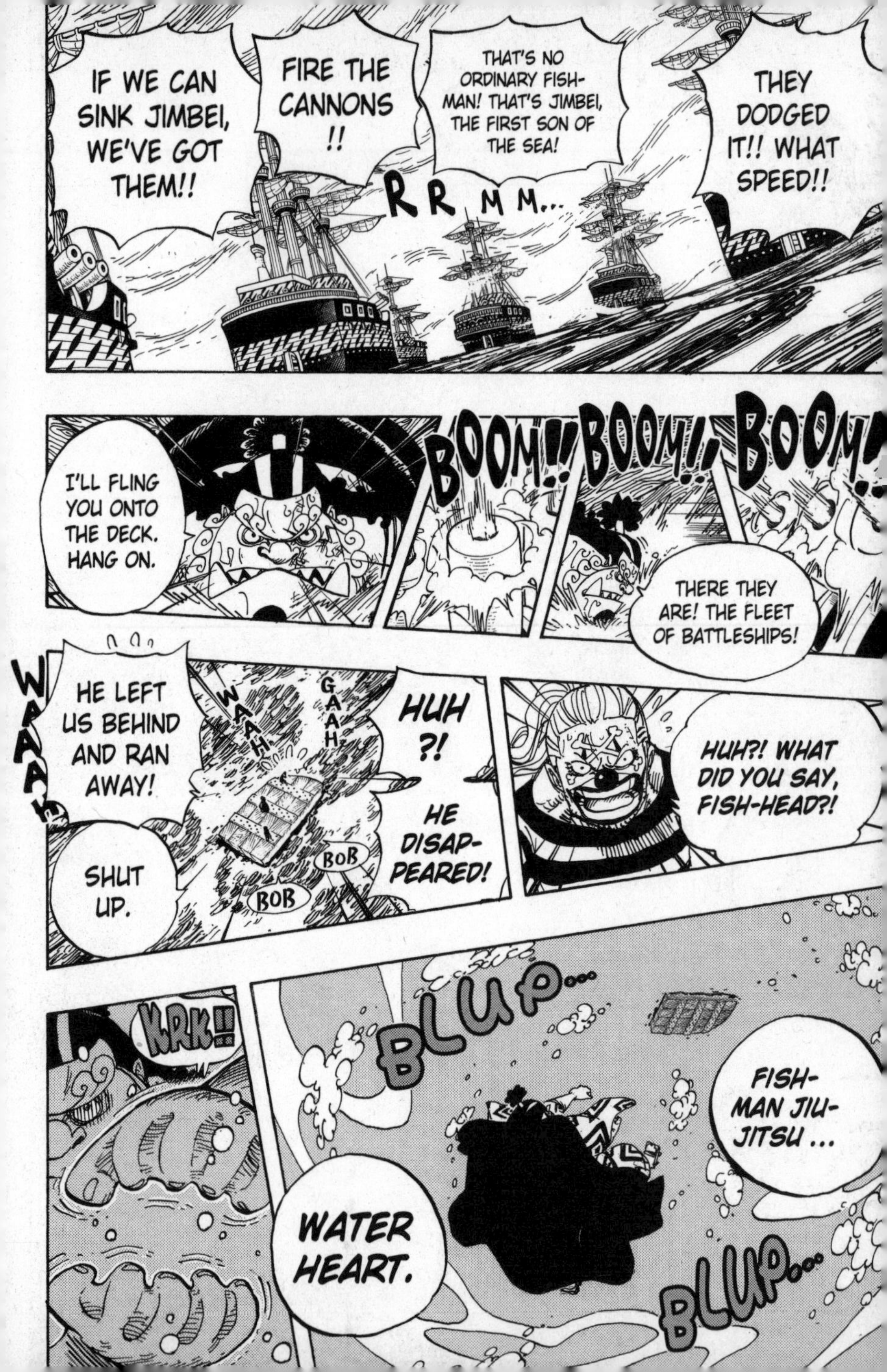
THEY DODGED IT!! WHAT SPEED!!
THAT'S NO ORDINARY FISH-MAN! THAT'S JIMBEI, THE FIRST SON OF THE SEA!
RRMM...
FIRE THE CANNONS!!
IF WE CAN SINK JIMBEI, WE'VE GOT THEM!!
BOOM!!
THERE THEY ARE! THE FLEET OF BATTLESHIPS!
BOOM!!
BOOM!!
I'LL FLING YOU ONTO THE DECK. HANG ON.
HUH?! WHAT DID YOU SAY, FISH-HEAD?!
HUH?!
HE DISAPPEARED!
GAAH
WAAH
BOB
BOB
HE LEFT US BEHIND AND RAN AWAY!
SHUT UP.
WAAAAH
FISH-MAN JIU-JITSU ...
BLUP...
WATER HEART.
BLUP...
KRK!!

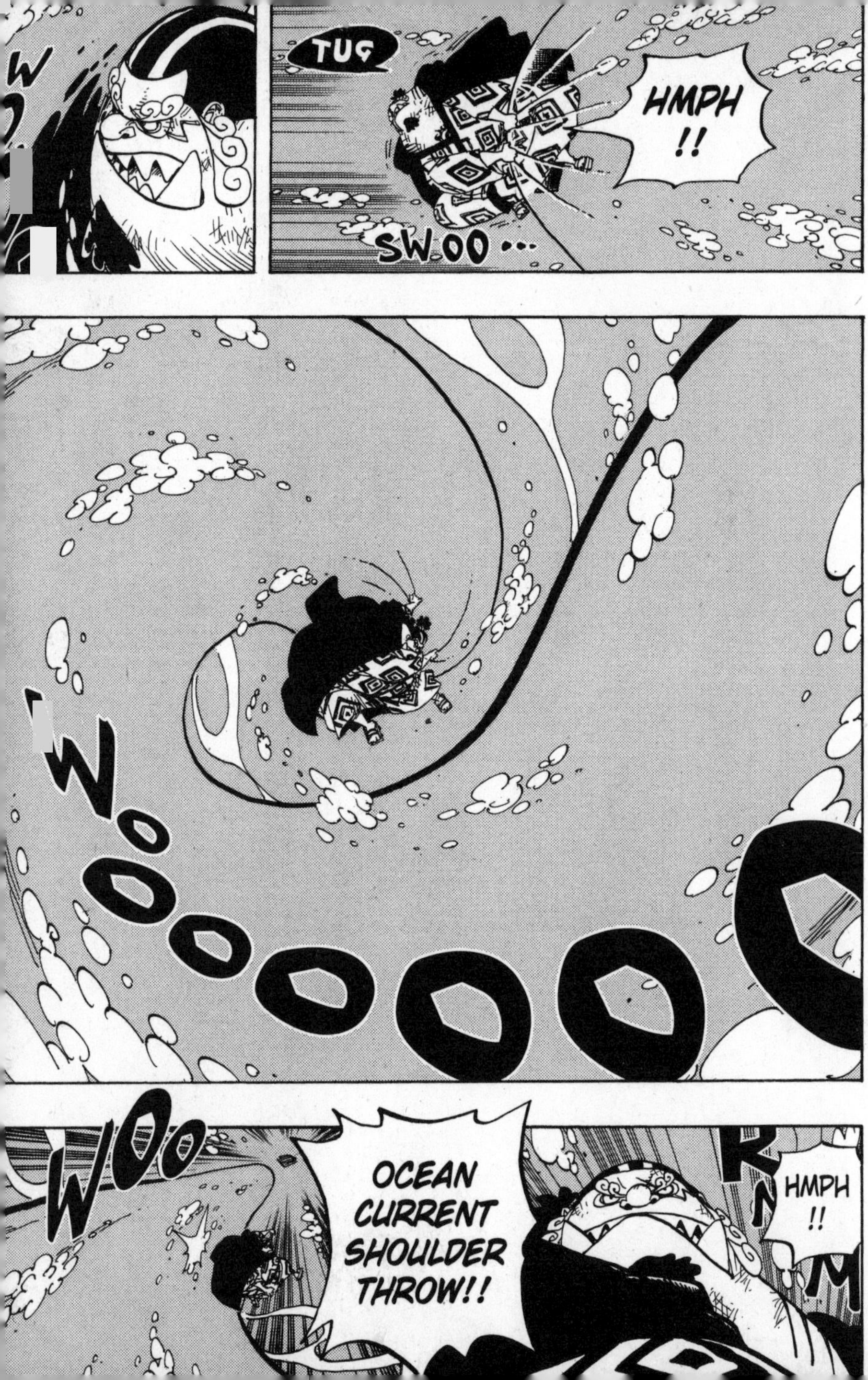

HMPH!!
TUG
SWOO...
W
WOOOOOOO
HMPH!!
OCEAN CURRENT SHOULDER THROW!!
WOO

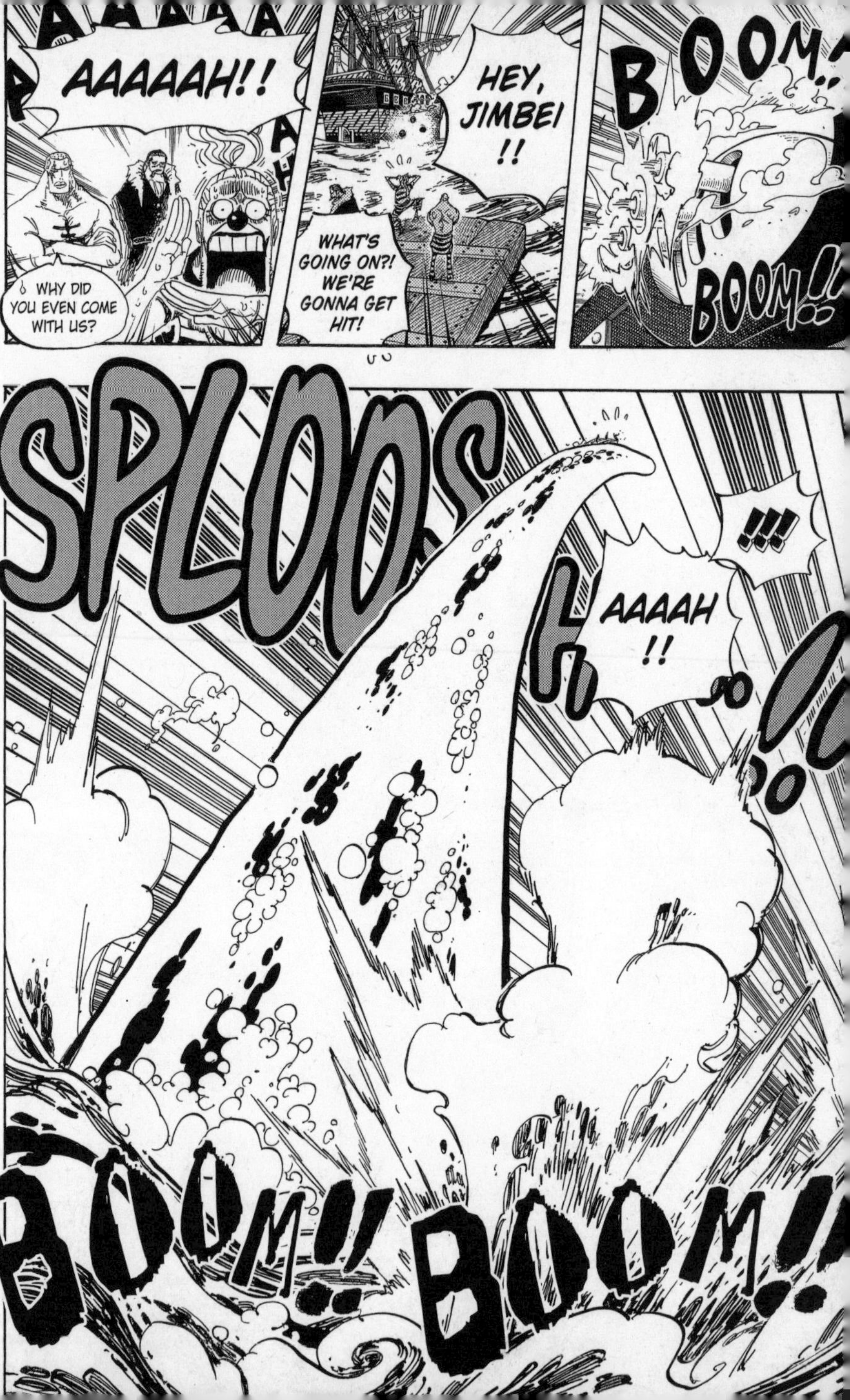

BOOM!!
BOOM!!
HEY, JIMBEI!!
WHAT'S GOING ON?! WE'RE GONNA GET HIT!
AAAAAH!!
WHY DID YOU EVEN COME WITH US?
!!!
AAAAH!!
SPLOOSH
BOOM!!
BOOM!!

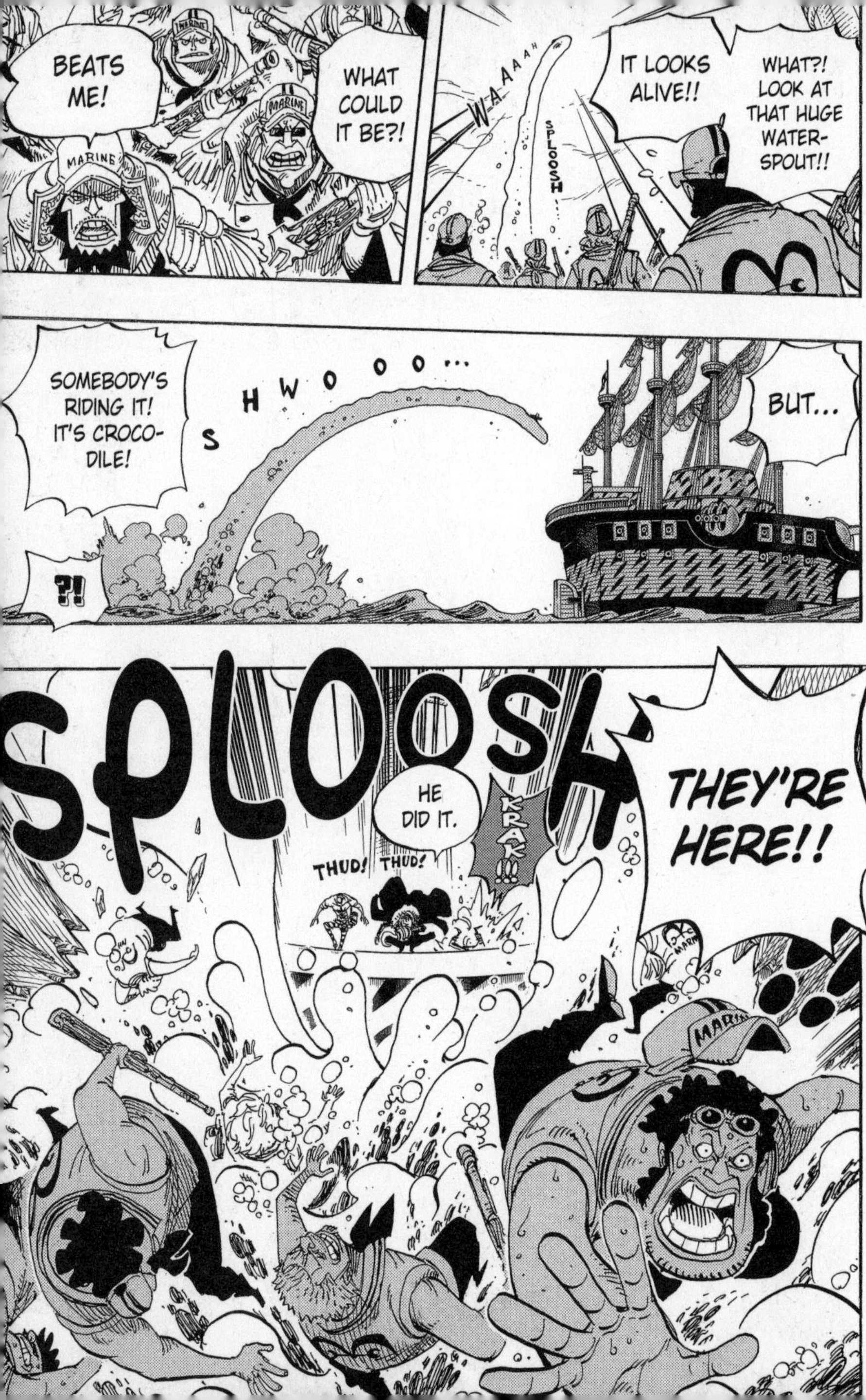
WHAT?! LOOK AT THAT HUGE WATER-SPOUT!!
IT LOOKS ALIVE!!
WAAAAAH
SPLOOSH
WHAT COULD IT BE?!
BEATS ME!
BUT...
SHWOOO...
SOMEBODY'S RIDING IT! IT'S CROCODILE!
?!
THEY'RE HERE!!
SPLOOSH
KRAK!!
HE DID IT.
THUD! THUD!

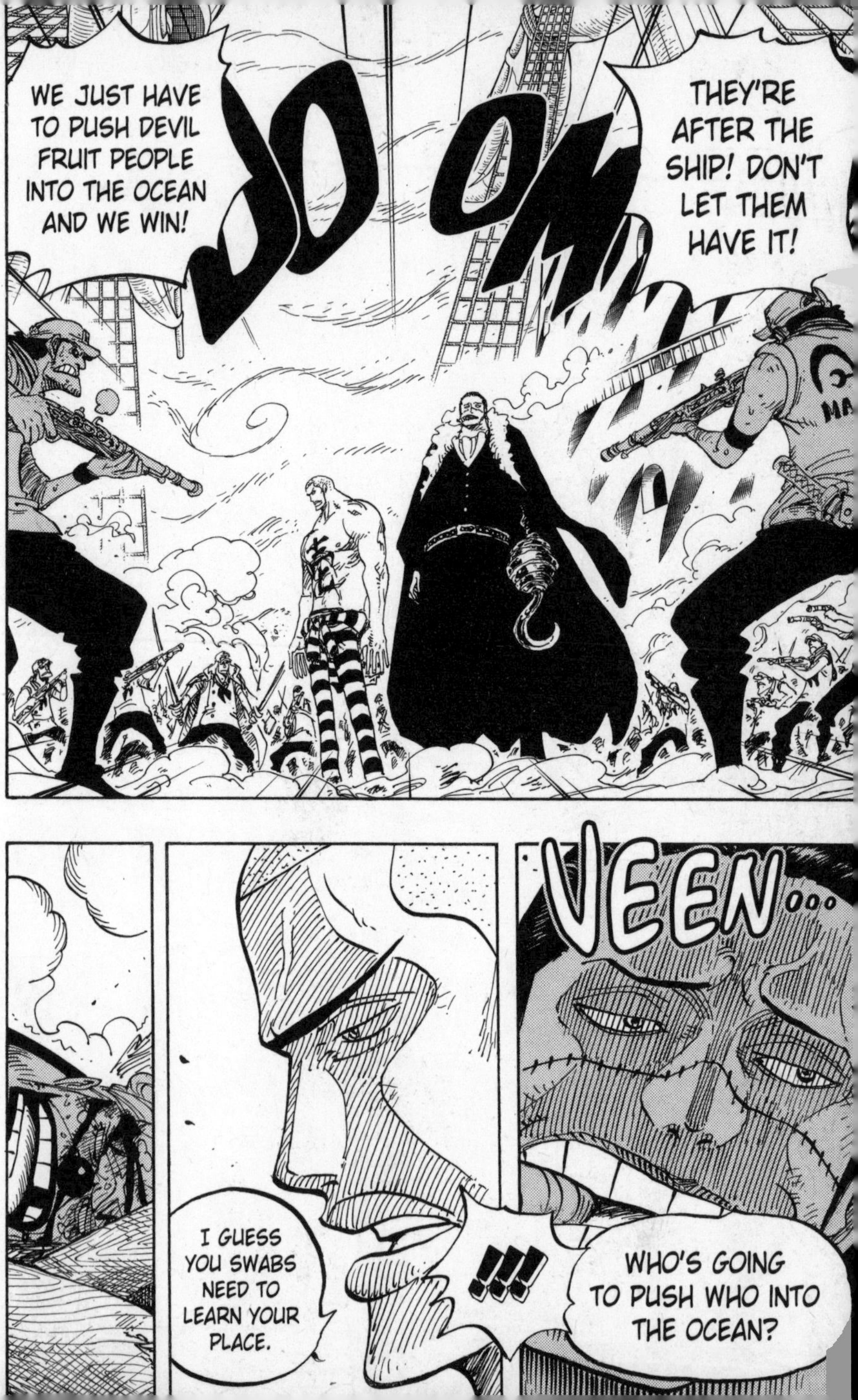
THEY'RE AFTER THE SHIP! DON'T LET THEM HAVE IT!
DOOM
WE JUST HAVE TO PUSH DEVIL FRUIT PEOPLE INTO THE OCEAN AND WE WIN!
VEEN...
WHO'S GOING TO PUSH WHO INTO THE OCEAN?
!!!
I GUESS YOU SWABS NEED TO LEARN YOUR PLACE.

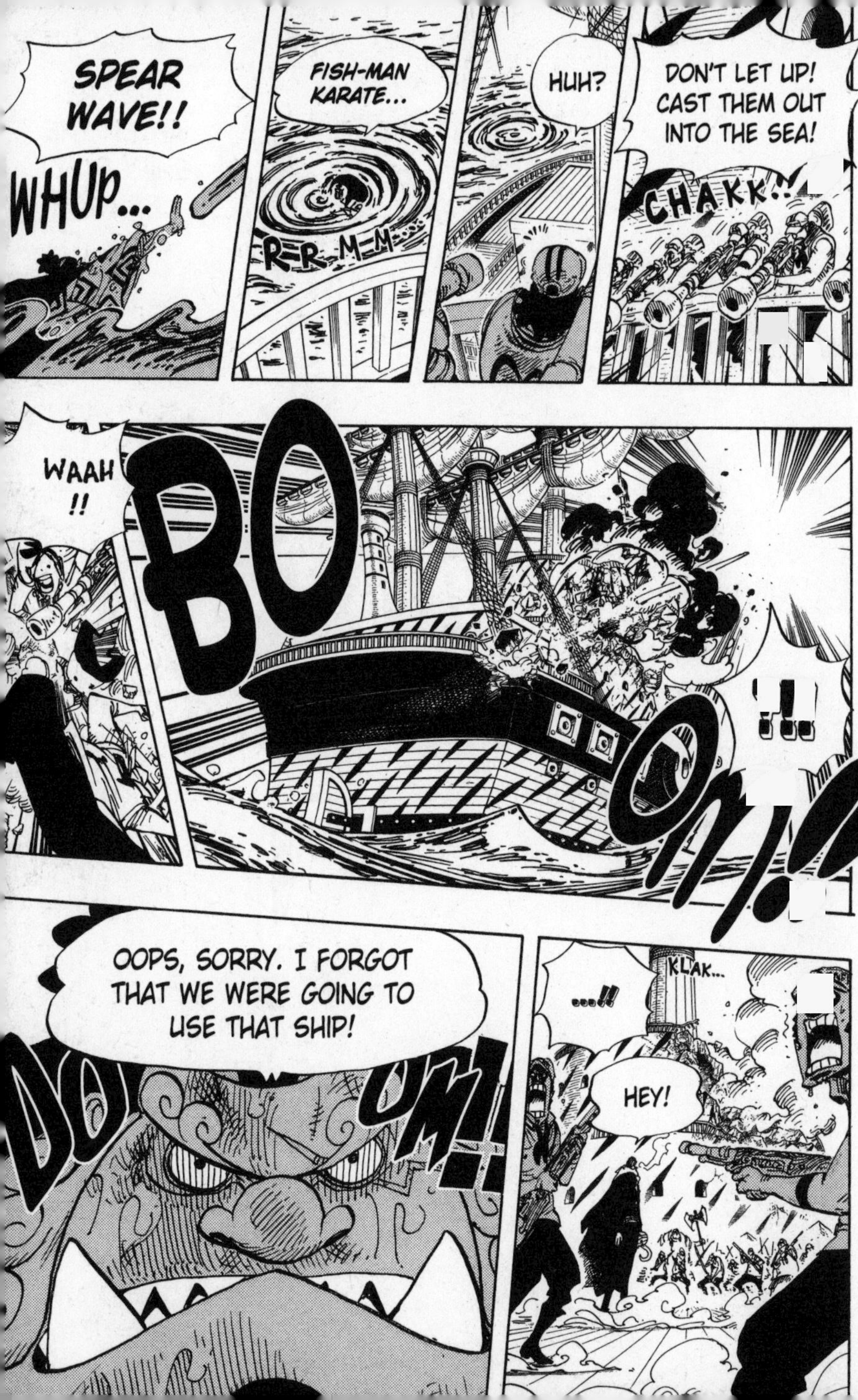
DON'T LET UP! CAST THEM OUT INTO THE SEA!
CHAKK
HUH?
FISH-MAN KARATE...
R-R-M-M
SPEAR WAVE!!
WHUP...
BOOM!!
WAAH !!
KLAK...
...!!
HEY!
OOPS, SORRY. I FORGOT THAT WE WERE GOING TO USE THAT SHIP!
DOOM!!

ISLAND RIPPER

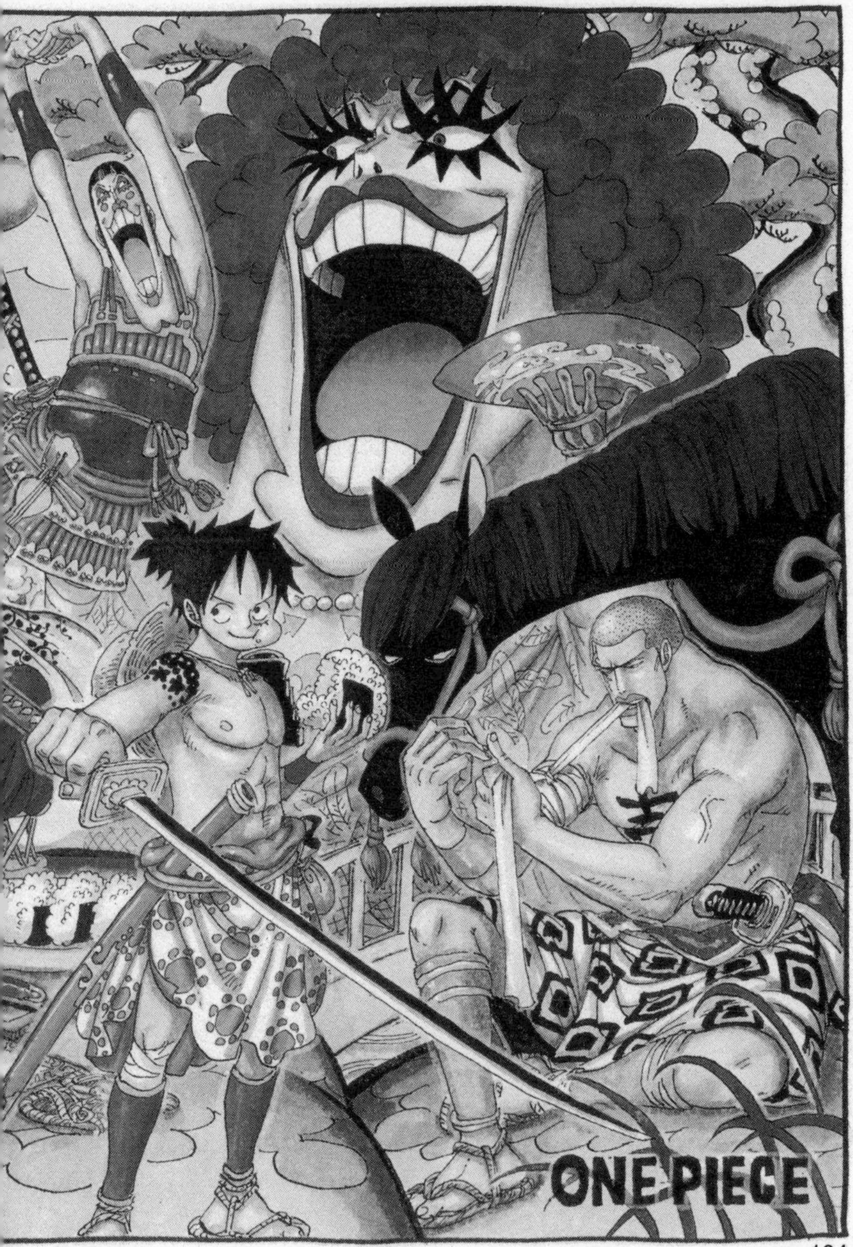
ONE PIECE

Chapter 547

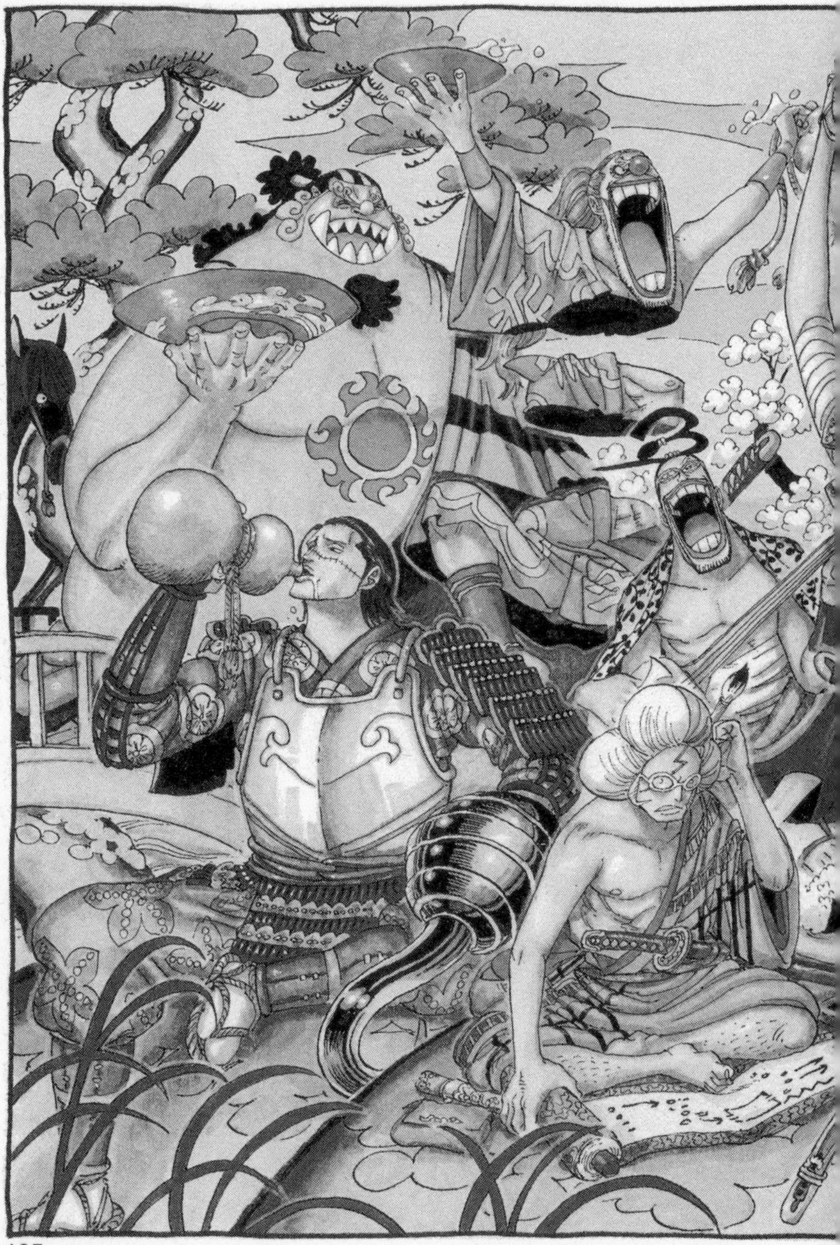

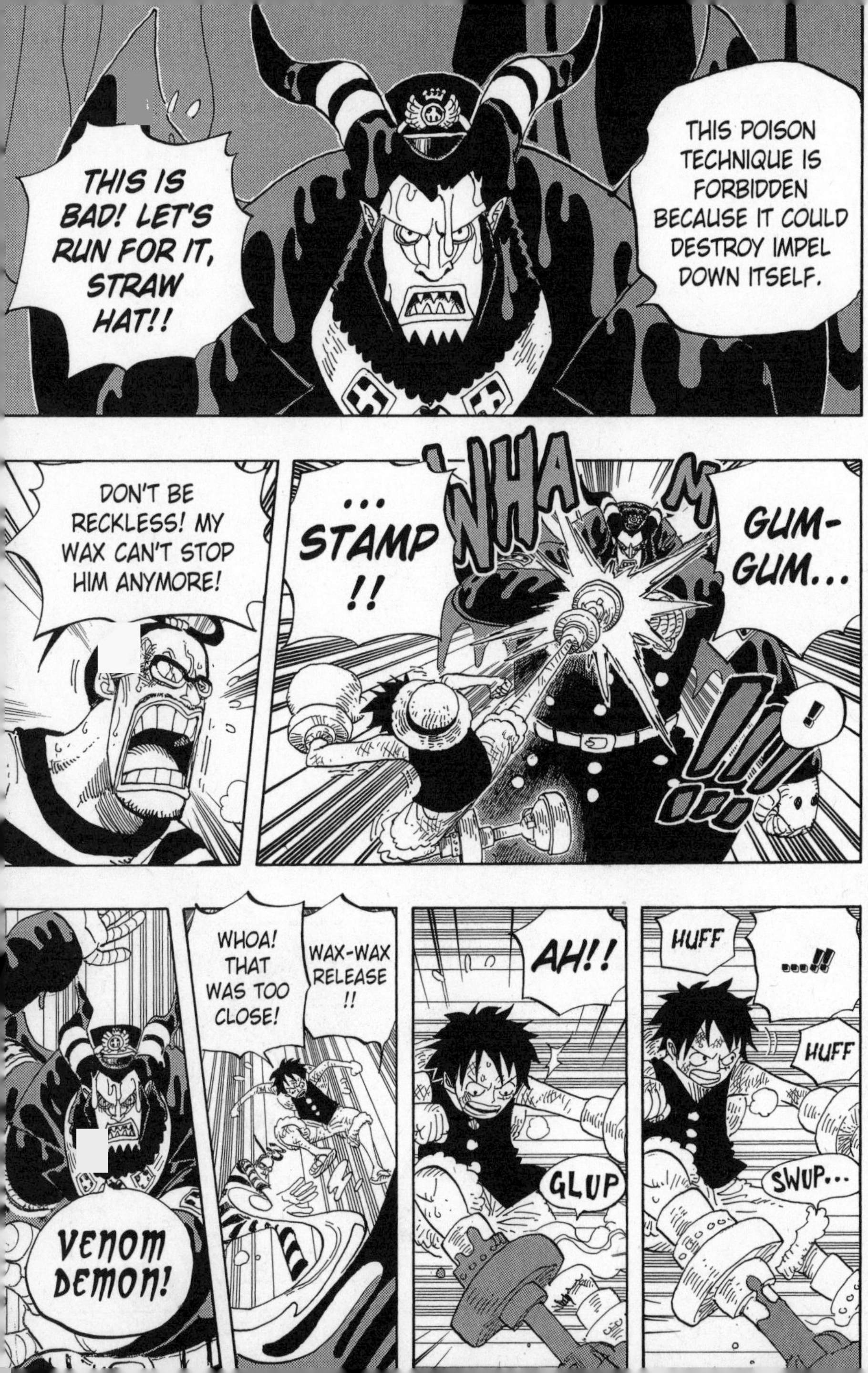
THIS POISON TECHNIQUE IS FORBIDDEN BECAUSE IT COULD DESTROY IMPEL DOWN ITSELF.
THIS IS BAD! LET'S RUN FOR IT, STRAW HAT!!
GUM-GUM...
WHAM
...STAMP!!
!
DON'T BE RECKLESS! MY WAX CAN'T STOP HIM ANYMORE!
HUFF
...!!
HUFF
SWUP...
AH!!
GLUP
WAX-WAX RELEASE!!
WHOA! THAT WAS TOO CLOSE!
VENOM DEMON!

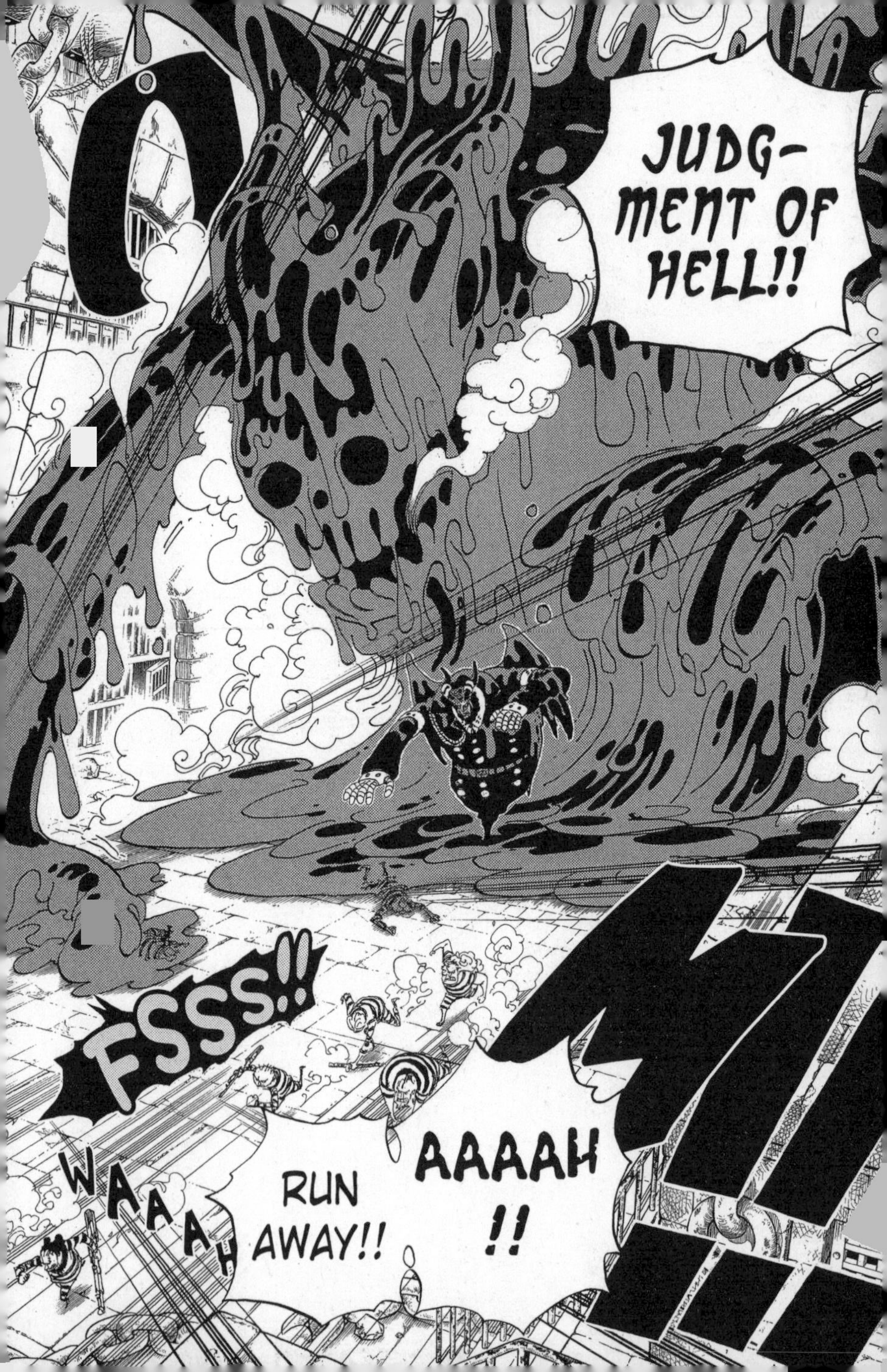
JUDG-MENT OF HELL!!
FSSS!!
AAAAH!!
RUN AWAY!!
WAAAAH

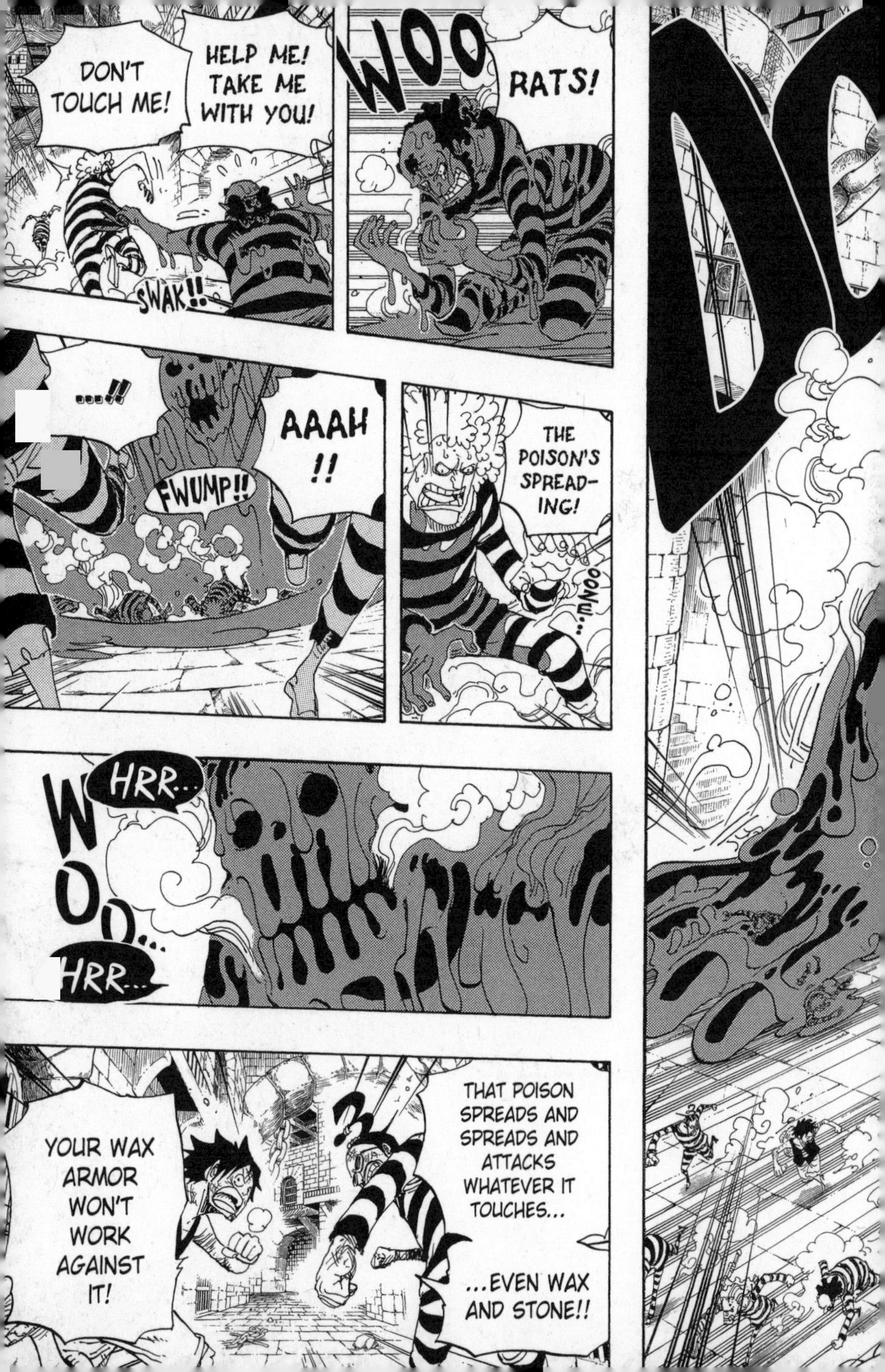
DO
WOO
RATS!
HELP ME! TAKE ME WITH YOU!
DON'T TOUCH ME!
SWAK!!
THE POISON'S SPREAD-ING!
OOZE...
AAAH!!
...!!
FWUMP!!
WOOO...
HRR...
HRR...
THAT POISON SPREADS AND SPREADS AND ATTACKS WHATEVER IT TOUCHES...
...EVEN WAX AND STONE!!
YOUR WAX ARMOR WON'T WORK AGAINST IT!

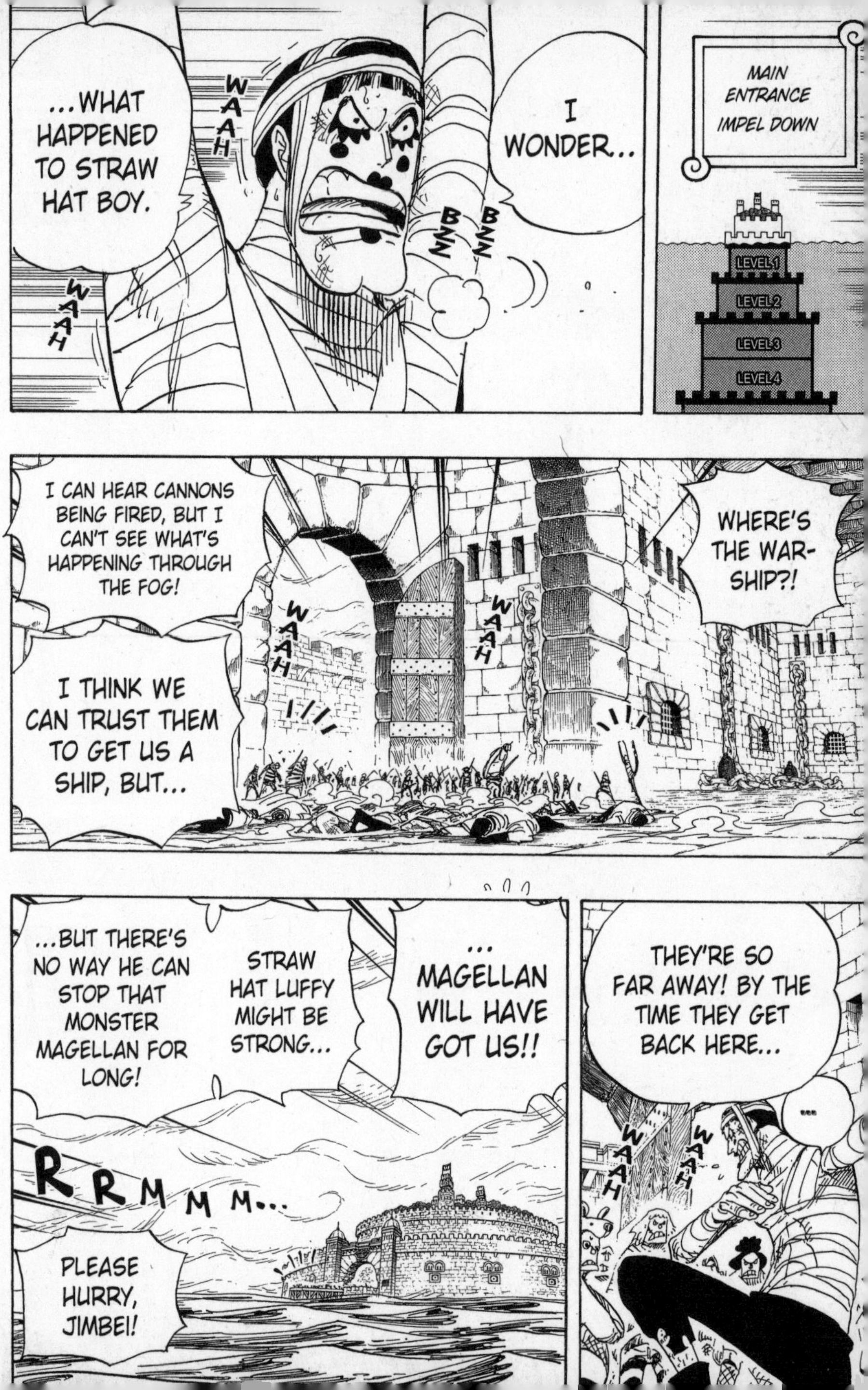
MAIN ENTRANCE IMPEL DOWN
LEVEL 1
LEVEL 2
LEVEL 3
LEVEL 4
...WHAT HAPPENED TO STRAW HAT BOY.
I WONDER...
WAAH
BZZ BZZ
WAAH
WHERE'S THE WAR-SHIP?!
I CAN HEAR CANNONS BEING FIRED, BUT I CAN'T SEE WHAT'S HAPPENING THROUGH THE FOG!
WAAH
WAAH
I THINK WE CAN TRUST THEM TO GET US A SHIP, BUT...
THEY'RE SO FAR AWAY! BY THE TIME THEY GET BACK HERE...
...
WAAH
WAAH
... MAGELLAN WILL HAVE GOT US!!
STRAW HAT LUFFY MIGHT BE STRONG...
...BUT THERE'S NO WAY HE CAN STOP THAT MONSTER MAGELLAN FOR LONG!
RRMMM...
PLEASE HURRY, JIMBEI!

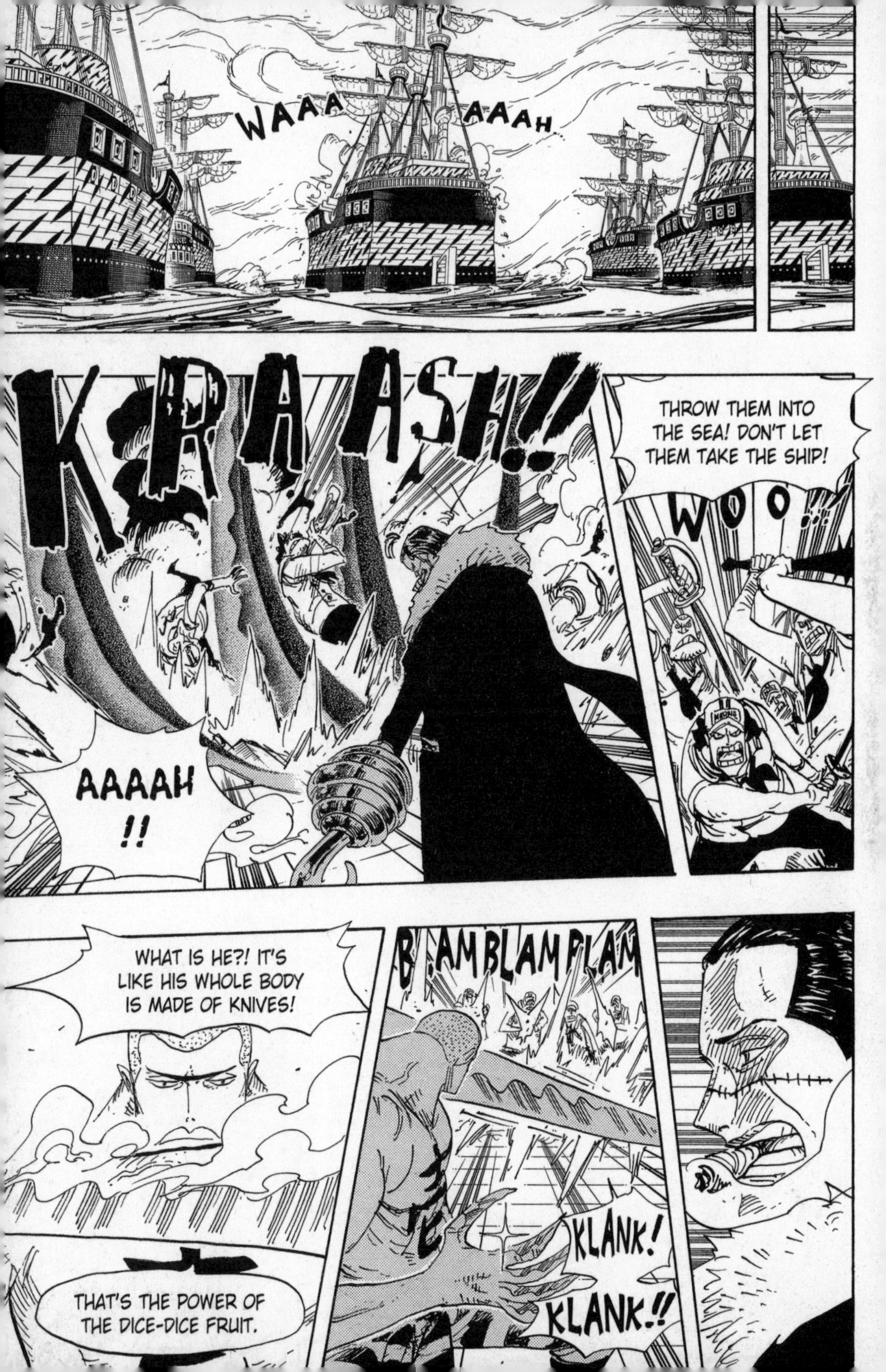
WAAA AAAH
THROW THEM INTO THE SEA! DON'T LET THEM TAKE THE SHIP!
WOO!!
KRAASH!!
AAAAH!!
BLAMBLAMBLAM
KLANK!
KLANK!!
WHAT IS HE?! IT'S LIKE HIS WHOLE BODY IS MADE OF KNIVES!
THAT'S THE POWER OF THE DICE-DICE FRUIT.

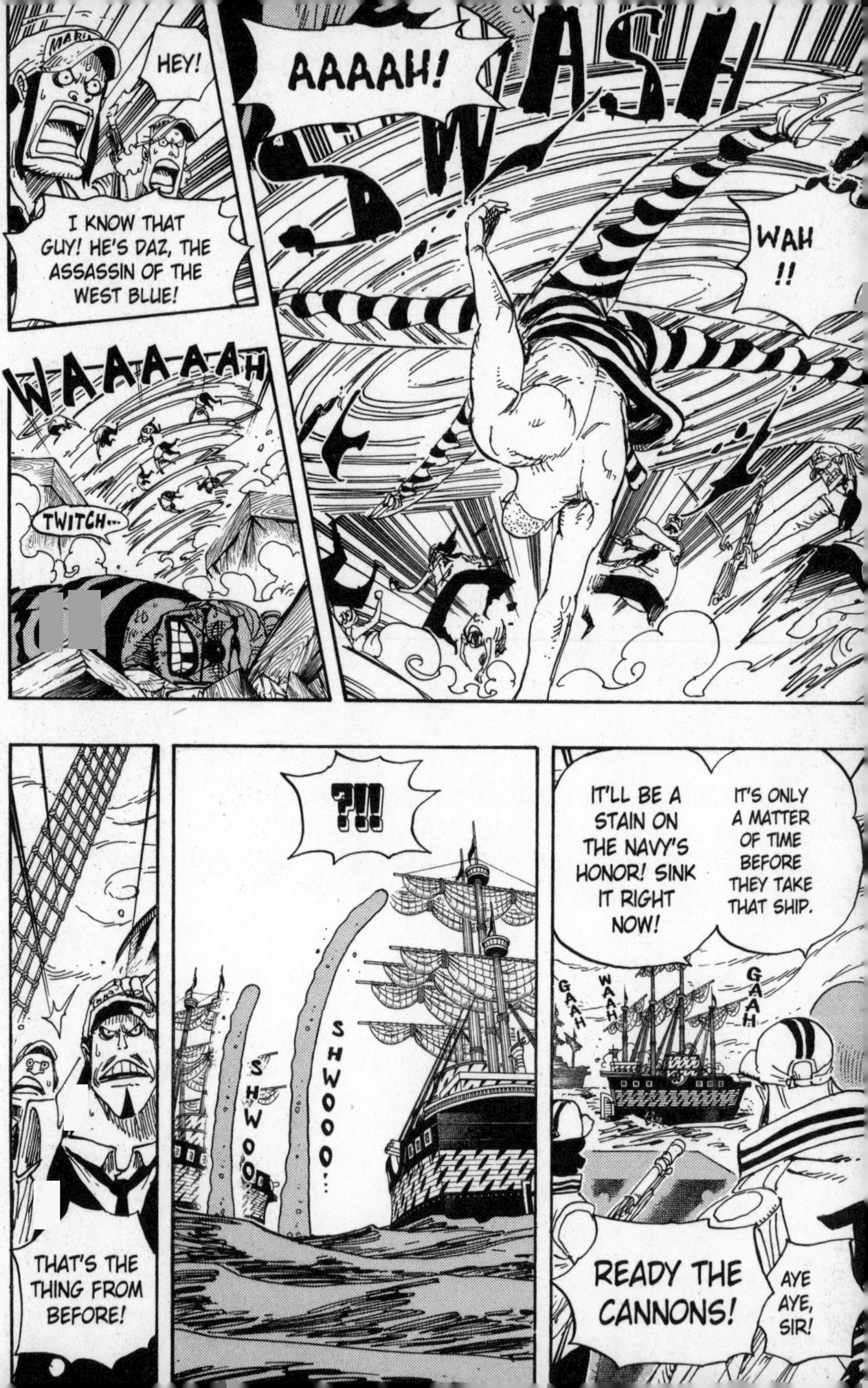
AAAAH!
SWASH
WAH !!
HEY!
I KNOW THAT GUY! HE'S DAZ, THE ASSASSIN OF THE WEST BLUE!
WAAAAAH
TWITCH...
IT'S ONLY A MATTER OF TIME BEFORE THEY TAKE THAT SHIP.
IT'LL BE A STAIN ON THE NAVY'S HONOR! SINK IT RIGHT NOW!
GAAH
WAAH
GAAH
READY THE CANNONS!
AYE AYE, SIR!
?!!
SHWOOO...
SHWOOO
THAT'S THE THING FROM BEFORE!

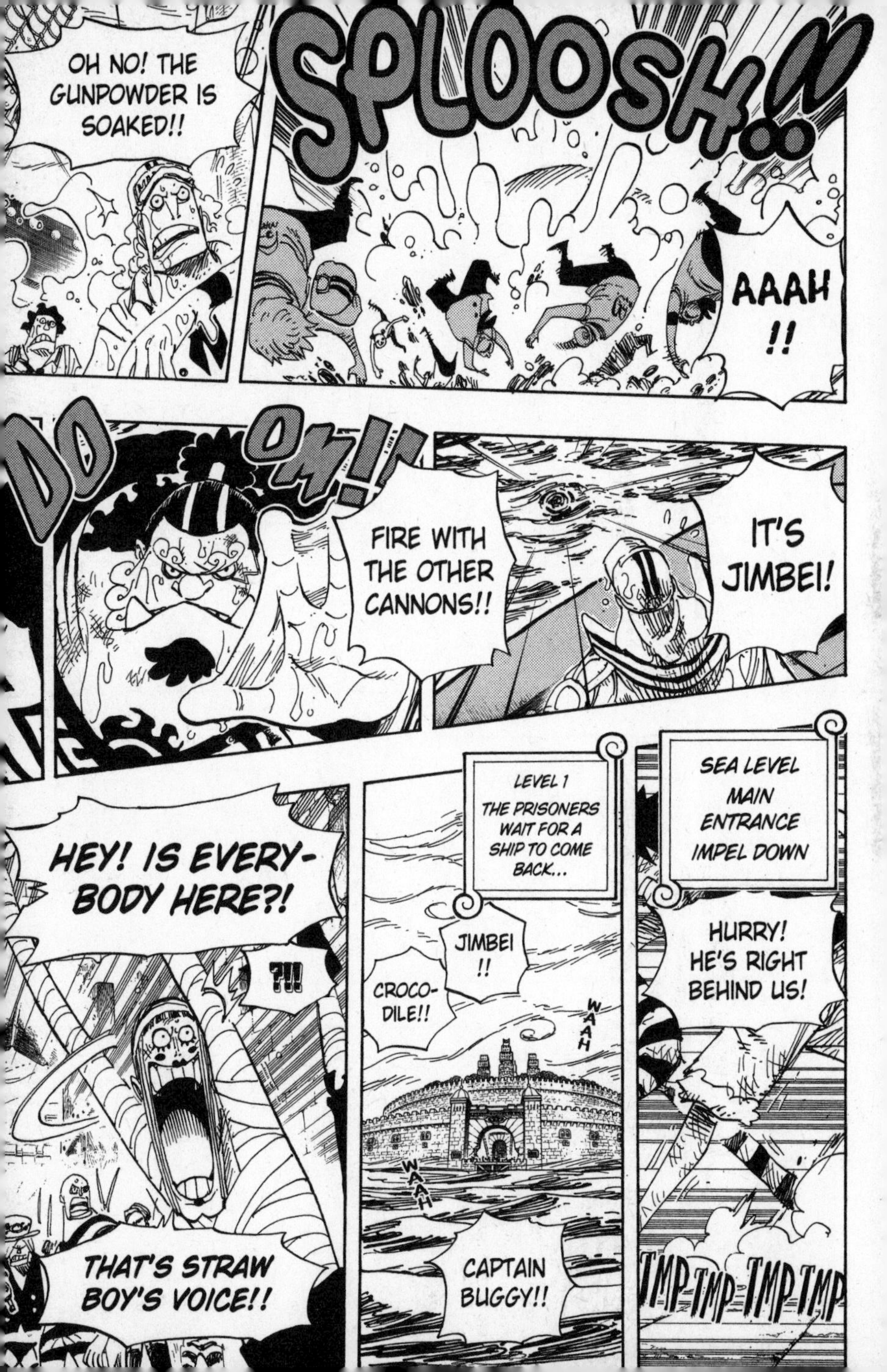
SPLOOSH!!
AAAH !!
OH NO! THE GUNPOWDER IS SOAKED!!
IT'S JIMBEI!
DOOM!!
FIRE WITH THE OTHER CANNONS!!
SEA LEVEL MAIN ENTRANCE IMPEL DOWN
HURRY! HE'S RIGHT BEHIND US!
TMP TMP TMP TMP
LEVEL 1 THE PRISONERS WAIT FOR A SHIP TO COME BACK...
JIMBEI !!
CROCO-DILE!!
WAAH
WAAH
CAPTAIN BUGGY!!
HEY! IS EVERY-BODY HERE?!
?!!
THAT'S STRAW BOY'S VOICE!!

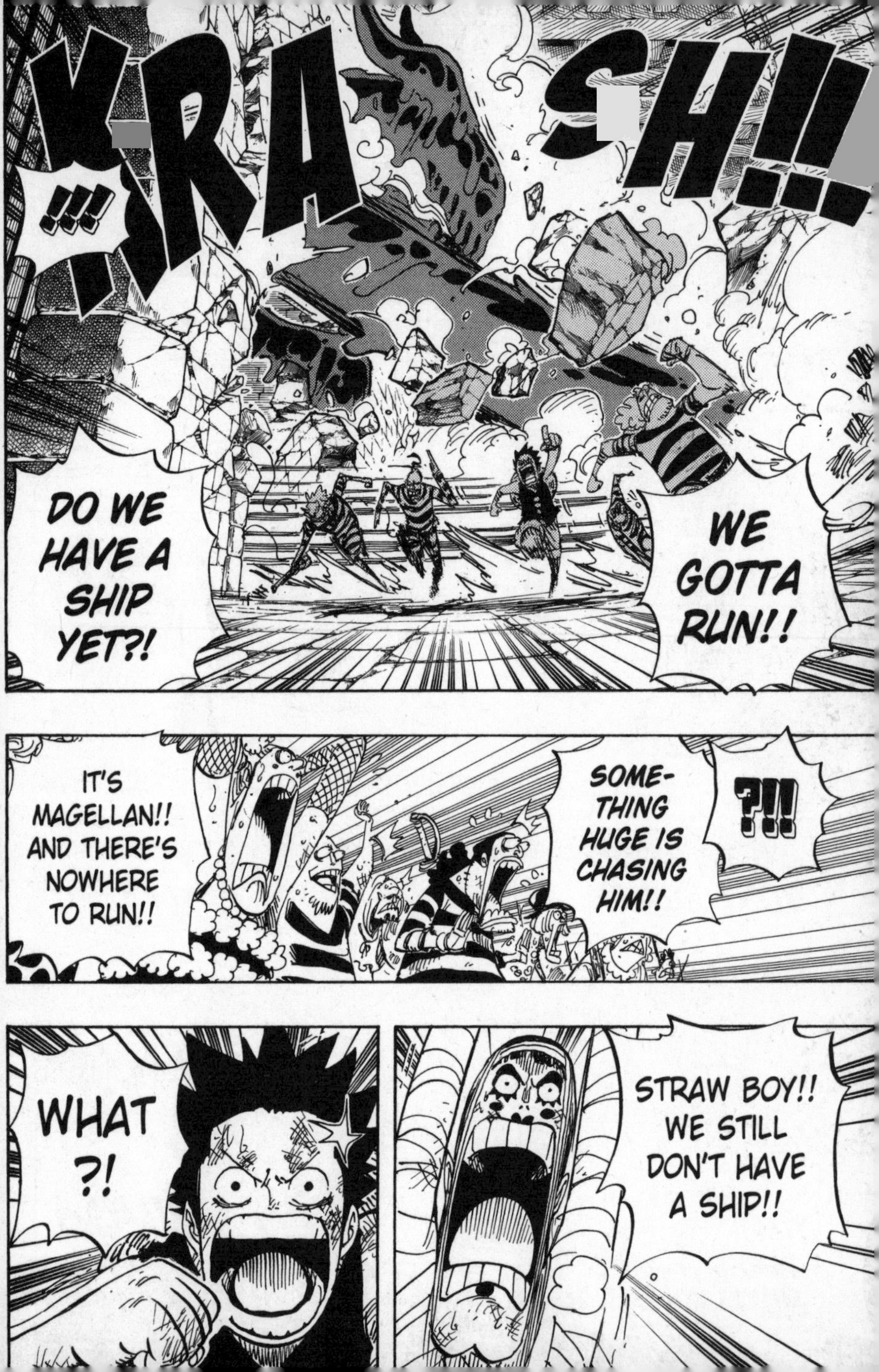
KRASH!!
WE GOTTA RUN!!
DO WE HAVE A SHIP YET?!
!!!
?!!
SOME-THING HUGE IS CHASING HIM!!
IT'S MAGELLAN!! AND THERE'S NOWHERE TO RUN!!
STRAW BOY!! WE STILL DON'T HAVE A SHIP!!
WHAT?!

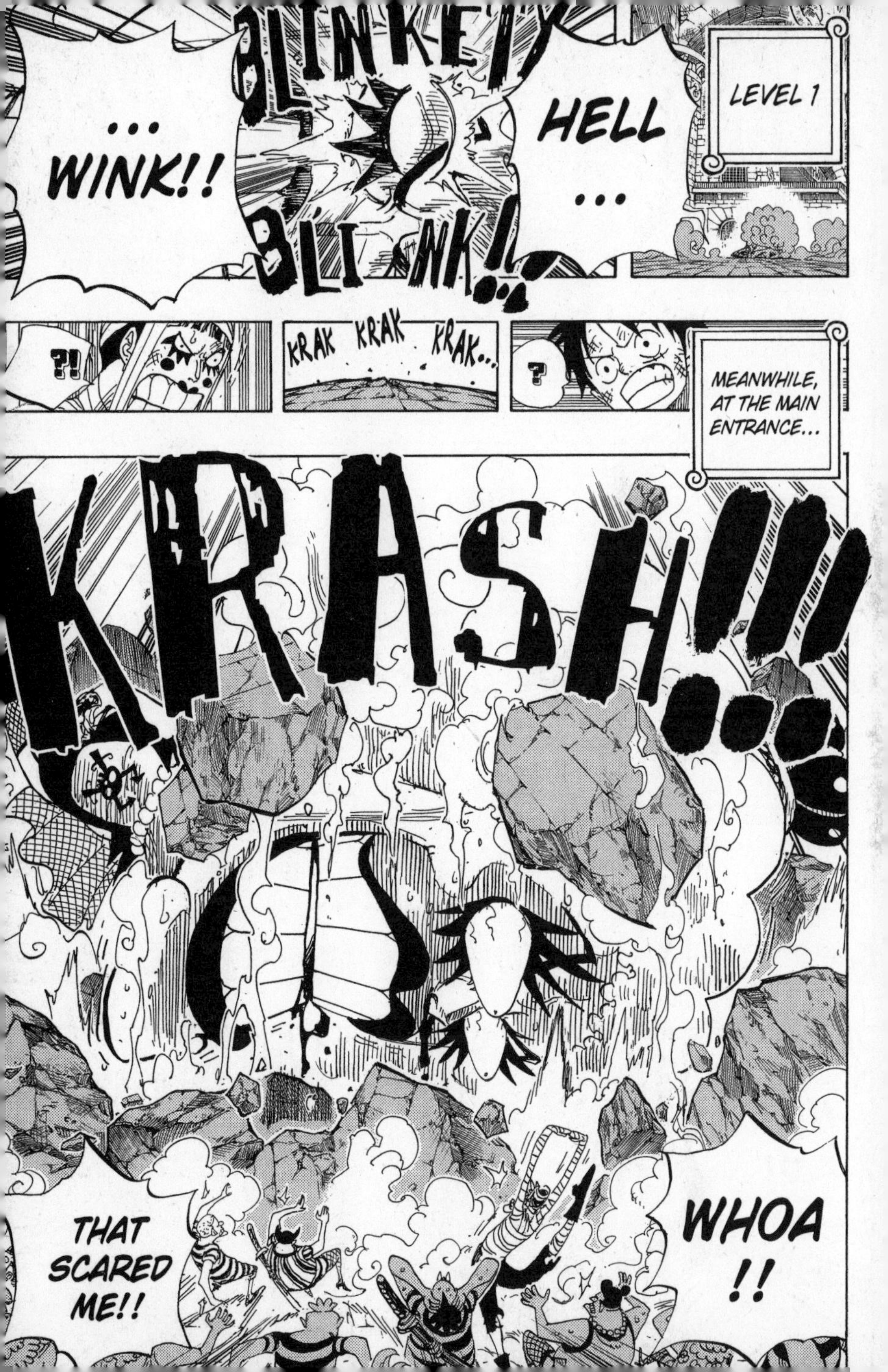
LEVEL 1
HELL ...
BLINKETY
BLINK!!
... WINK!!
MEANWHILE, AT THE MAIN ENTRANCE...
?
KRAK KRAK KRAK...
?!
KRASH!!!!
WHOA !!
THAT SCARED ME!!

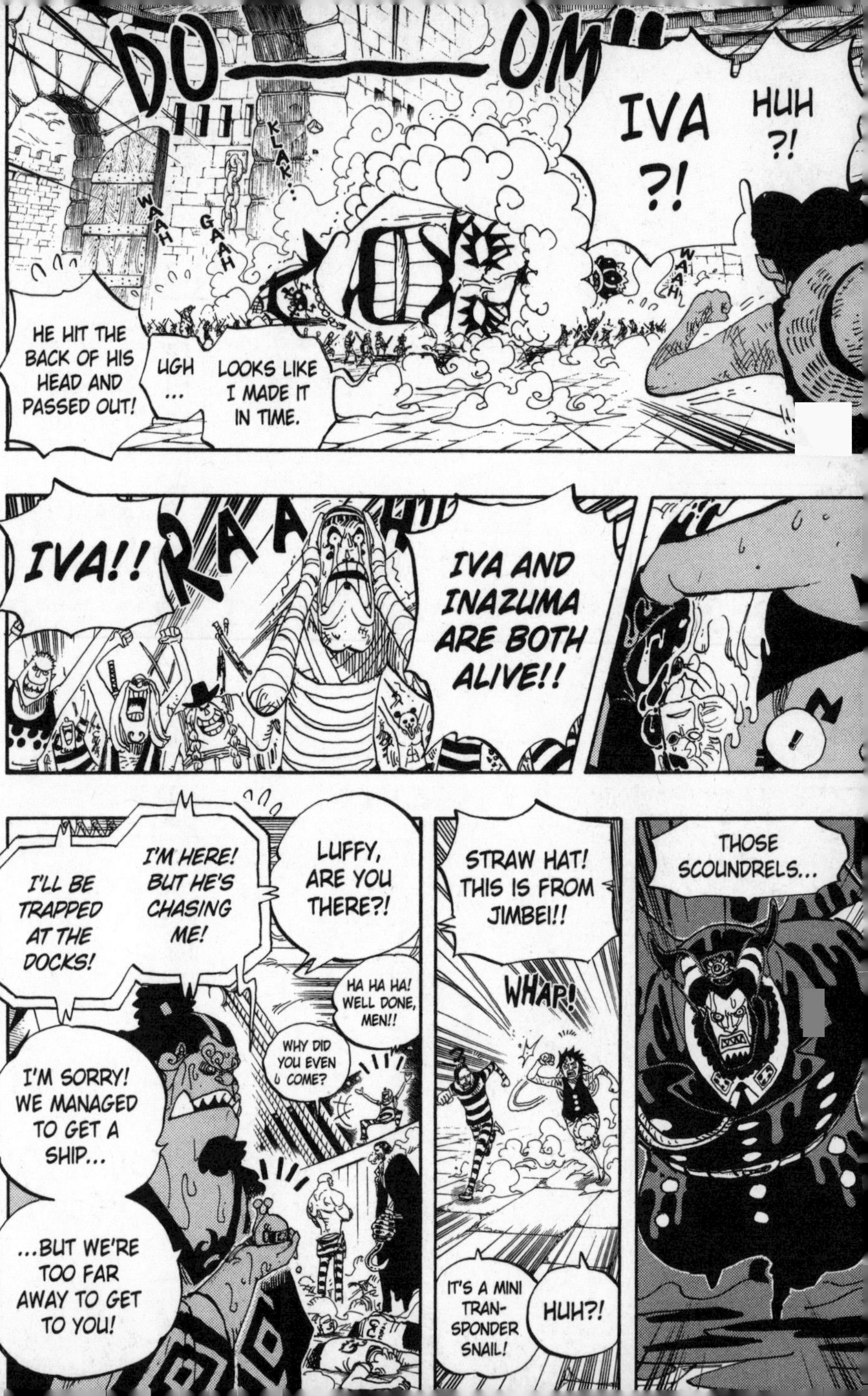
DO—OM!!
HUH ?!
IVA ?!
KLAK...
WAAH
GAAH
WAAH
LOOKS LIKE I MADE IT IN TIME.
UGH ...
HE HIT THE BACK OF HIS HEAD AND PASSED OUT!
!
IVA AND INAZUMA ARE BOTH ALIVE!!
RAAAH
IVA!!
THOSE SCOUNDRELS...
STRAW HAT! THIS IS FROM JIMBEI!!
WHAP!
HUH?!
IT'S A MINI TRAN-SPONDER SNAIL!
LUFFY, ARE YOU THERE?!
I'M HERE! BUT HE'S CHASING ME!
I'LL BE TRAPPED AT THE DOCKS!
HA HA HA! WELL DONE, MEN!!
WHY DID YOU EVEN COME?
I'M SORRY! WE MANAGED TO GET A SHIP...
...BUT WE'RE TOO FAR AWAY TO GET TO YOU!

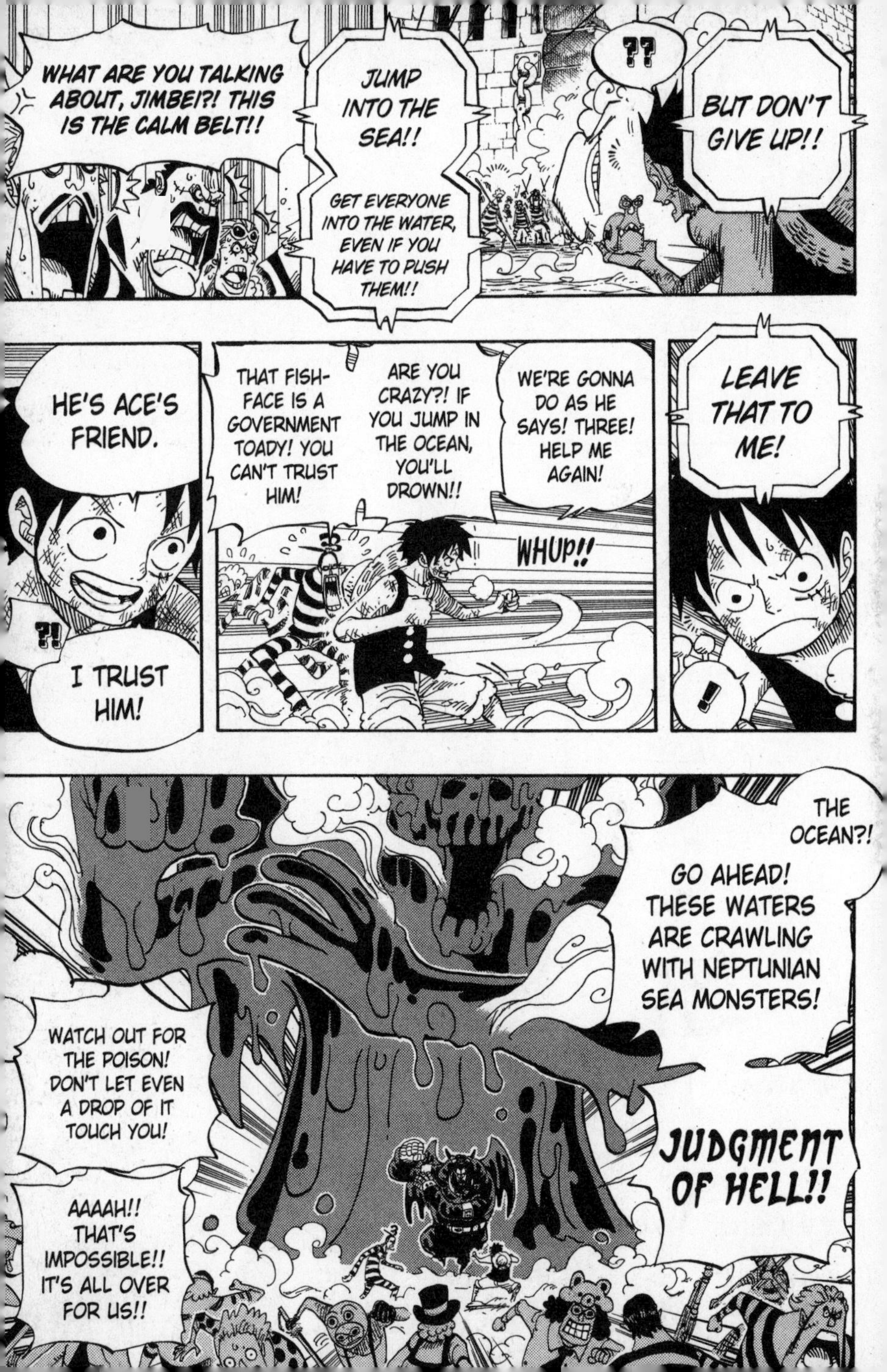
??
BUT DON'T GIVE UP!!
JUMP INTO THE SEA!!
GET EVERYONE INTO THE WATER, EVEN IF YOU HAVE TO PUSH THEM!!
WHAT ARE YOU TALKING ABOUT, JIMBEI?! THIS IS THE CALM BELT!!
LEAVE THAT TO ME!
!
WE'RE GONNA DO AS HE SAYS! THREE! HELP ME AGAIN!
ARE YOU CRAZY?! IF YOU JUMP IN THE OCEAN, YOU'LL DROWN!!
THAT FISH-FACE IS A GOVERNMENT TOADY! YOU CAN'T TRUST HIM!
WHUP!!
HE'S ACE'S FRIEND.
?!
I TRUST HIM!
THE OCEAN?!
GO AHEAD! THESE WATERS ARE CRAWLING WITH NEPTUNIAN SEA MONSTERS!
JUDGMENT OF HELL!!
WATCH OUT FOR THE POISON! DON'T LET EVEN A DROP OF IT TOUCH YOU!
AAAAH!! THAT'S IMPOSSIBLE!! IT'S ALL OVER FOR US!!

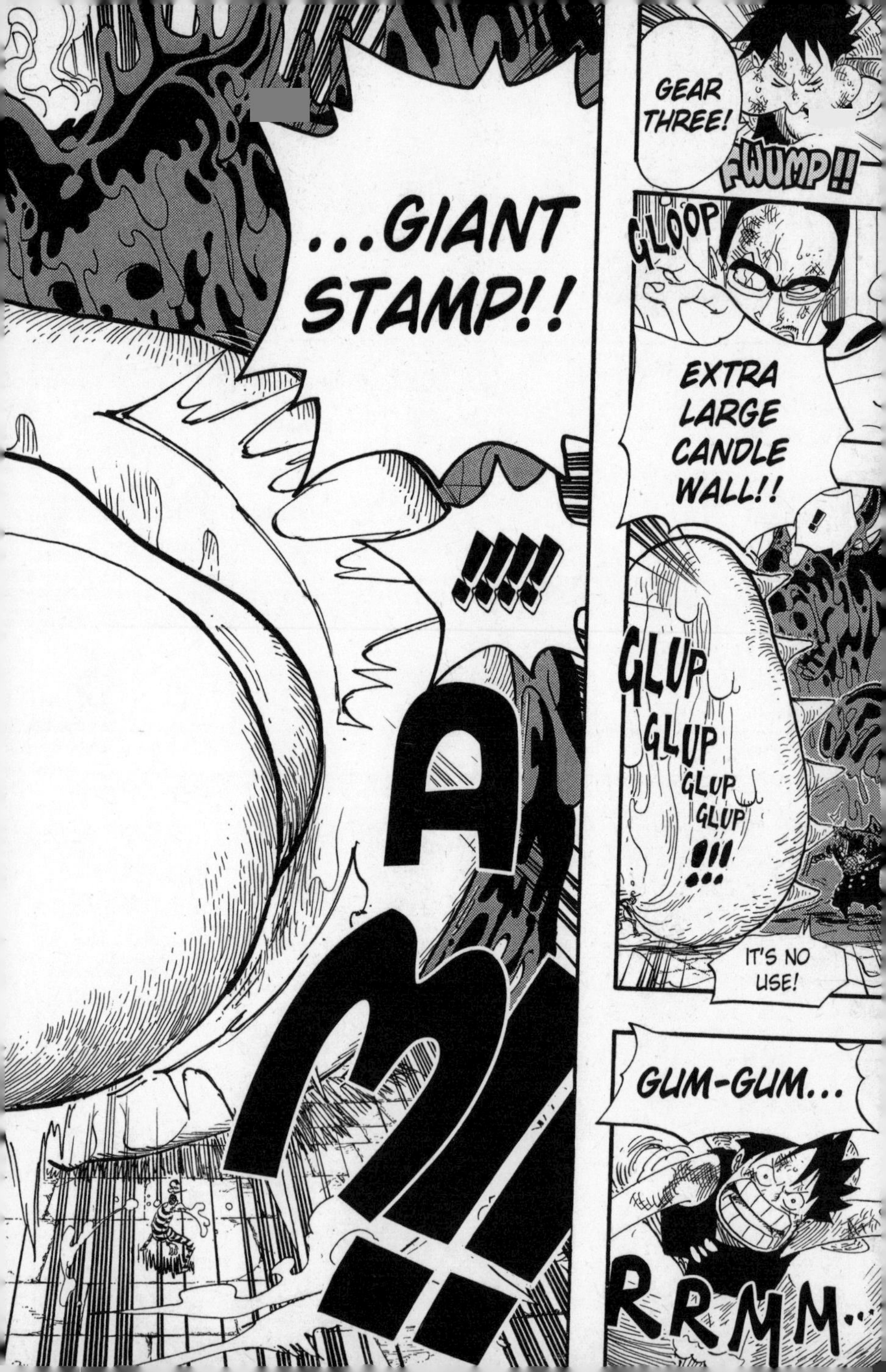
GEAR THREE!
FWUMP!!
GLOOP
EXTRA LARGE CANDLE WALL!!
!
GLUP
GLUP
GLUP
GLUP
!!!
IT'S NO USE!
GUM-GUM...
RRMM...
...GIANT STAMP!!
!!!!

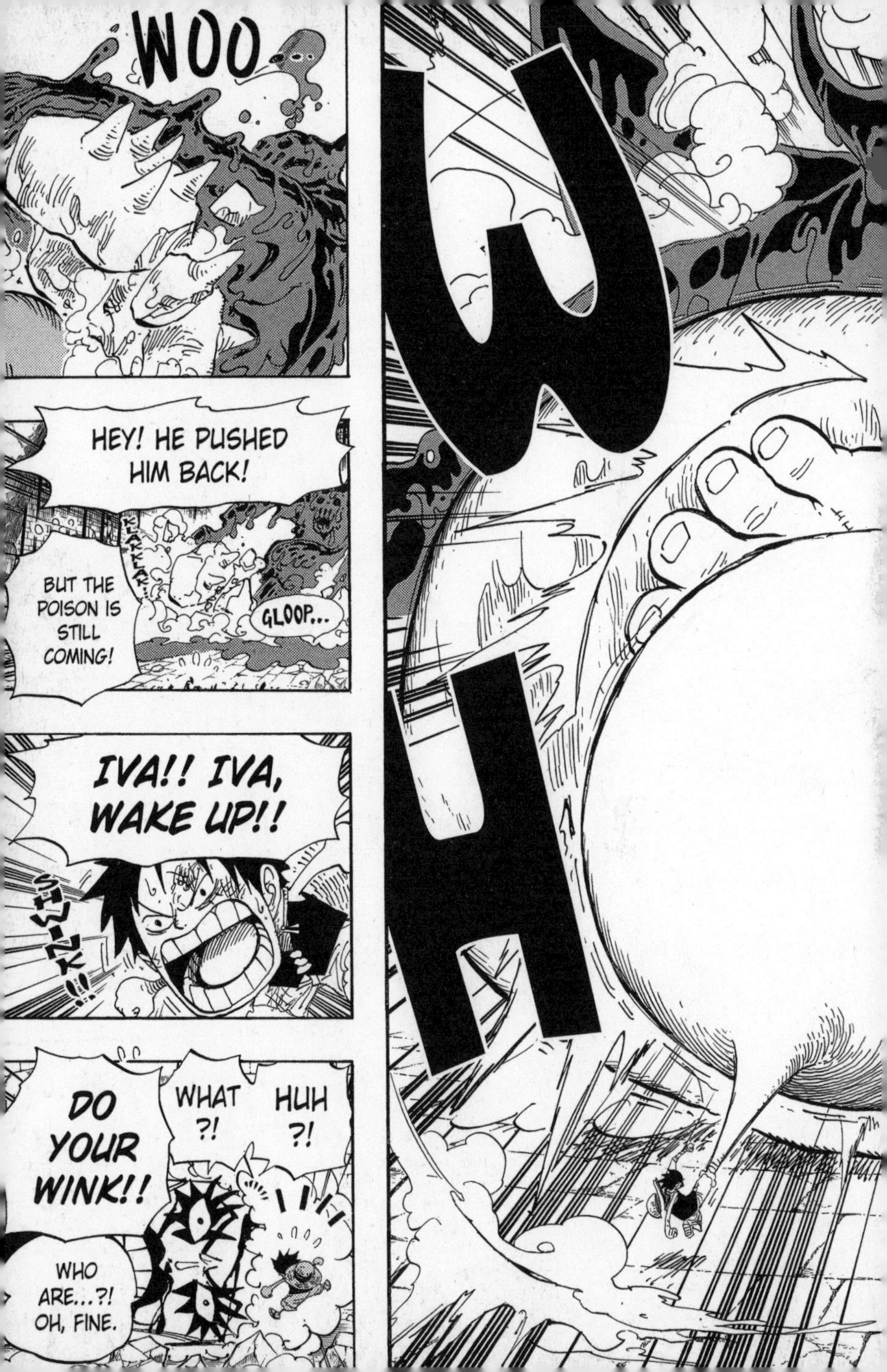
WOO
HEY! HE PUSHED HIM BACK!
KLAKKLAK!!
GLOOP...
BUT THE POISON IS STILL COMING!
IVA!! IVA, WAKE UP!!
SHWINK!!
HUH ?!
WHAT ?!
DO YOUR WINK!!
WHO ARE...?! OH, FINE.

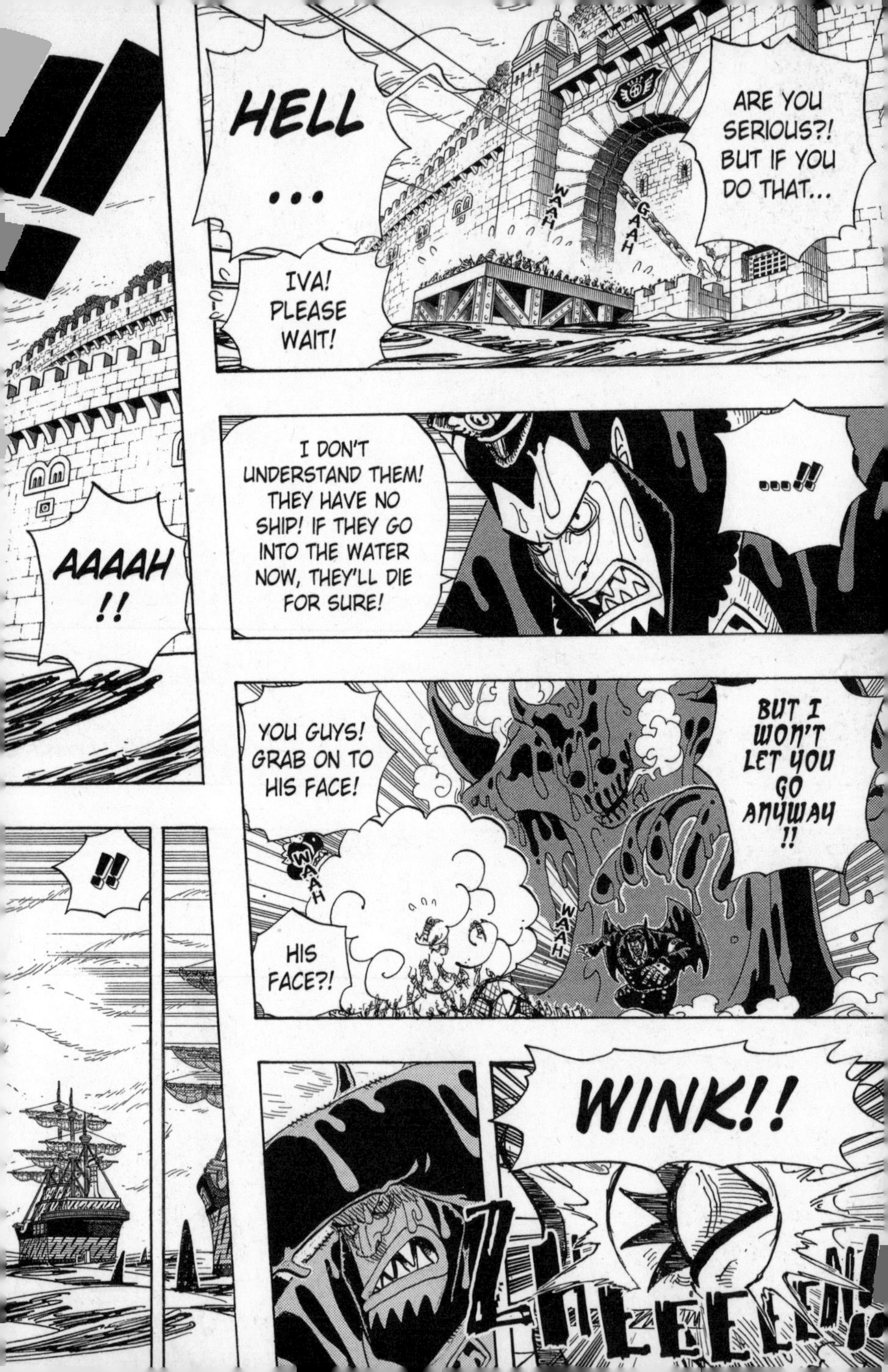
ARE YOU SERIOUS?! BUT IF YOU DO THAT...
HELL ...
WAAH
GAAH
IVA! PLEASE WAIT!
...!!
I DON'T UNDERSTAND THEM! THEY HAVE NO SHIP! IF THEY GO INTO THE WATER NOW, THEY'LL DIE FOR SURE!
BUT I WON'T LET YOU GO ANYWAY!!
YOU GUYS! GRAB ON TO HIS FACE!
WAAH
WAAH
HIS FACE?!
WINK!!
AAAAH!!
!!

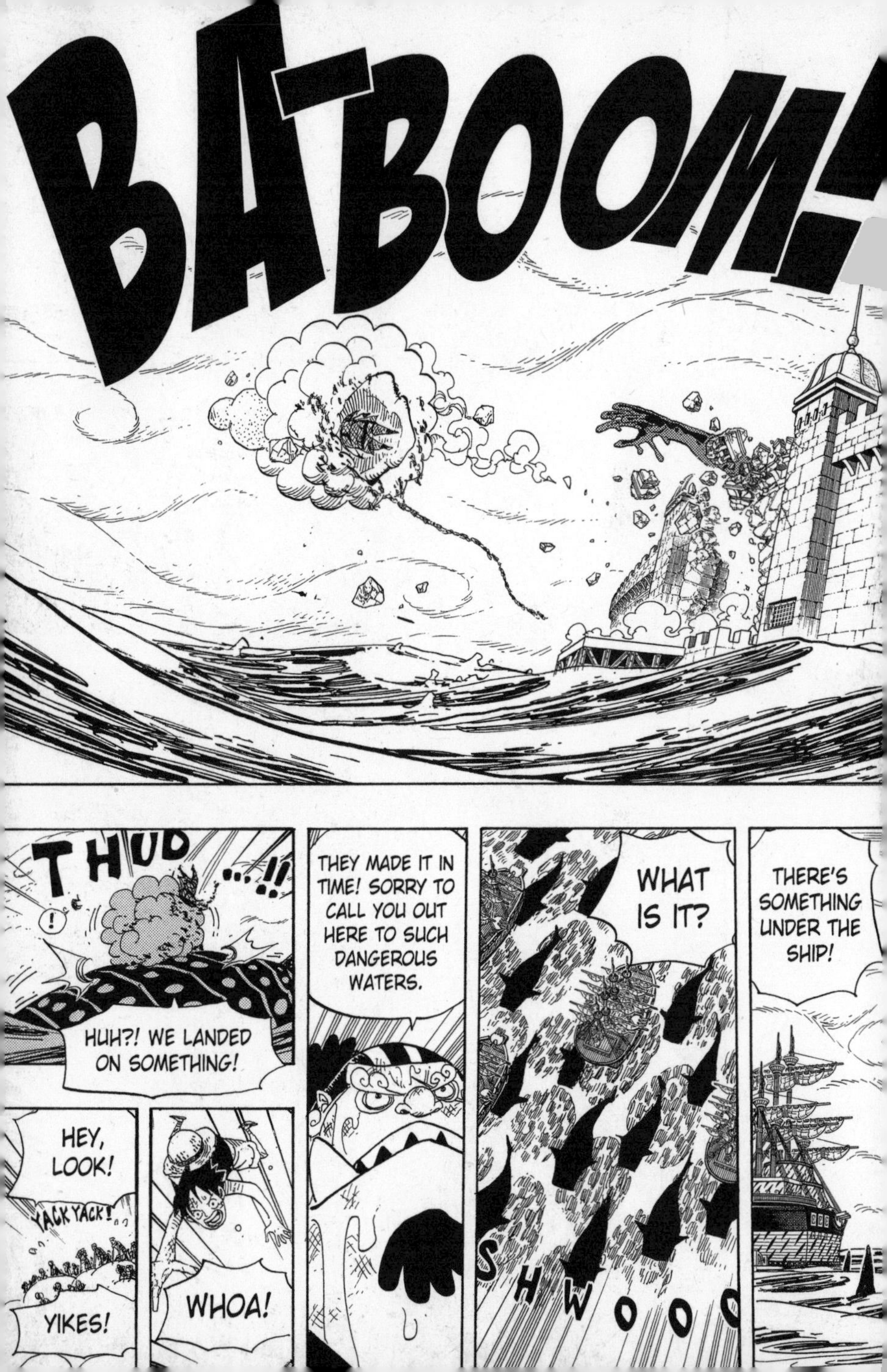
BA-BOOM!
THERE'S SOMETHING UNDER THE SHIP!
WHAT IS IT?
SHWOOO
THEY MADE IT IN TIME! SORRY TO CALL YOU OUT HERE TO SUCH DANGEROUS WATERS.
THUD
...!!
!
HUH?! WE LANDED ON SOMETHING!
WHOA!
HEY, LOOK!
YACK YACK!
YIKES!

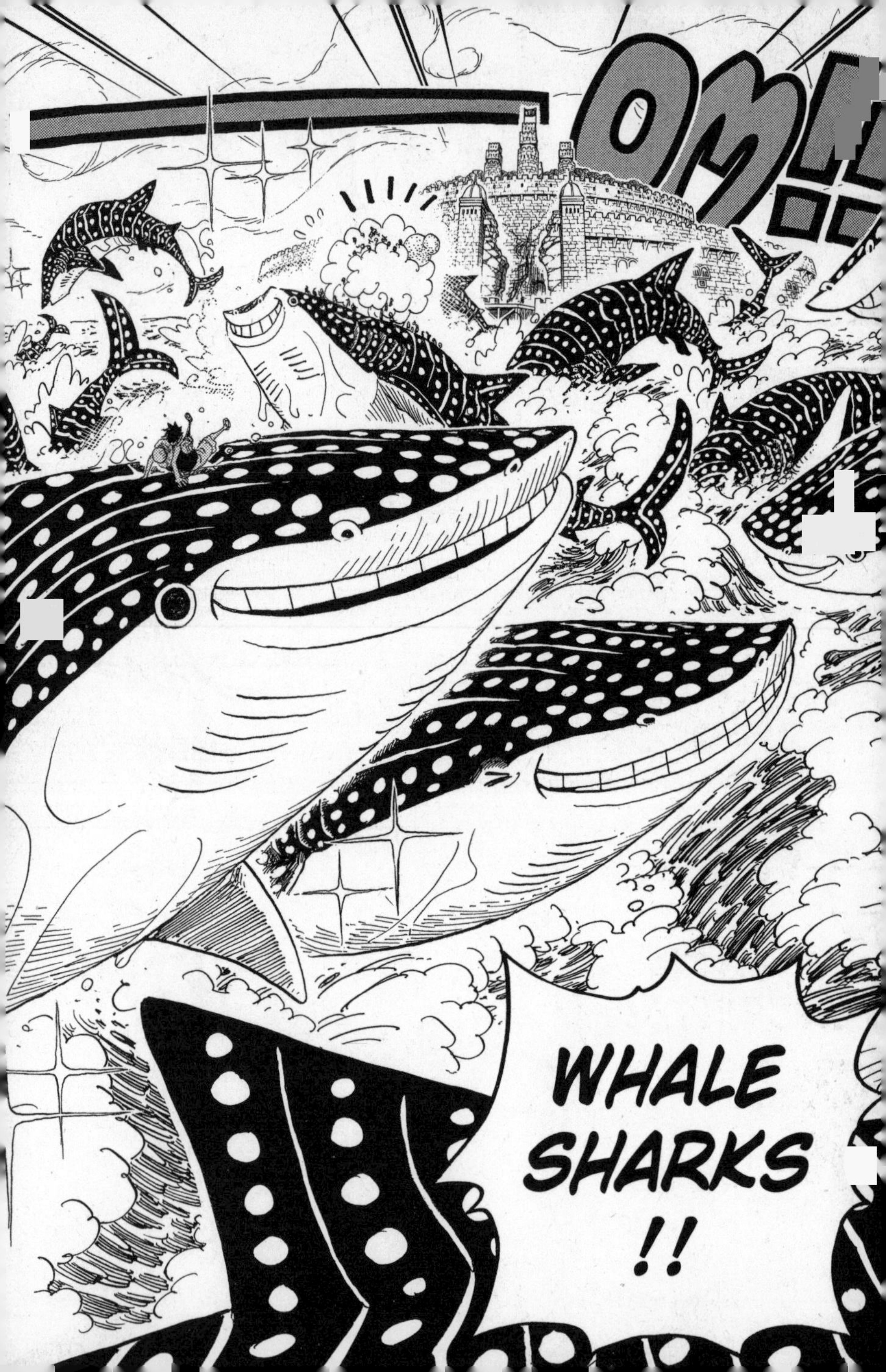
WHALE SHARKS !!

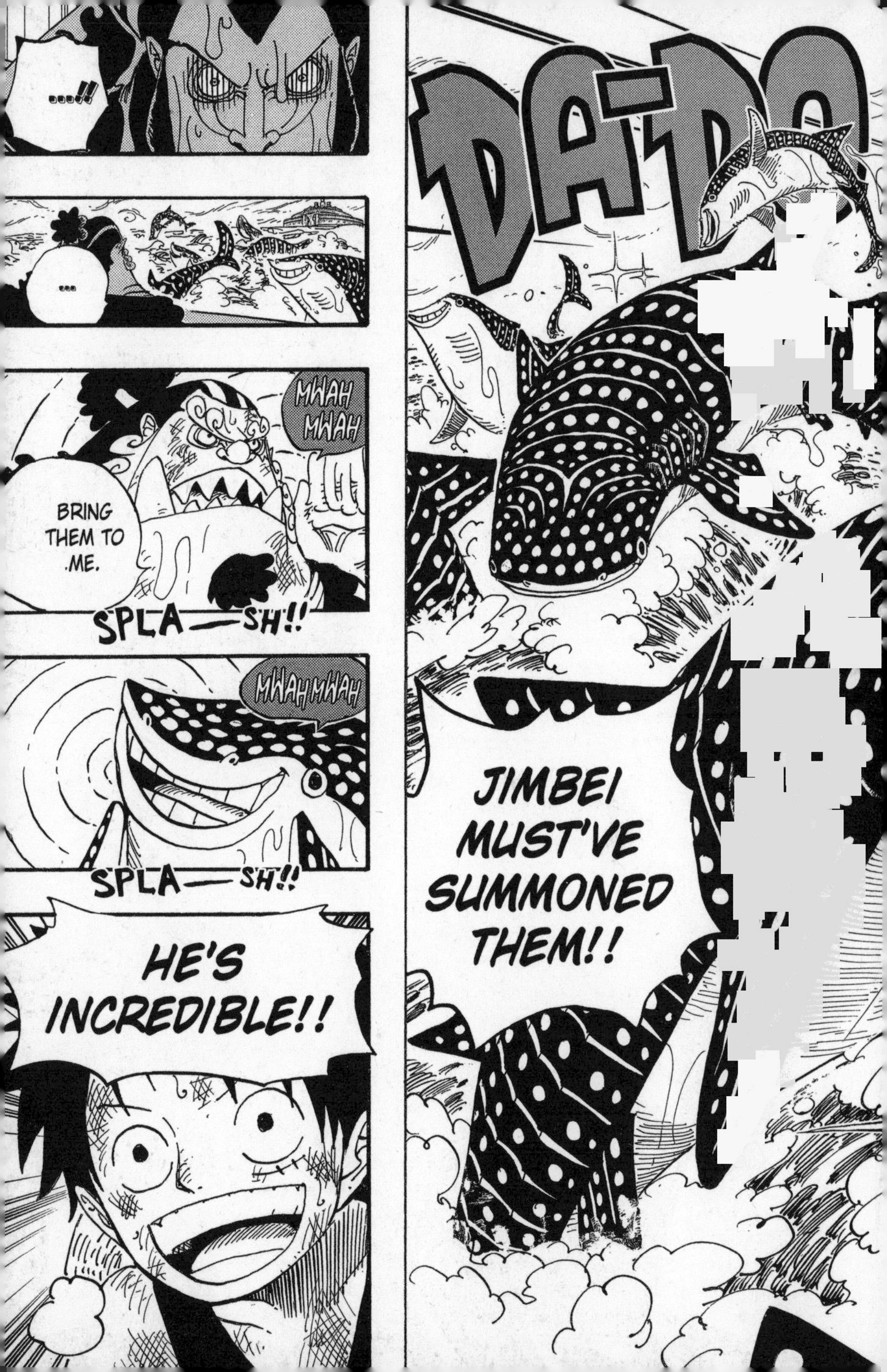
DA-DO
JIMBEI MUST'VE SUMMONED THEM!!
...!!
...
MWAH MWAH
BRING THEM TO ME.
SPLA—SH!!
MWAH MWAH
SPLA—SH!!
HE'S INCREDIBLE!!

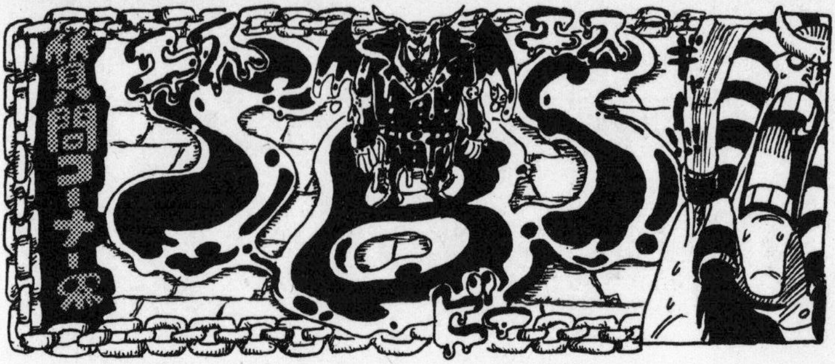
SBS

(Ponio-san, Aichi)

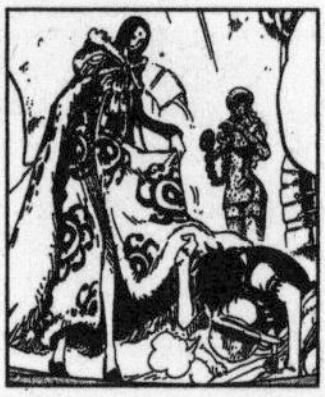

Q: One thing that got my attention is the fourth panel on page 5 of chapter 526. Luffy didn't come out of Hancock's cape! He came out from under her skirt! What really happened?! I was so preoccupied with this that I answered "Lagoon" as "Laboon" on my geography test! It's all your fault!

--Sanctuary inside the Skirt♡

A: I can't really take responsibility for your test results, but yes, Luffy was hiding not inside the cape, but under the skirt. Well, he was inside that Chinese dress, to be exact. If he didn't do that, they could just turn over her cape and find him there. He was grabbing onto Hancock directly under her clothes. Hey! Hey! It's nothing weird like that! Geez! The two of them were in a serious situation! If they'd found him, it would have cost lives! Whoops, now I have a nosebleed.

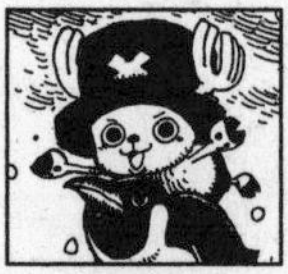

Q: If you cross a raccoon dog and a reindeer, you get Chopper?

--Sugacchi

A: Yes. What? This nosebleed? I just, uh, tripped. Yeah, I tripped earlier.

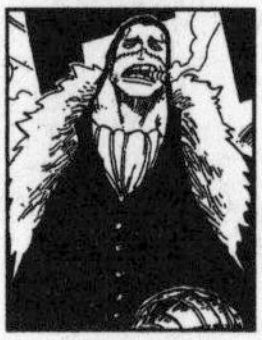

Q: Master Oda. Knowing you, you'd probably respond with "Yes, one of the guard's rooms was nearby and the prisoner's personal belongings were kept there. He dropped by that area to grab his clothes and cigar. As expected of Crocodile, what a guy, always caring about his fashion." But I will still ask you this. In chapter 540, Crocodile was still wearing his prisoner's uniform, but why was he in his usual clothes with a cigar in his mouth when he appears next?

--Bluebeard

A: You already know most of what's going on! But I'll still answer you. There is a place where they keep the personal belongings of the prisoners. Because the people of Kama Land keep going there to steal more clothes, Kama Land is filled with all kinds of outfits; that includes cigars and whatnot. I skipped the part where it shows that, but Luffy and that group stopped by Kama Land, so he took someone's clothes there. As expected of Crocodile, what a guy, always caring about his fashion.

Chapter 548:
THANK YOU

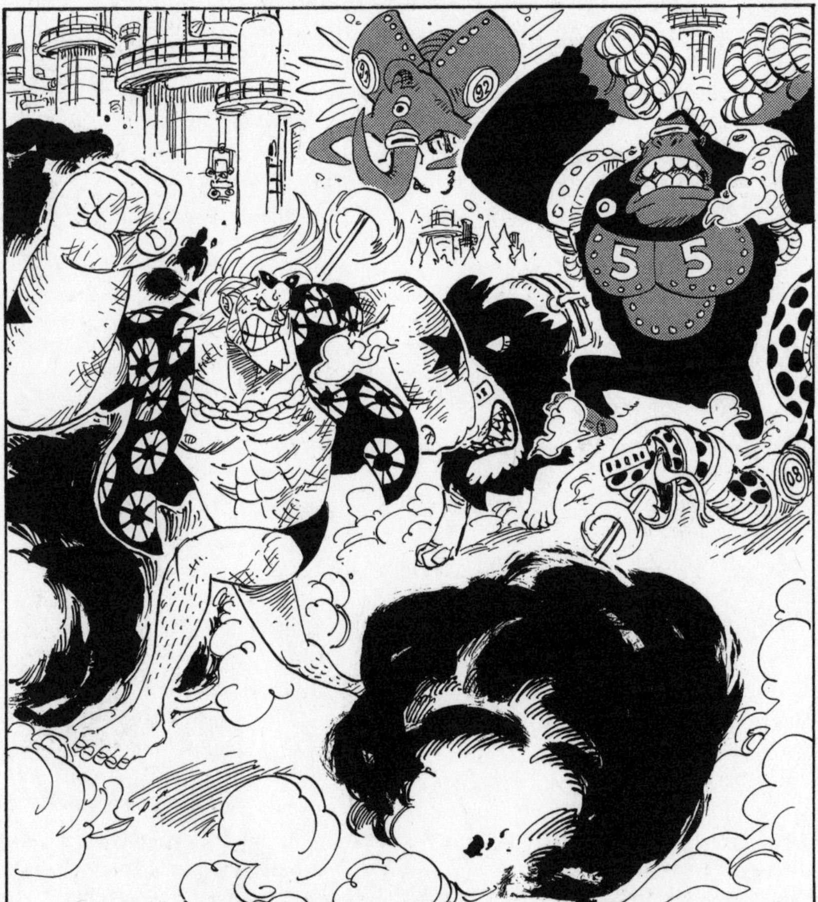

55

LIMITED COVER SERIES, NO. 13:
FRANKY'S "I'M NO GOOD THIS WEEK"
VOL. 1: "FREE ROAMING CYBORG ANIMALS"

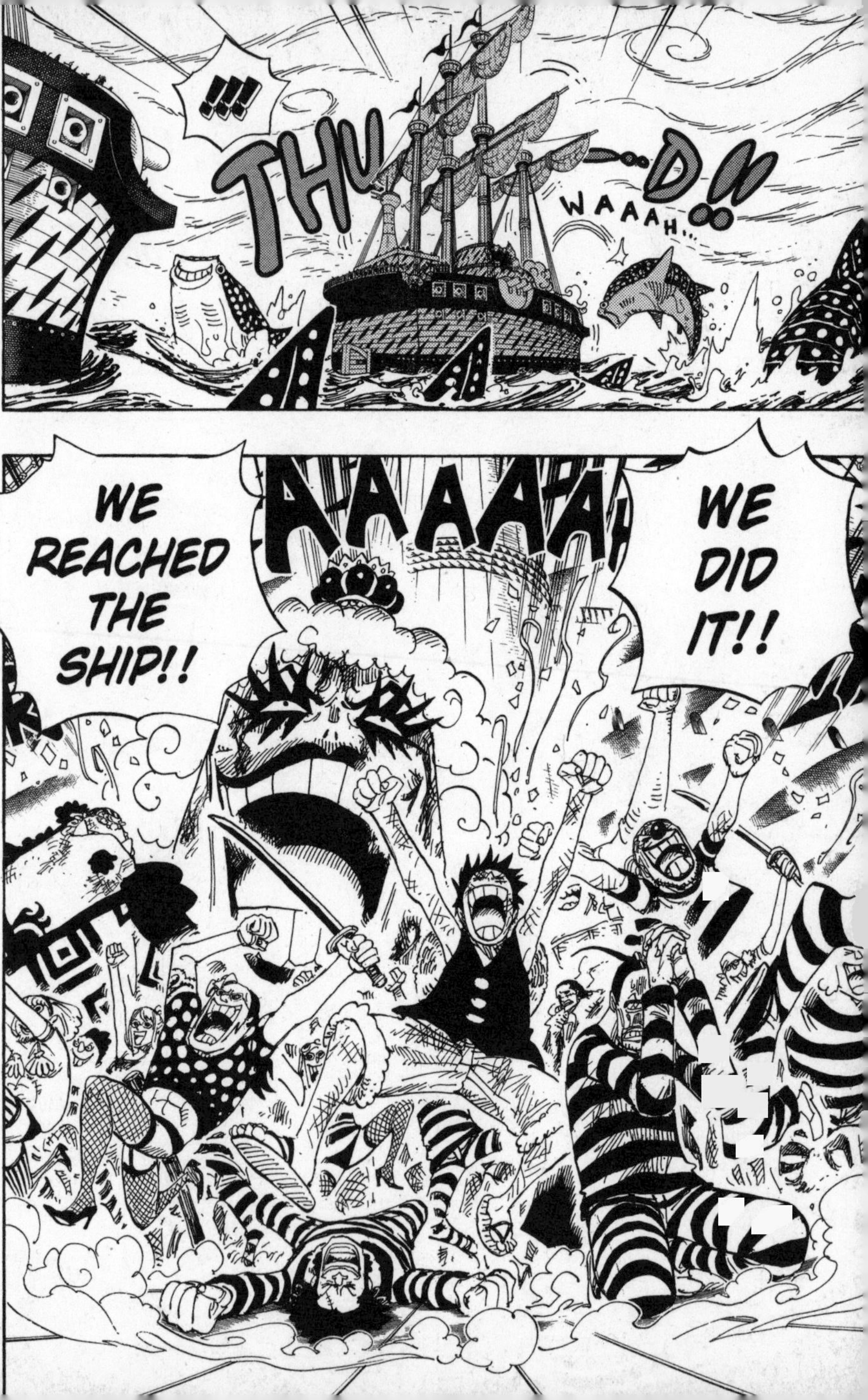
!!!
THU--D!!
WAAAH...
WE DID IT!!
AAAAAH
WE REACHED THE SHIP!!

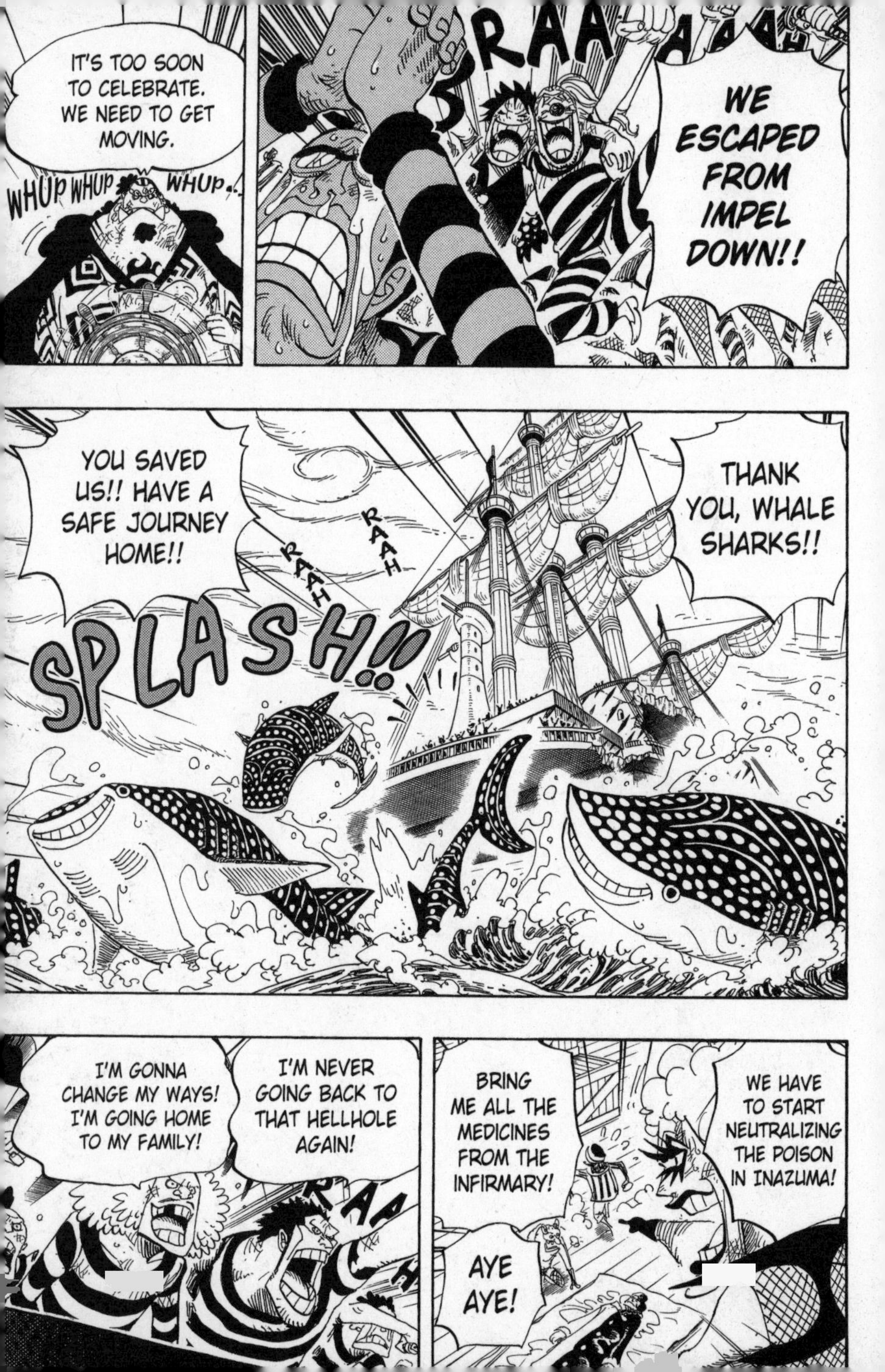
RAAAAAH
WE ESCAPED FROM IMPEL DOWN!!
IT'S TOO SOON TO CELEBRATE. WE NEED TO GET MOVING.
WHUP WHUP WHUP...
THANK YOU, WHALE SHARKS!!
RAAH
RAAH
YOU SAVED US!! HAVE A SAFE JOURNEY HOME!!
SPLASH!!
WE HAVE TO START NEUTRALIZING THE POISON IN INAZUMA!
BRING ME ALL THE MEDICINES FROM THE INFIRMARY!
AYE AYE!
I'M NEVER GOING BACK TO THAT HELLHOLE AGAIN!
I'M GONNA CHANGE MY WAYS! I'M GOING HOME TO MY FAMILY!
RAAH

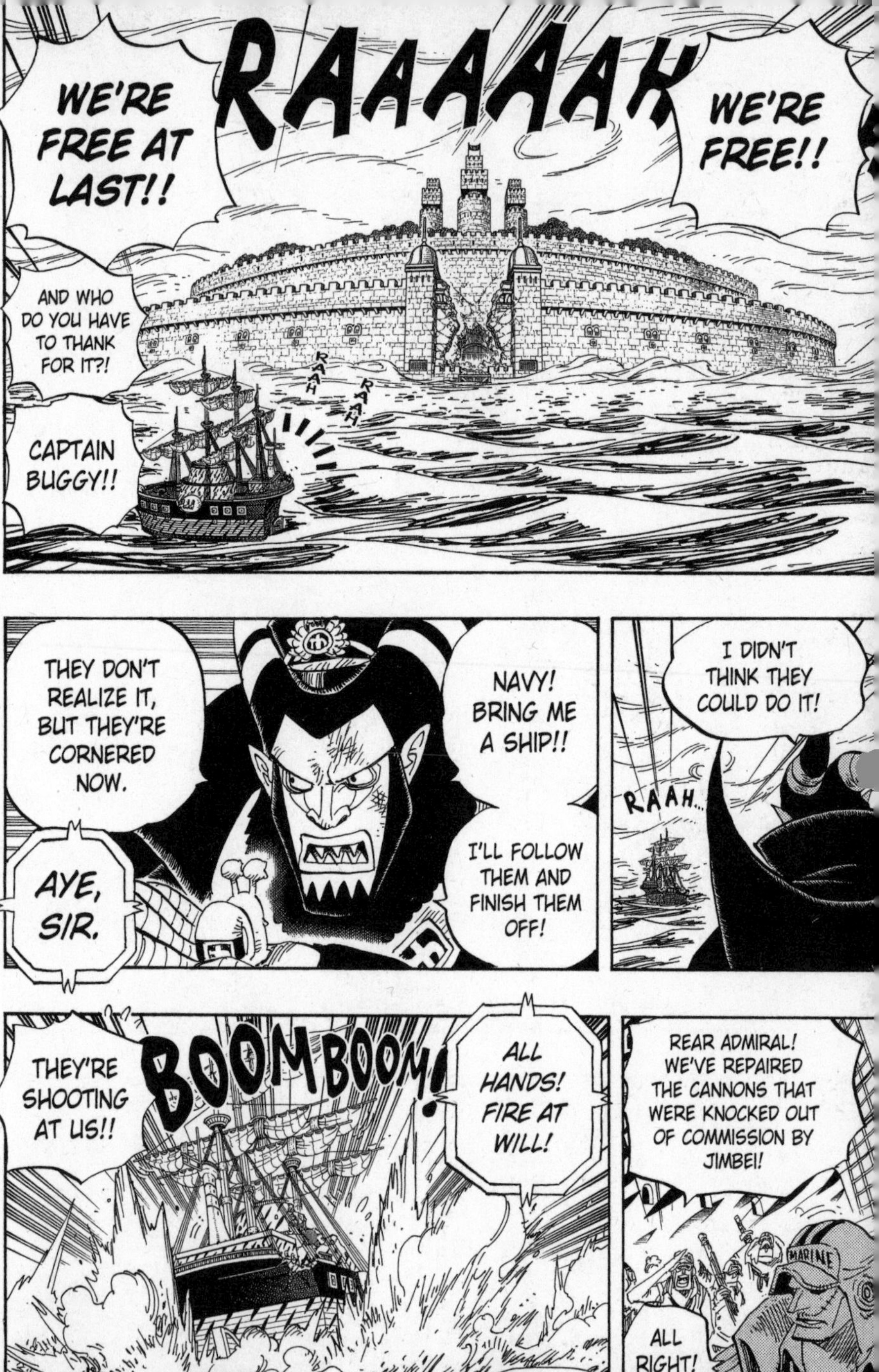
WE'RE FREE!!
RAAAAAK
WE'RE FREE AT LAST!!
RAAH
RAAH
AND WHO DO YOU HAVE TO THANK FOR IT?!
CAPTAIN BUGGY!!
I DIDN'T THINK THEY COULD DO IT!
RAAH...
NAVY! BRING ME A SHIP!!
I'LL FOLLOW THEM AND FINISH THEM OFF!
THEY DON'T REALIZE IT, BUT THEY'RE CORNERED NOW.
AYE, SIR.
REAR ADMIRAL! WE'VE REPAIRED THE CANNONS THAT WERE KNOCKED OUT OF COMMISSION BY JIMBEI!
MARINE
ALL RIGHT!
ALL HANDS! FIRE AT WILL!
BOOMBOOM
THEY'RE SHOOTING AT US!!

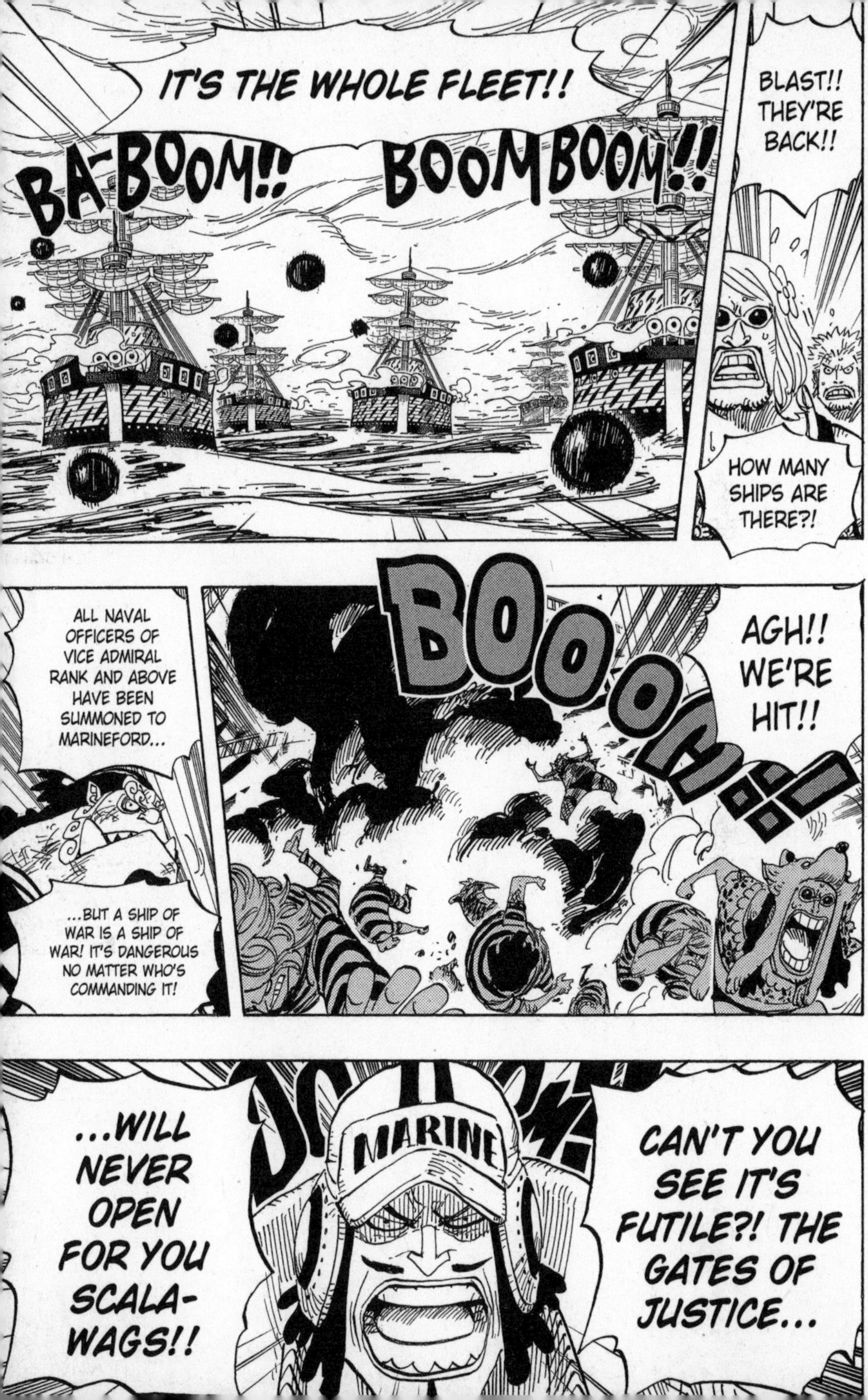
BLAST!! THEY'RE BACK!!
HOW MANY SHIPS ARE THERE?!
IT'S THE WHOLE FLEET!!
BA-BOOM!!
BOOMBOOM!!
BOOOOM!!
AGH!! WE'RE HIT!!
ALL NAVAL OFFICERS OF VICE ADMIRAL RANK AND ABOVE HAVE BEEN SUMMONED TO MARINEFORD...
...BUT A SHIP OF WAR IS A SHIP OF WAR! IT'S DANGEROUS NO MATTER WHO'S COMMANDING IT!
MARINE
CAN'T YOU SEE IT'S FUTILE?! THE GATES OF JUSTICE...
...WILL NEVER OPEN FOR YOU SCALA-WAGS!!

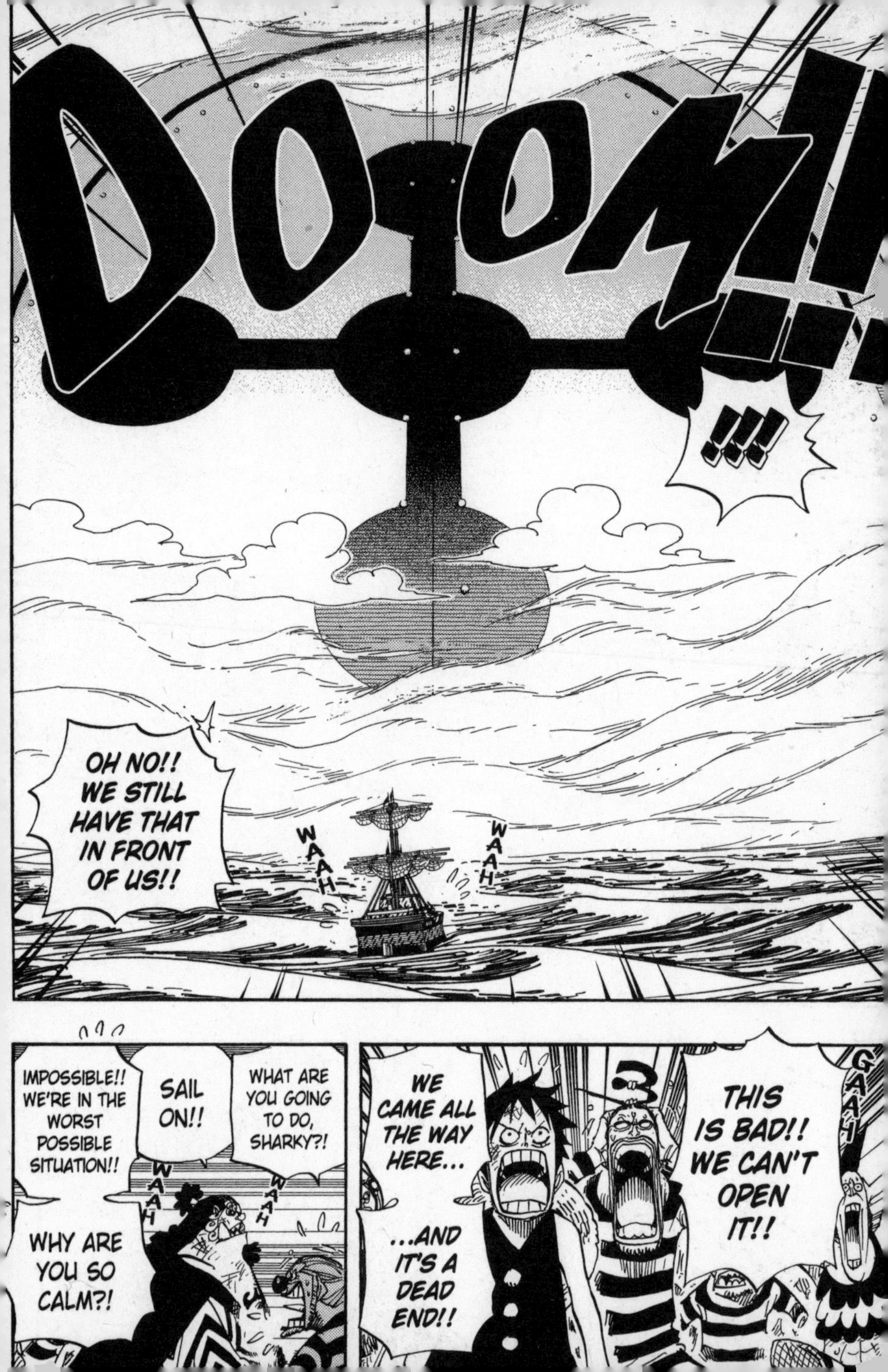
DOOM!!
!!!
OH NO!! WE STILL HAVE THAT IN FRONT OF US!!
WAAH
WAAH
THIS IS BAD!! WE CAN'T OPEN IT!!
WE CAME ALL THE WAY HERE...
...AND IT'S A DEAD END!!
WHAT ARE YOU GOING TO DO, SHARKY?!
SAIL ON!!
IMPOSSIBLE!! WE'RE IN THE WORST POSSIBLE SITUATION!!
WAAH
WAAH
WHY ARE YOU SO CALM?!

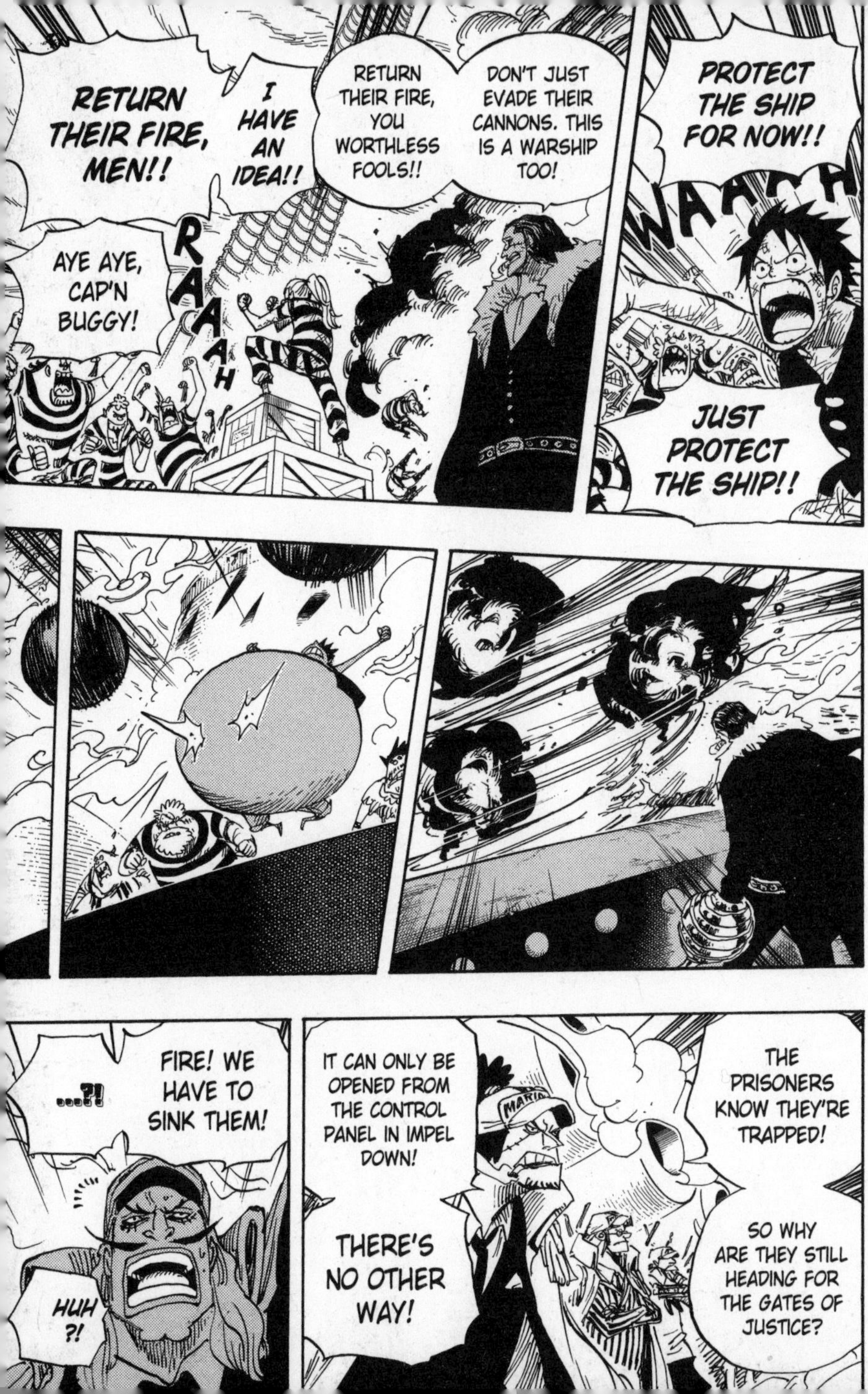
PROTECT THE SHIP FOR NOW!!
WAAAH
JUST PROTECT THE SHIP!!
DON'T JUST EVADE THEIR CANNONS. THIS IS A WARSHIP TOO!
RETURN THEIR FIRE, YOU WORTHLESS FOOLS!!
I HAVE AN IDEA!!
RETURN THEIR FIRE, MEN!!
RAAAH
AYE AYE, CAP'N BUGGY!
THE PRISONERS KNOW THEY'RE TRAPPED!
SO WHY ARE THEY STILL HEADING FOR THE GATES OF JUSTICE?
IT CAN ONLY BE OPENED FROM THE CONTROL PANEL IN IMPEL DOWN!
THERE'S NO OTHER WAY!
FIRE! WE HAVE TO SINK THEM!
...?!
HUH ?!

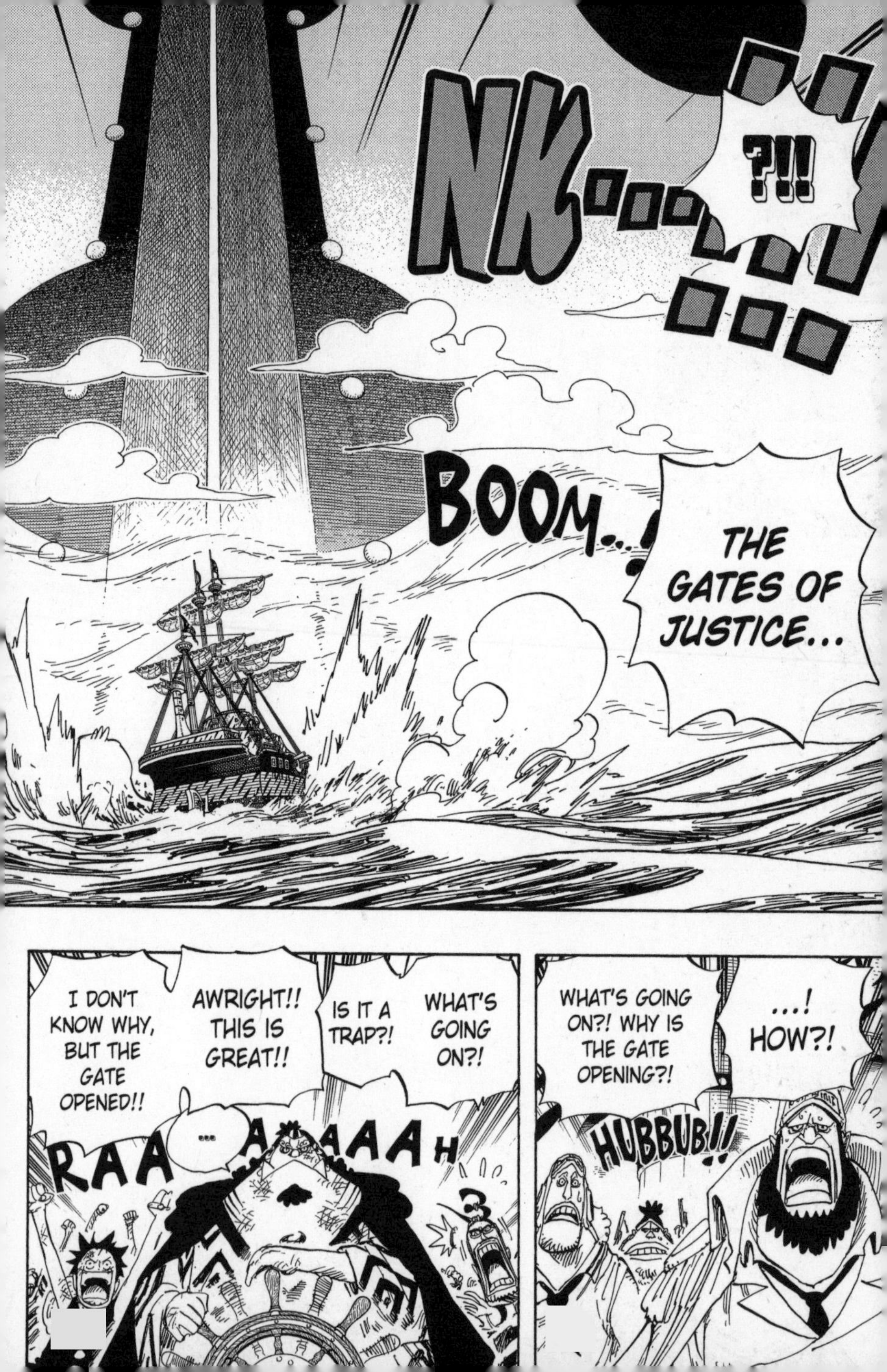
?!!
NK...
BOOM...!
THE GATES OF JUSTICE...
...! HOW?!
WHAT'S GOING ON?! WHY IS THE GATE OPENING?!
HUBBUB!!
WHAT'S GOING ON?!
IS IT A TRAP?!
AWRIGHT!! THIS IS GREAT!!
I DON'T KNOW WHY, BUT THE GATE OPENED!!
...
RAAAAAAAH

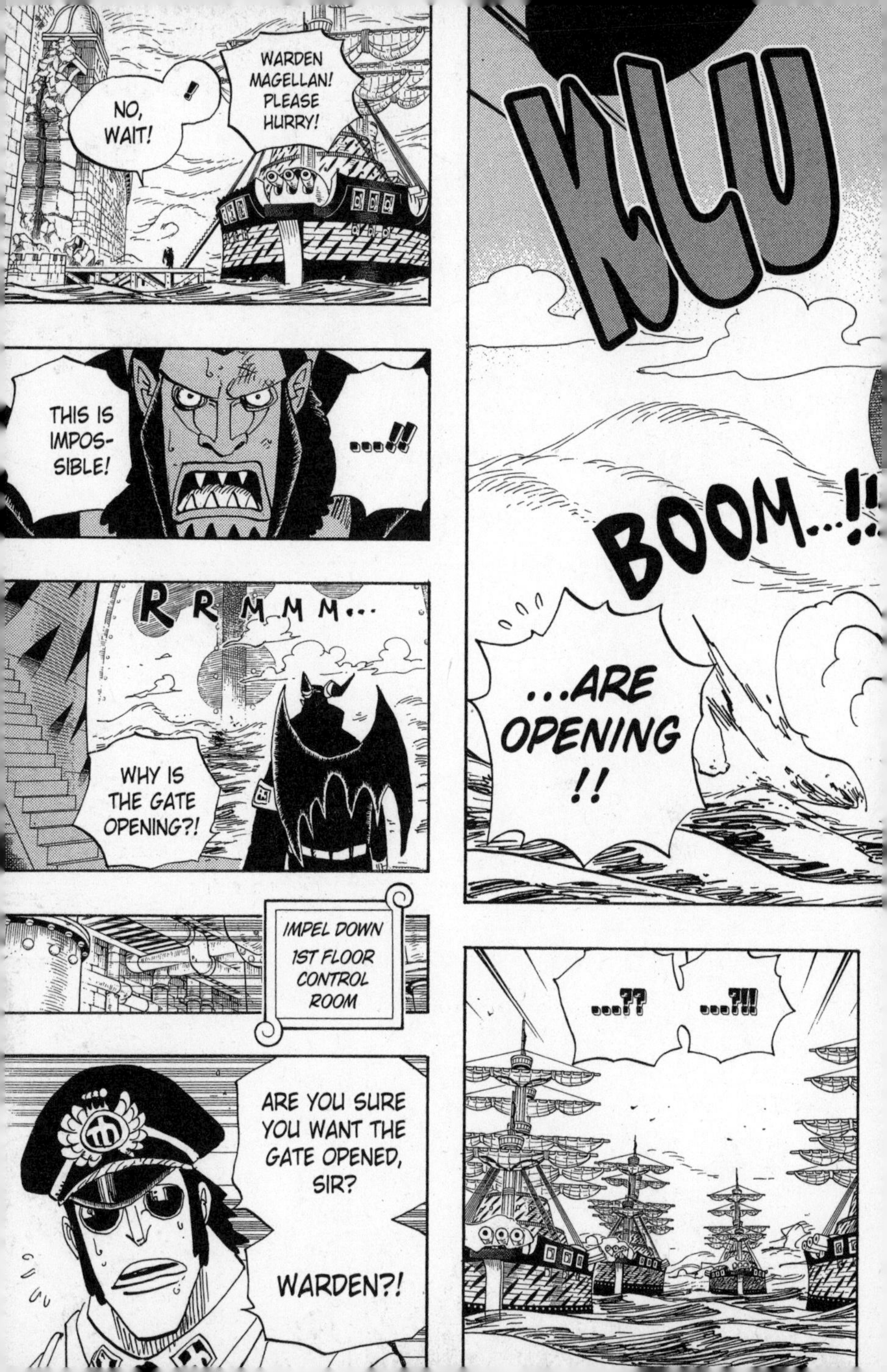
KLLU
BOOM...!!
...ARE OPENING!!
WARDEN MAGELLAN! PLEASE HURRY!
!
NO, WAIT!
THIS IS IMPOSSIBLE!
...!!
RRMMM...
WHY IS THE GATE OPENING?!
...??
...?!!
IMPEL DOWN 1ST FLOOR CONTROL ROOM
ARE YOU SURE YOU WANT THE GATE OPENED, SIR?
WARDEN?!

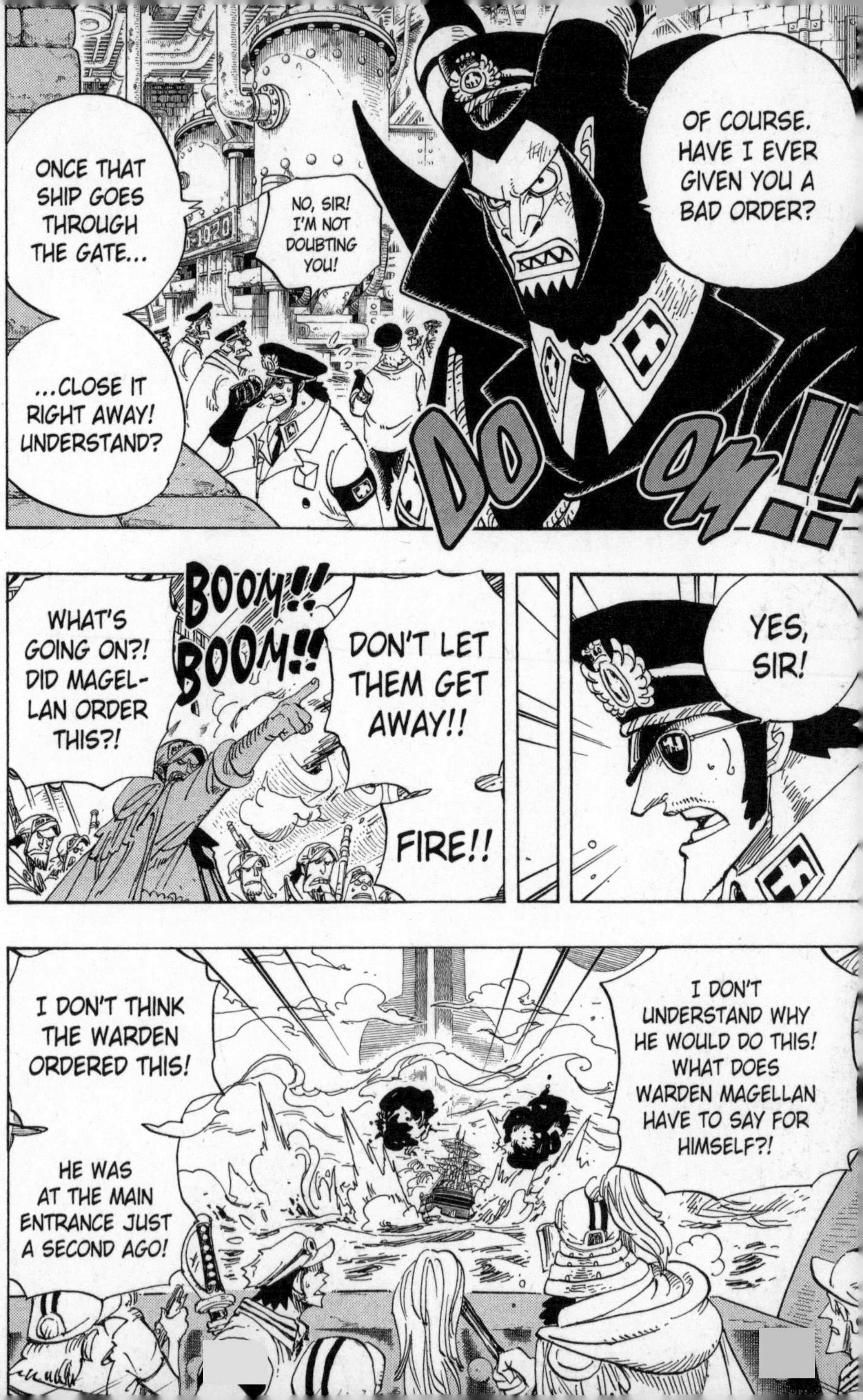
OF COURSE. HAVE I EVER GIVEN YOU A BAD ORDER?
NO, SIR! I'M NOT DOUBTING YOU!
ONCE THAT SHIP GOES THROUGH THE GATE...
...CLOSE IT RIGHT AWAY! UNDERSTAND?
DOOM!!
YES, SIR!
BOOM!! BOOM!!
DON'T LET THEM GET AWAY!!
WHAT'S GOING ON?! DID MAGEL-LAN ORDER THIS?!
FIRE!!
I DON'T UNDERSTAND WHY HE WOULD DO THIS! WHAT DOES WARDEN MAGELLAN HAVE TO SAY FOR HIMSELF?!
I DON'T THINK THE WARDEN ORDERED THIS!
HE WAS AT THE MAIN ENTRANCE JUST A SECOND AGO!

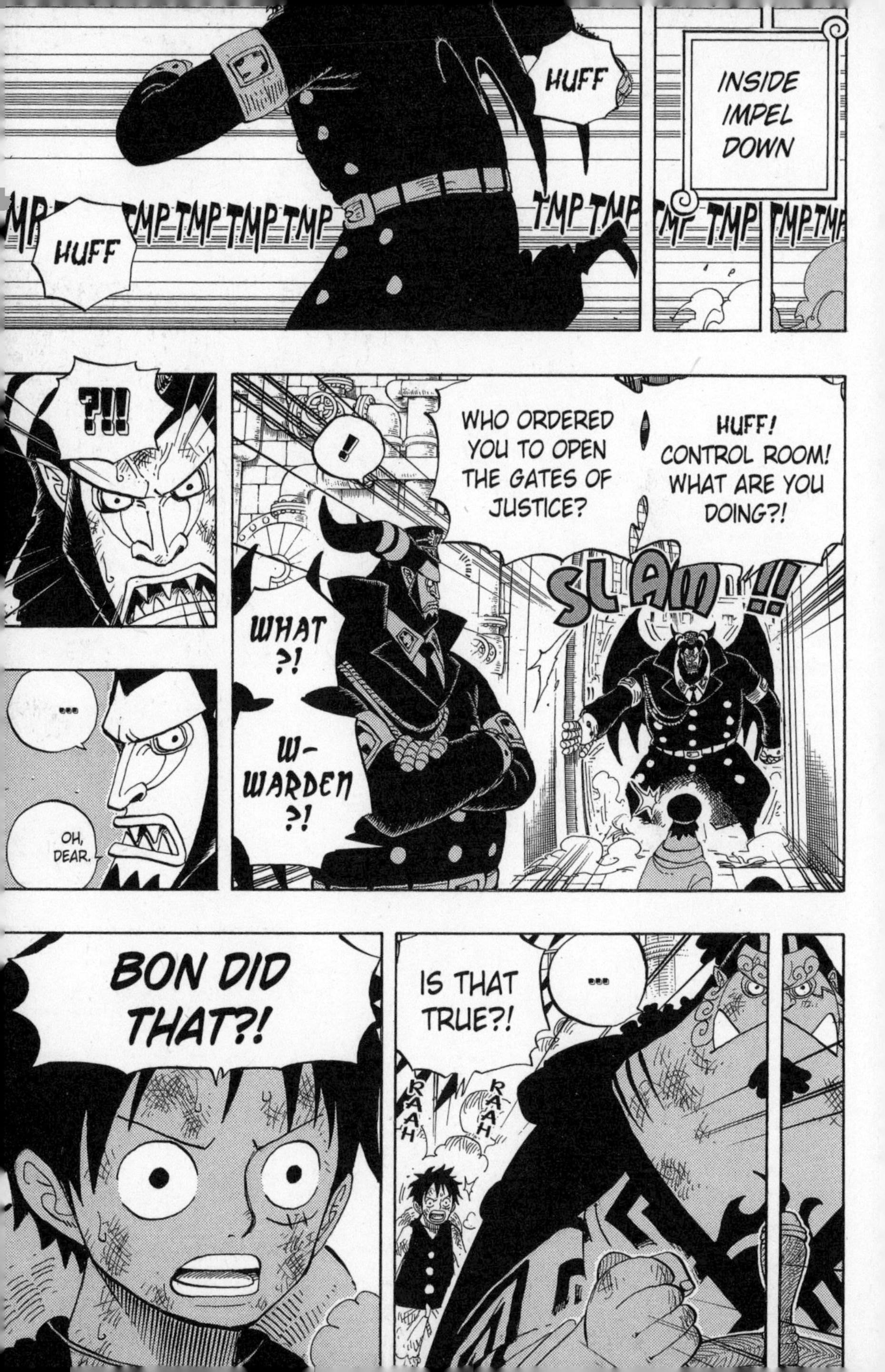
INSIDE IMPEL DOWN
TMP TMP TMP TMP TMP
HUFF
TMP TMP
HUFF
TMP TMP TMP TMP
HUFF! CONTROL ROOM! WHAT ARE YOU DOING?!
SLAM!!
WHO ORDERED YOU TO OPEN THE GATES OF JUSTICE?
!
WHAT?!
W-WARDEN?!
?!!
...
OH, DEAR.
...
IS THAT TRUE?!
RAAAH
RAAAH
BON DID THAT?!

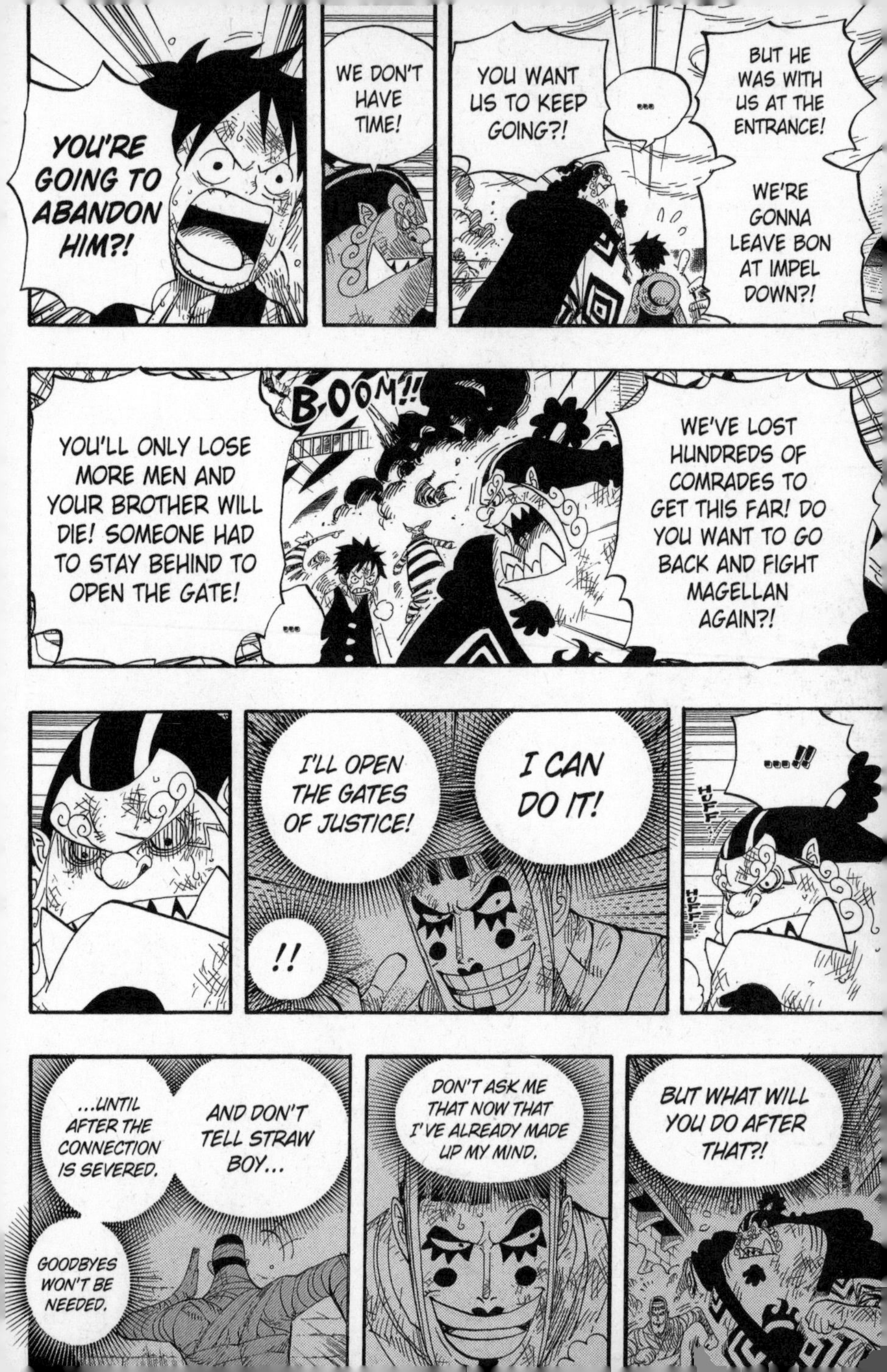
BUT HE WAS WITH US AT THE ENTRANCE!
WE'RE GONNA LEAVE BON AT IMPEL DOWN?!
...
YOU WANT US TO KEEP GOING?!
WE DON'T HAVE TIME!
YOU'RE GOING TO ABANDON HIM?!
WE'VE LOST HUNDREDS OF COMRADES TO GET THIS FAR! DO YOU WANT TO GO BACK AND FIGHT MAGELLAN AGAIN?!
BOOM!!
YOU'LL ONLY LOSE MORE MEN AND YOUR BROTHER WILL DIE! SOMEONE HAD TO STAY BEHIND TO OPEN THE GATE!
...
...!!
HUFF
HUFF
I CAN DO IT!
I'LL OPEN THE GATES OF JUSTICE!
!!
BUT WHAT WILL YOU DO AFTER THAT?!
DON'T ASK ME THAT NOW THAT I'VE ALREADY MADE UP MY MIND.
AND DON'T TELL STRAW BOY...
...UNTIL AFTER THE CONNECTION IS SEVERED.
GOODBYES WON'T BE NEEDED.

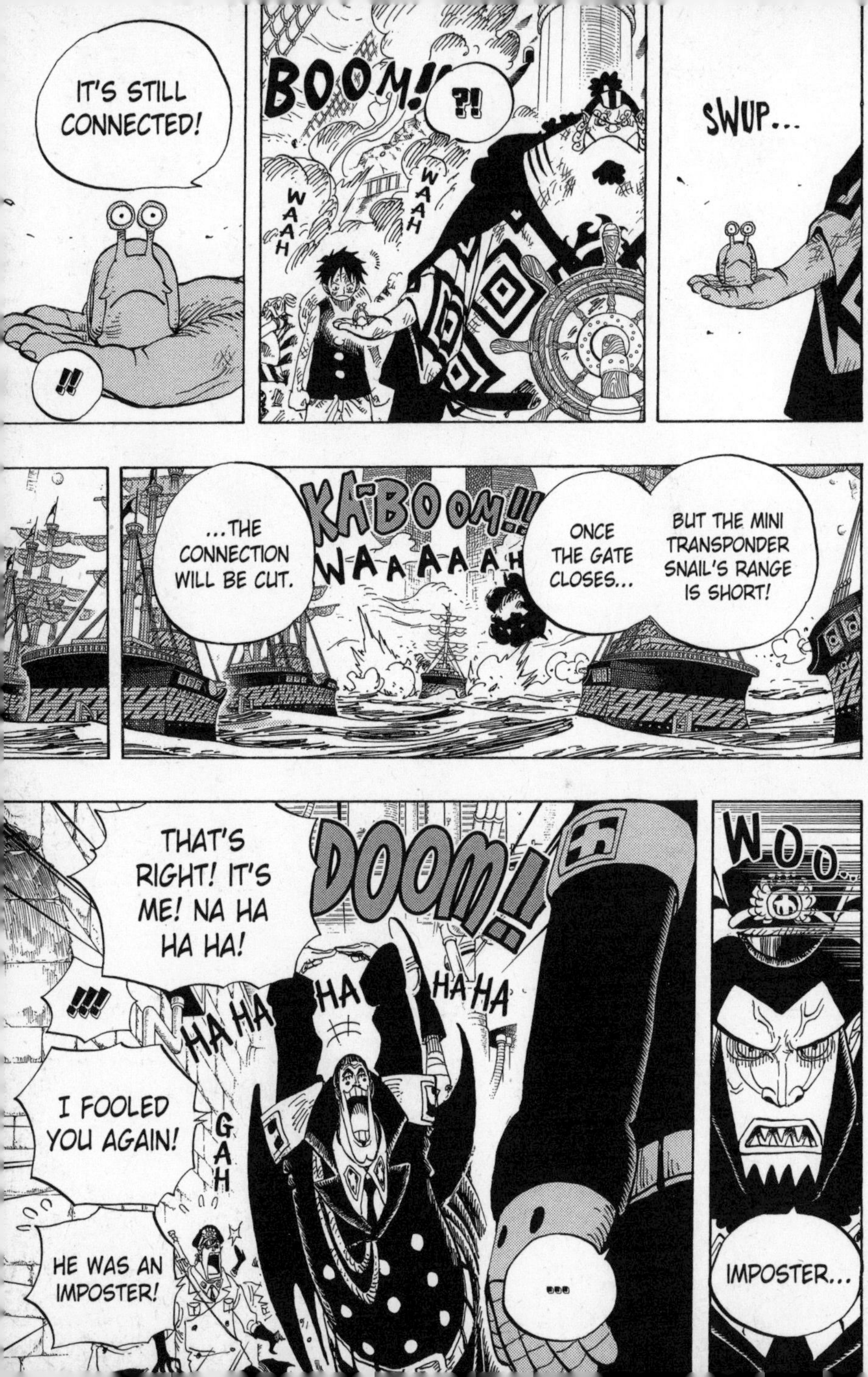
SWUP...
BOOM!!
?!
WAAAH
WAAAH
IT'S STILL CONNECTED!
!!
KA-BOOM!!!
WAAAAAH
BUT THE MINI TRANSPONDER SNAIL'S RANGE IS SHORT!
ONCE THE GATE CLOSES...
...THE CONNECTION WILL BE CUT.
WOO...
IMPOSTER...
DOOM!!
THAT'S RIGHT! IT'S ME! NA HA HA HA!
HA HA HA HA HA
!!!
I FOOLED YOU AGAIN!
GAH
HE WAS AN IMPOSTER!
...

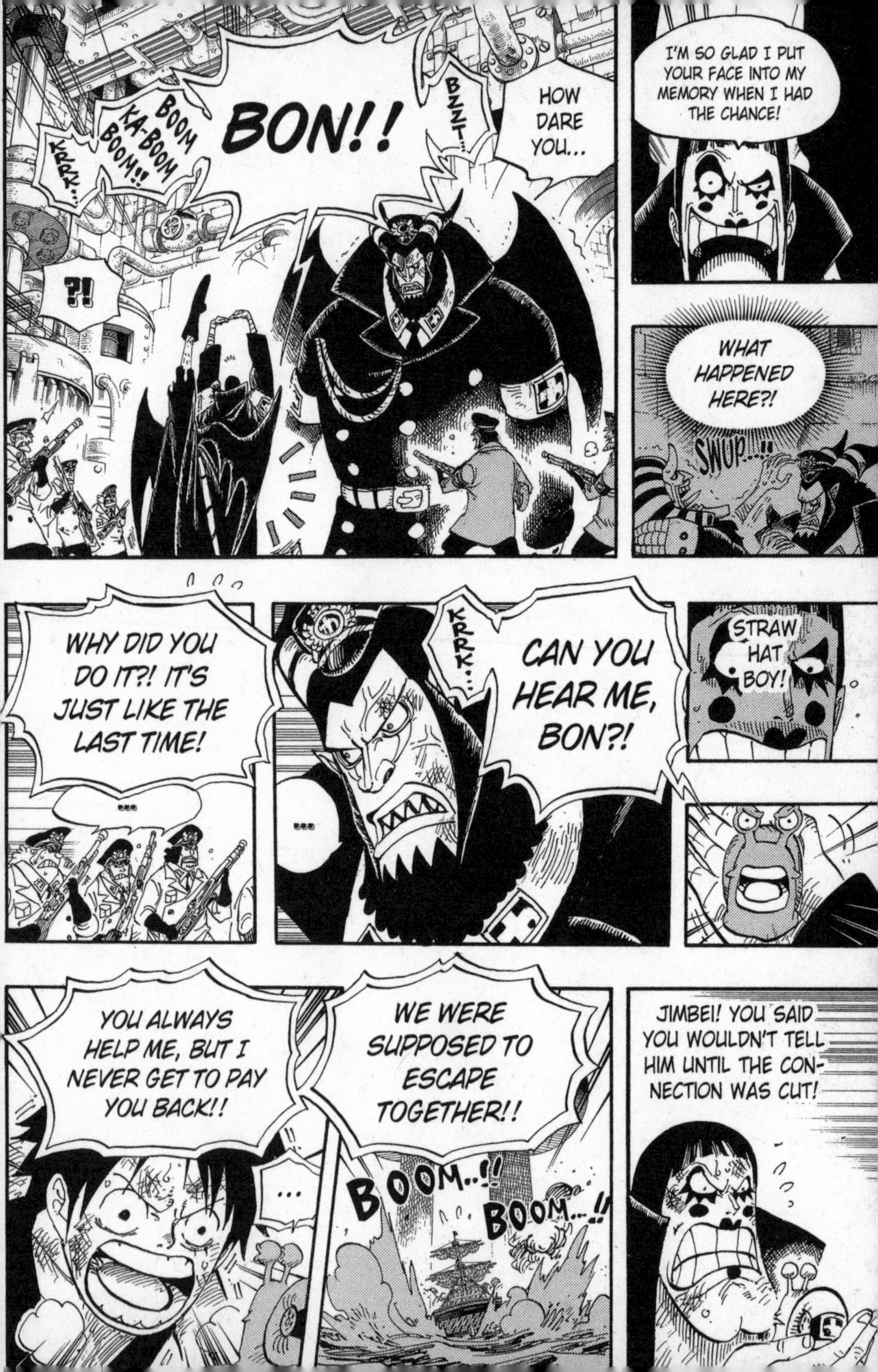

I'M SO GLAD I PUT YOUR FACE INTO MY MEMORY WHEN I HAD THE CHANCE!
WHAT HAPPENED HERE?!
SWUP...!!
HOW DARE YOU...
BZZT...
BON!!
BOOM KA-BOOM BOOM!!
KRRK...
?!
STRAW HAT BOY!
KRRK...
CAN YOU HEAR ME, BON?!
...
WHY DID YOU DO IT?! IT'S JUST LIKE THE LAST TIME!
...
JIMBEI! YOU SAID YOU WOULDN'T TELL HIM UNTIL THE CON-NECTION WAS CUT!
WE WERE SUPPOSED TO ESCAPE TOGETHER!!
BOOM..!!
BOOM...!!
YOU ALWAYS HELP ME, BUT I NEVER GET TO PAY YOU BACK!!
...

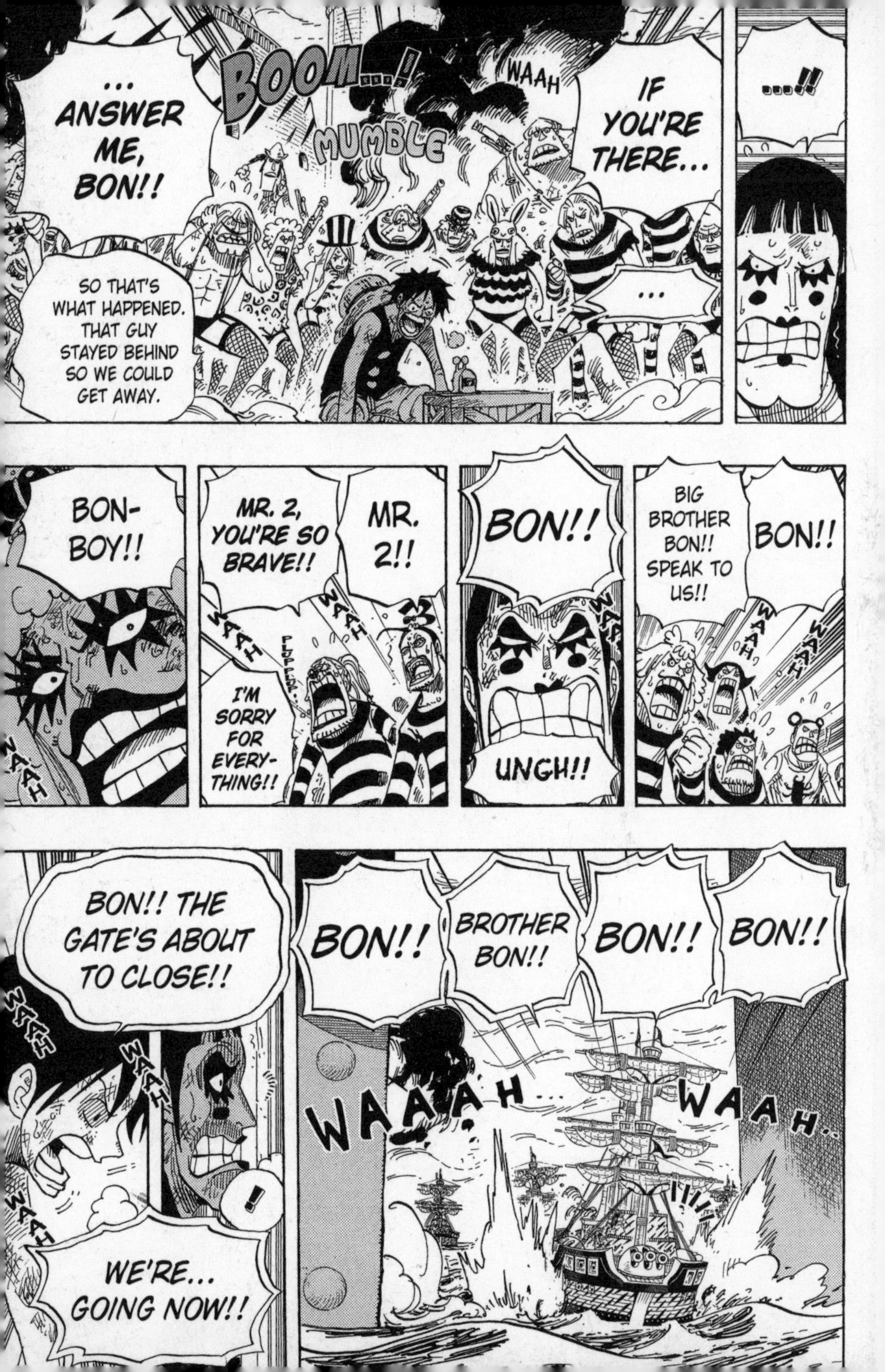
...!!
WAAH
IF YOU'RE THERE...
BOOM...!
MUMBLE
... ANSWER ME, BON!!
...
SO THAT'S WHAT HAPPENED. THAT GUY STAYED BEHIND SO WE COULD GET AWAY.
BON!!
BIG BROTHER BON!! SPEAK TO US!!
WAAH
WAAH
BON!!
WAAH
UNGH!!
MR. 2!!
MR. 2, YOU'RE SO BRAVE!!
WAAH
WAAH
PLUP PLUP
I'M SORRY FOR EVERYTHING!!
BON-BOY!!
WAAH
BON!!
BON!!
BROTHER BON!!
BON!!
WAAH...
WAAH...
!!!!
BON!! THE GATE'S ABOUT TO CLOSE!!
WAAH
WAAH
!
WE'RE... GOING NOW!!
WAAH

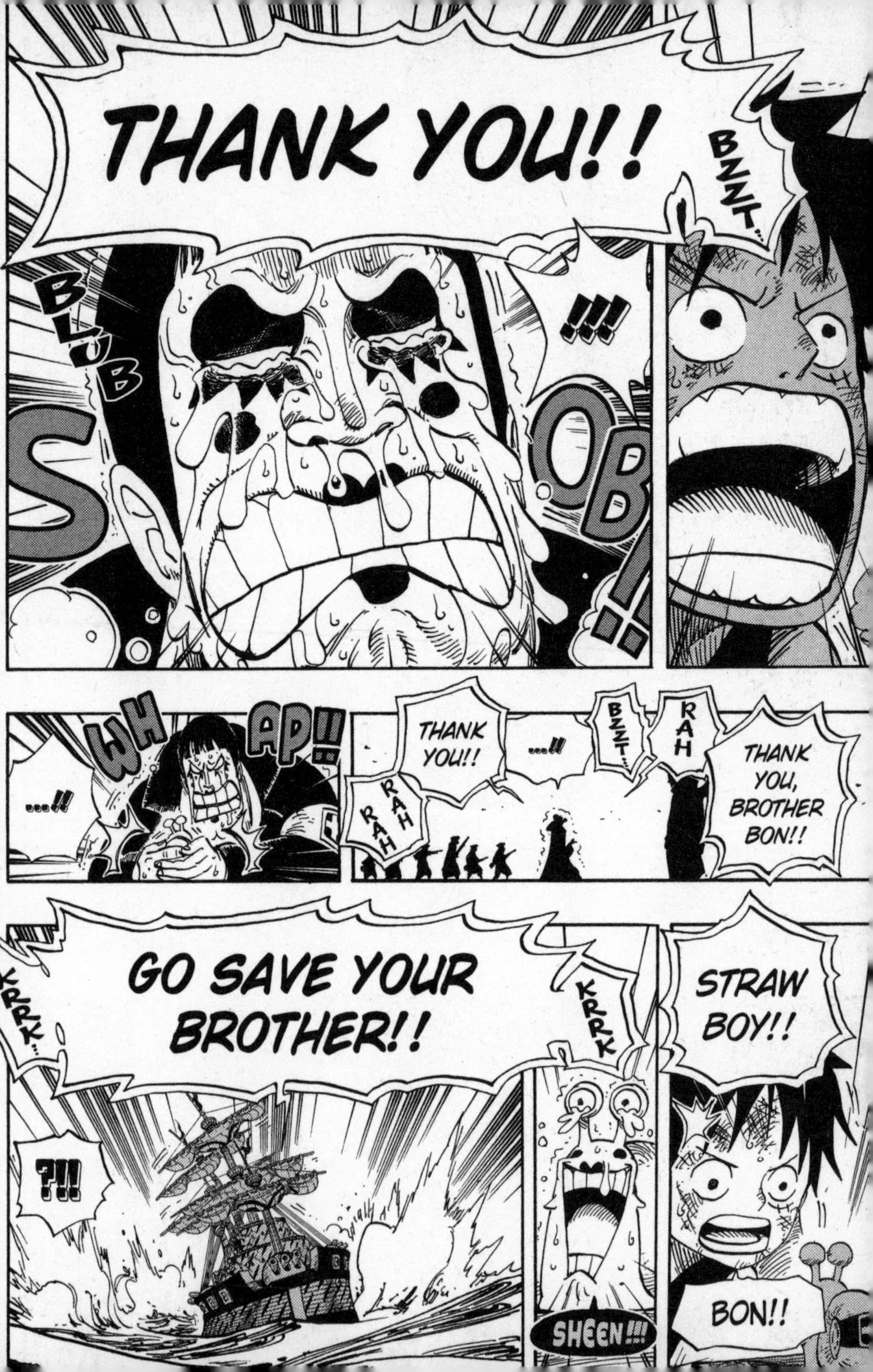
BZZZT...
THANK YOU!!
!!!
BLUB
SOB!!
THANK YOU, BROTHER BON!!
RAH
BZZT...
...!!
THANK YOU!!
RAH RAH RAH
WHAP!!
...!!
STRAW BOY!!
BON!!
KRRRK...
SHEEN!!!
GO SAVE YOUR BROTHER!!
KRRRK...
?!!

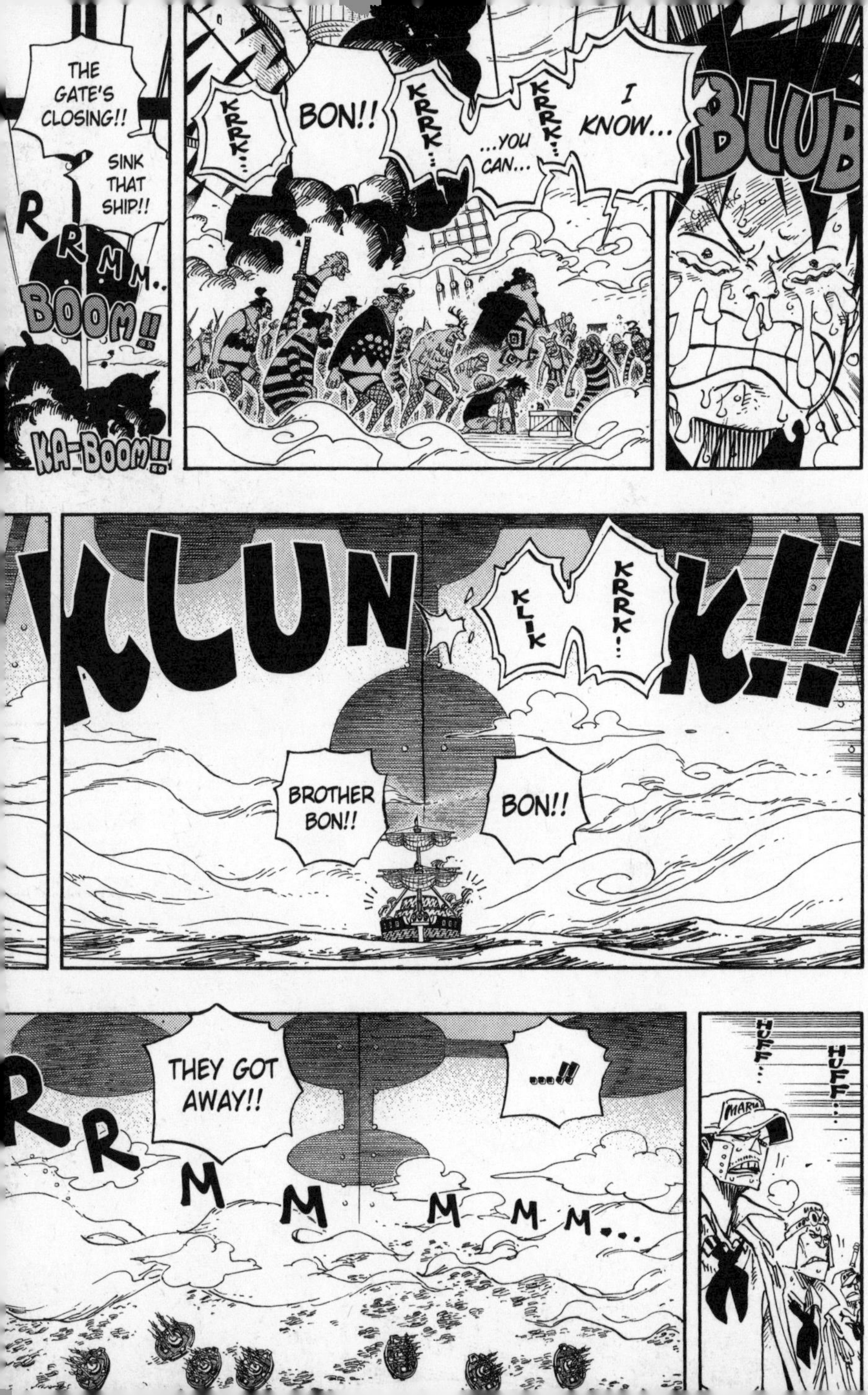
BLUB
I KNOW...
KRRRK...
...YOU CAN...
KRRRK...
BON!!
KRRK...
THE GATE'S CLOSING!!
SINK THAT SHIP!!
RRMM..
BOOM!!
KA-BOOM!!
KLUNK!!
KRRRK!
KLIK
BON!!
BROTHER BON!!
HUFF...
HUFF...
...!!
THEY GOT AWAY!!
RRMMMMM...

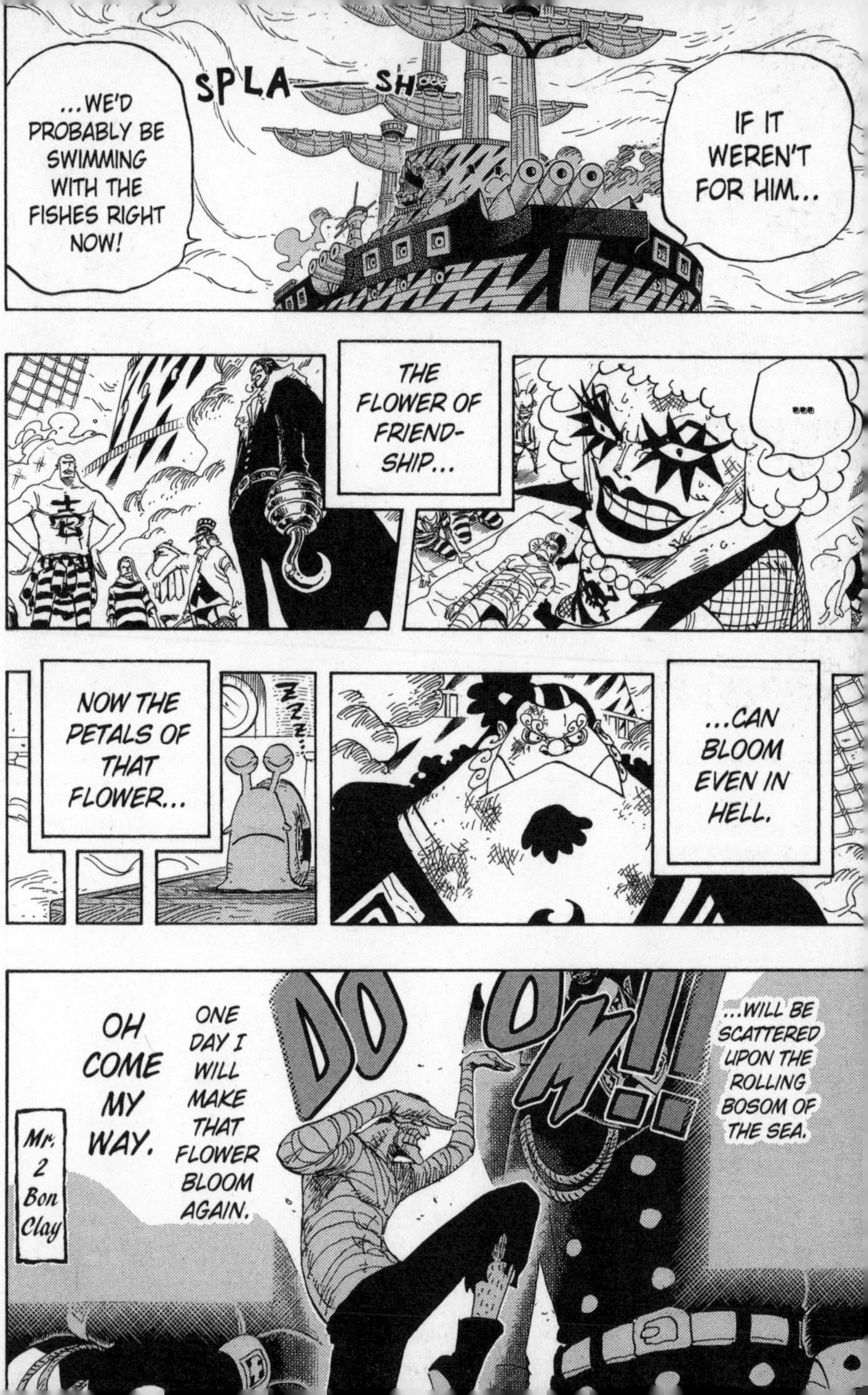
IF IT WEREN'T FOR HIM...
SPLA—SH
...WE'D PROBABLY BE SWIMMING WITH THE FISHES RIGHT NOW!
...
THE FLOWER OF FRIEND-SHIP...
...CAN BLOOM EVEN IN HELL.
Z Z Z...
NOW THE PETALS OF THAT FLOWER...
...WILL BE SCATTERED UPON THE ROLLING BOSOM OF THE SEA.
DOOM!!
ONE DAY I WILL MAKE THAT FLOWER BLOOM AGAIN.
OH COME MY WAY.
Mr. 2 Bon Clay

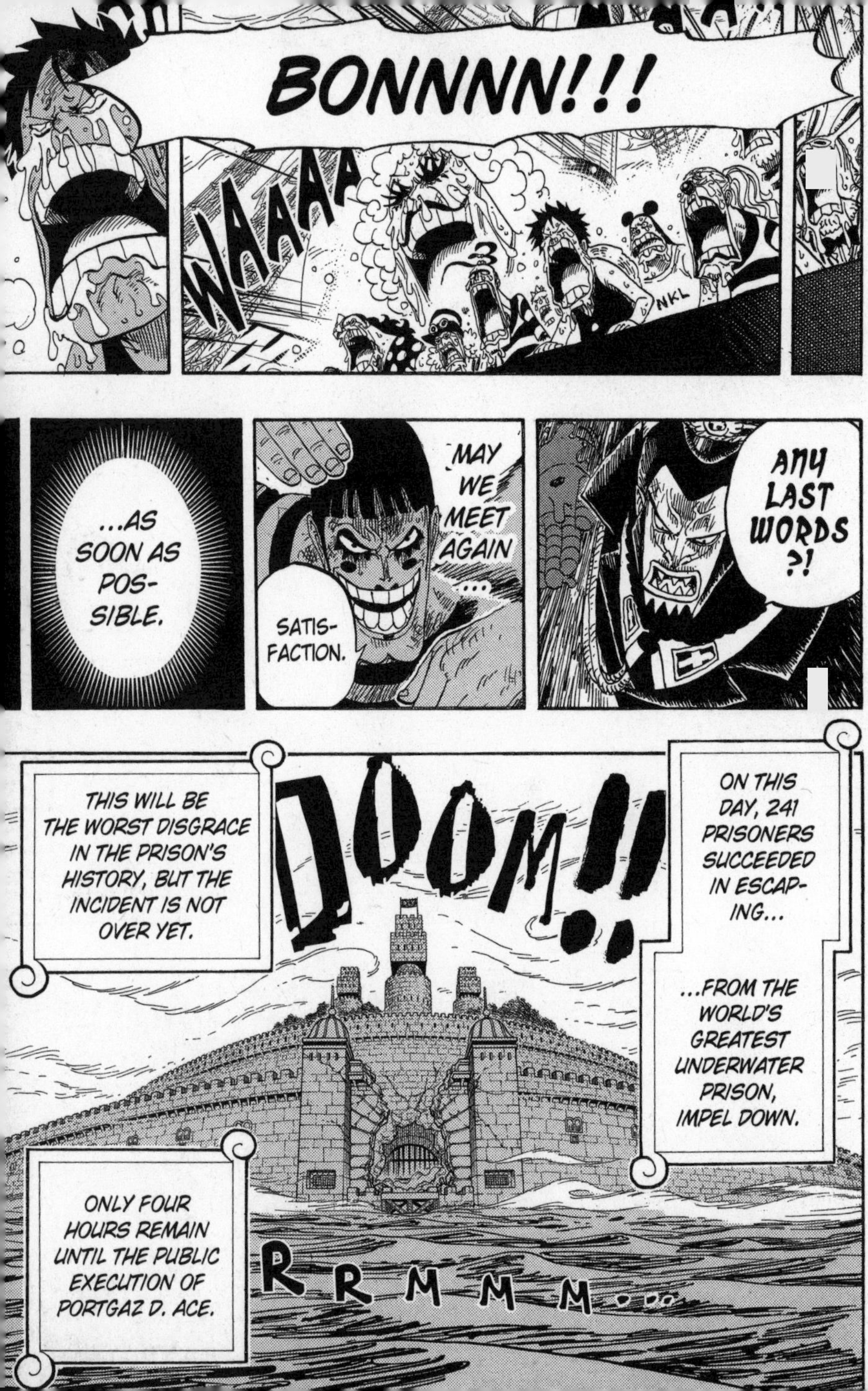
BONNNN!!!
WAAAA
ANY LAST WORDS?!
MAY WE MEET AGAIN...
SATIS-FACTION.
...AS SOON AS POS-SIBLE.
ON THIS DAY, 241 PRISONERS SUCCEEDED IN ESCAP-ING...
...FROM THE WORLD'S GREATEST UNDERWATER PRISON, IMPEL DOWN.
DOOM!!
THIS WILL BE THE WORST DISGRACE IN THE PRISON'S HISTORY, BUT THE INCIDENT IS NOT OVER YET.
ONLY FOUR HOURS REMAIN UNTIL THE PUBLIC EXECUTION OF PORTGAZ D. ACE.
RRMMM...

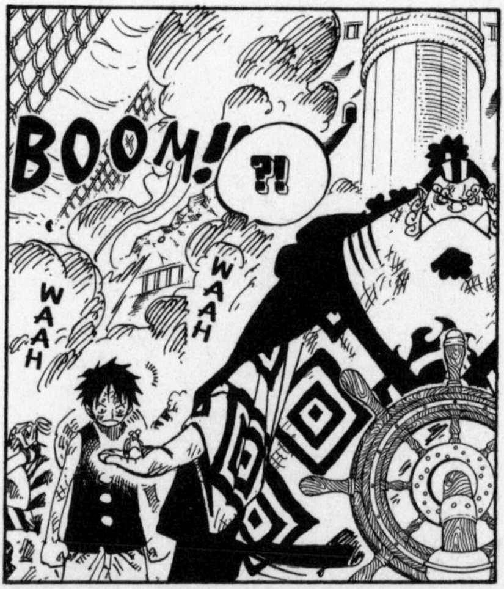
?!
BOOM!!
WAAH
WAAH

Chapter 549:
BATTLESHIP

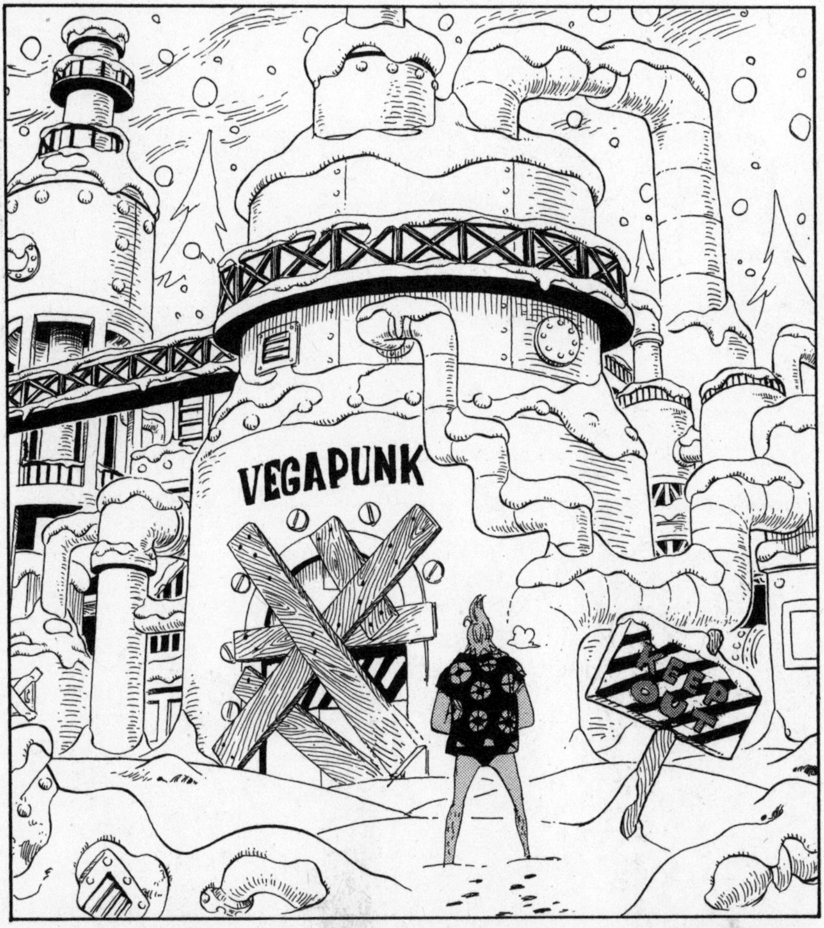
VEGAPUNK
KEEP OUT

FRANKY'S "I'M NO GOOD THIS WEEK" FINAL VOLUME:
"THE HOUSE WHERE DR. VEGAPUNK WAS BORN"

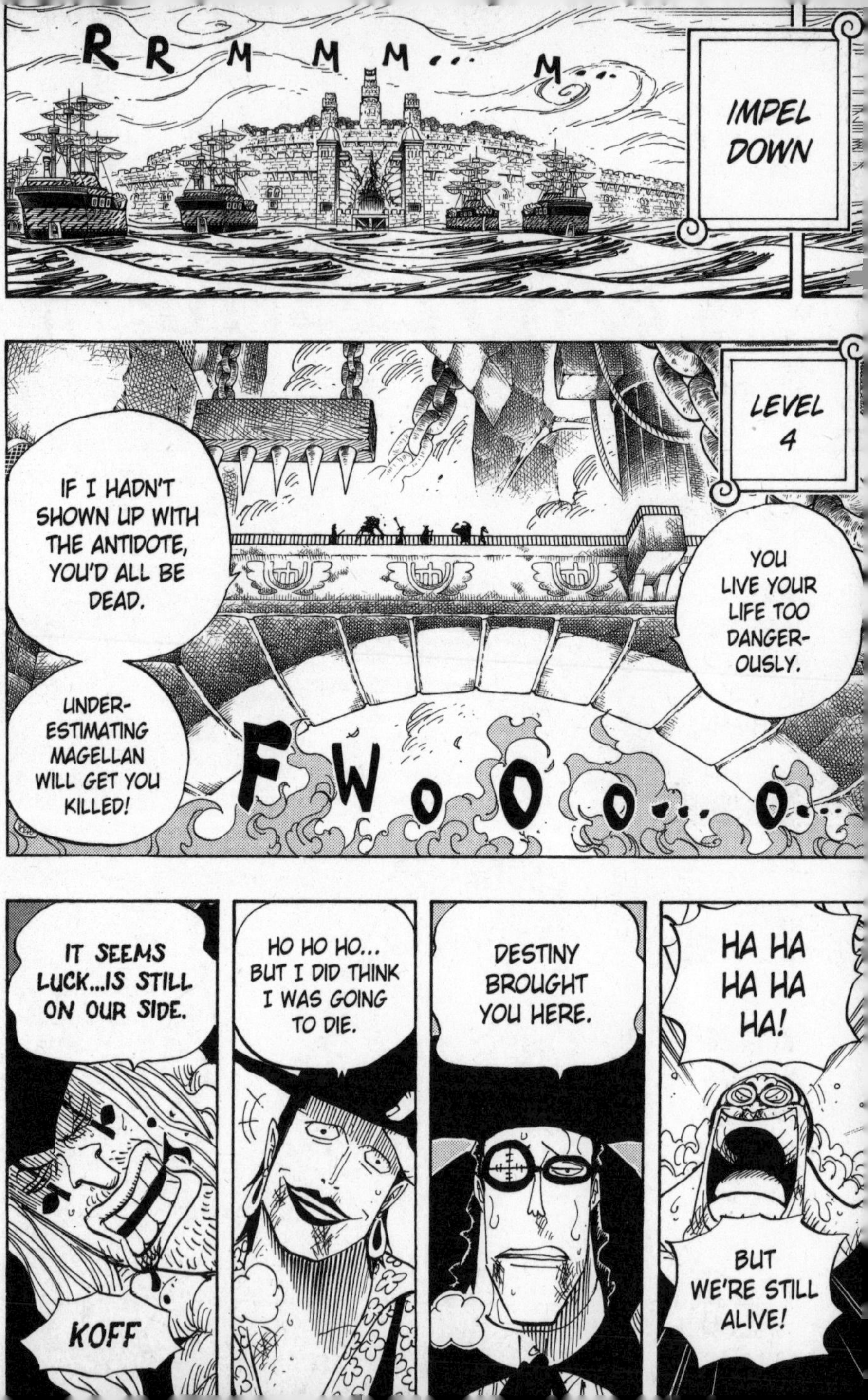

RRMMM...M...
IMPEL DOWN
LEVEL 4
IF I HADN'T SHOWN UP WITH THE ANTIDOTE, YOU'D ALL BE DEAD.
YOU LIVE YOUR LIFE TOO DANGER-OUSLY.
UNDER-ESTIMATING MAGELLAN WILL GET YOU KILLED!
FWOOO...O...
HA HA HA HA HA!
BUT WE'RE STILL ALIVE!
DESTINY BROUGHT YOU HERE.
HO HO HO... BUT I DID THINK I WAS GOING TO DIE.
IT SEEMS LUCK...IS STILL ON OUR SIDE.
KOFF

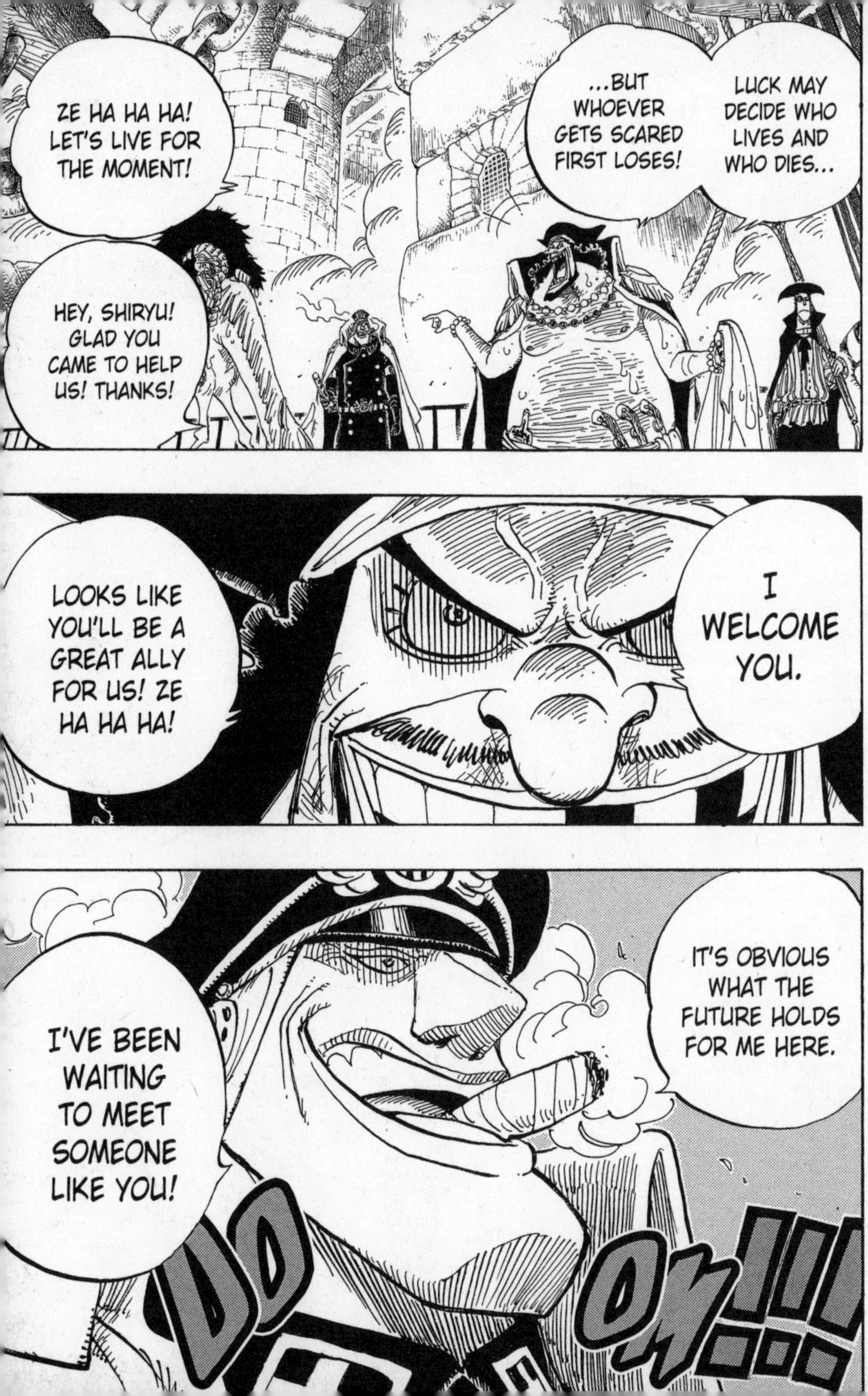
LUCK MAY DECIDE WHO LIVES AND WHO DIES...
...BUT WHOEVER GETS SCARED FIRST LOSES!
ZE HA HA HA! LET'S LIVE FOR THE MOMENT!
HEY, SHIRYU! GLAD YOU CAME TO HELP US! THANKS!
I WELCOME YOU.
LOOKS LIKE YOU'LL BE A GREAT ALLY FOR US! ZE HA HA HA!
IT'S OBVIOUS WHAT THE FUTURE HOLDS FOR ME HERE.
I'VE BEEN WAITING TO MEET SOMEONE LIKE YOU!
DOOM!!!

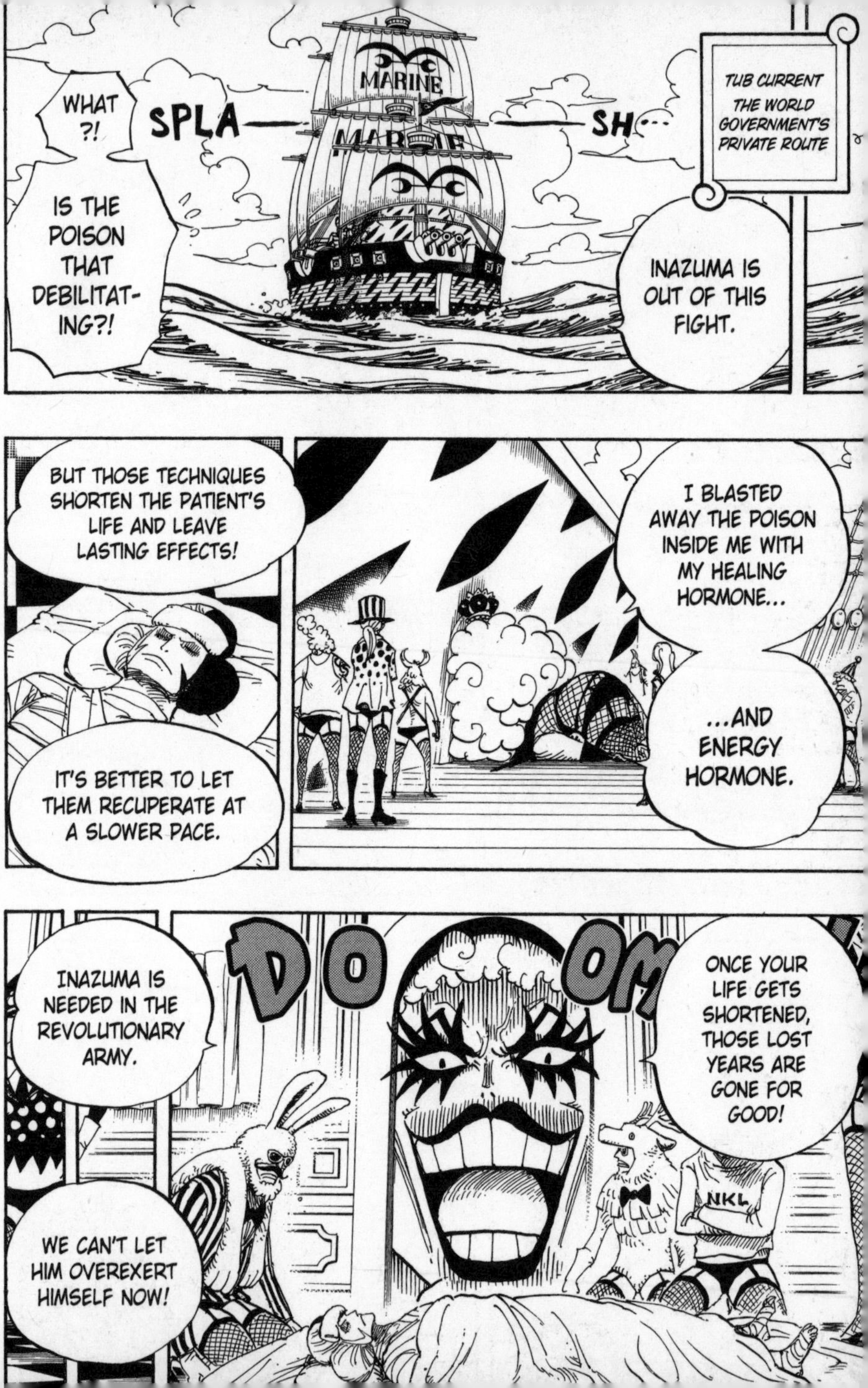
TUB CURRENT THE WORLD GOVERNMENT'S PRIVATE ROUTE
MARINE
SPLA——SH...
INAZUMA IS OUT OF THIS FIGHT.
WHAT?!
IS THE POISON THAT DEBILITATING?!
I BLASTED AWAY THE POISON INSIDE ME WITH MY HEALING HORMONE...
...AND ENERGY HORMONE.
BUT THOSE TECHNIQUES SHORTEN THE PATIENT'S LIFE AND LEAVE LASTING EFFECTS!
IT'S BETTER TO LET THEM RECUPERATE AT A SLOWER PACE.
DO OM
ONCE YOUR LIFE GETS SHORTENED, THOSE LOST YEARS ARE GONE FOR GOOD!
NKL
INAZUMA IS NEEDED IN THE REVOLUTIONARY ARMY.
WE CAN'T LET HIM OVEREXERT HIMSELF NOW!

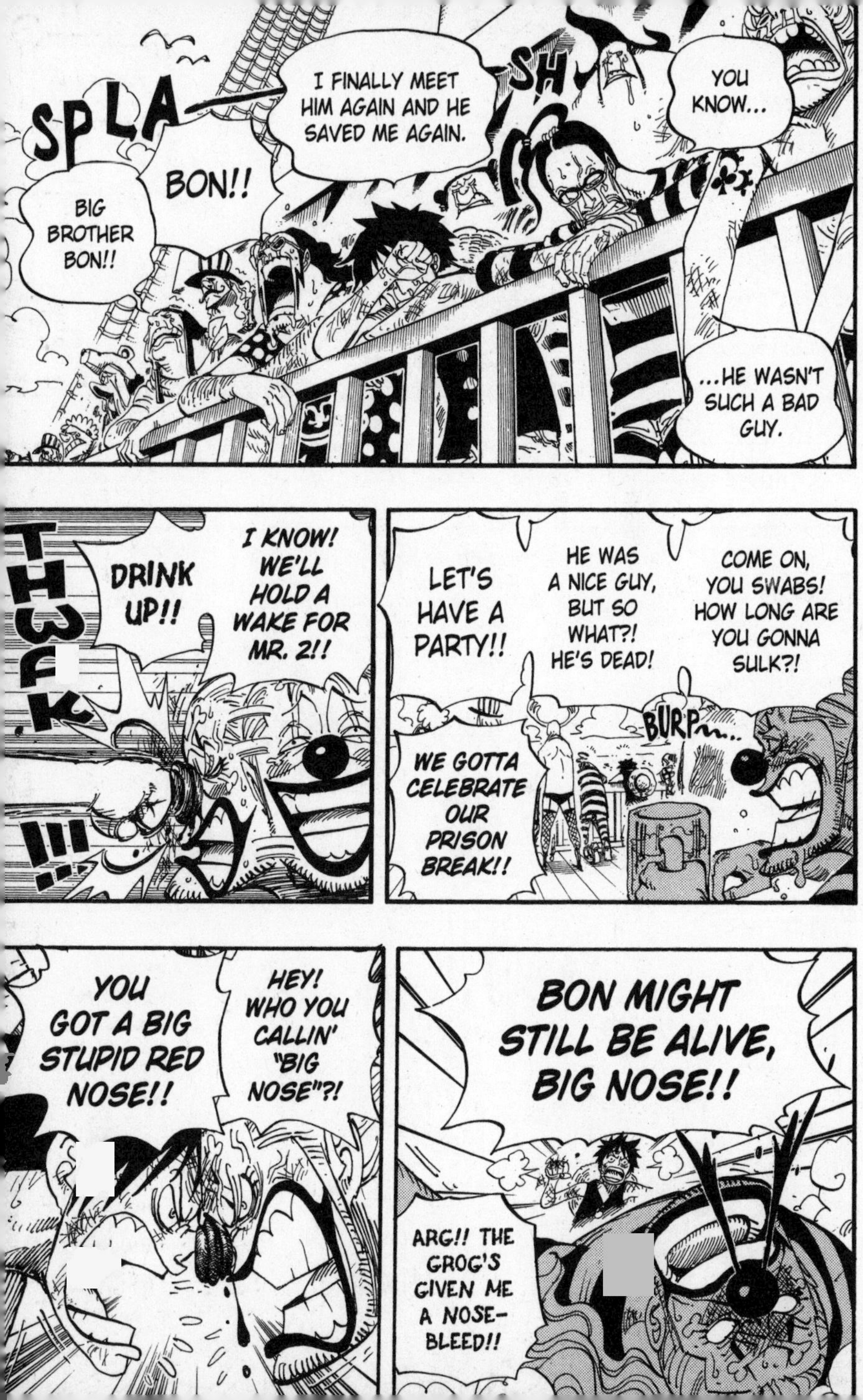
YOU KNOW...
...HE WASN'T SUCH A BAD GUY.
SH
I FINALLY MEET HIM AGAIN AND HE SAVED ME AGAIN.
BON!!
BIG BROTHER BON!!
SPLA
COME ON, YOU SWABS! HOW LONG ARE YOU GONNA SULK?!
HE WAS A NICE GUY, BUT SO WHAT?! HE'S DEAD!
LET'S HAVE A PARTY!!
BURP...
WE GOTTA CELEBRATE OUR PRISON BREAK!!
I KNOW! WE'LL HOLD A WAKE FOR MR. 2!!
DRINK UP!!
THWAK!!!
BON MIGHT STILL BE ALIVE, BIG NOSE!!
ARG!! THE GROG'S GIVEN ME A NOSE-BLEED!!
HEY! WHO YOU CALLIN' "BIG NOSE"?!
YOU GOT A BIG STUPID RED NOSE!!

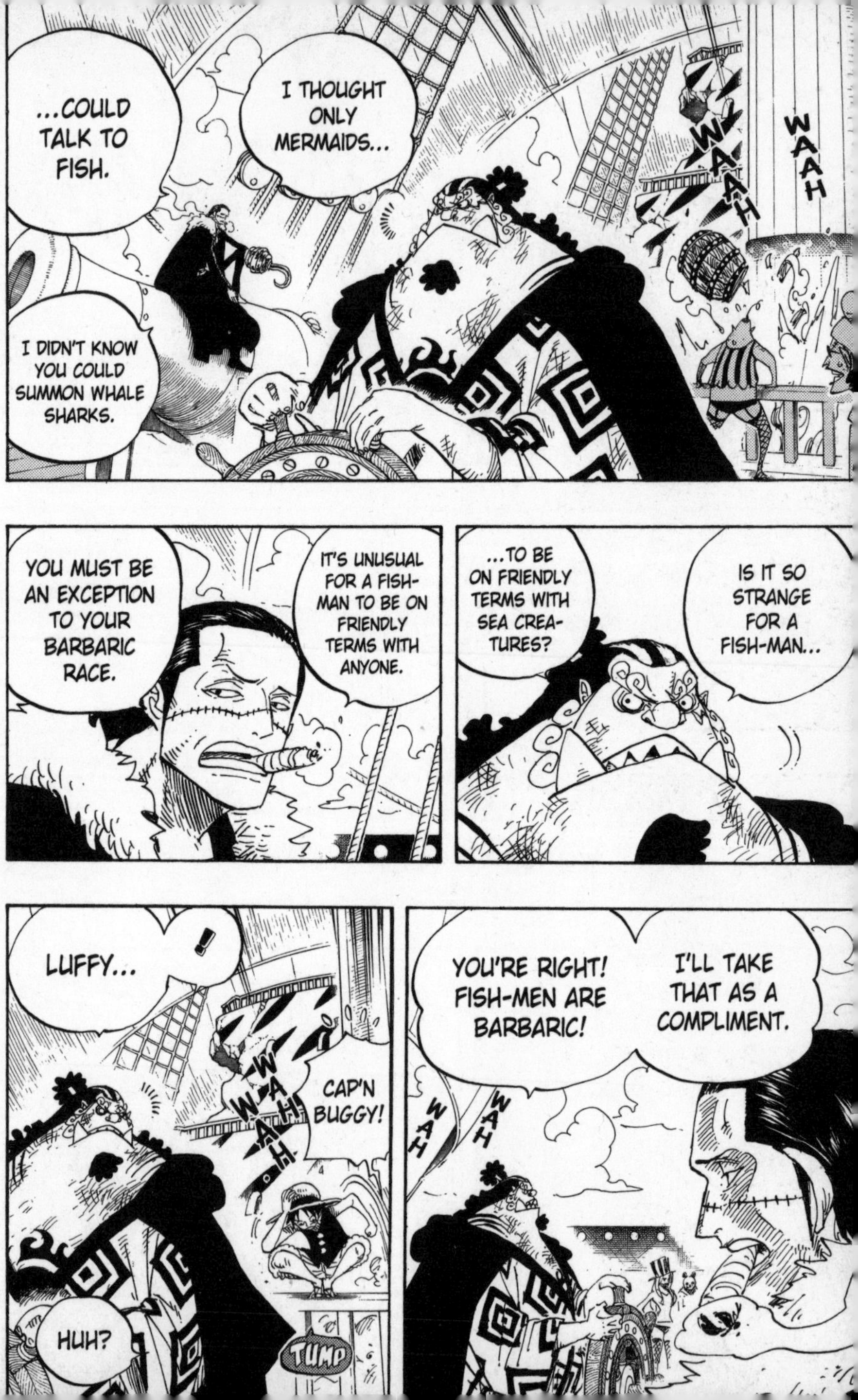
WAAH
WAAH
I THOUGHT ONLY MERMAIDS...
...COULD TALK TO FISH.
I DIDN'T KNOW YOU COULD SUMMON WHALE SHARKS.
IS IT SO STRANGE FOR A FISH-MAN...
...TO BE ON FRIENDLY TERMS WITH SEA CREA-TURES?
IT'S UNUSUAL FOR A FISH-MAN TO BE ON FRIENDLY TERMS WITH ANYONE.
YOU MUST BE AN EXCEPTION TO YOUR BARBARIC RACE.
I'LL TAKE THAT AS A COMPLIMENT.
YOU'RE RIGHT! FISH-MEN ARE BARBARIC!
WAH
WAH
!
LUFFY...
CAP'N BUGGY!
WAH
WAH
WAH
HUH?
TUMP

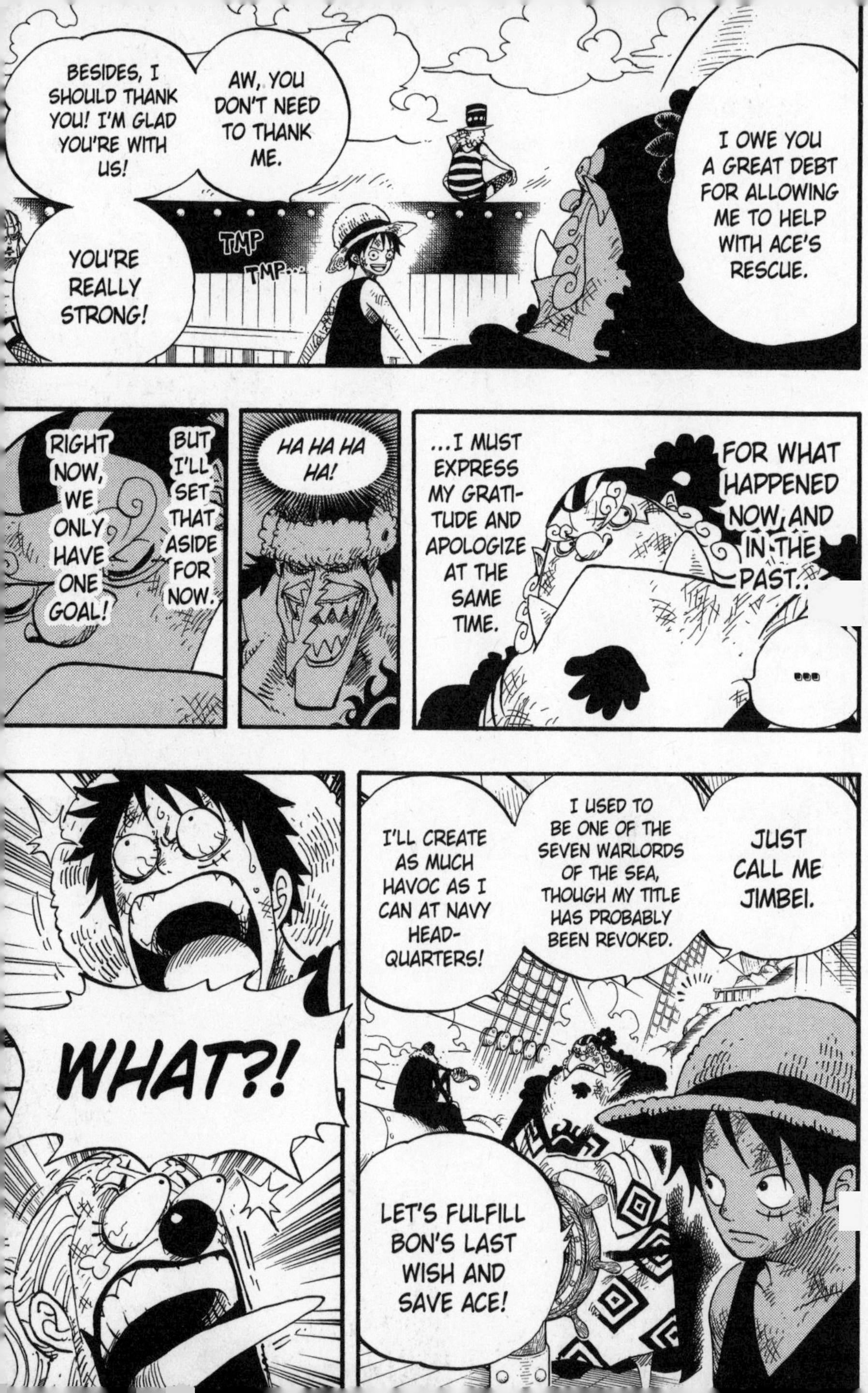
I OWE YOU A GREAT DEBT FOR ALLOWING ME TO HELP WITH ACE'S RESCUE.
AW, YOU DON'T NEED TO THANK ME.
BESIDES, I SHOULD THANK YOU! I'M GLAD YOU'RE WITH US!
TMP
TMP...
YOU'RE REALLY STRONG!
FOR WHAT HAPPENED NOW, AND IN THE PAST...
...I MUST EXPRESS MY GRATITUDE AND APOLOGIZE AT THE SAME TIME.
...
HA HA HA HA!
BUT I'LL SET THAT ASIDE FOR NOW.
RIGHT NOW, WE ONLY HAVE ONE GOAL!
JUST CALL ME JIMBEI.
I USED TO BE ONE OF THE SEVEN WARLORDS OF THE SEA, THOUGH MY TITLE HAS PROBABLY BEEN REVOKED.
I'LL CREATE AS MUCH HAVOC AS I CAN AT NAVY HEADQUARTERS!
LET'S FULFILL BON'S LAST WISH AND SAVE ACE!
WHAT?!

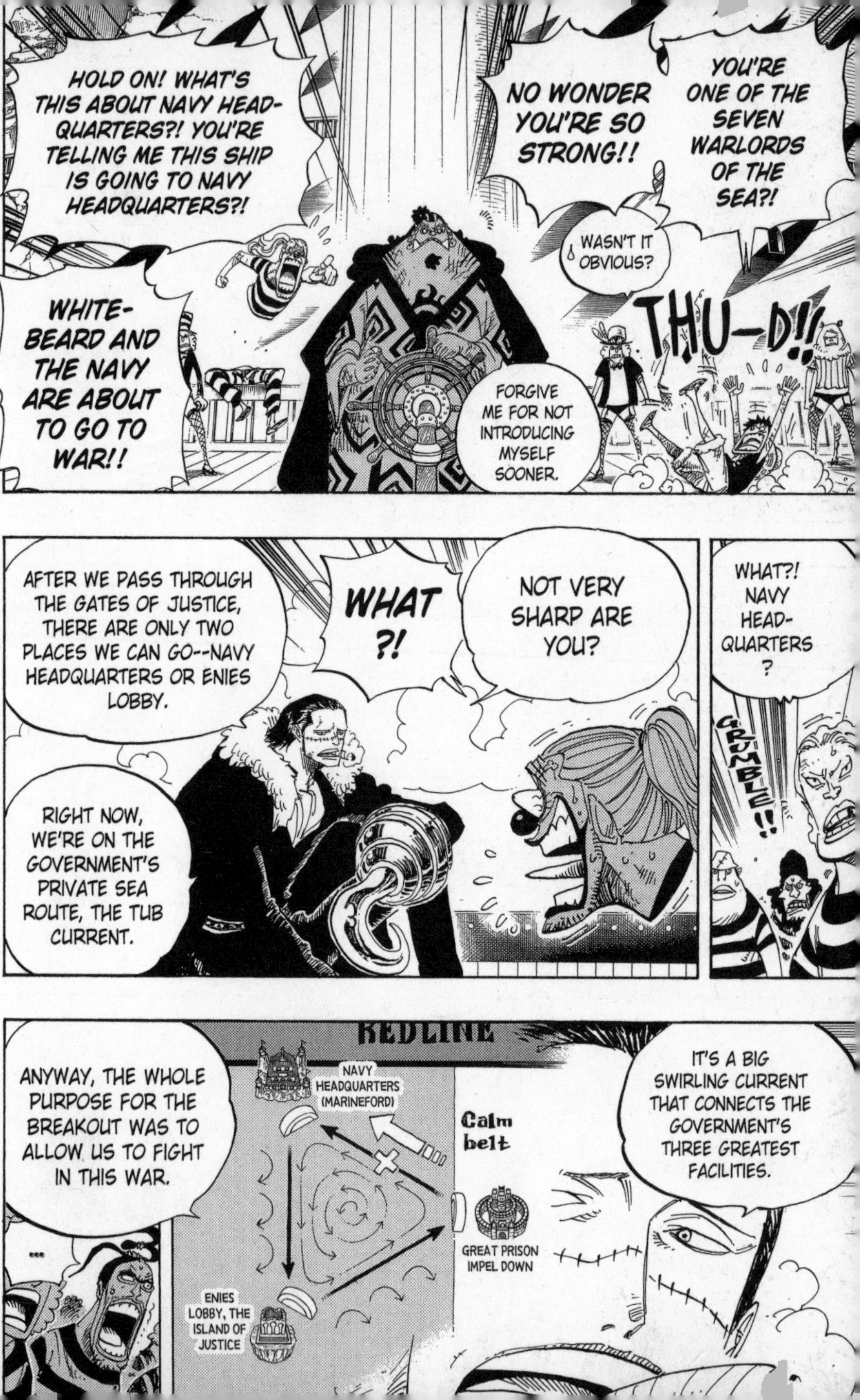
YOU'RE ONE OF THE SEVEN WARLORDS OF THE SEA?!
NO WONDER YOU'RE SO STRONG!!
HOLD ON! WHAT'S THIS ABOUT NAVY HEAD-QUARTERS?! YOU'RE TELLING ME THIS SHIP IS GOING TO NAVY HEADQUARTERS?!
WASN'T IT OBVIOUS?
THU-D!!
FORGIVE ME FOR NOT INTRODUCING MYSELF SOONER.
WHITE-BEARD AND THE NAVY ARE ABOUT TO GO TO WAR!!
WHAT?! NAVY HEAD-QUARTERS ?
GRUMBLE!!
NOT VERY SHARP ARE YOU?
WHAT ?!
AFTER WE PASS THROUGH THE GATES OF JUSTICE, THERE ARE ONLY TWO PLACES WE CAN GO--NAVY HEADQUARTERS OR ENIES LOBBY.
RIGHT NOW, WE'RE ON THE GOVERNMENT'S PRIVATE SEA ROUTE, THE TUB CURRENT.
IT'S A BIG SWIRLING CURRENT THAT CONNECTS THE GOVERNMENT'S THREE GREATEST FACILITIES.
REDLINE
Calm belt
NAVY HEADQUARTERS (MARINEFORD)
GREAT PRISON IMPEL DOWN
ENIES LOBBY, THE ISLAND OF JUSTICE
ANYWAY, THE WHOLE PURPOSE FOR THE BREAKOUT WAS TO ALLOW US TO FIGHT IN THIS WAR.
...

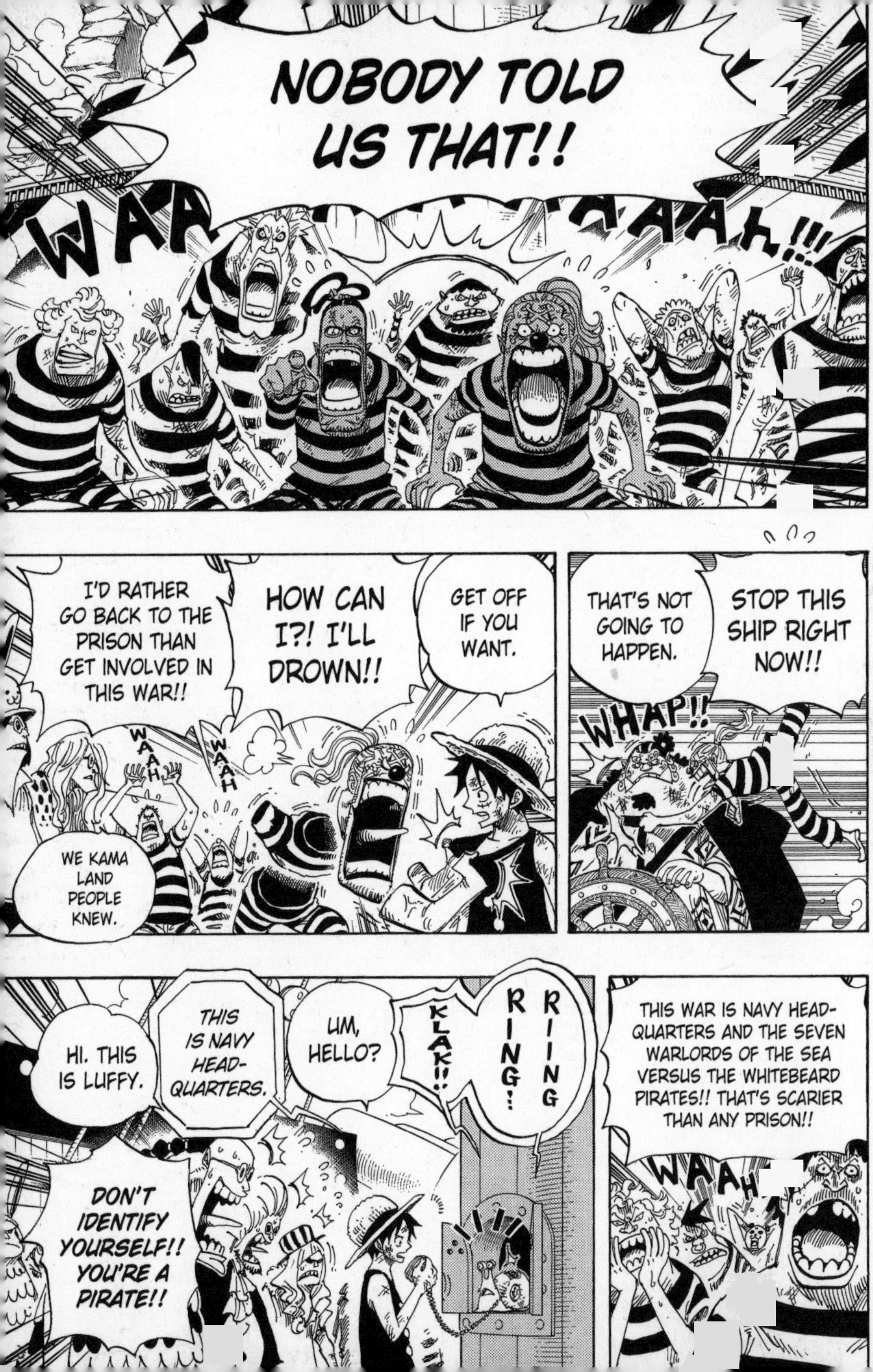
NOBODY TOLD US THAT!!
WAA
AAAAh!!!
STOP THIS SHIP RIGHT NOW!!
THAT'S NOT GOING TO HAPPEN.
WHAP!!
GET OFF IF YOU WANT.
HOW CAN I?! I'LL DROWN!!
I'D RATHER GO BACK TO THE PRISON THAN GET INVOLVED IN THIS WAR!!
WAAH
WAAH
WE KAMA LAND PEOPLE KNEW.
THIS WAR IS NAVY HEAD-QUARTERS AND THE SEVEN WARLORDS OF THE SEA VERSUS THE WHITEBEARD PIRATES!! THAT'S SCARIER THAN ANY PRISON!!
WAAH
RIING
RING!
KLAK!!
UM, HELLO?
THIS IS NAVY HEAD-QUARTERS.
HI. THIS IS LUFFY.
DON'T IDENTIFY YOURSELF!! YOU'RE A PIRATE!!

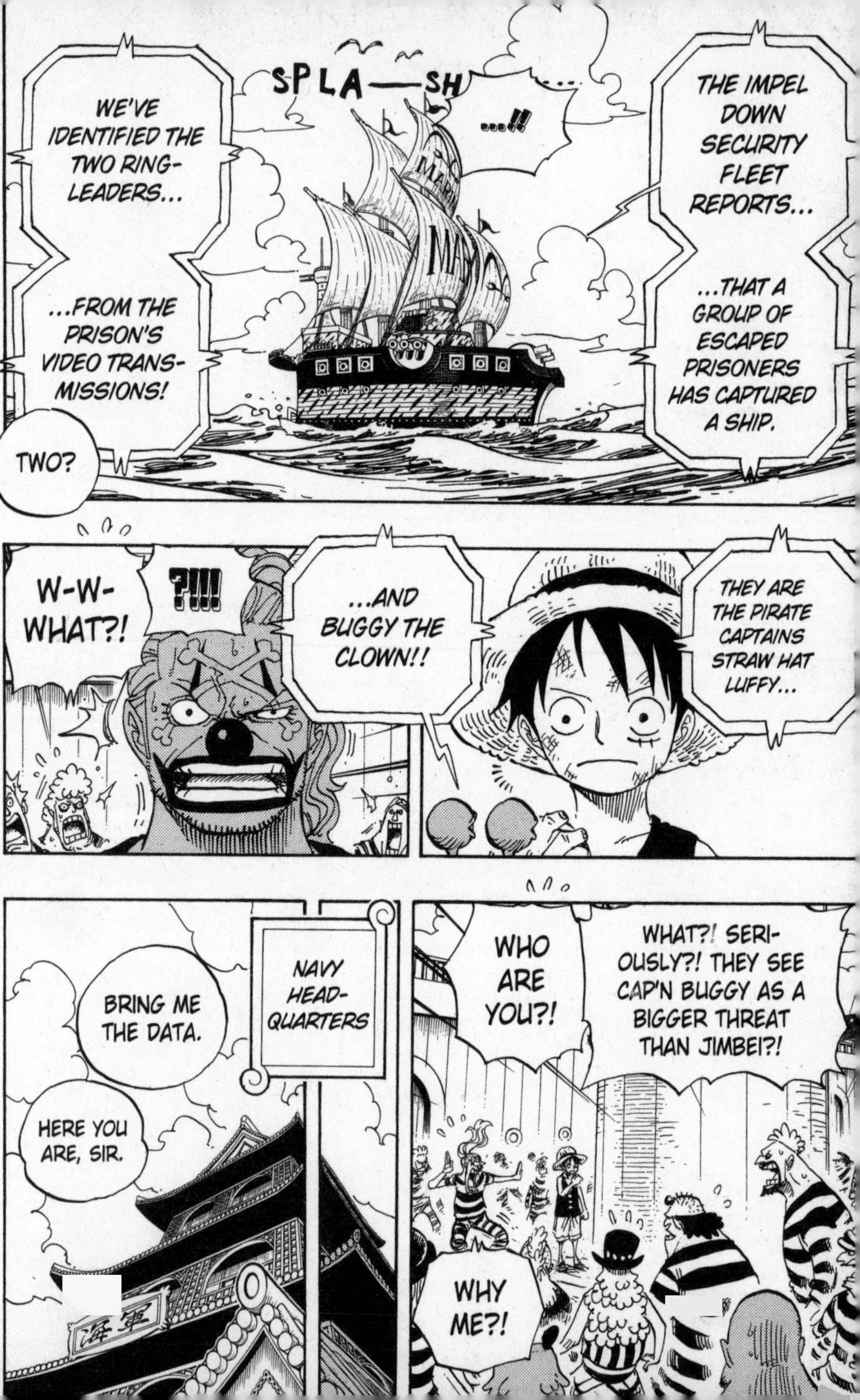
THE IMPEL DOWN SECURITY FLEET REPORTS...
...THAT A GROUP OF ESCAPED PRISONERS HAS CAPTURED A SHIP.
SPLA—SH
...!!
WE'VE IDENTIFIED THE TWO RING-LEADERS...
...FROM THE PRISON'S VIDEO TRANS-MISSIONS!
TWO?
THEY ARE THE PIRATE CAPTAINS STRAW HAT LUFFY...
...AND BUGGY THE CLOWN!!
?!!!
W-W-WHAT?!
WHAT?! SERI-OUSLY?! THEY SEE CAP'N BUGGY AS A BIGGER THREAT THAN JIMBEI?!
WHO ARE YOU?!
WHY ME?!
NAVY HEAD-QUARTERS
BRING ME THE DATA.
HERE YOU ARE, SIR.
海軍

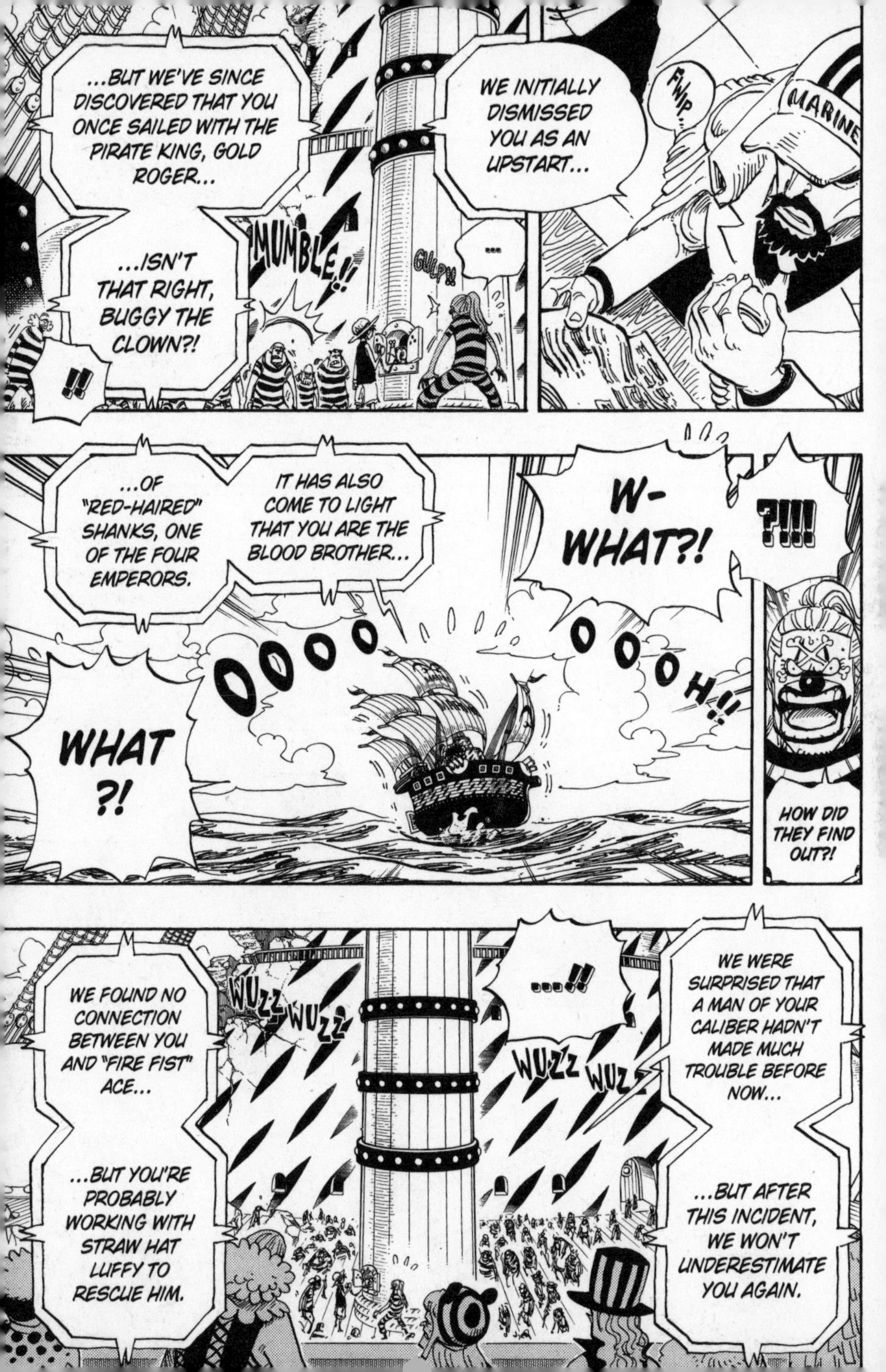
FWIP...
WE INITIALLY DISMISSED YOU AS AN UPSTART...
...BUT WE'VE SINCE DISCOVERED THAT YOU ONCE SAILED WITH THE PIRATE KING, GOLD ROGER...
MUMBLE!!
GULP!!
...
...ISN'T THAT RIGHT, BUGGY THE CLOWN?!
!!
?!!!
HOW DID THEY FIND OUT?!
IT HAS ALSO COME TO LIGHT THAT YOU ARE THE BLOOD BROTHER...
...OF "RED-HAIRED" SHANKS, ONE OF THE FOUR EMPERORS.
W- WHAT?!
OOOOH!!
OOOO
WHAT ?!
WE WERE SURPRISED THAT A MAN OF YOUR CALIBER HADN'T MADE MUCH TROUBLE BEFORE NOW...
...BUT AFTER THIS INCIDENT, WE WON'T UNDERESTIMATE YOU AGAIN.
...!!
WUZZ WUZZ
WE FOUND NO CONNECTION BETWEEN YOU AND "FIRE FIST" ACE...
...BUT YOU'RE PROBABLY WORKING WITH STRAW HAT LUFFY TO RESCUE HIM.
WUZZ WUZZ

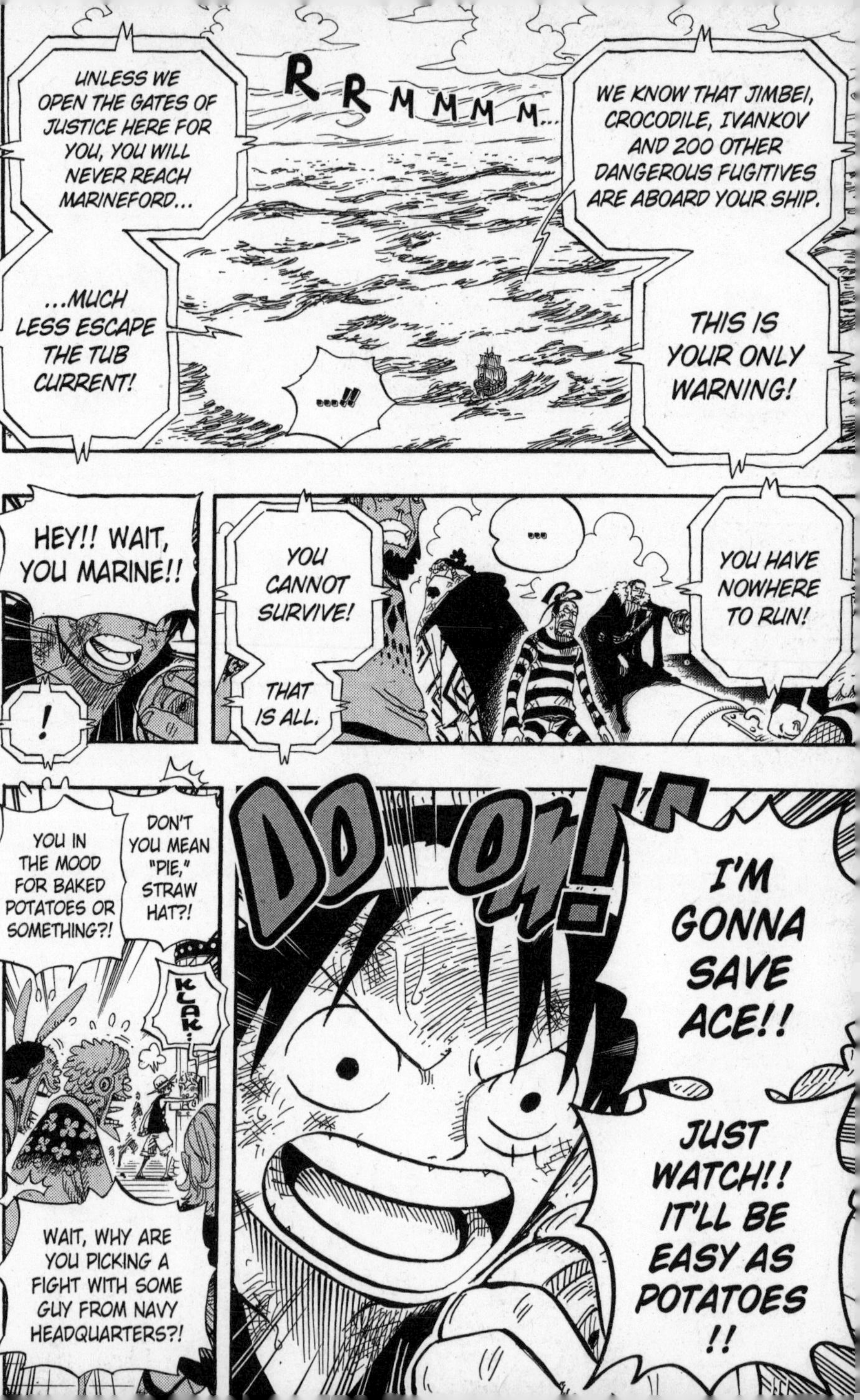
WE KNOW THAT JIMBEI, CROCODILE, IVANKOV AND 200 OTHER DANGEROUS FUGITIVES ARE ABOARD YOUR SHIP.
THIS IS YOUR ONLY WARNING!
RRMMMM...
UNLESS WE OPEN THE GATES OF JUSTICE HERE FOR YOU, YOU WILL NEVER REACH MARINEFORD...
...MUCH LESS ESCAPE THE TUB CURRENT!
...!!
YOU HAVE NOWHERE TO RUN!
...
YOU CANNOT SURVIVE!
THAT IS ALL.
HEY!! WAIT, YOU MARINE!!
!
DOON!!
I'M GONNA SAVE ACE!!
JUST WATCH!! IT'LL BE EASY AS POTATOES!!
DON'T YOU MEAN "PIE," STRAW HAT?!
YOU IN THE MOOD FOR BAKED POTATOES OR SOMETHING?!
KLAK!
WAIT, WHY ARE YOU PICKING A FIGHT WITH SOME GUY FROM NAVY HEADQUARTERS?!

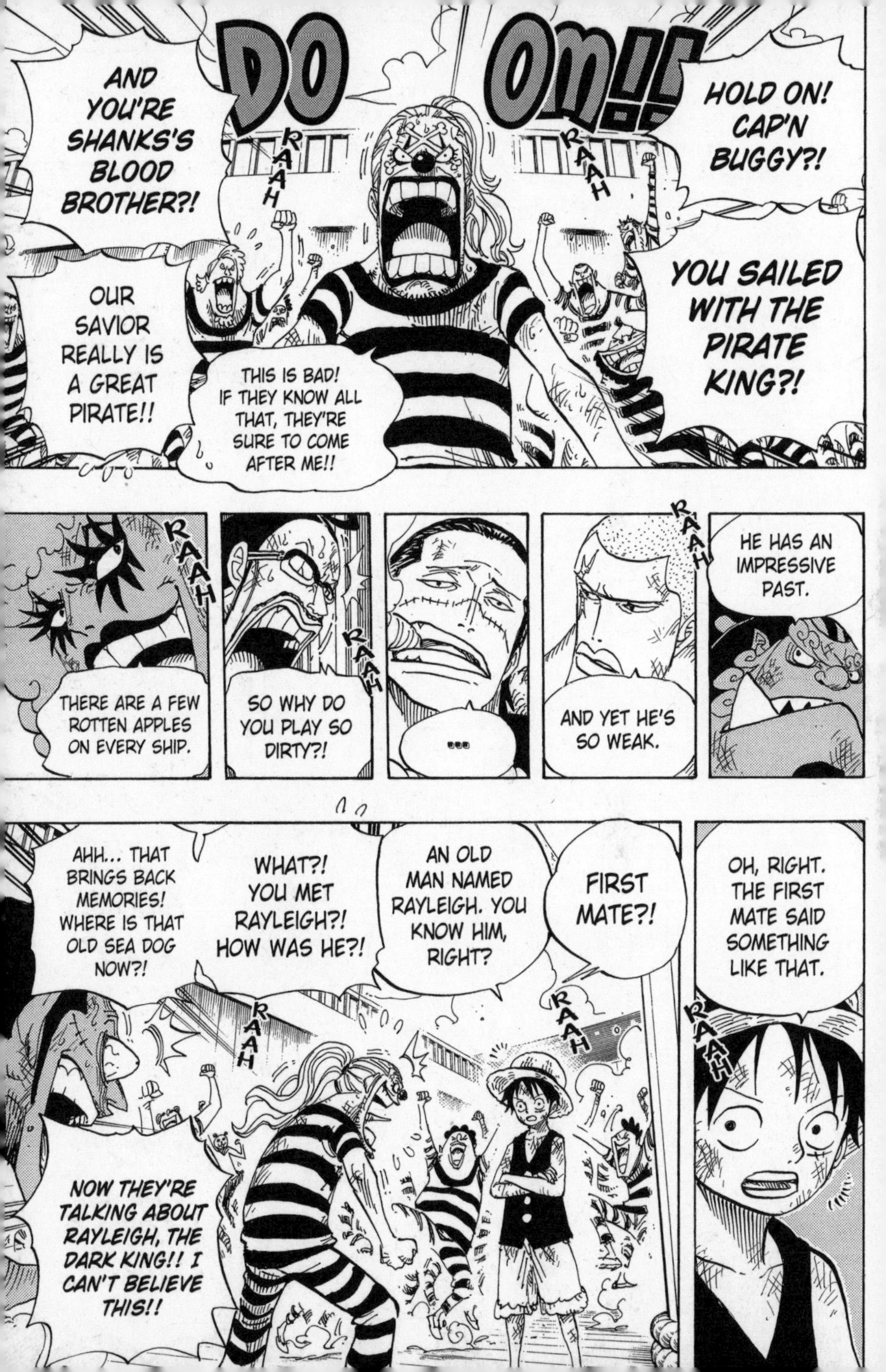
DOOM!!
HOLD ON! CAP'N BUGGY?!
RAAH
RAAH
AND YOU'RE SHANKS'S BLOOD BROTHER?!
YOU SAILED WITH THE PIRATE KING?!
OUR SAVIOR REALLY IS A GREAT PIRATE!!
THIS IS BAD! IF THEY KNOW ALL THAT, THEY'RE SURE TO COME AFTER ME!!
HE HAS AN IMPRESSIVE PAST.
RAAH
AND YET HE'S SO WEAK.
...
RAAH
SO WHY DO YOU PLAY SO DIRTY?!
RAAH
THERE ARE A FEW ROTTEN APPLES ON EVERY SHIP.
OH, RIGHT. THE FIRST MATE SAID SOMETHING LIKE THAT.
RAAH
FIRST MATE?!
AN OLD MAN NAMED RAYLEIGH. YOU KNOW HIM, RIGHT?
RAAH
WHAT?! YOU MET RAYLEIGH?! HOW WAS HE?!
AHH... THAT BRINGS BACK MEMORIES! WHERE IS THAT OLD SEA DOG NOW?!
RAAH
NOW THEY'RE TALKING ABOUT RAYLEIGH, THE DARK KING!! I CAN'T BELIEVE THIS!!

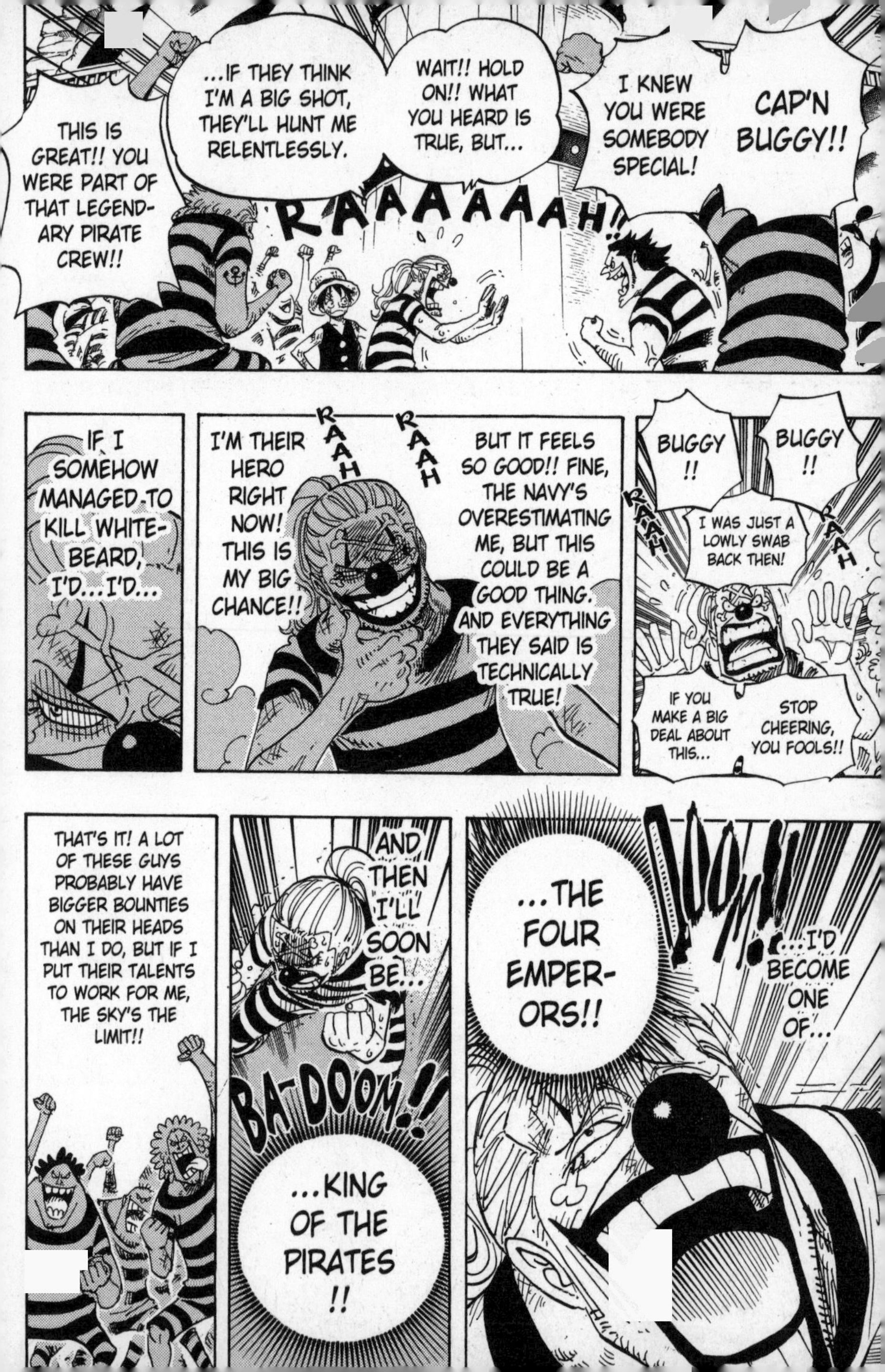
CAP'N BUGGY!!
I KNEW YOU WERE SOMEBODY SPECIAL!
WAIT!! HOLD ON!! WHAT YOU HEARD IS TRUE, BUT...
...IF THEY THINK I'M A BIG SHOT, THEY'LL HUNT ME RELENTLESSLY.
THIS IS GREAT!! YOU WERE PART OF THAT LEGENDARY PIRATE CREW!!
RAAAAAAAH!!
BUGGY!!
BUGGY!!
RAAH
RAAH
I WAS JUST A LOWLY SWAB BACK THEN!
STOP CHEERING, YOU FOOLS!!
IF YOU MAKE A BIG DEAL ABOUT THIS...
BUT IT FEELS SO GOOD!! FINE, THE NAVY'S OVERESTIMATING ME, BUT THIS COULD BE A GOOD THING. AND EVERYTHING THEY SAID IS TECHNICALLY TRUE!
RAAH
RAAH
I'M THEIR HERO RIGHT NOW! THIS IS MY BIG CHANCE!!
IF I SOMEHOW MANAGED TO KILL WHITEBEARD, I'D...I'D...
DOOM!!
...I'D BECOME ONE OF...
...THE FOUR EMPERORS!!
AND THEN I'LL SOON BE...
...KING OF THE PIRATES!!
BA-DOOM!!
THAT'S IT! A LOT OF THESE GUYS PROBABLY HAVE BIGGER BOUNTIES ON THEIR HEADS THAN I DO, BUT IF I PUT THEIR TALENTS TO WORK FOR ME, THE SKY'S THE LIMIT!!

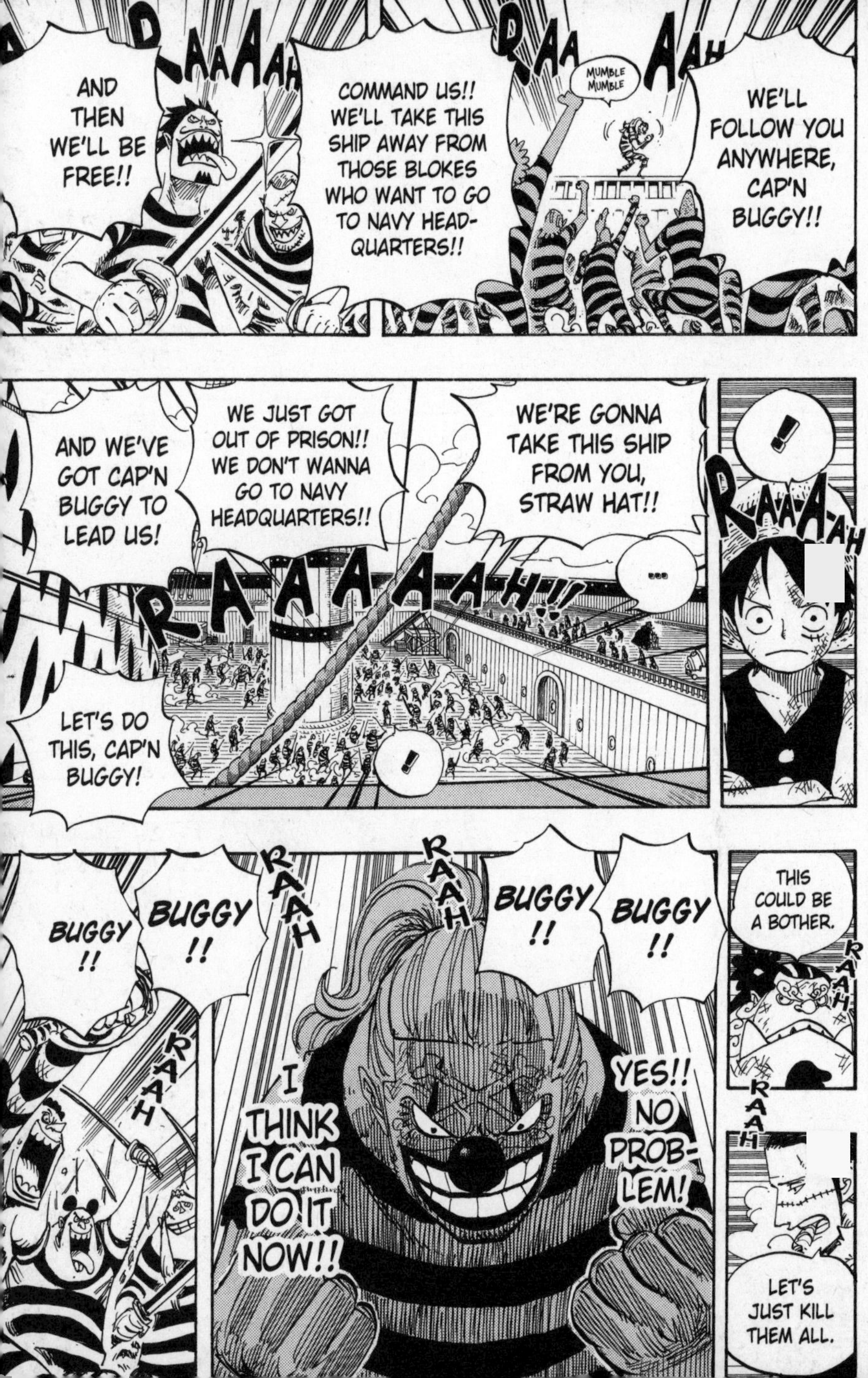
DAAAAH
MUMBLE MUMBLE
WE'LL FOLLOW YOU ANYWHERE, CAP'N BUGGY!!
COMMAND US!! WE'LL TAKE THIS SHIP AWAY FROM THOSE BLOKES WHO WANT TO GO TO NAVY HEAD-QUARTERS!!
AND THEN WE'LL BE FREE!!
DAAAAAH
!
RAAAAAH
WE'RE GONNA TAKE THIS SHIP FROM YOU, STRAW HAT!!
WE JUST GOT OUT OF PRISON!! WE DON'T WANNA GO TO NAVY HEADQUARTERS!!
AND WE'VE GOT CAP'N BUGGY TO LEAD US!
RAAAAAH!!
...
LET'S DO THIS, CAP'N BUGGY!
!
THIS COULD BE A BOTHER.
RAAH
RAAH
LET'S JUST KILL THEM ALL.
BUGGY!!
BUGGY!!
RAAH
BUGGY!!
RAAH
BUGGY!!
YES!! NO PROB-LEM!
I THINK I CAN DO IT NOW!!
RAAH

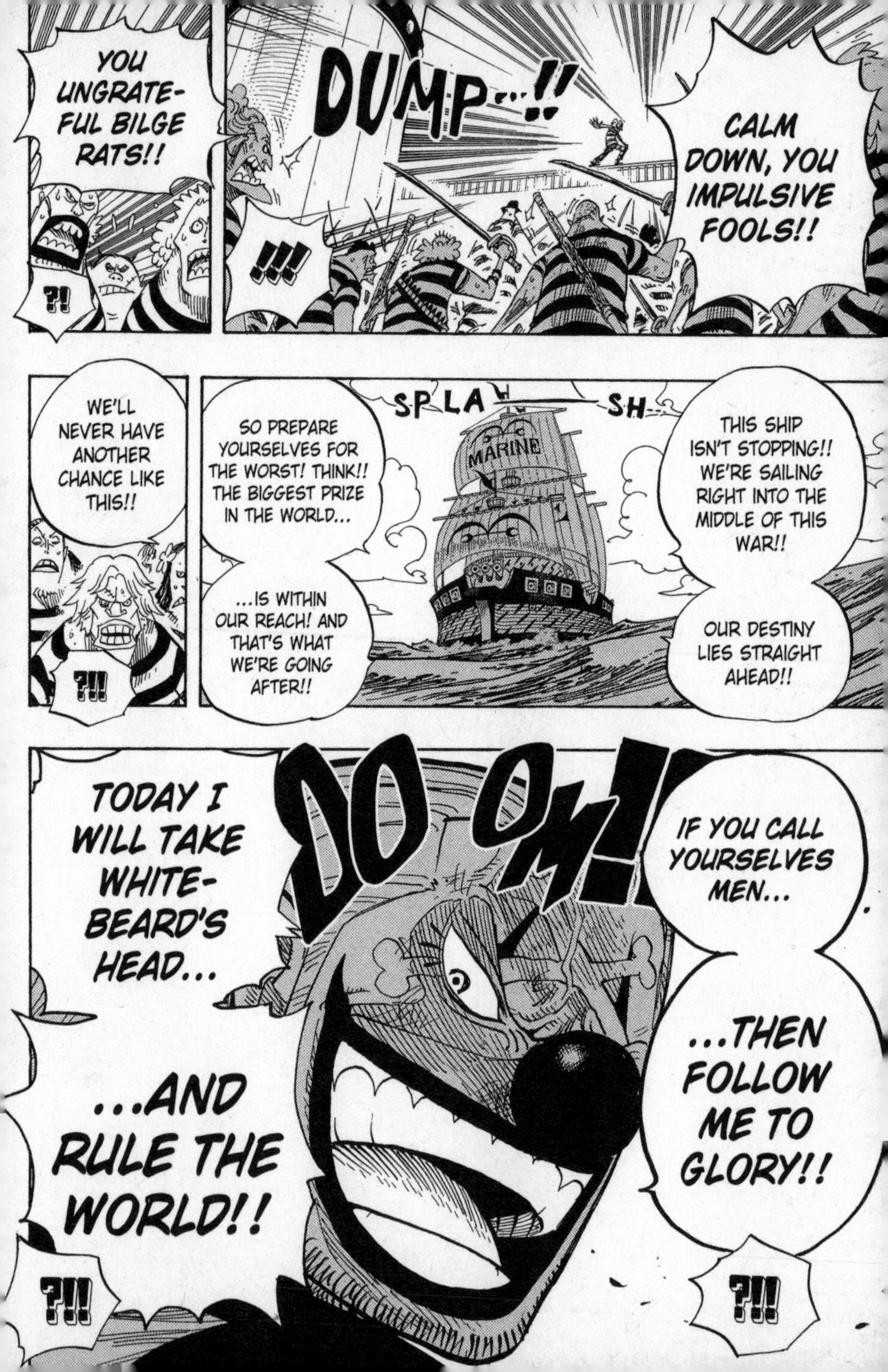
CALM DOWN, YOU IMPULSIVE FOOLS!!
DUMP...!!
!!!
YOU UNGRATE-FUL BILGE RATS!!
?!
SPLA—SH
THIS SHIP ISN'T STOPPING!! WE'RE SAILING RIGHT INTO THE MIDDLE OF THIS WAR!!
OUR DESTINY LIES STRAIGHT AHEAD!!
MARINE
SO PREPARE YOURSELVES FOR THE WORST! THINK!! THE BIGGEST PRIZE IN THE WORLD...
...IS WITHIN OUR REACH! AND THAT'S WHAT WE'RE GOING AFTER!!
WE'LL NEVER HAVE ANOTHER CHANCE LIKE THIS!!
?!!
IF YOU CALL YOURSELVES MEN...
DOOM!!
...THEN FOLLOW ME TO GLORY!!
?!!
TODAY I WILL TAKE WHITE-BEARD'S HEAD...
...AND RULE THE WORLD!!
?!!

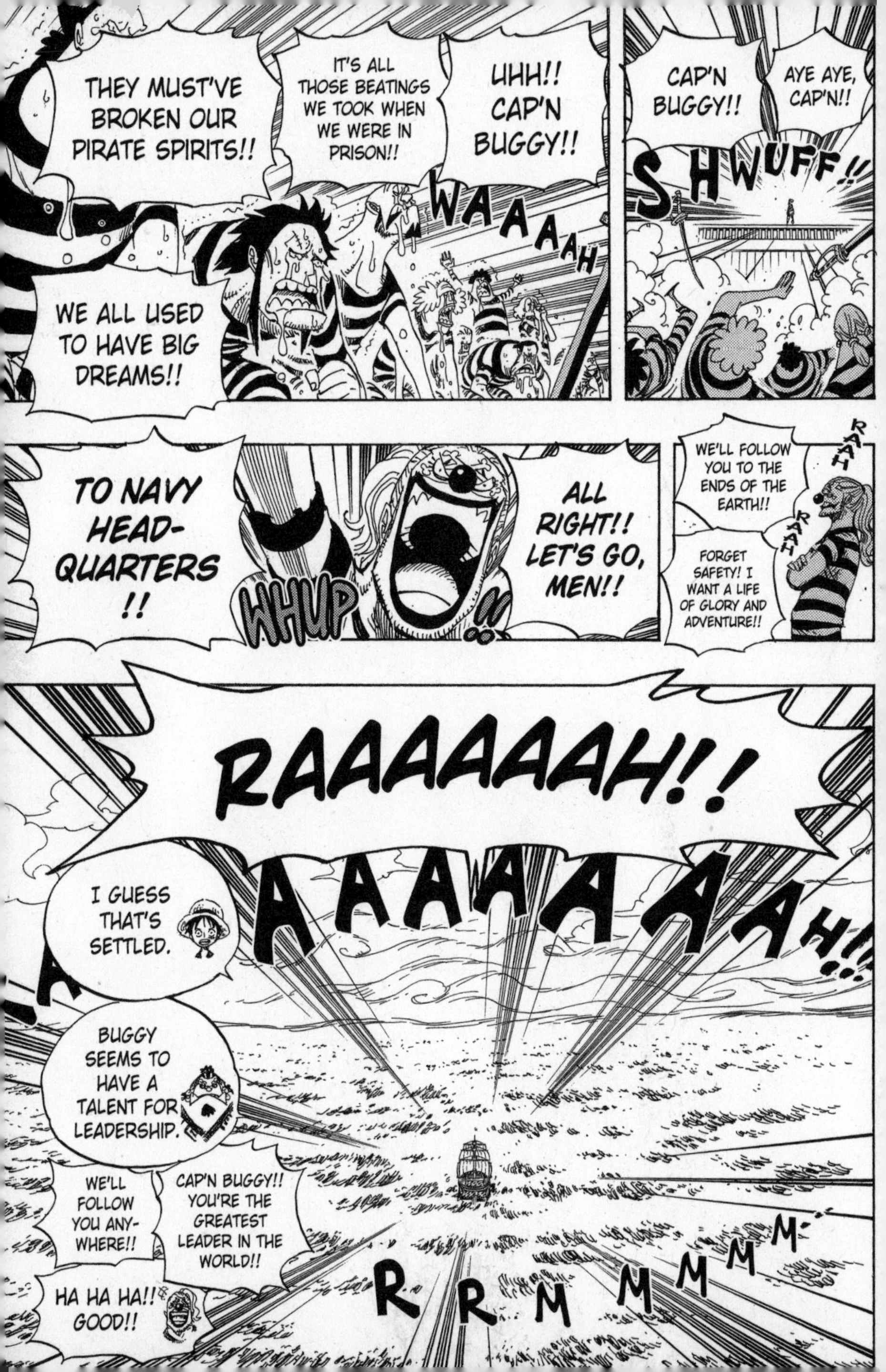
AYE AYE, CAP'N!!
CAP'N BUGGY!!
SHWUFF!!
UHH!! CAP'N BUGGY!!
IT'S ALL THOSE BEATINGS WE TOOK WHEN WE WERE IN PRISON!!
THEY MUST'VE BROKEN OUR PIRATE SPIRITS!!
WAAAAH
WE ALL USED TO HAVE BIG DREAMS!!
RAAAH
WE'LL FOLLOW YOU TO THE ENDS OF THE EARTH!!
RAAH
FORGET SAFETY! I WANT A LIFE OF GLORY AND ADVENTURE!!
ALL RIGHT!! LET'S GO, MEN!!
WHUP
TO NAVY HEAD-QUARTERS!!
RAAAAAAH!!
AAAAAAAAAH!!!
I GUESS THAT'S SETTLED.
BUGGY SEEMS TO HAVE A TALENT FOR LEADERSHIP.
CAP'N BUGGY!! YOU'RE THE GREATEST LEADER IN THE WORLD!!
WE'LL FOLLOW YOU ANY-WHERE!!
RRMMMMMM
HA HA HA!! GOOD!!

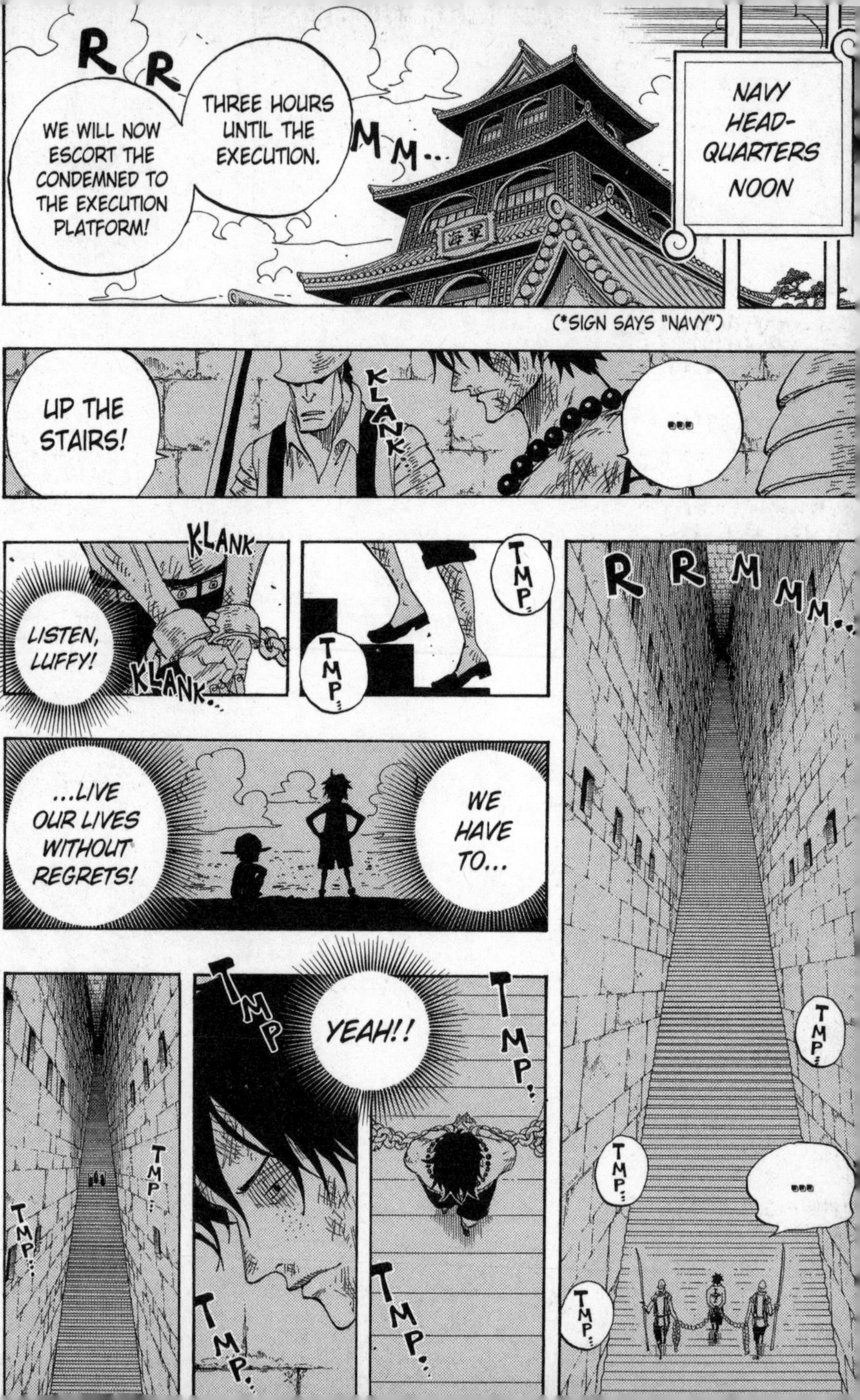
NAVY HEADQUARTERS NOON
RRRMMM...
THREE HOURS UNTIL THE EXECUTION.
WE WILL NOW ESCORT THE CONDEMNED TO THE EXECUTION PLATFORM!
(*SIGN SAYS "NAVY")
...
KLANK...
UP THE STAIRS!
RRRMMMM...
TMP...
...
TMP...
TMP...
TMP...
TMP...
KLANK
LISTEN, LUFFY!
KLANK...
WE HAVE TO...
...LIVE OUR LIVES WITHOUT REGRETS!
TMP
TMP...
YEAH!!
TMP
TMP...
TMP...
TMP...
TMP...

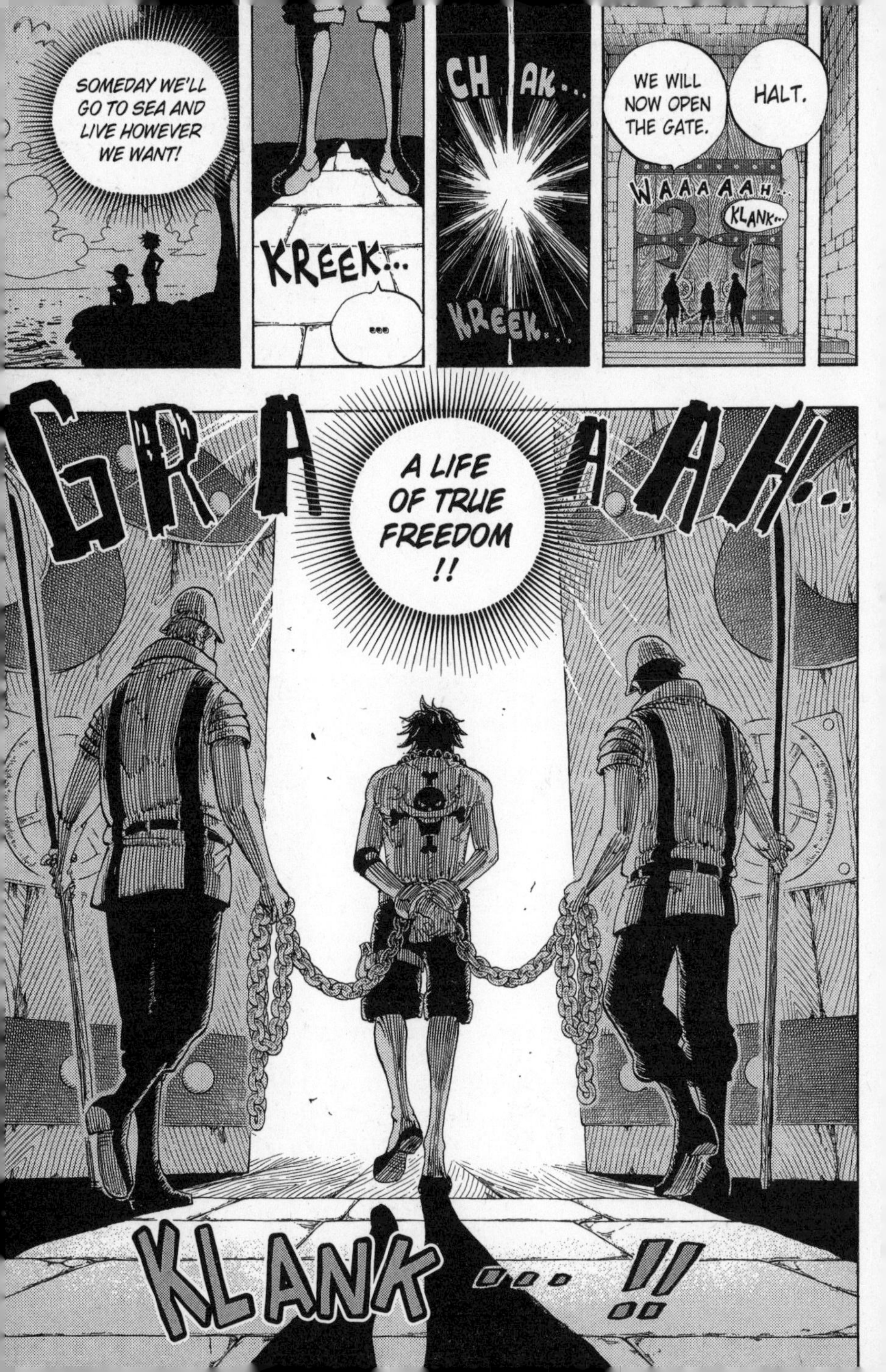
HALT.
WE WILL NOW OPEN THE GATE.
WAAAAAH...
KLANK...
CHAK...
KREEK...
KREEK...
...
SOMEDAY WE'LL GO TO SEA AND LIVE HOWEVER WE WANT!
GRAAAH...
A LIFE OF TRUE FREEDOM!!
KLANK...!!

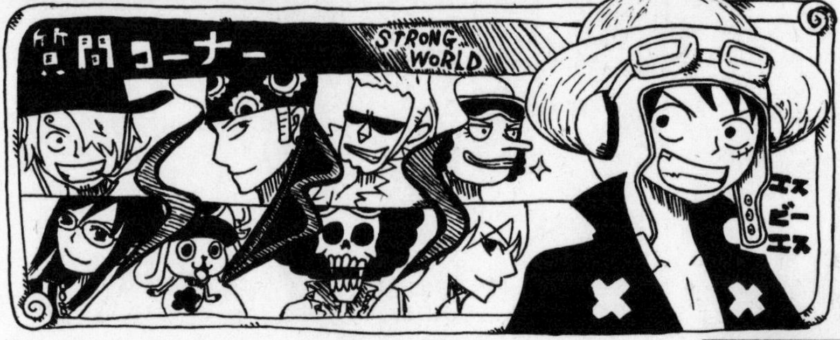
質問コーナー
STRONG WORLD
エスビーエス

(Chonkichi, Kanagawa)

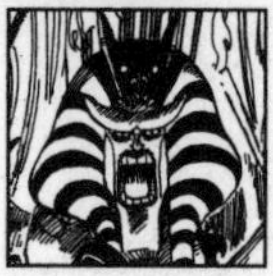

Q: What's inside Hannyabal's chin? Is it filled with dreams?

--Sappina

A: Yeah, I guess. It's filled with dreams by the name of ambition.

Q: Nice to meet you, Mr. Oda. I have a question. If *One Piece* took place in the real world, where would each of the Straw Hat Pirates be from?

--Michale Jackson's Brother

A: I didn't really put too much thought into this, but this would fit with their images.

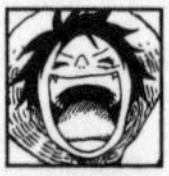
Luffy (Brazil)

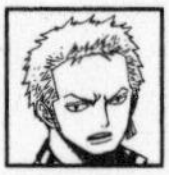
Zolo (Japan)

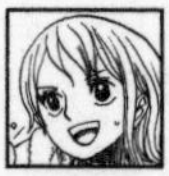
Nami (Sweden)

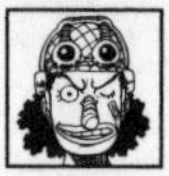
Usopp (Africa)

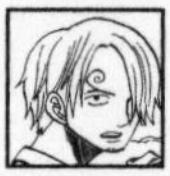
Sanji (France)

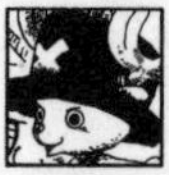
Chopper (Canada)

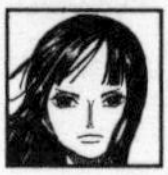
Robin (Russia)

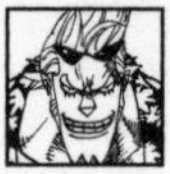
Franky (America)

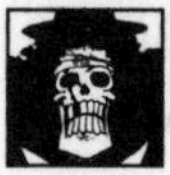
Brook (Austria)

Q: Iva's Death Wink creates some really weird sound effects. Tell me how I'm supposed to say them! ♡

--Muffy the Straw Hat

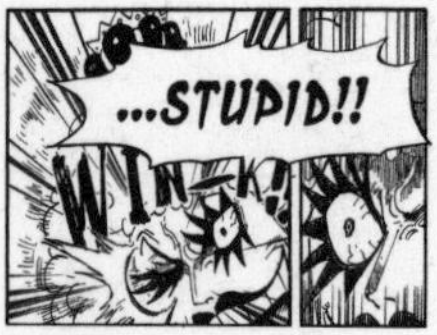
...STUPID!!

A: You sure got a sharp eye there. I gave it that particular sound effect because no ordinary sound effect could completely express what a powerful blast it is. Sometimes, I forget about it when drawing the drafts, but I always end up adding it back in. Say it with me, everybody! Blinkity Blink! Anyways, that's it for this volume's Question Corner! The voice actor Question Corner will also be taking a break this time around. See you next volume!

Chapter 550:
NAVY HEADQUARTERS

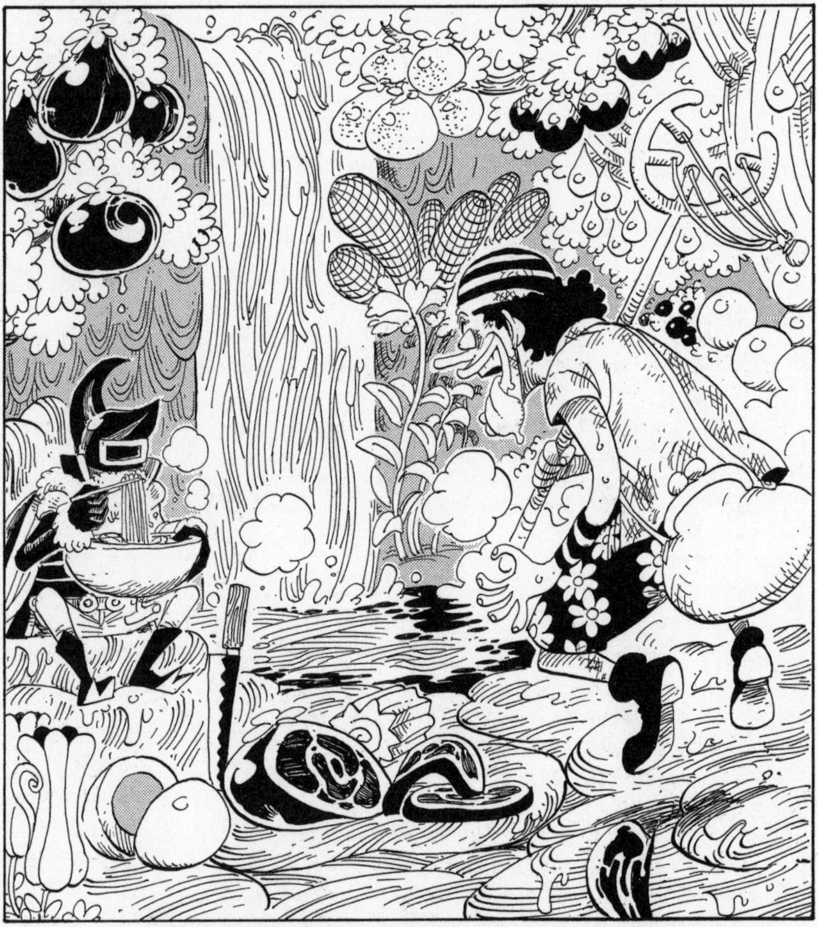

LIMITED COVER SERIES, NO. 14: USOPP'S "I'LL DIE IF I'M ALONE DISEASE" VOL. 1: "BOWIN ISLAND IS A FOREST OF GLUTTONY"

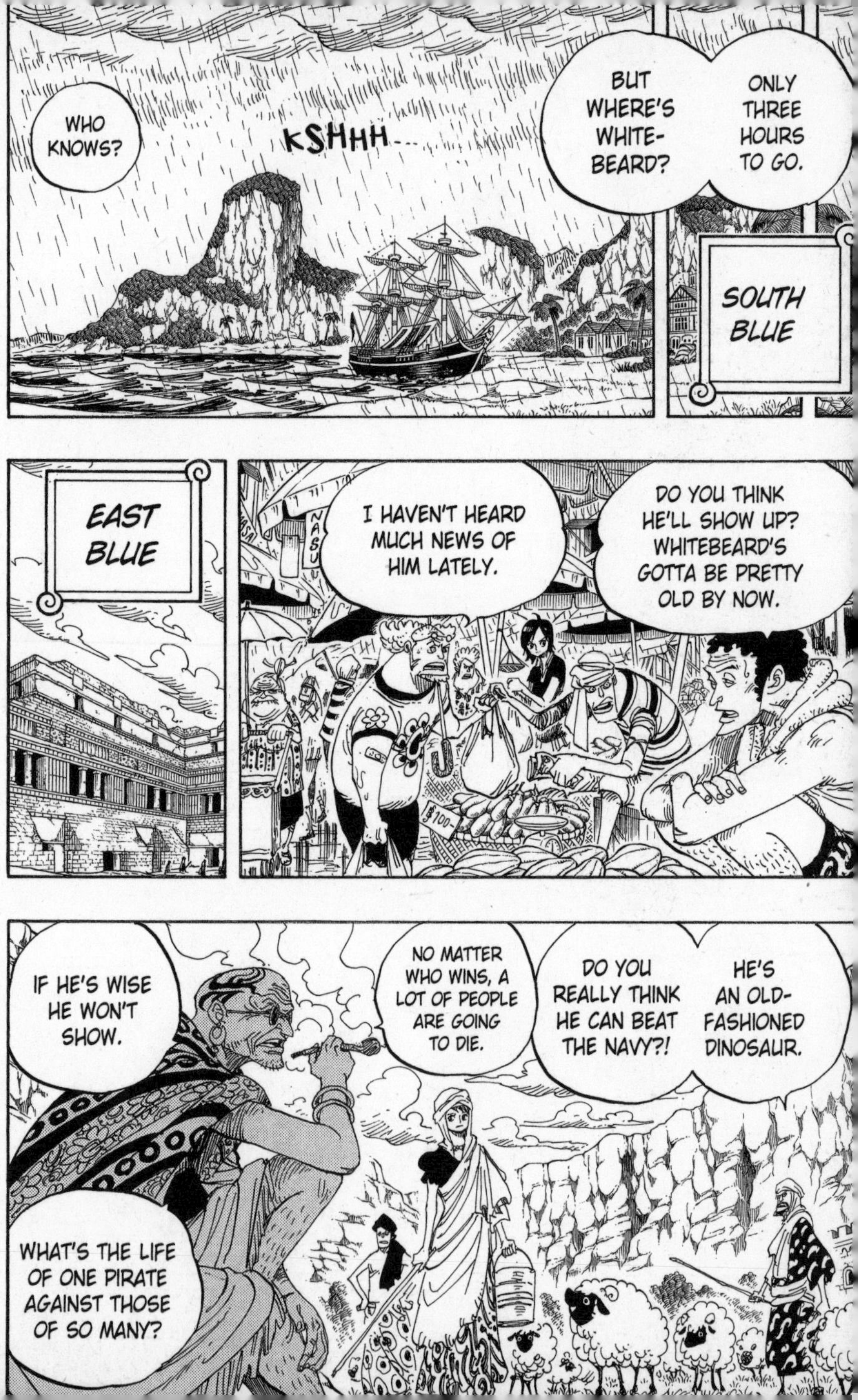
SOUTH BLUE
ONLY THREE HOURS TO GO.
BUT WHERE'S WHITE-BEARD?
KSHHH...
WHO KNOWS?
DO YOU THINK HE'LL SHOW UP? WHITEBEARD'S GOTTA BE PRETTY OLD BY NOW.
I HAVEN'T HEARD MUCH NEWS OF HIM LATELY.
EAST BLUE
HE'S AN OLD-FASHIONED DINOSAUR.
DO YOU REALLY THINK HE CAN BEAT THE NAVY?!
NO MATTER WHO WINS, A LOT OF PEOPLE ARE GOING TO DIE.
IF HE'S WISE HE WON'T SHOW.
WHAT'S THE LIFE OF ONE PIRATE AGAINST THOSE OF SO MANY?

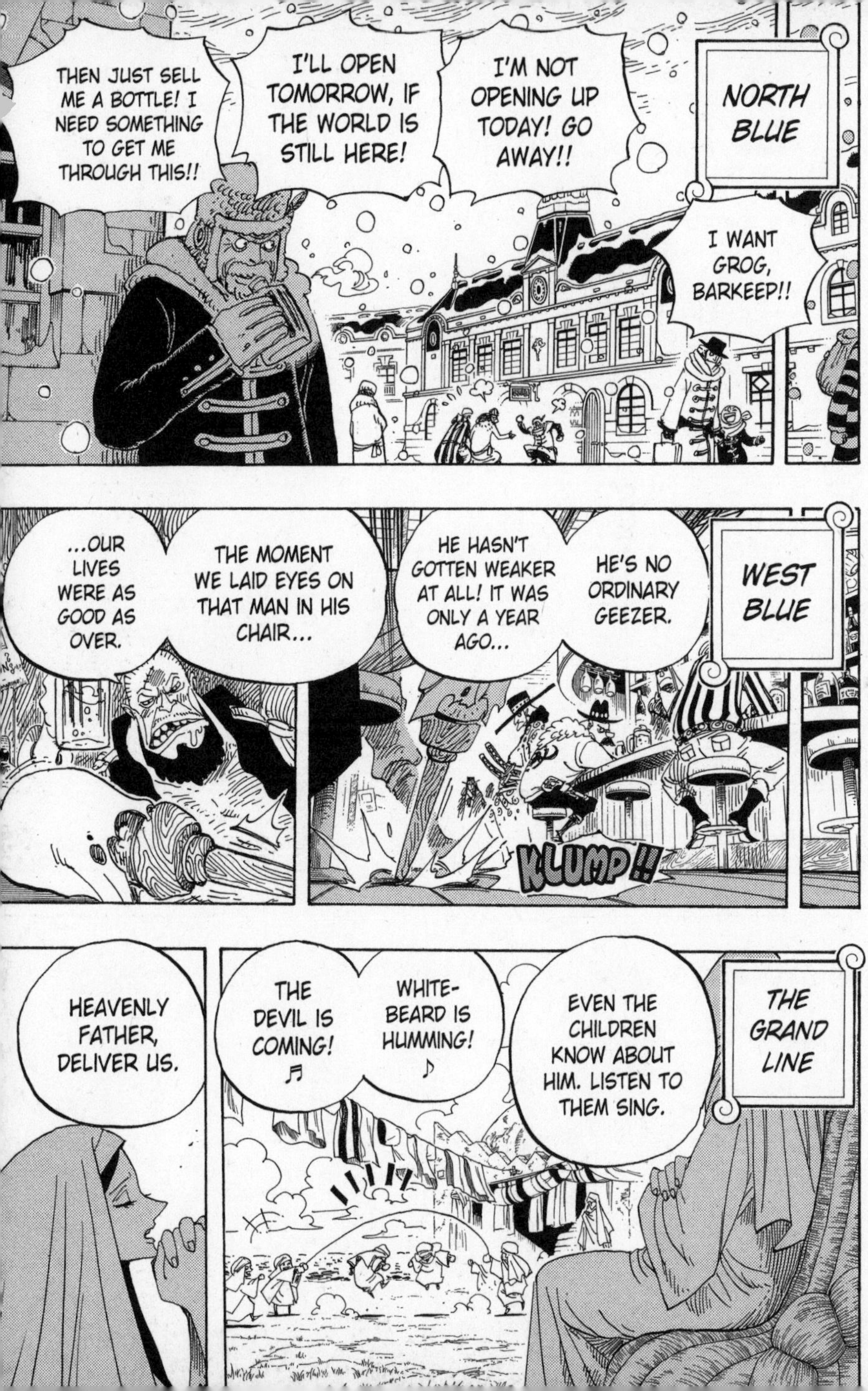
NORTH BLUE
I WANT GROG, BARKEEP!!
I'M NOT OPENING UP TODAY! GO AWAY!!
I'LL OPEN TOMORROW, IF THE WORLD IS STILL HERE!
THEN JUST SELL ME A BOTTLE! I NEED SOMETHING TO GET ME THROUGH THIS!!
WEST BLUE
HE'S NO ORDINARY GEEZER.
HE HASN'T GOTTEN WEAKER AT ALL! IT WAS ONLY A YEAR AGO...
KLUMP!!
THE MOMENT WE LAID EYES ON THAT MAN IN HIS CHAIR...
...OUR LIVES WERE AS GOOD AS OVER.
THE GRAND LINE
EVEN THE CHILDREN KNOW ABOUT HIM. LISTEN TO THEM SING.
WHITE-BEARD IS HUMMING! ♪
THE DEVIL IS COMING! ♬
HEAVENLY FATHER, DELIVER US.

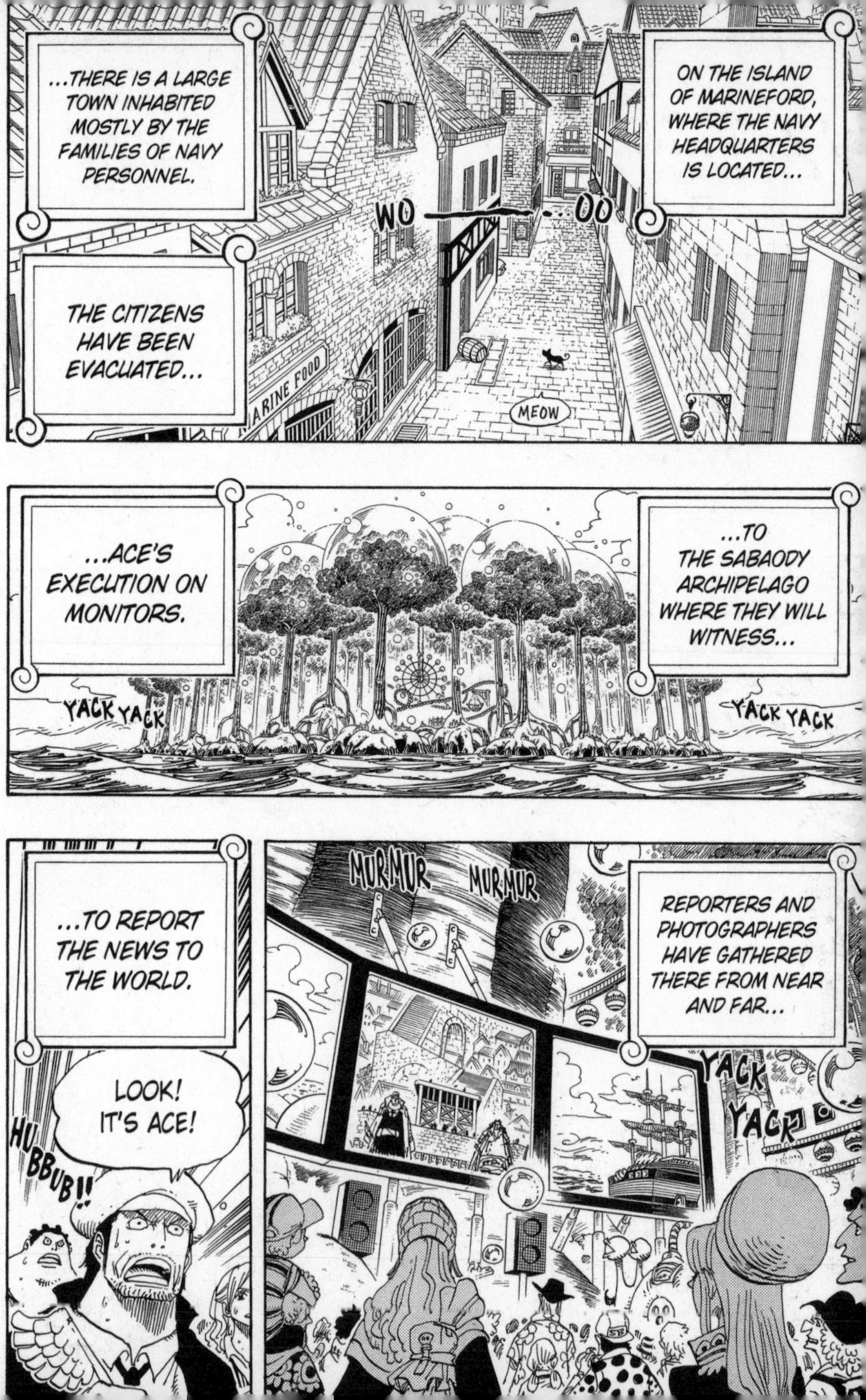
ON THE ISLAND OF MARINEFORD, WHERE THE NAVY HEADQUARTERS IS LOCATED...
...THERE IS A LARGE TOWN INHABITED MOSTLY BY THE FAMILIES OF NAVY PERSONNEL.
WO—OO
THE CITIZENS HAVE BEEN EVACUATED...
ARINE FOOD
MEOW
...TO THE SABAODY ARCHIPELAGO WHERE THEY WILL WITNESS...
...ACE'S EXECUTION ON MONITORS.
YACK YACK
YACK YACK
REPORTERS AND PHOTOGRAPHERS HAVE GATHERED THERE FROM NEAR AND FAR...
MURMUR
MURMUR
YACK YACK
...TO REPORT THE NEWS TO THE WORLD.
LOOK! IT'S ACE!
HUBBUB!!

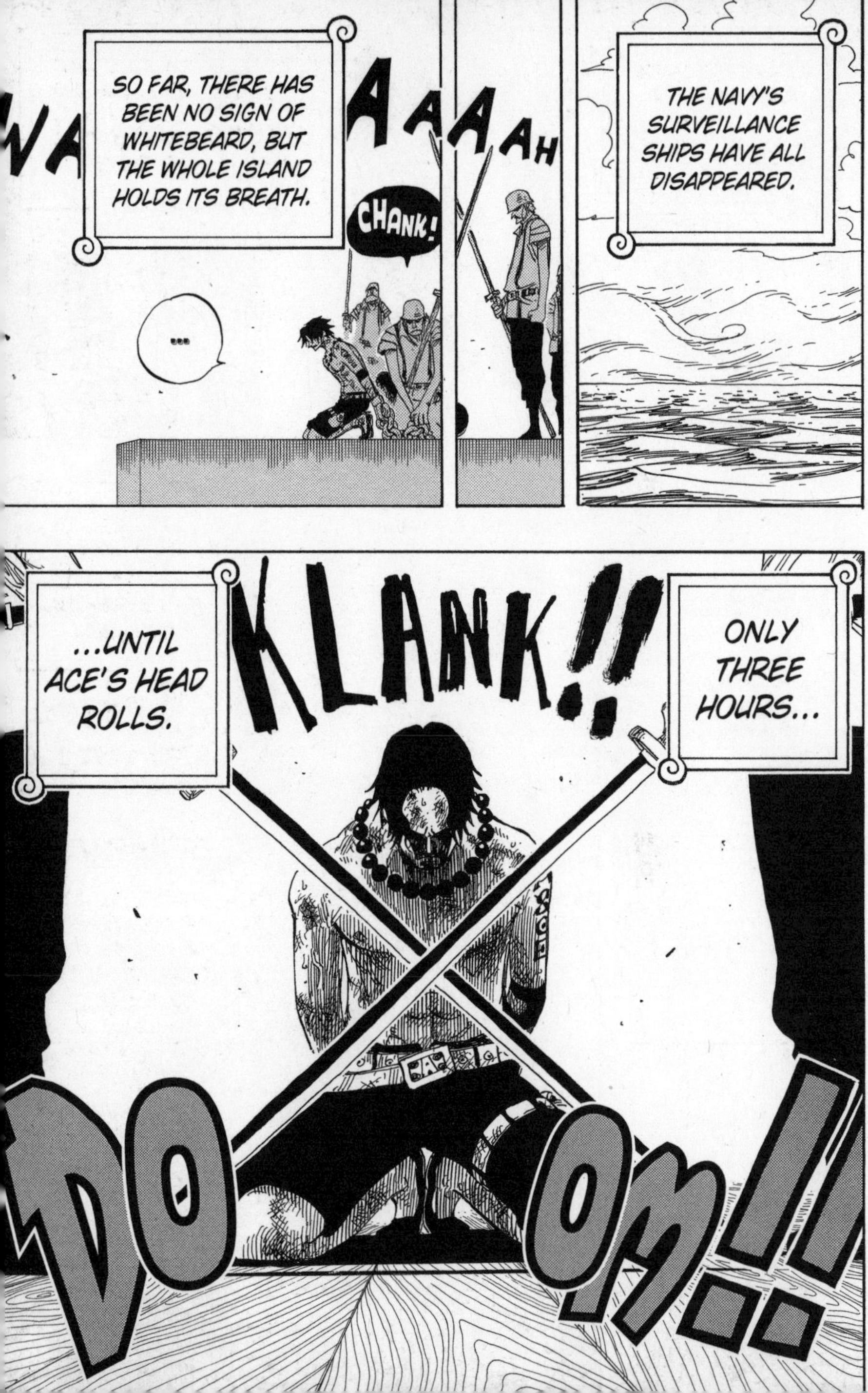
THE NAVY'S SURVEILLANCE SHIPS HAVE ALL DISAPPEARED.
SO FAR, THERE HAS BEEN NO SIGN OF WHITEBEARD, BUT THE WHOLE ISLAND HOLDS ITS BREATH.
WAAAAAH
CHANK!
...
ONLY THREE HOURS...
KLANK!!
...UNTIL ACE'S HEAD ROLLS.
DOOM!!

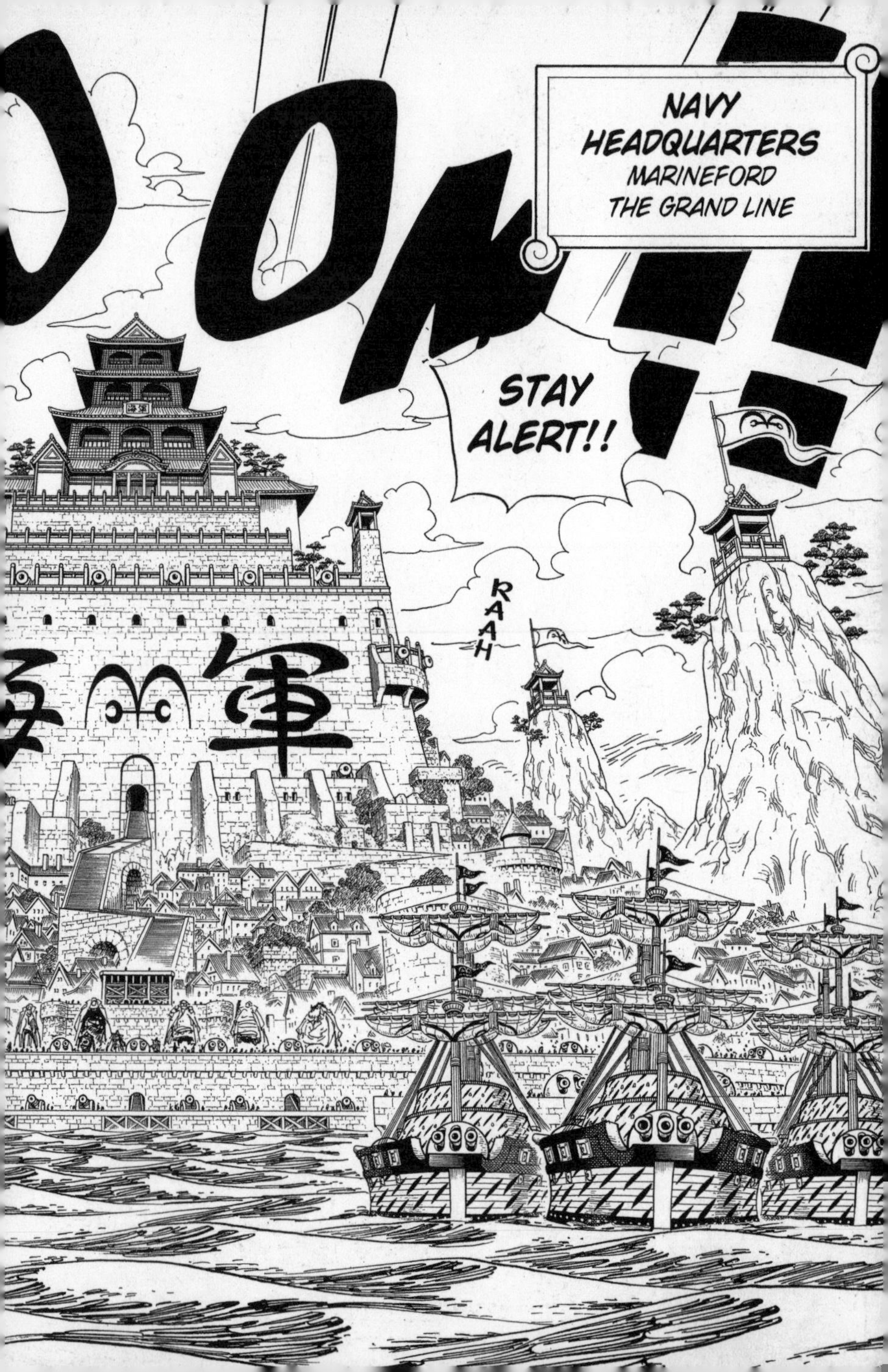
NAVY HEADQUARTERS
MARINEFORD
THE GRAND LINE
STAY ALERT!!
RAAAH

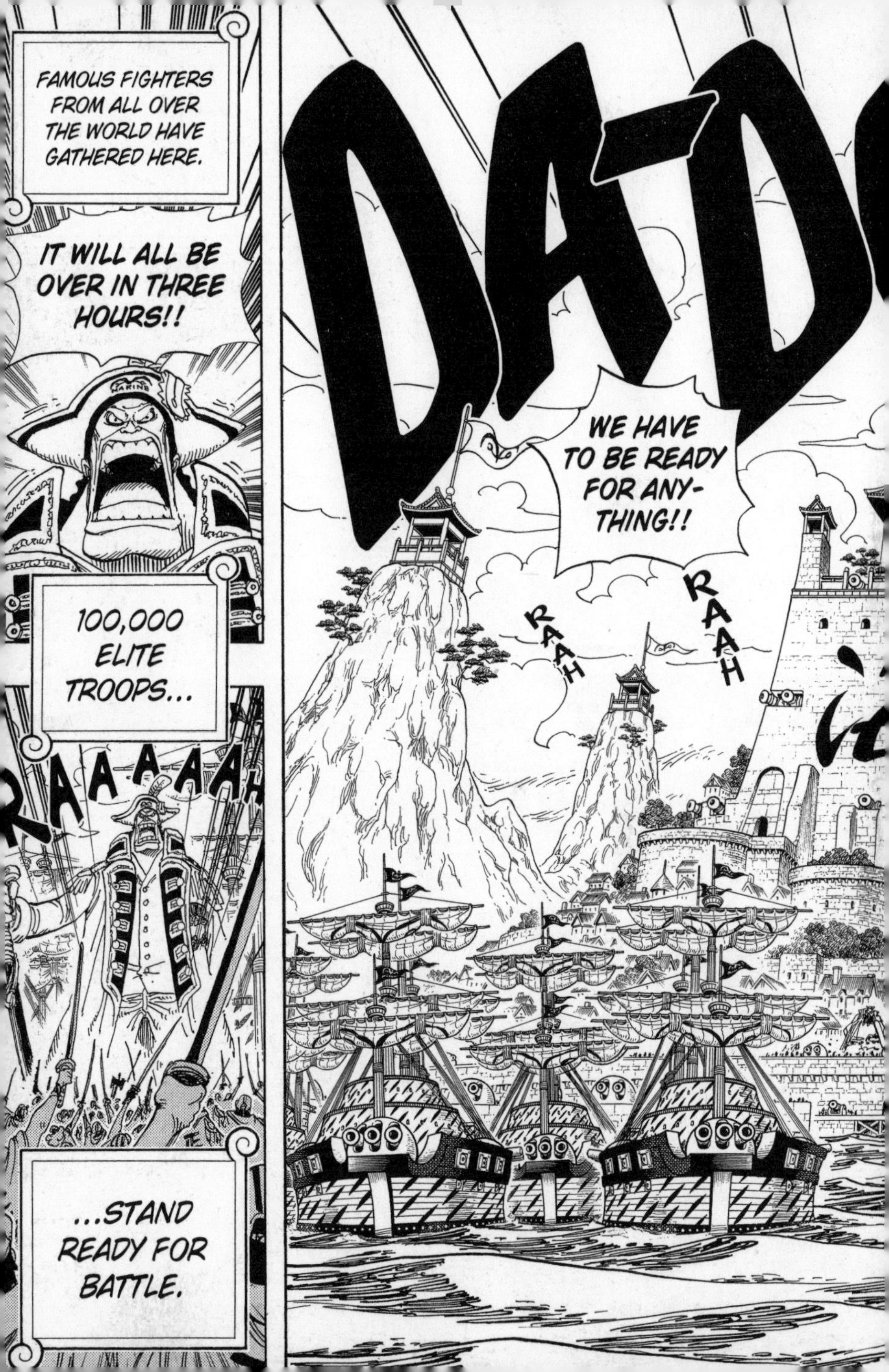
DA-D
WE HAVE TO BE READY FOR ANYTHING!!
RAAH
RAAH
FAMOUS FIGHTERS FROM ALL OVER THE WORLD HAVE GATHERED HERE.
IT WILL ALL BE OVER IN THREE HOURS!!
100,000 ELITE TROOPS...
RAAAAAAH
...STAND READY FOR BATTLE.

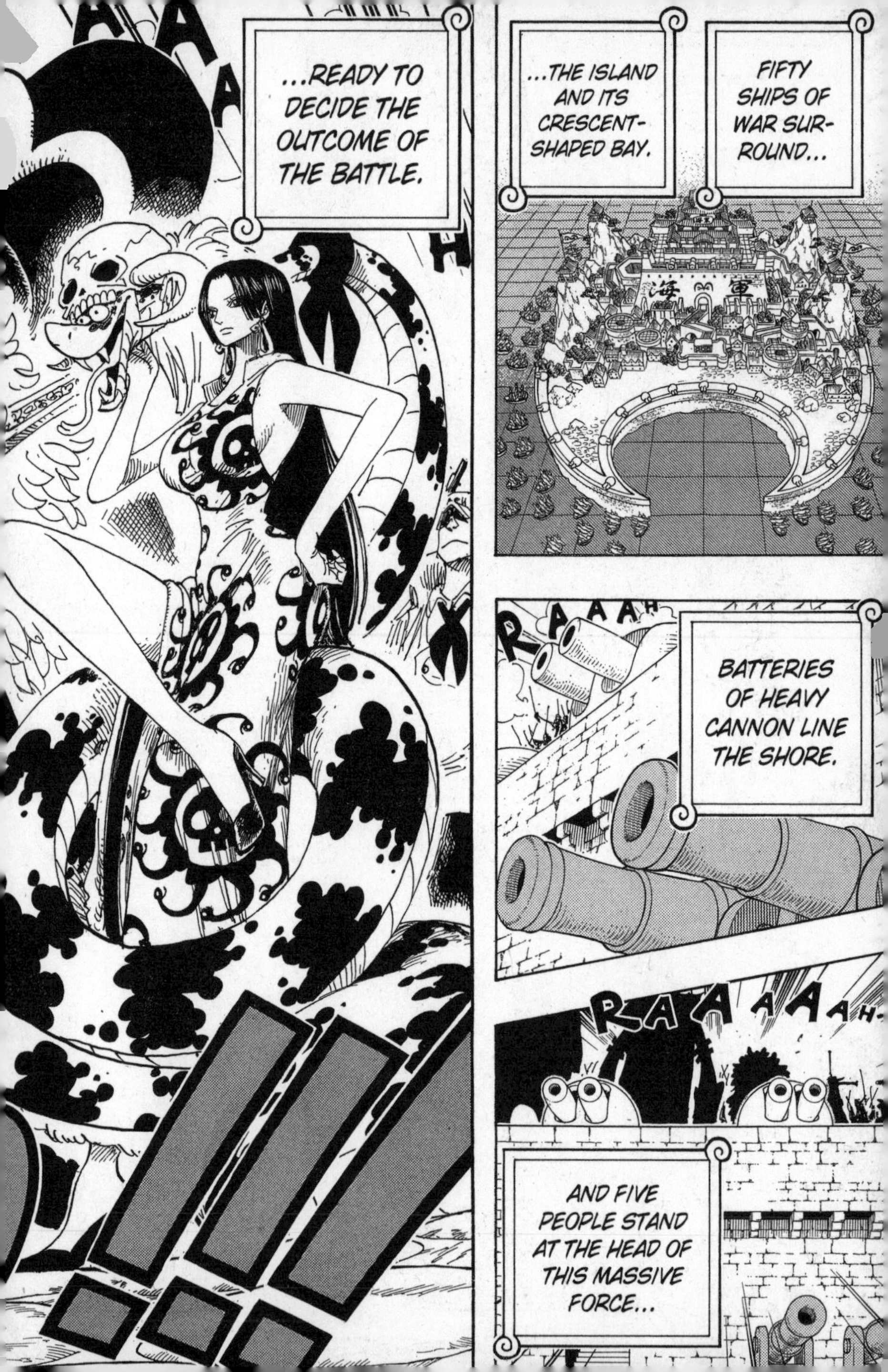
FIFTY SHIPS OF WAR SURROUND...
...THE ISLAND AND ITS CRESCENT-SHAPED BAY.
海軍
RAAAH
BATTERIES OF HEAVY CANNON LINE THE SHORE.
RAAAAAH-
AND FIVE PEOPLE STAND AT THE HEAD OF THIS MASSIVE FORCE...
...READY TO DECIDE THE OUTCOME OF THE BATTLE.

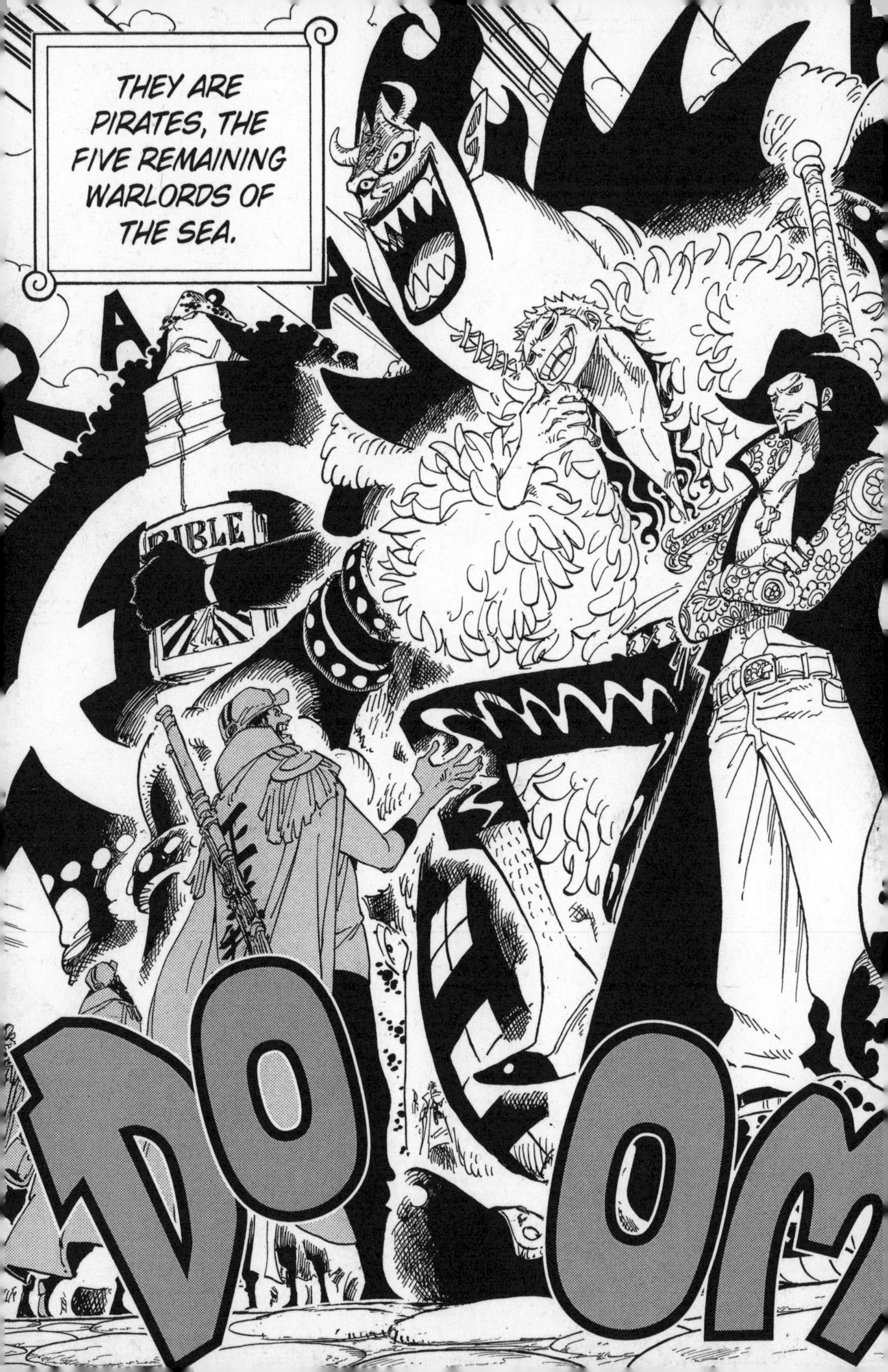
THEY ARE PIRATES, THE FIVE REMAINING WARLORDS OF THE SEA.
BIBLE
DOOM

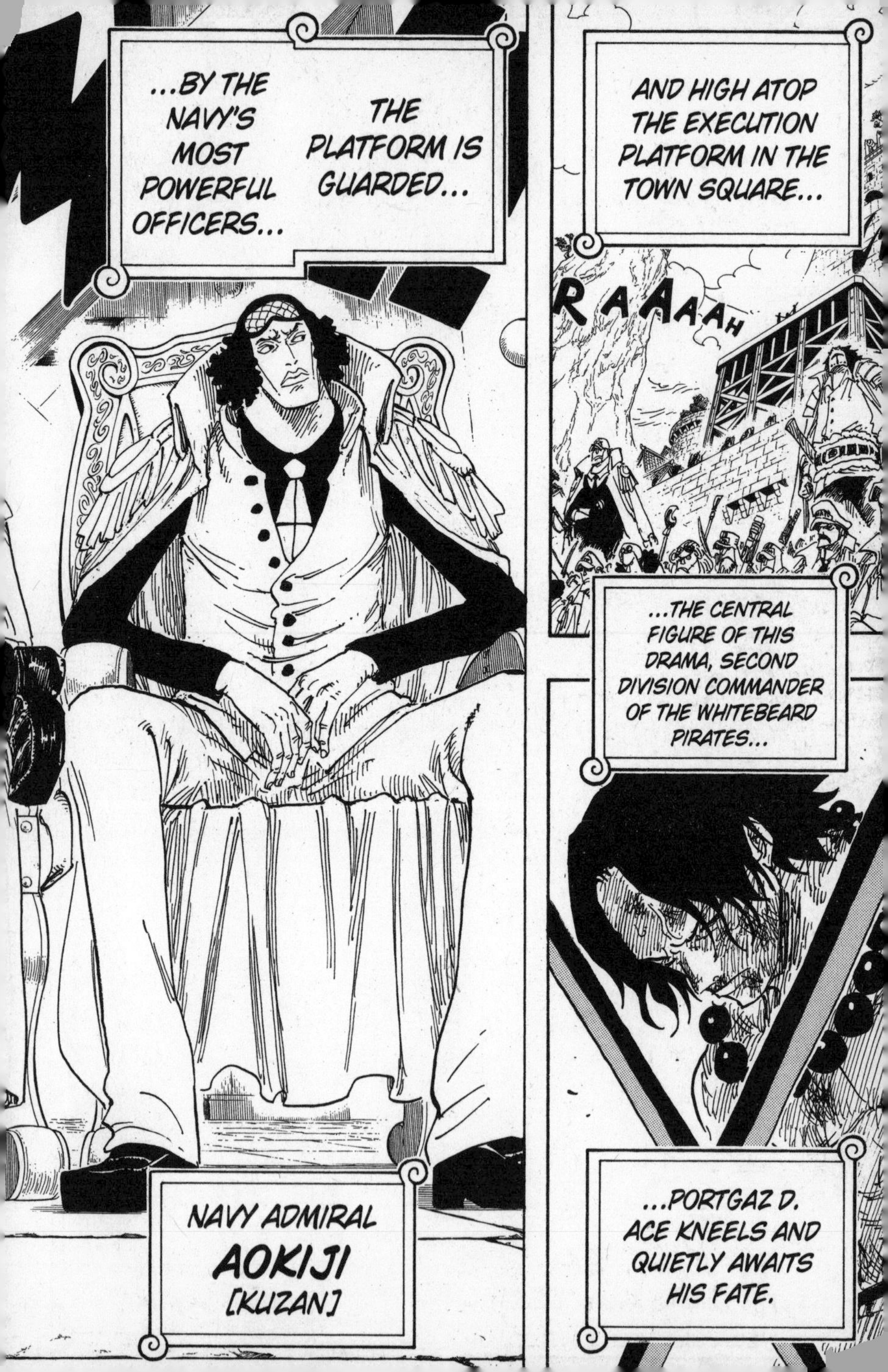
AND HIGH ATOP THE EXECUTION PLATFORM IN THE TOWN SQUARE...
RAAAAAH
...THE CENTRAL FIGURE OF THIS DRAMA, SECOND DIVISION COMMANDER OF THE WHITEBEARD PIRATES...
...PORTGAZ D. ACE KNEELS AND QUIETLY AWAITS HIS FATE.
THE PLATFORM IS GUARDED...
...BY THE NAVY'S MOST POWERFUL OFFICERS...
NAVY ADMIRAL
AOKIJI
[KUZAN]

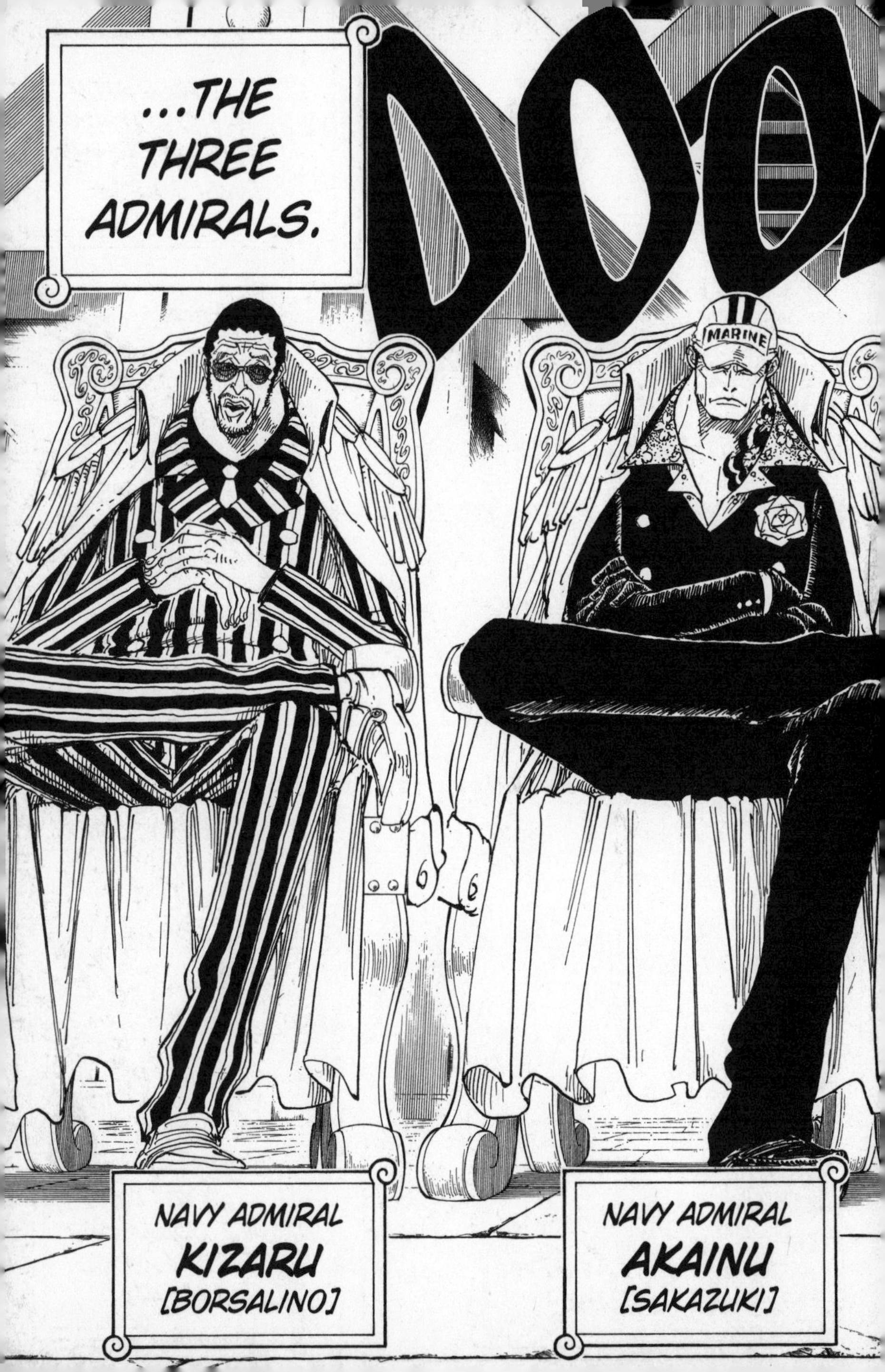
DOO
...THE THREE ADMIRALS.
NAVY ADMIRAL AKAINU [SAKAZUKI]
NAVY ADMIRAL KIZARU [BORSALINO]

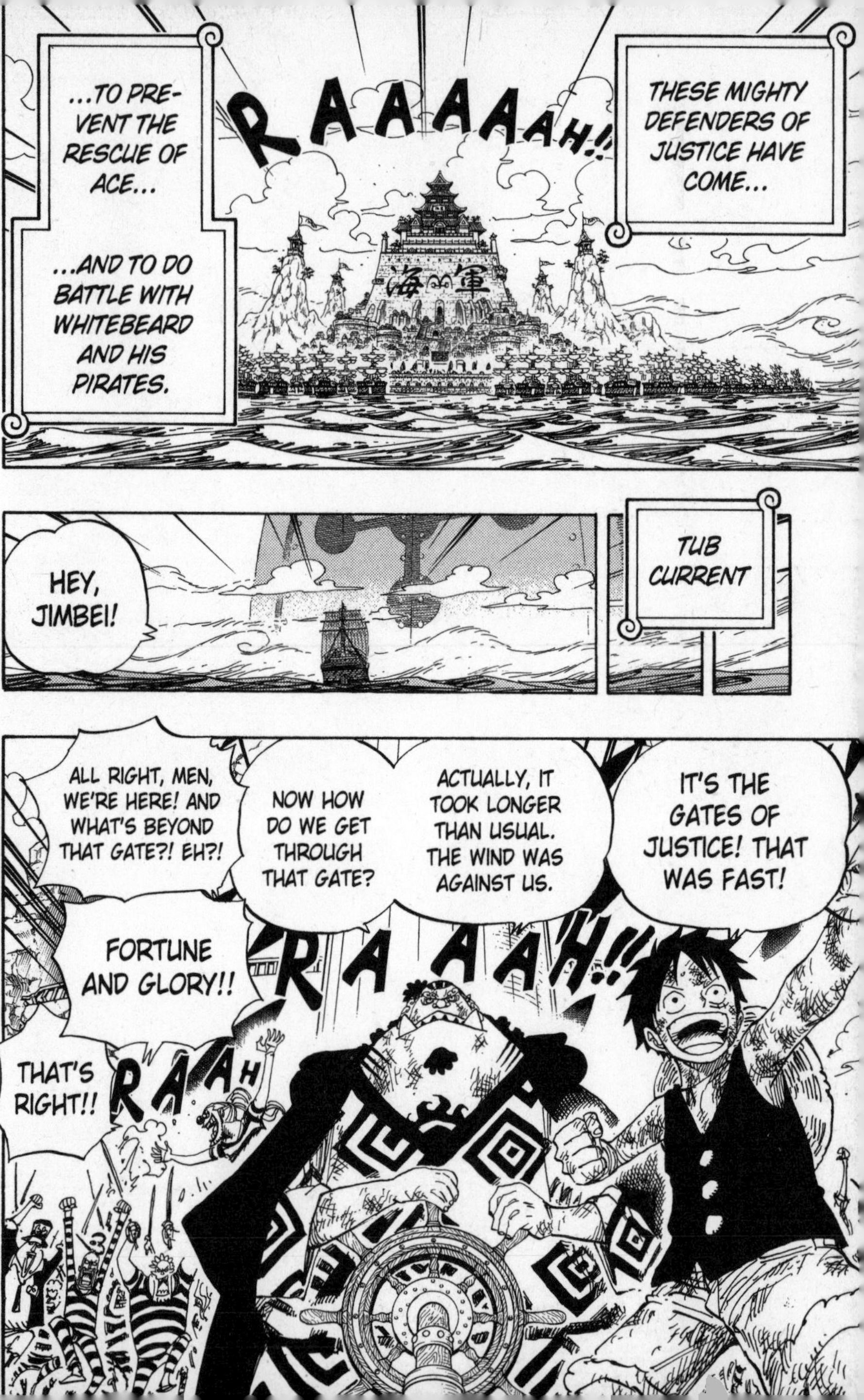
THESE MIGHTY DEFENDERS OF JUSTICE HAVE COME...
RAAAAAAH!!
海軍
...TO PRE-VENT THE RESCUE OF ACE...
...AND TO DO BATTLE WITH WHITEBEARD AND HIS PIRATES.
TUB CURRENT
HEY, JIMBEI!
IT'S THE GATES OF JUSTICE! THAT WAS FAST!
ACTUALLY, IT TOOK LONGER THAN USUAL. THE WIND WAS AGAINST US.
NOW HOW DO WE GET THROUGH THAT GATE?
ALL RIGHT, MEN, WE'RE HERE! AND WHAT'S BEYOND THAT GATE?! EH?!
RAAAH!!
FORTUNE AND GLORY!!
RAAAH
THAT'S RIGHT!!

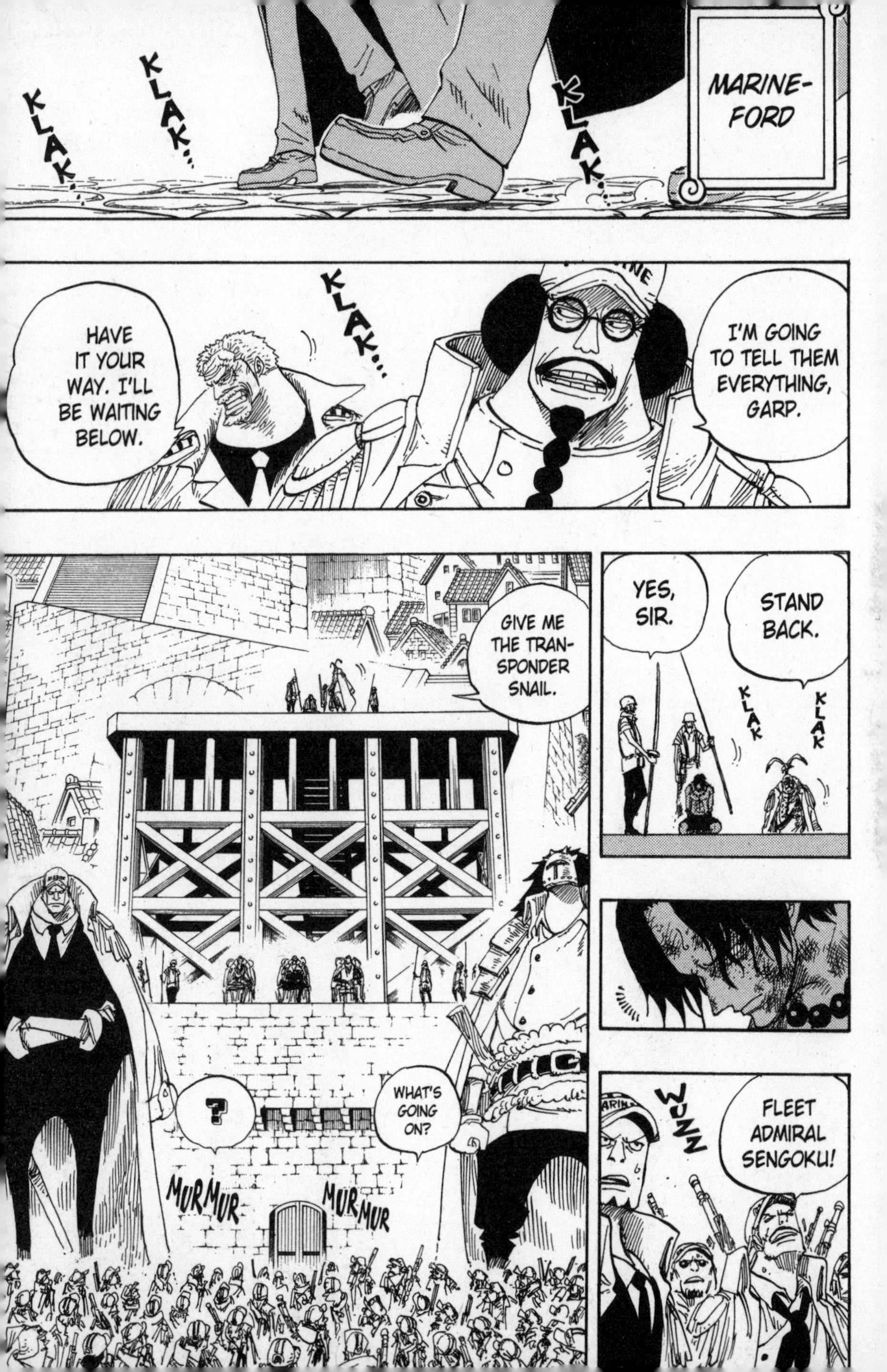
MARINE-FORD
KLAK...
KLAK...
KLAK...
I'M GOING TO TELL THEM EVERYTHING, GARP.
KLAK...
HAVE IT YOUR WAY. I'LL BE WAITING BELOW.
STAND BACK.
YES, SIR.
KLAK
KLAK
FLEET ADMIRAL SENGOKU!
WUZZ
GIVE ME THE TRAN-SPONDER SNAIL.
WHAT'S GOING ON?
?
MUR-MUR
MURMUR

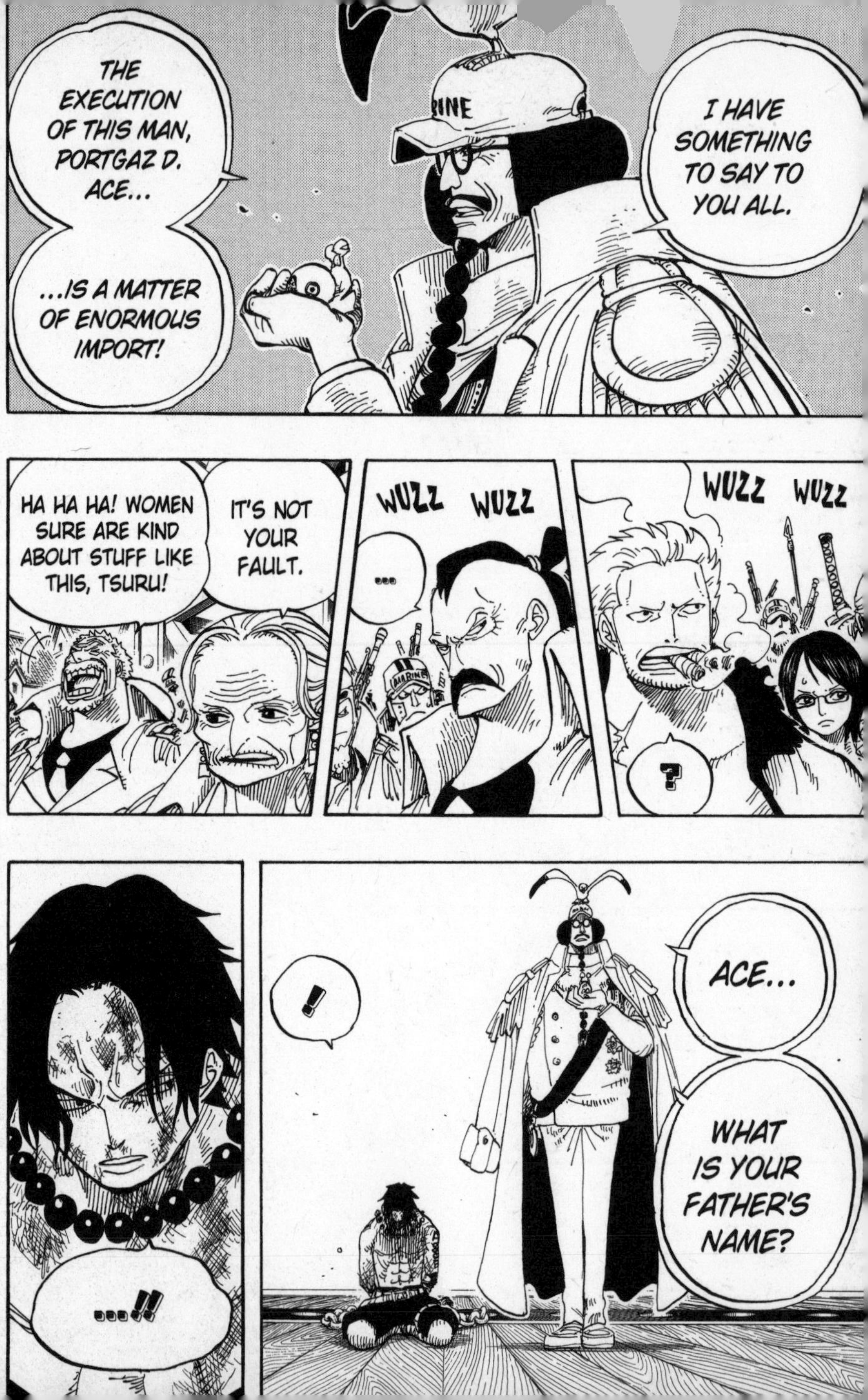
I HAVE SOMETHING TO SAY TO YOU ALL.
THE EXECUTION OF THIS MAN, PORTGAZ D. ACE...
...IS A MATTER OF ENORMOUS IMPORT!
WUZZ WUZZ
?
WUZZ WUZZ
...
IT'S NOT YOUR FAULT.
HA HA HA! WOMEN SURE ARE KIND ABOUT STUFF LIKE THIS, TSURU!
ACE...
WHAT IS YOUR FATHER'S NAME?
!
...!!

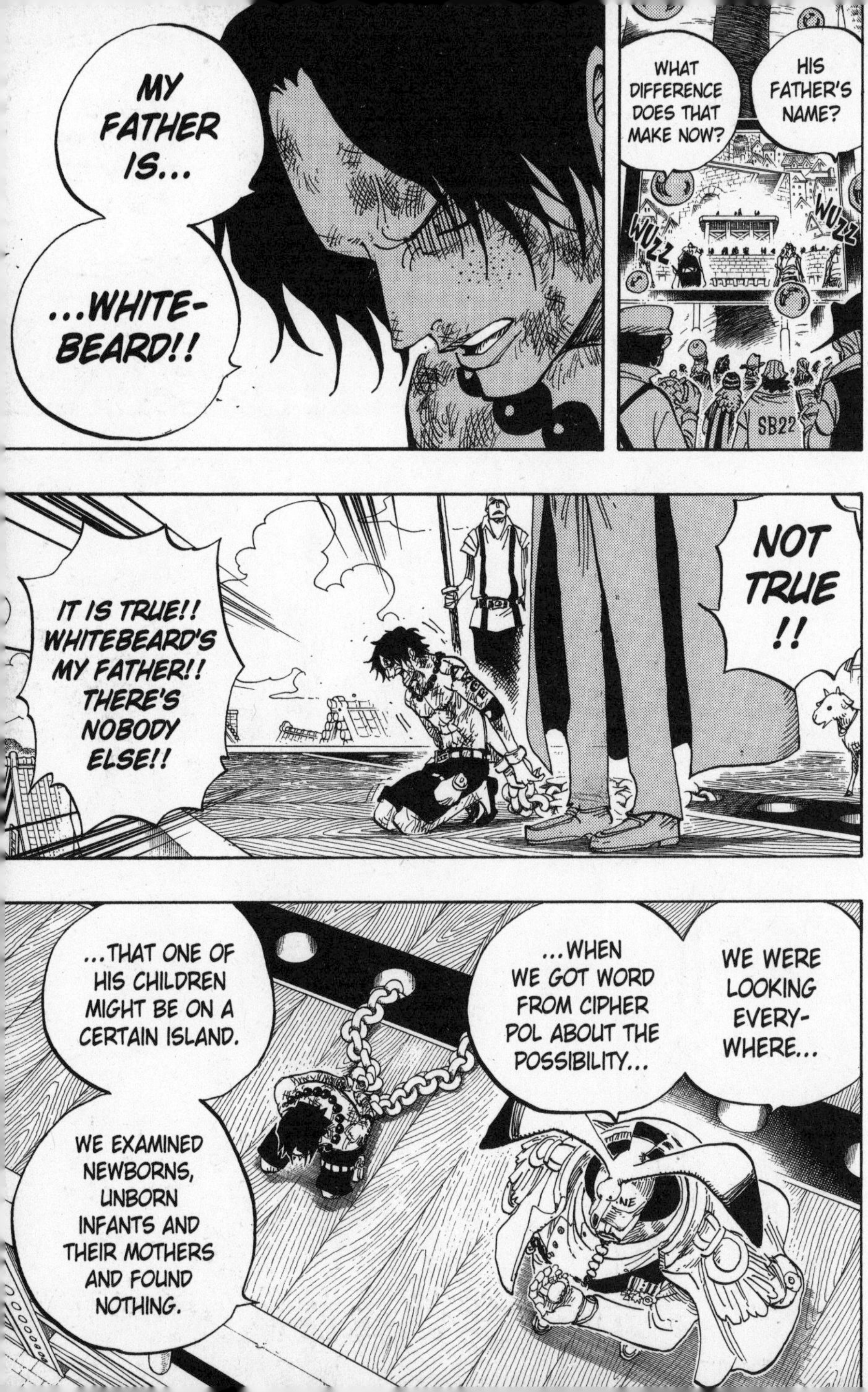
HIS FATHER'S NAME?
WHAT DIFFERENCE DOES THAT MAKE NOW?
WUZZ
WUZZ
MY FATHER IS...
...WHITE-BEARD!!
NOT TRUE!!
IT IS TRUE!! WHITEBEARD'S MY FATHER!! THERE'S NOBODY ELSE!!
WE WERE LOOKING EVERY-WHERE...
...WHEN WE GOT WORD FROM CIPHER POL ABOUT THE POSSIBILITY...
...THAT ONE OF HIS CHILDREN MIGHT BE ON A CERTAIN ISLAND.
WE EXAMINED NEWBORNS, UNBORN INFANTS AND THEIR MOTHERS AND FOUND NOTHING.

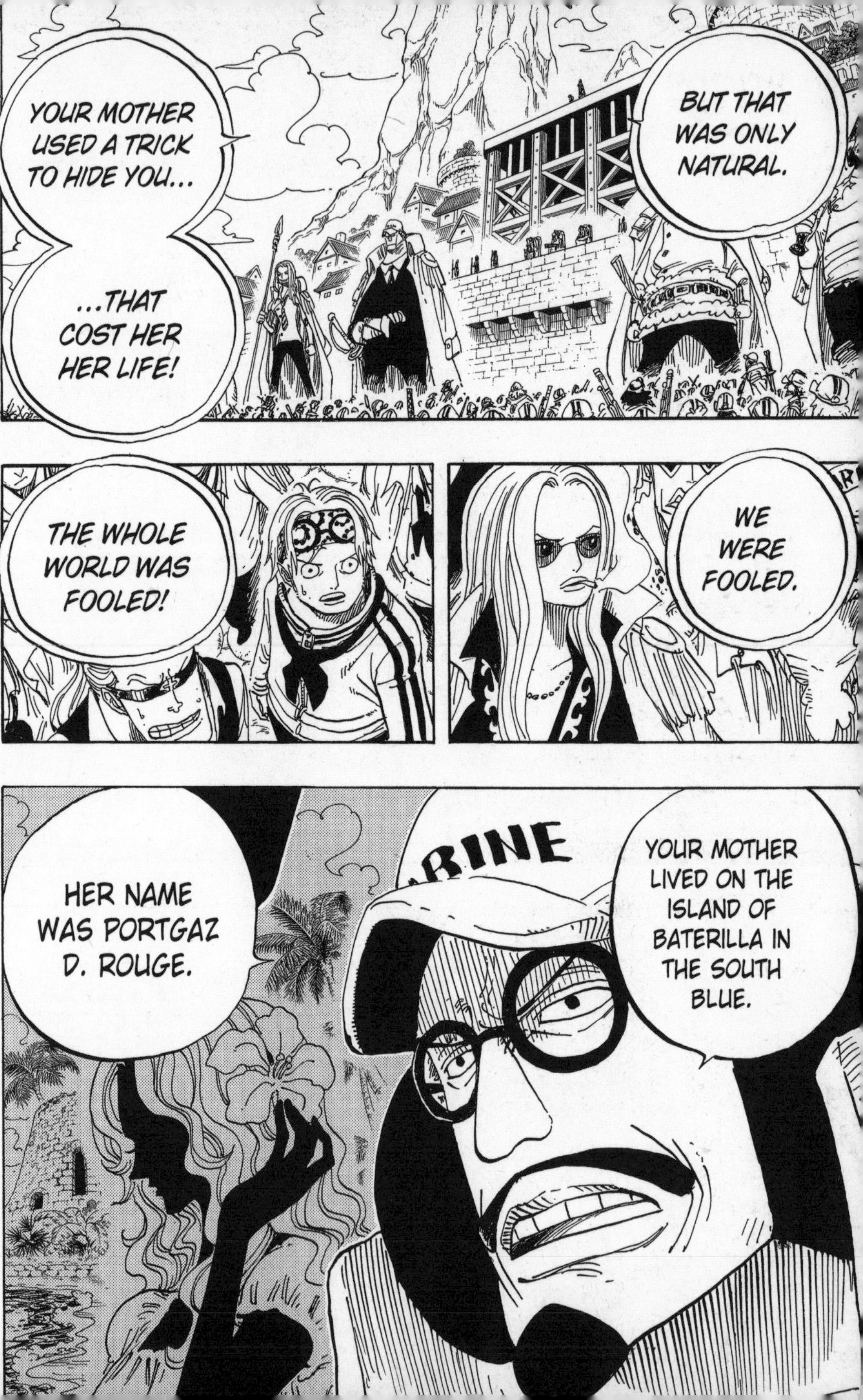
BUT THAT WAS ONLY NATURAL.
YOUR MOTHER USED A TRICK TO HIDE YOU...
...THAT COST HER HER LIFE!
WE WERE FOOLED.
THE WHOLE WORLD WAS FOOLED!
YOUR MOTHER LIVED ON THE ISLAND OF BATERILLA IN THE SOUTH BLUE.
HER NAME WAS PORTGAZ D. ROUGE.

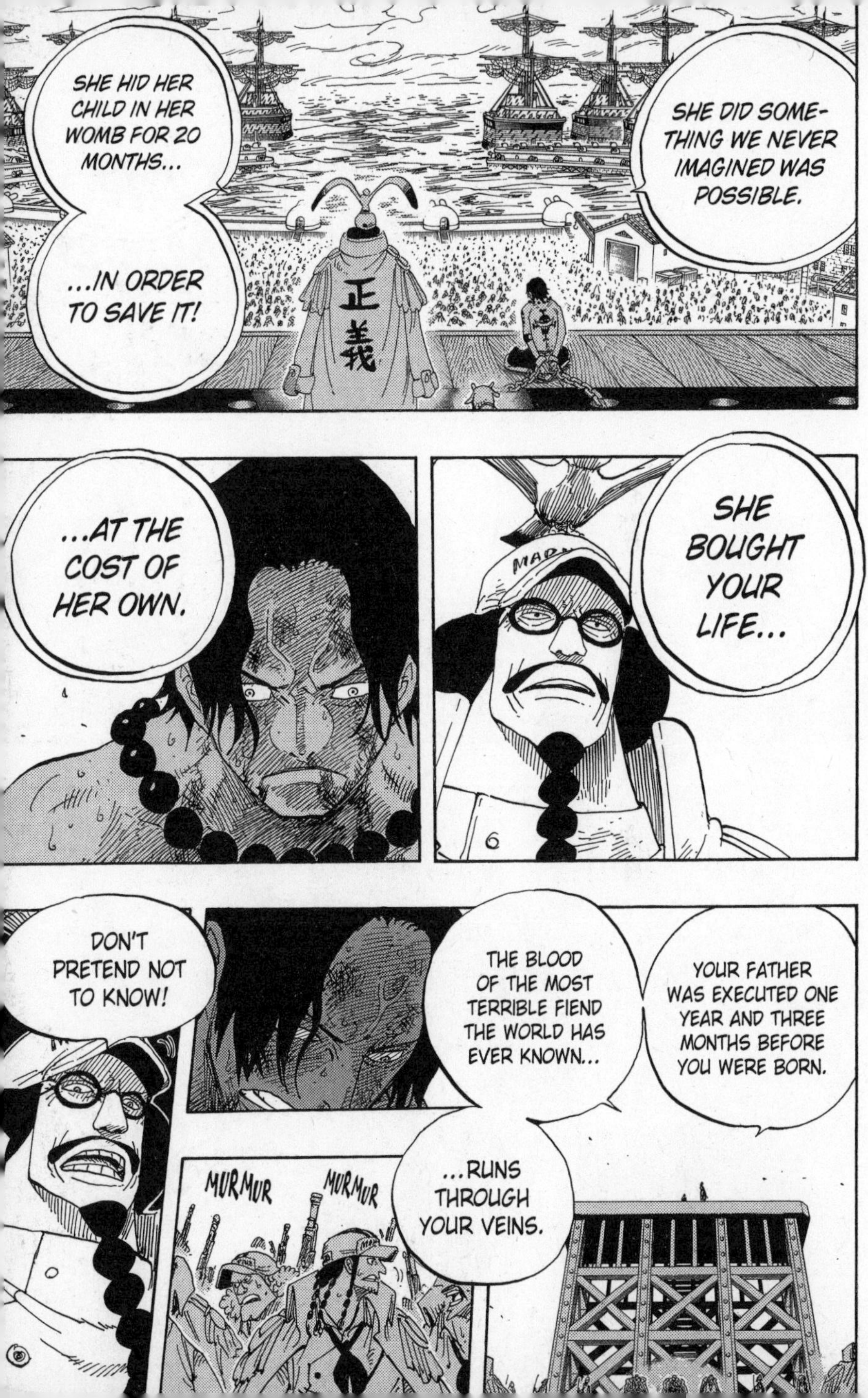
SHE DID SOME-THING WE NEVER IMAGINED WAS POSSIBLE.
SHE HID HER CHILD IN HER WOMB FOR 20 MONTHS...
...IN ORDER TO SAVE IT!
SHE BOUGHT YOUR LIFE...
...AT THE COST OF HER OWN.
YOUR FATHER WAS EXECUTED ONE YEAR AND THREE MONTHS BEFORE YOU WERE BORN.
THE BLOOD OF THE MOST TERRIBLE FIEND THE WORLD HAS EVER KNOWN...
...RUNS THROUGH YOUR VEINS.
MURMUR
MURMUR
DON'T PRETEND NOT TO KNOW!

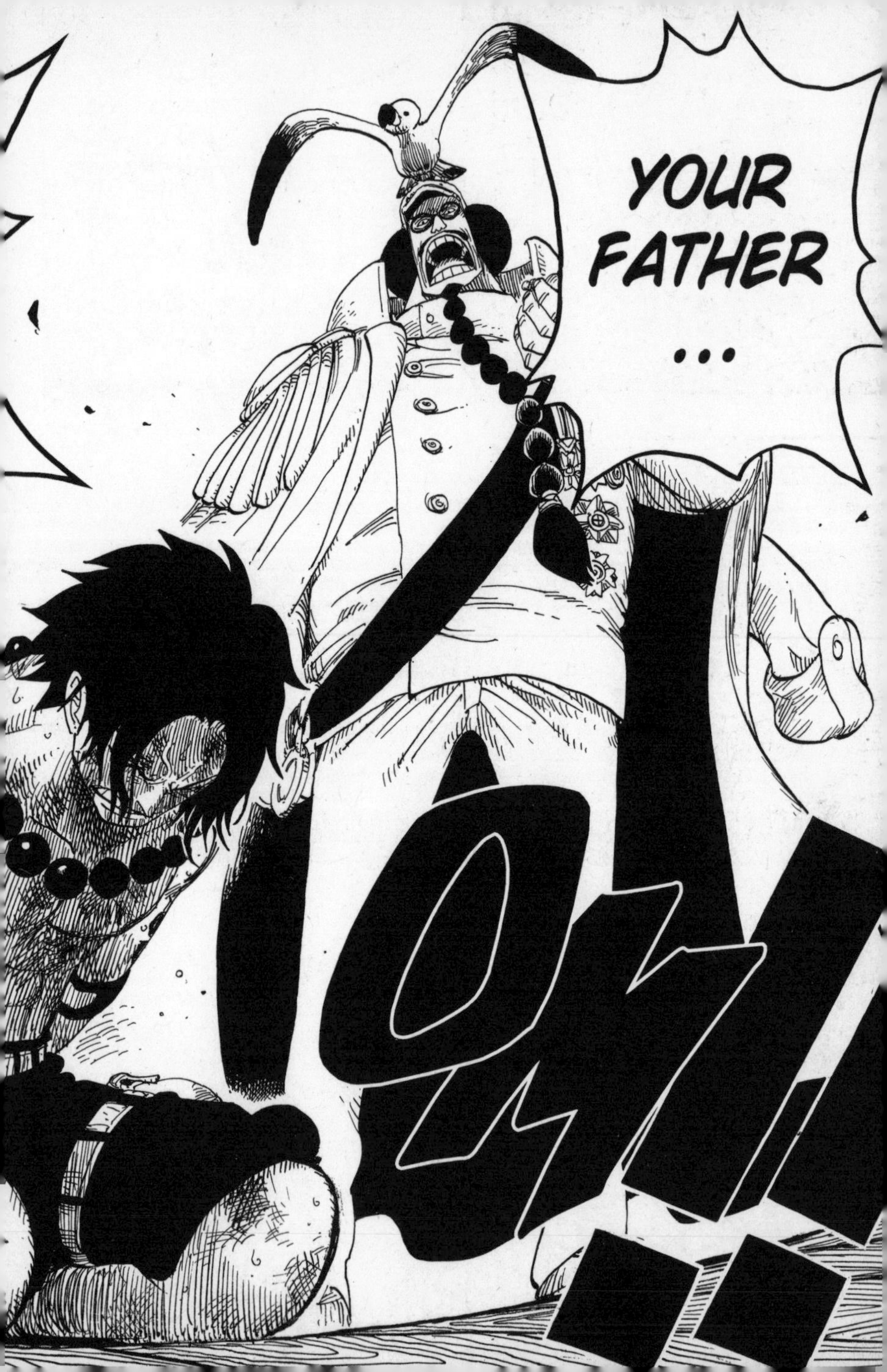
YOUR FATHER ...

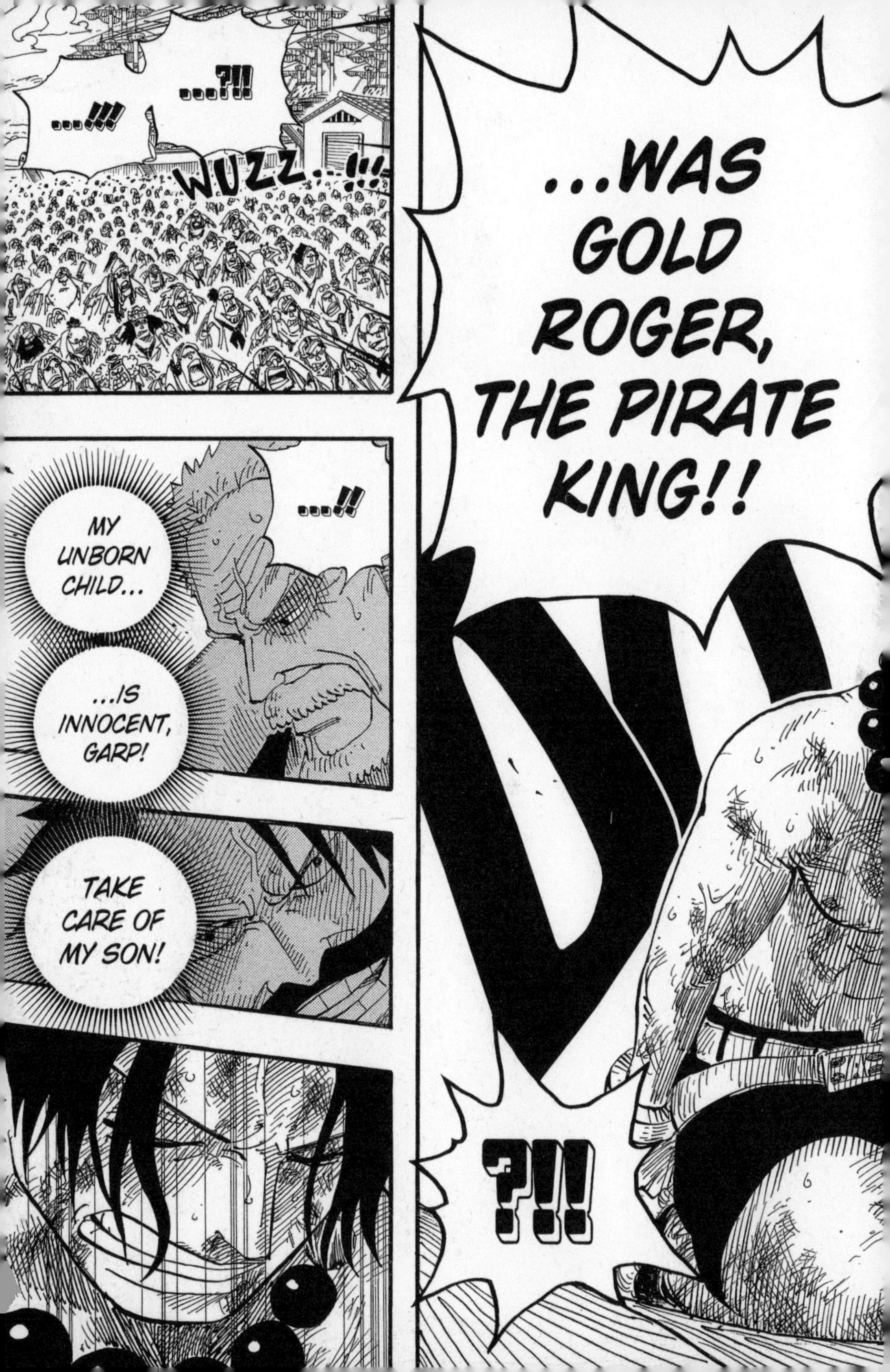
...WAS GOLD ROGER, THE PIRATE KING!!
?!!
...?!!
...!!!
WUZZ...!!!
...!!
MY UNBORN CHILD...
...IS INNOCENT, GARP!
TAKE CARE OF MY SON!

ONE PIECE vol.56

Chapter 551: WHITEBEARD OF THE FOUR EMPERORS

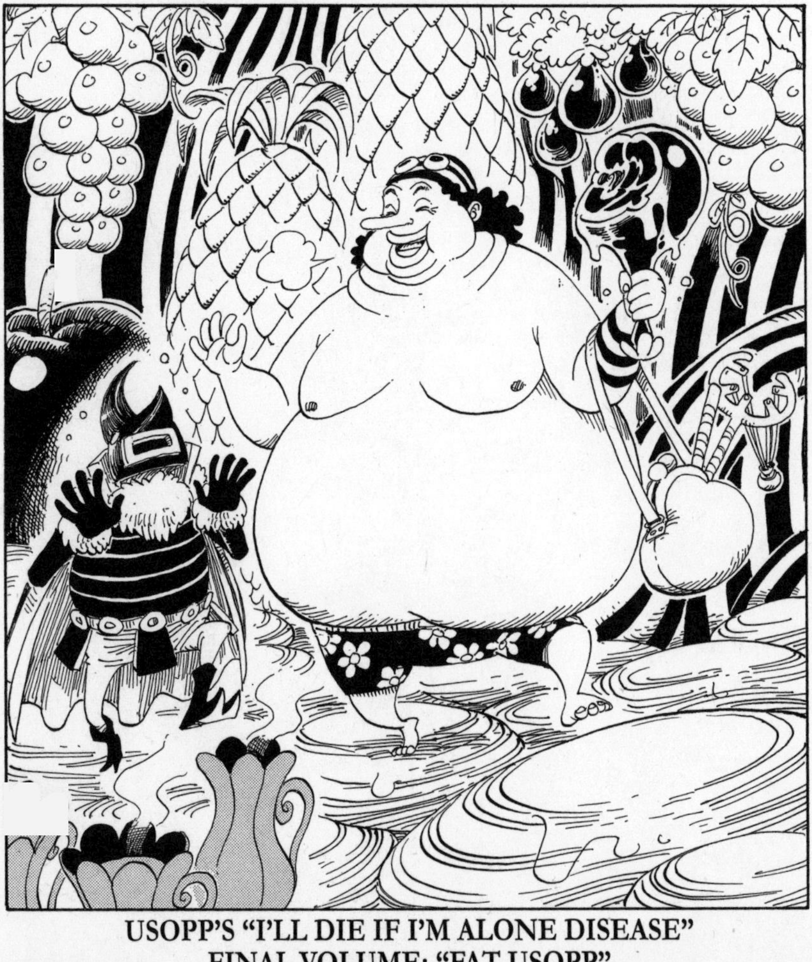

USOPP'S "I'LL DIE IF I'M ALONE DISEASE"
FINAL VOLUME: "FAT USOPP"

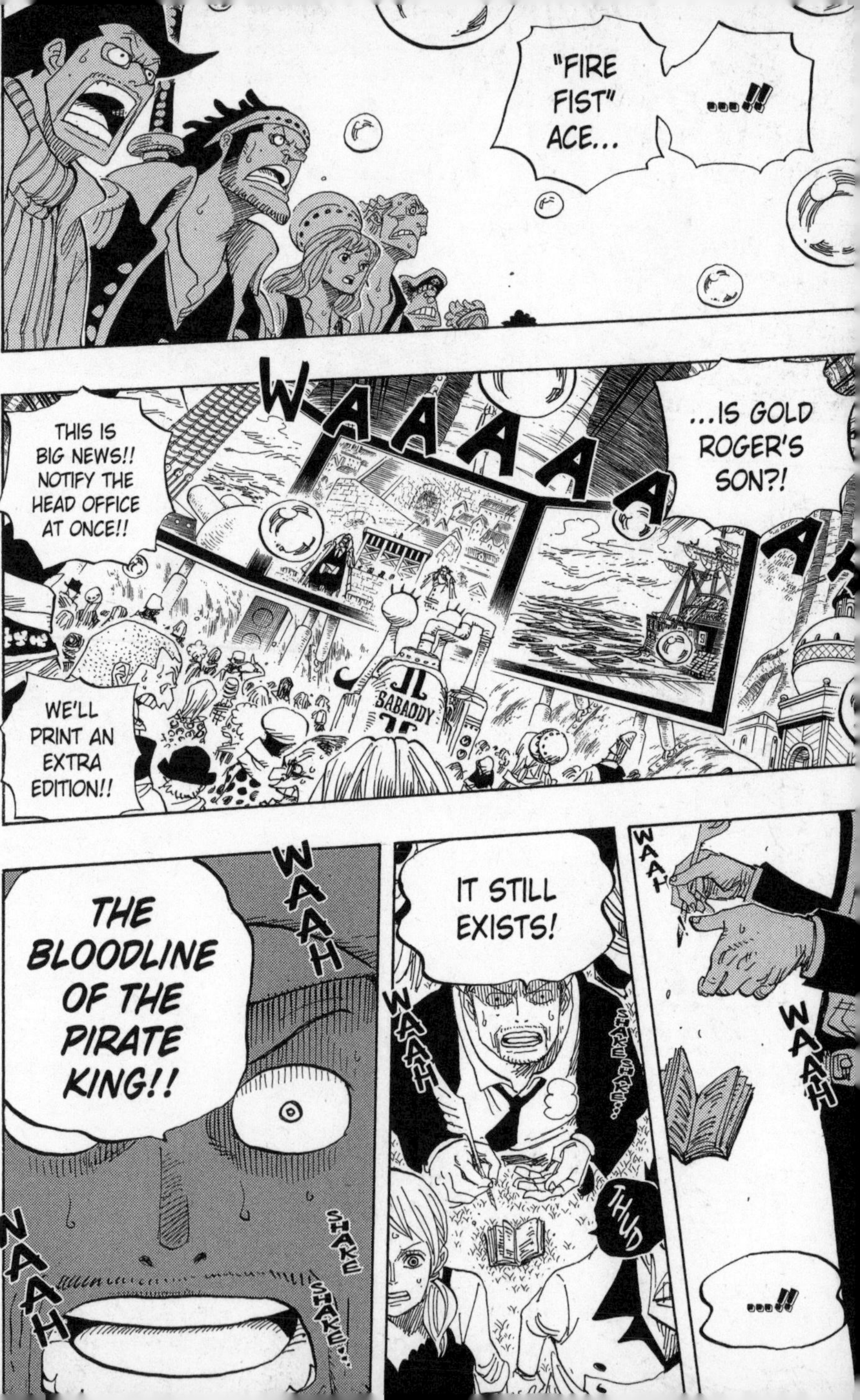
...!!
"FIRE FIST" ACE...
...IS GOLD ROGER'S SON?!
WAAAAAAAH
THIS IS BIG NEWS!! NOTIFY THE HEAD OFFICE AT ONCE!!
SABADDY
WE'LL PRINT AN EXTRA EDITION!!
WAAH
WAAH
...!!
IT STILL EXISTS!
WAAH
SHAKE SHAKE...
THUD
WAAH
THE BLOODLINE OF THE PIRATE KING!!
WAAH
SHAKE SHAKE...

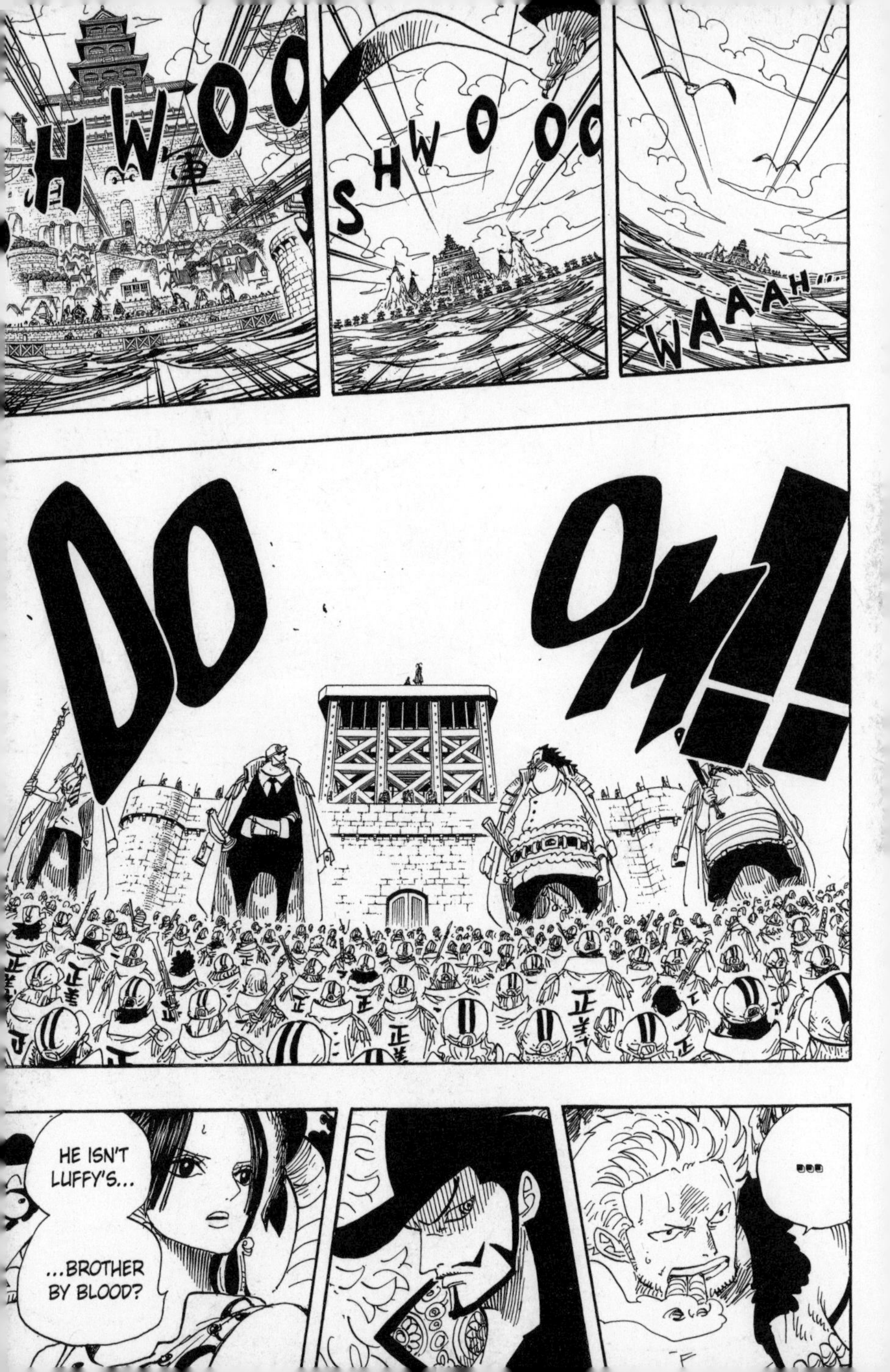
WAAAH
SHWOO
HWOO
DOOM!!
...
HE ISN'T LUFFY'S...
...BROTHER BY BLOOD?

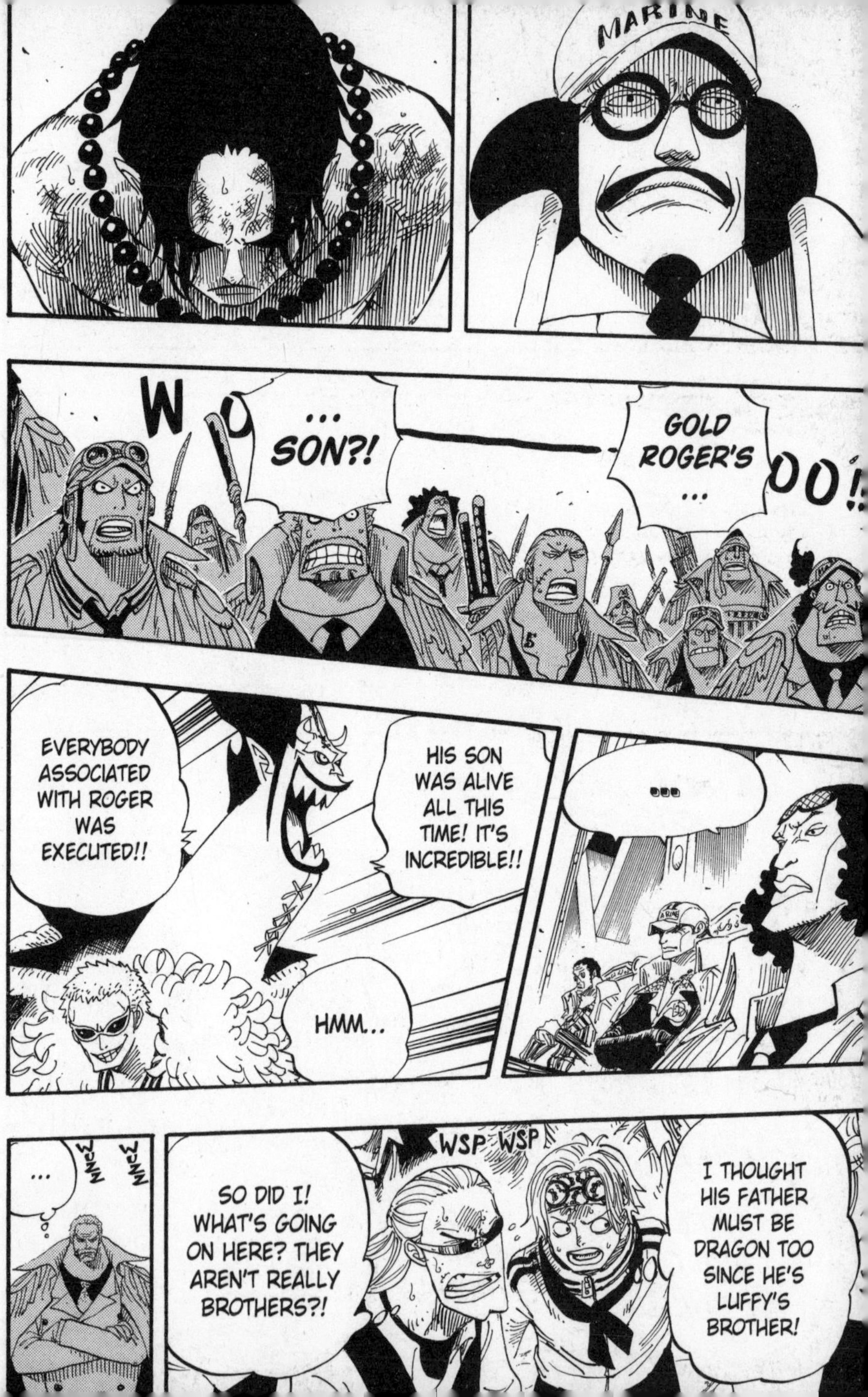

MARINE
GOLD ROGER'S ...
... SON?!
WOOO!!
...
HIS SON WAS ALIVE ALL THIS TIME! IT'S INCREDIBLE!!
EVERYBODY ASSOCIATED WITH ROGER WAS EXECUTED!!
HMM..
WSP WSP
I THOUGHT HIS FATHER MUST BE DRAGON TOO SINCE HE'S LUFFY'S BROTHER!
SO DID I! WHAT'S GOING ON HERE? THEY AREN'T REALLY BROTHERS?!
MUNCH MUNCH
...

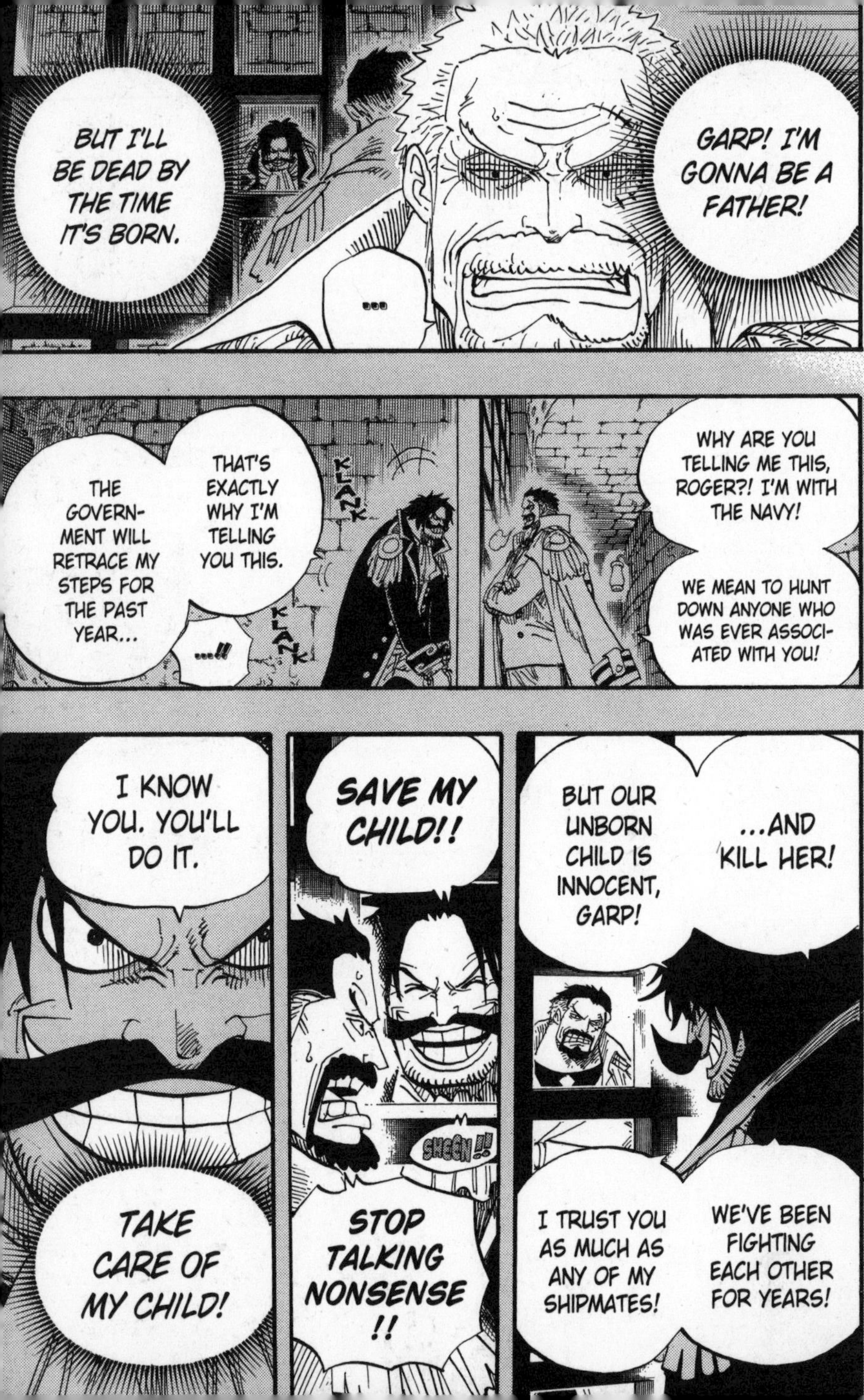
GARP! I'M GONNA BE A FATHER!
BUT I'LL BE DEAD BY THE TIME IT'S BORN.
...
WHY ARE YOU TELLING ME THIS, ROGER?! I'M WITH THE NAVY!
WE MEAN TO HUNT DOWN ANYONE WHO WAS EVER ASSOCIATED WITH YOU!
KLANK
THAT'S EXACTLY WHY I'M TELLING YOU THIS.
THE GOVERNMENT WILL RETRACE MY STEPS FOR THE PAST YEAR...
KLANK
...!!
...AND KILL HER!
BUT OUR UNBORN CHILD IS INNOCENT, GARP!
WE'VE BEEN FIGHTING EACH OTHER FOR YEARS!
I TRUST YOU AS MUCH AS ANY OF MY SHIPMATES!
SAVE MY CHILD!!
SHEEN!!
STOP TALKING NONSENSE!!
I KNOW YOU. YOU'LL DO IT.
TAKE CARE OF MY CHILD!

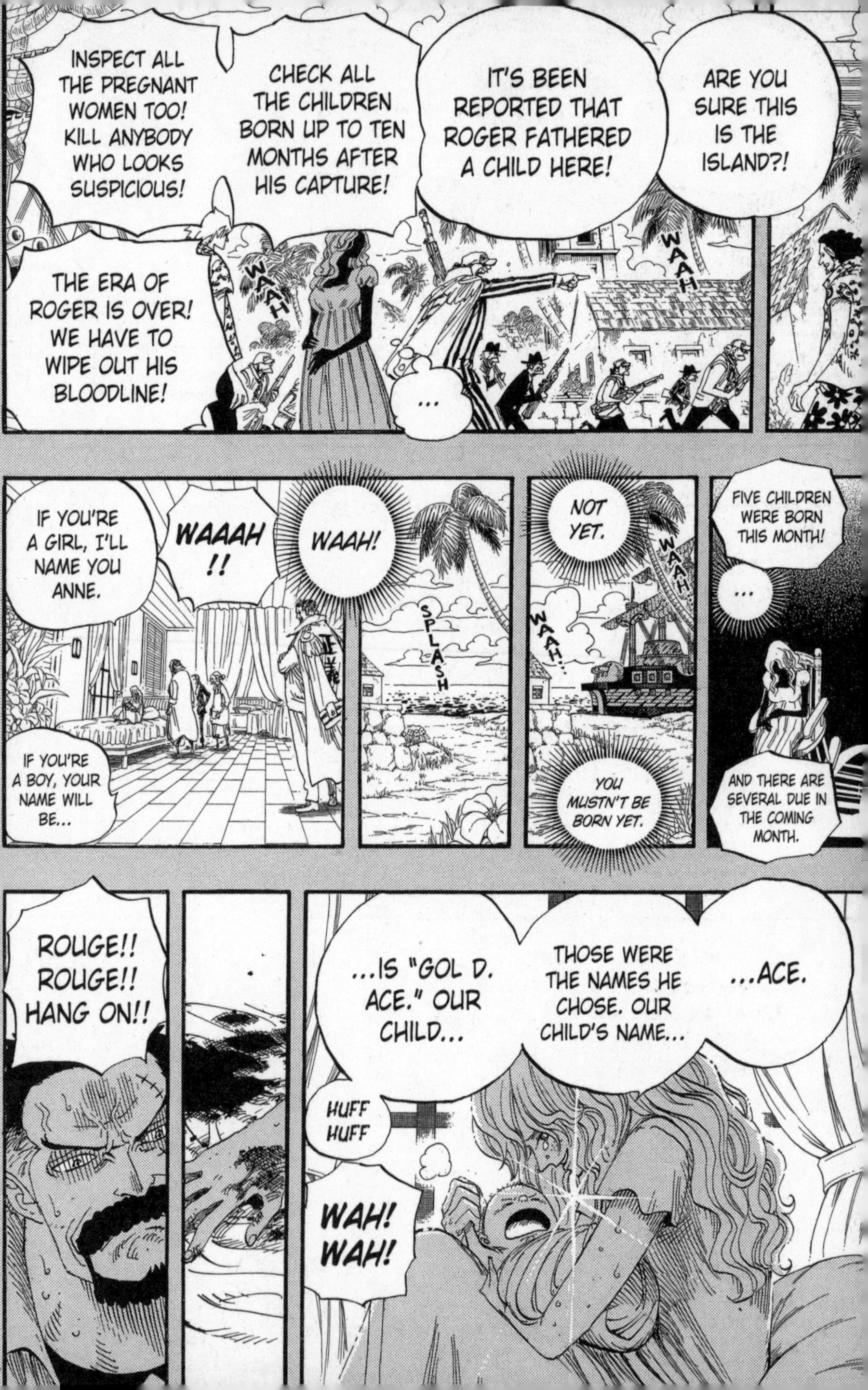
ARE YOU SURE THIS IS THE ISLAND?!
WAAH
IT'S BEEN REPORTED THAT ROGER FATHERED A CHILD HERE!
CHECK ALL THE CHILDREN BORN UP TO TEN MONTHS AFTER HIS CAPTURE!
INSPECT ALL THE PREGNANT WOMEN TOO! KILL ANYBODY WHO LOOKS SUSPICIOUS!
WAAH
...
THE ERA OF ROGER IS OVER! WE HAVE TO WIPE OUT HIS BLOODLINE!
FIVE CHILDREN WERE BORN THIS MONTH!
...
AND THERE ARE SEVERAL DUE IN THE COMING MONTH.
NOT YET.
WAAH
WAAH...
YOU MUSTN'T BE BORN YET.
SPLASH
WAAH!
WAAAH!!
IF YOU'RE A GIRL, I'LL NAME YOU ANNE.
IF YOU'RE A BOY, YOUR NAME WILL BE...
...ACE.
THOSE WERE THE NAMES HE CHOSE. OUR CHILD'S NAME...
...IS "GOL D. ACE." OUR CHILD...
HUFF HUFF
WAH! WAH!
ROUGE!! ROUGE!! HANG ON!!

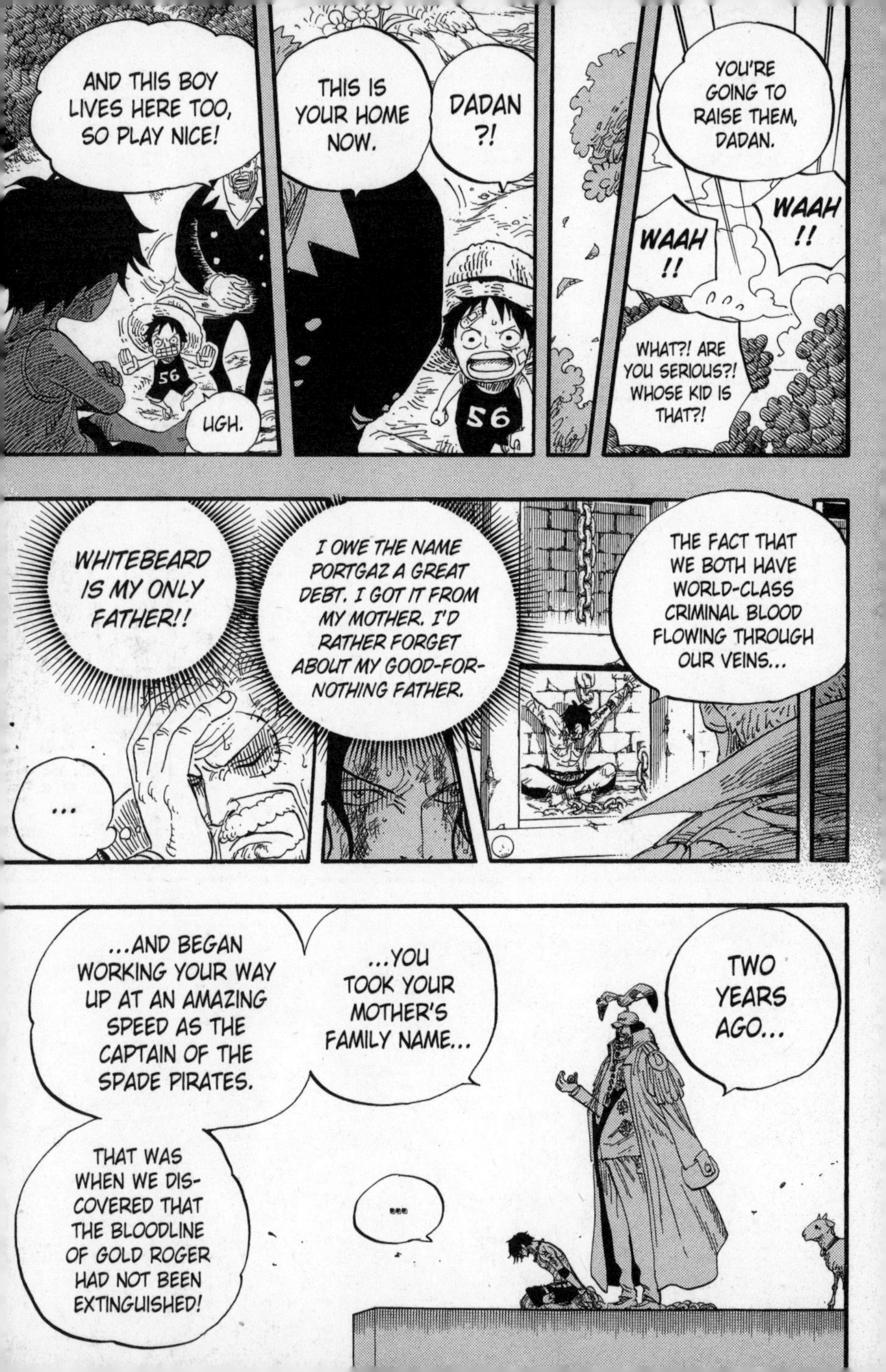
YOU'RE GOING TO RAISE THEM, DADAN.
WAAH!!
WAAH!!
WHAT?! ARE YOU SERIOUS?! WHOSE KID IS THAT?!
DADAN ?!
THIS IS YOUR HOME NOW.
AND THIS BOY LIVES HERE TOO, SO PLAY NICE!
UGH.
THE FACT THAT WE BOTH HAVE WORLD-CLASS CRIMINAL BLOOD FLOWING THROUGH OUR VEINS...
I OWE THE NAME PORTGAZ A GREAT DEBT. I GOT IT FROM MY MOTHER. I'D RATHER FORGET ABOUT MY GOOD-FOR-NOTHING FATHER.
WHITEBEARD IS MY ONLY FATHER!!
...
TWO YEARS AGO...
...YOU TOOK YOUR MOTHER'S FAMILY NAME...
...AND BEGAN WORKING YOUR WAY UP AT AN AMAZING SPEED AS THE CAPTAIN OF THE SPADE PIRATES.
THAT WAS WHEN WE DIS-COVERED THAT THE BLOODLINE OF GOLD ROGER HAD NOT BEEN EXTINGUISHED!
...

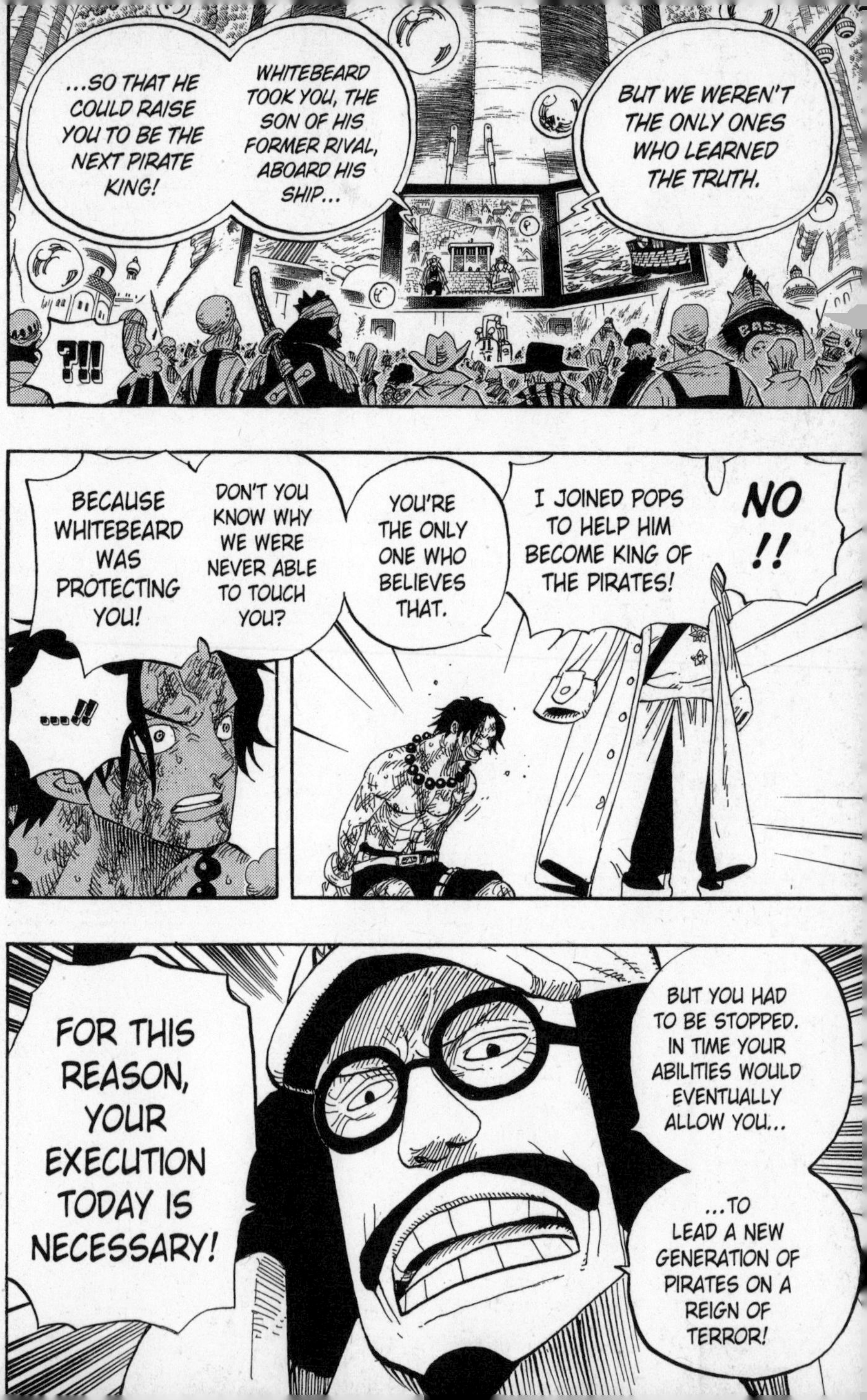
BUT WE WEREN'T THE ONLY ONES WHO LEARNED THE TRUTH.
WHITEBEARD TOOK YOU, THE SON OF HIS FORMER RIVAL, ABOARD HIS SHIP...
...SO THAT HE COULD RAISE YOU TO BE THE NEXT PIRATE KING!
?!!
NO !!
I JOINED POPS TO HELP HIM BECOME KING OF THE PIRATES!
YOU'RE THE ONLY ONE WHO BELIEVES THAT.
DON'T YOU KNOW WHY WE WERE NEVER ABLE TO TOUCH YOU?
BECAUSE WHITEBEARD WAS PROTECTING YOU!
...!!
BUT YOU HAD TO BE STOPPED. IN TIME YOUR ABILITIES WOULD EVENTUALLY ALLOW YOU...
...TO LEAD A NEW GENERATION OF PIRATES ON A REIGN OF TERROR!
FOR THIS REASON, YOUR EXECUTION TODAY IS NECESSARY!

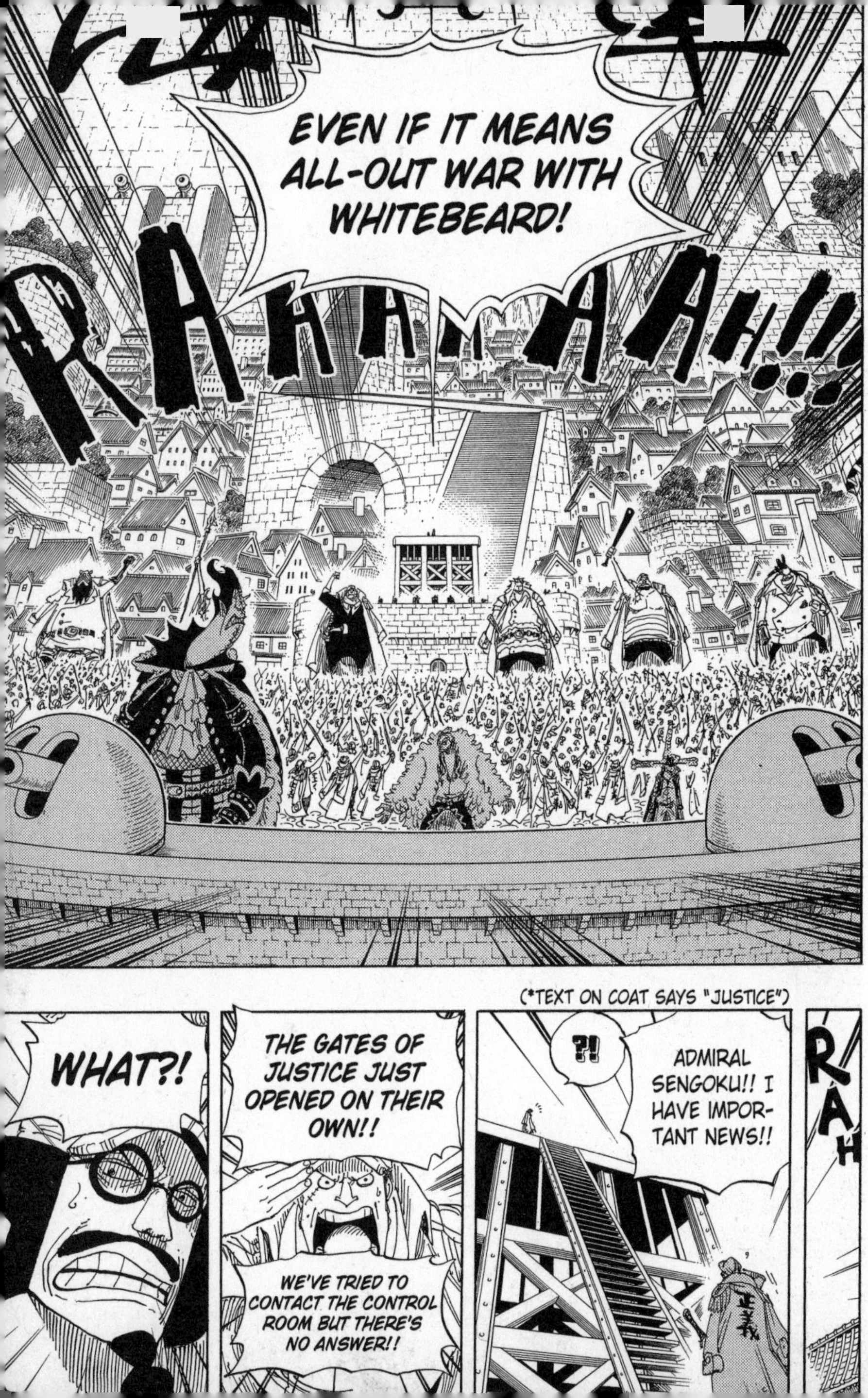
EVEN IF IT MEANS ALL-OUT WAR WITH WHITEBEARD!
RAAAAAAH!!!
RAH
?!
ADMIRAL SENGOKU!! I HAVE IMPORTANT NEWS!!
THE GATES OF JUSTICE JUST OPENED ON THEIR OWN!!
WE'VE TRIED TO CONTACT THE CONTROL ROOM BUT THERE'S NO ANSWER!!
WHAT?!
(*TEXT ON COAT SAYS "JUSTICE")

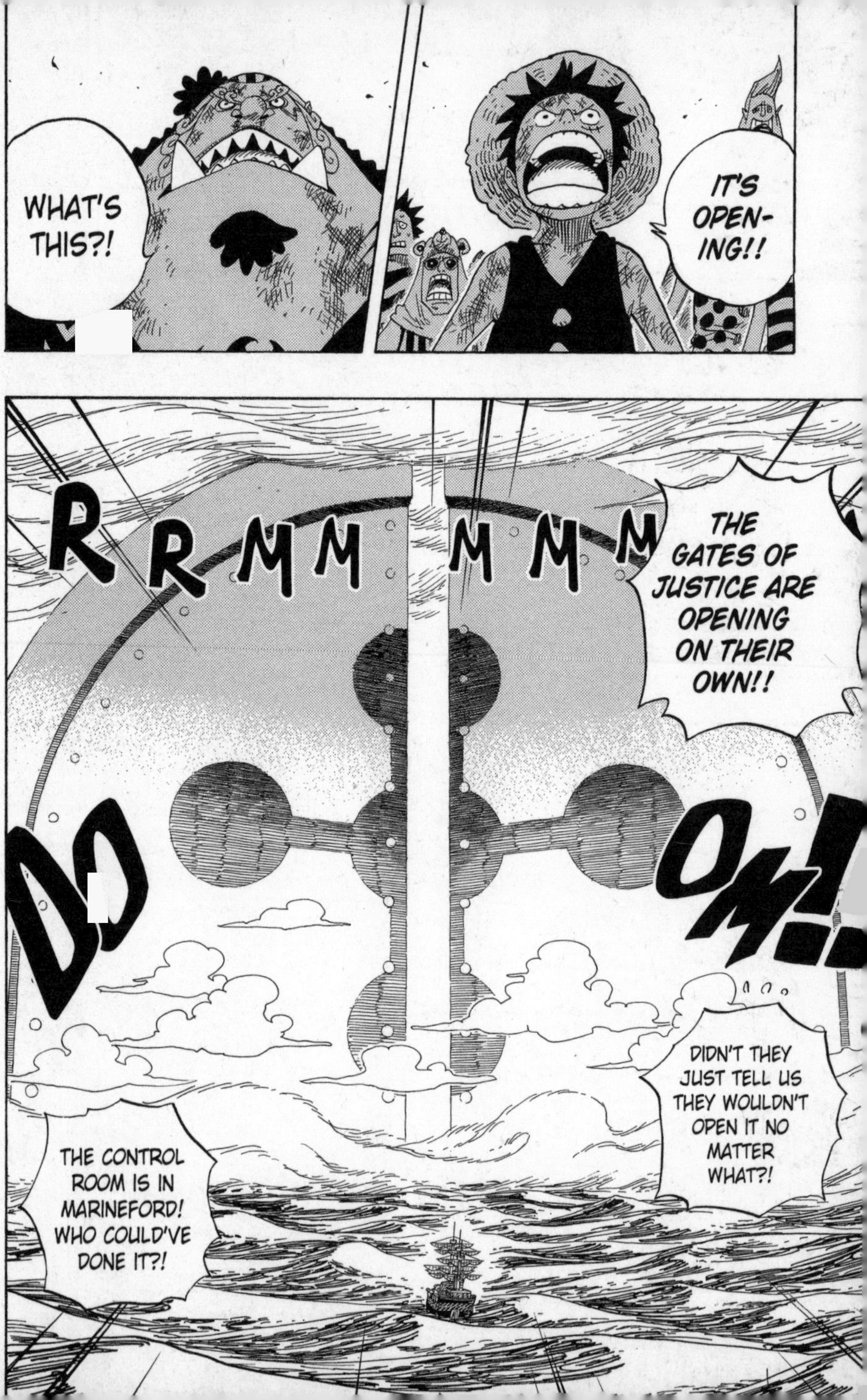
IT'S OPEN-ING!!
WHAT'S THIS?!
RRMMMMMM
THE GATES OF JUSTICE ARE OPENING ON THEIR OWN!!
DOOM!!
DIDN'T THEY JUST TELL US THEY WOULDN'T OPEN IT NO MATTER WHAT?!
THE CONTROL ROOM IS IN MARINEFORD! WHO COULD'VE DONE IT?!

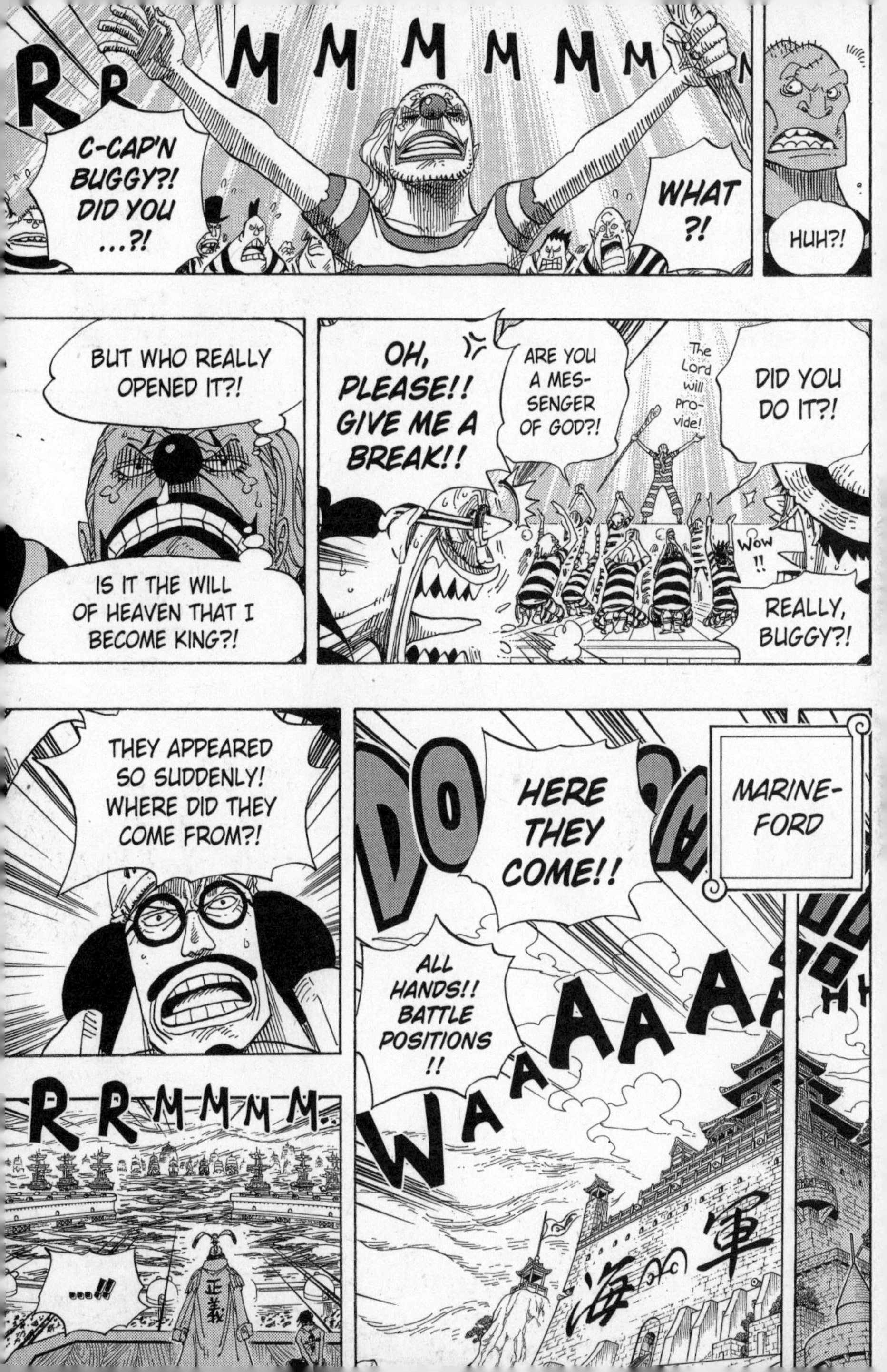
HUH?!
RRMMMMMMM
WHAT?!
C-CAP'N BUGGY?! DID YOU ...?!
DID YOU DO IT?!
The Lord will provide!
ARE YOU A MESSENGER OF GOD?!
OH, PLEASE!! GIVE ME A BREAK!!
WOW!!
REALLY, BUGGY?!
BUT WHO REALLY OPENED IT?!
IS IT THE WILL OF HEAVEN THAT I BECOME KING?!
MARINEFORD
DO
HERE THEY COME!!
ALL HANDS!! BATTLE POSITIONS!!
WAAAAAAA
海軍
THEY APPEARED SO SUDDENLY! WHERE DID THEY COME FROM?!
RRMMMMM
...!!

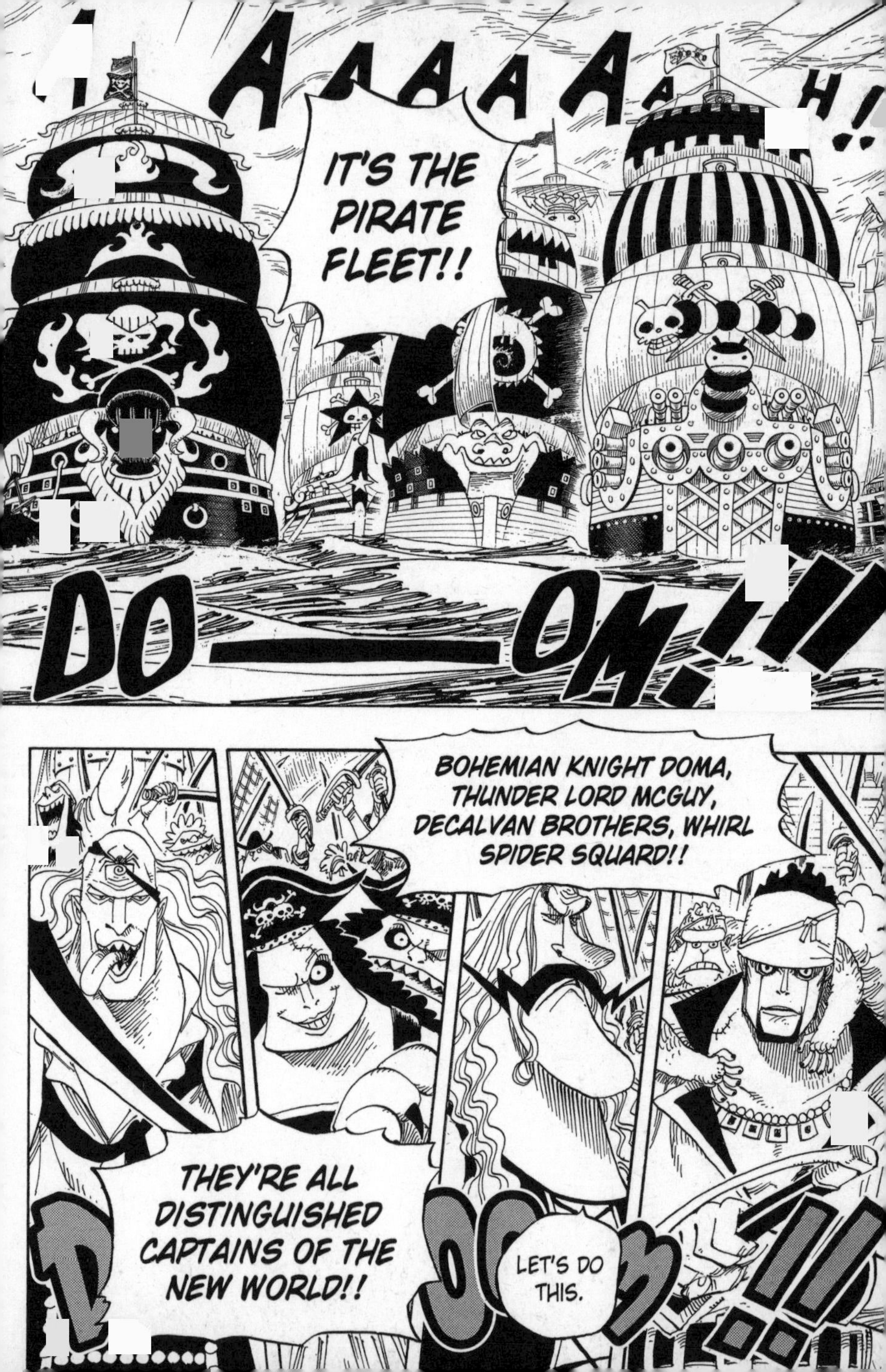
AAAAAAAH!!
IT'S THE PIRATE FLEET!!
DO—OM!!!
BOHEMIAN KNIGHT DOMA, THUNDER LORD MCGUY, DECALVAN BROTHERS, WHIRL SPIDER SQUARD!!
THEY'RE ALL DISTINGUISHED CAPTAINS OF THE NEW WORLD!!
LET'S DO THIS.

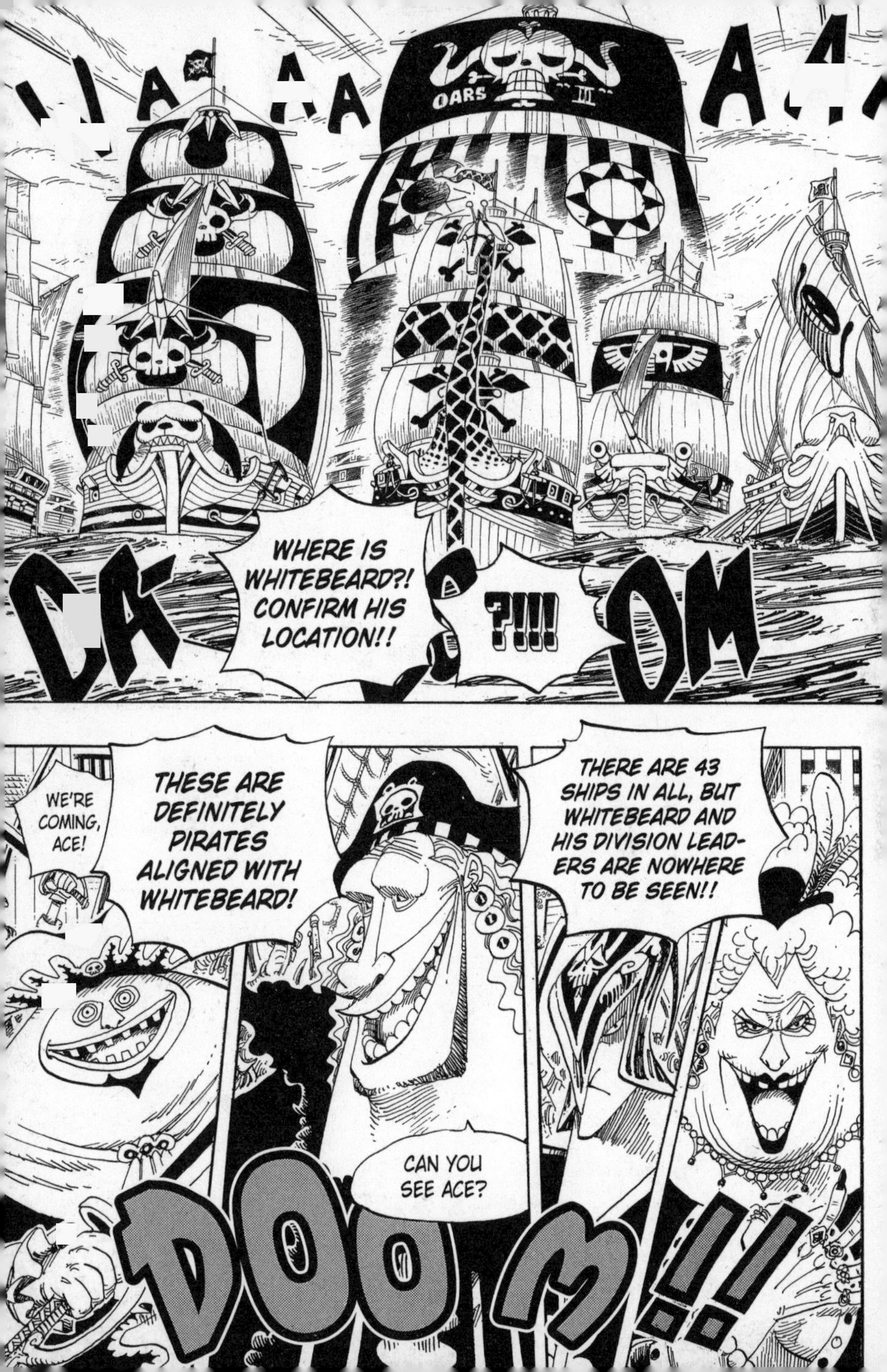
WHERE IS WHITEBEARD?! CONFIRM HIS LOCATION!!
?!!!
THERE ARE 43 SHIPS IN ALL, BUT WHITEBEARD AND HIS DIVISION LEADERS ARE NOWHERE TO BE SEEN!!
THESE ARE DEFINITELY PIRATES ALIGNED WITH WHITEBEARD!
WE'RE COMING, ACE!
CAN YOU SEE ACE?
DOOM!!

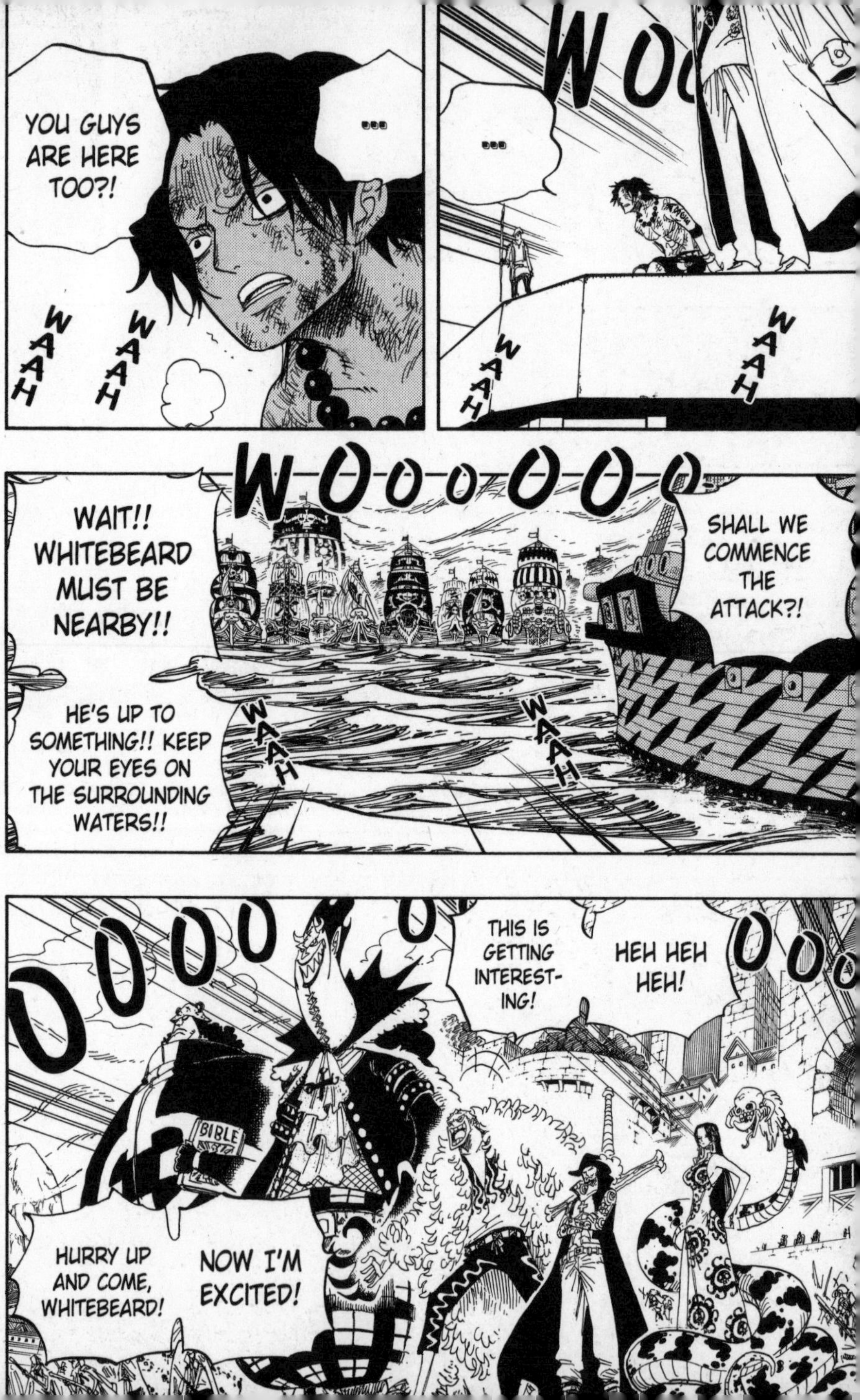
WOO
...
...
WAAH
WAAH
YOU GUYS ARE HERE TOO?!
...
WAAH
WAAH
SHALL WE COMMENCE THE ATTACK?!
WOOOOOOO
WAIT!! WHITEBEARD MUST BE NEARBY!!
HE'S UP TO SOMETHING!! KEEP YOUR EYES ON THE SURROUNDING WATERS!!
WAAH
WAAH
OOO
HEH HEH HEH!
THIS IS GETTING INTEREST-ING!
OOOO
NOW I'M EXCITED!
HURRY UP AND COME, WHITEBEARD!

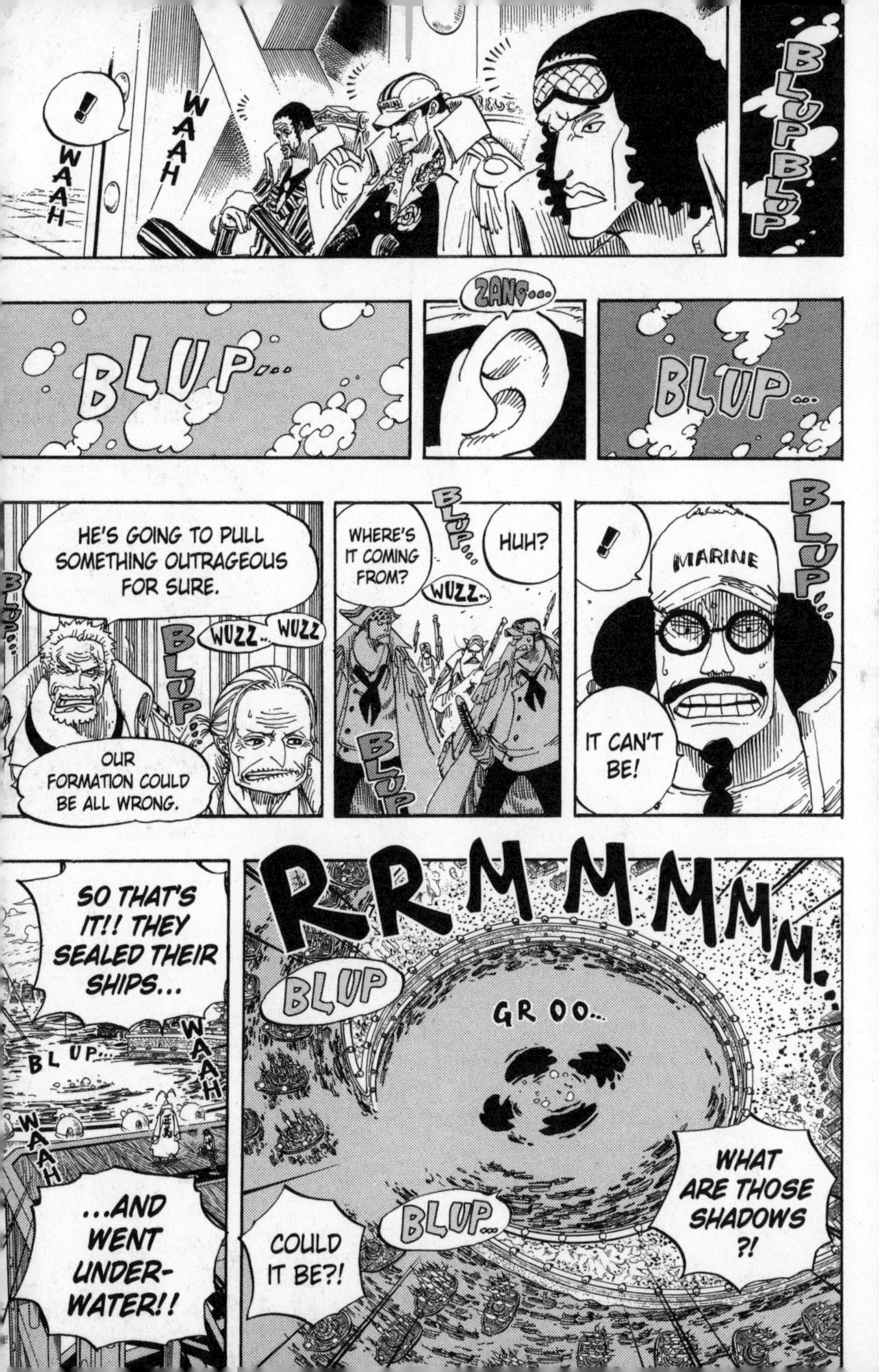
BLUPBLUP
WAAH
WAAH
!
BLUP...
ZANG...
BLUP...
!
BLUP...
IT CAN'T BE!
HUH?
BLUP...
WHERE'S IT COMING FROM?
WUZZ...
BLUP
HE'S GOING TO PULL SOMETHING OUTRAGEOUS FOR SURE.
WUZZ...
WUZZ
BLUP
OUR FORMATION COULD BE ALL WRONG.
BLUP...
RRMMMMM...
WHAT ARE THOSE SHADOWS?!
GROO...
BLUP
BLUP...
COULD IT BE?!
SO THAT'S IT!! THEY SEALED THEIR SHIPS...
WAAH
BLUP...
WAAH
...AND WENT UNDER-WATER!!

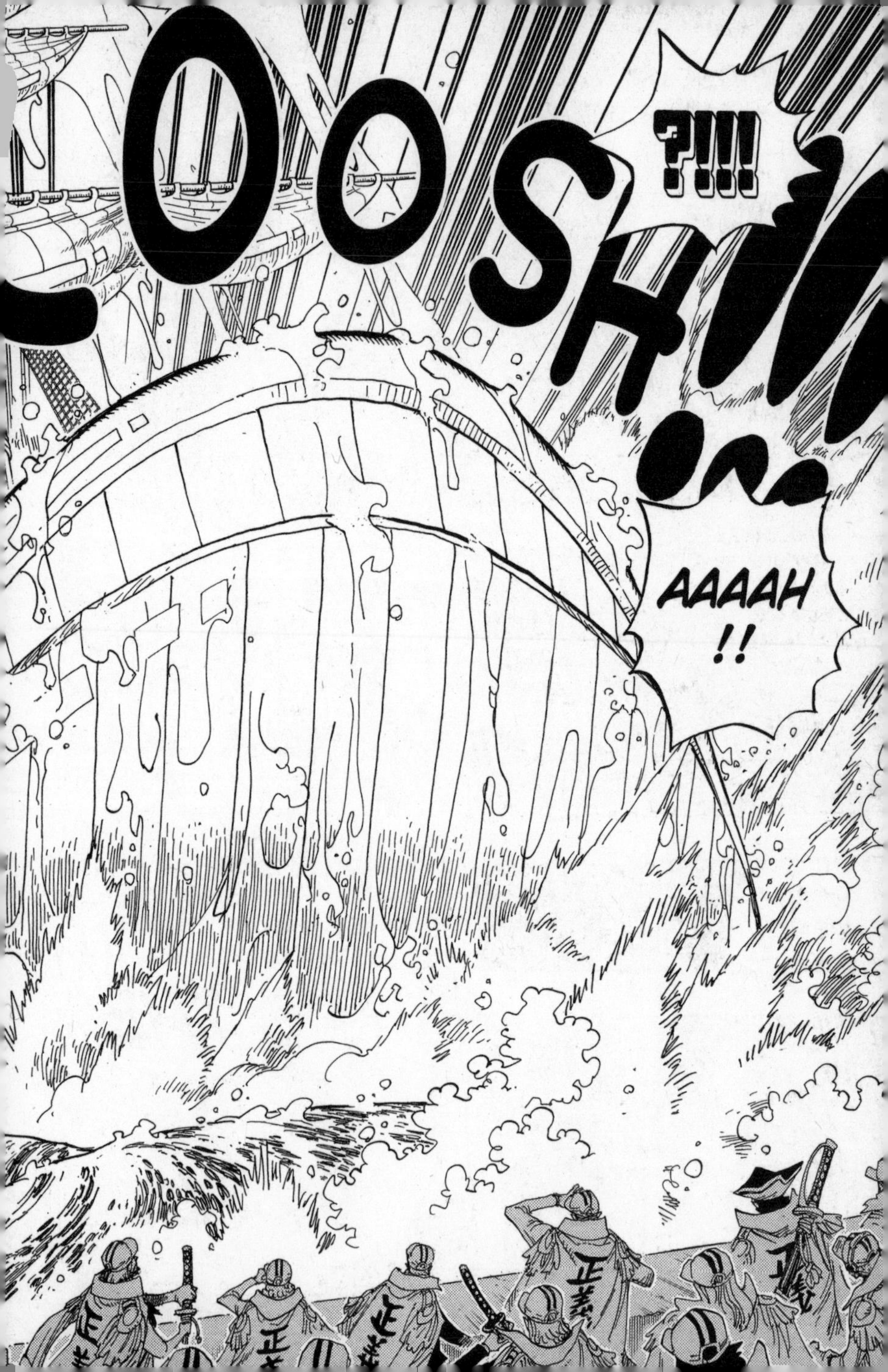

?!!!
AAAAH !!
SPLOOOSH...

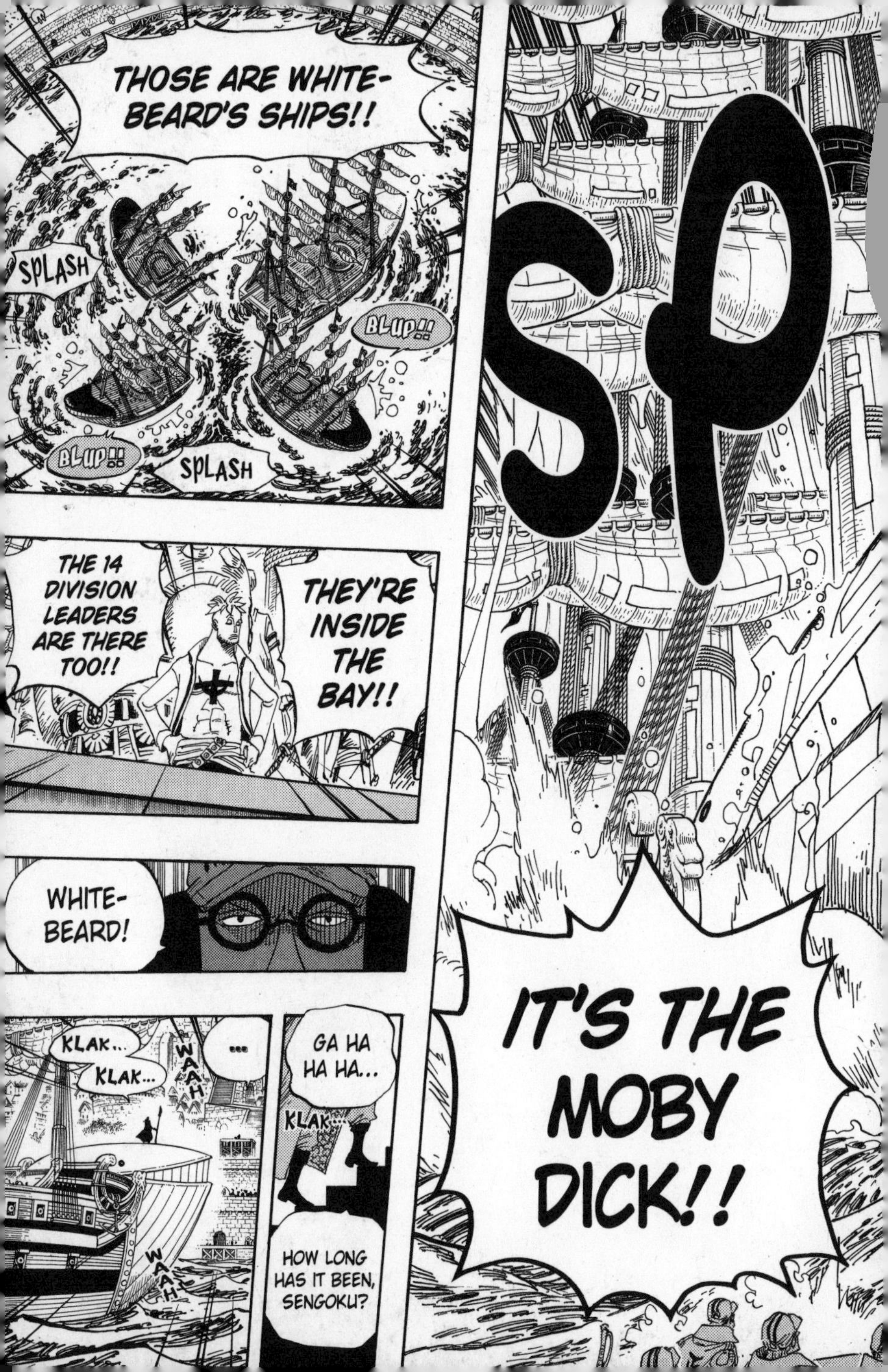
SP
IT'S THE MOBY DICK!!
THOSE ARE WHITE-BEARD'S SHIPS!!
BLUP!!
SPLASH
SPLASH
BLUP!!
THEY'RE INSIDE THE BAY!!
THE 14 DIVISION LEADERS ARE THERE TOO!!
WHITE-BEARD!
GA HA HA HA...
KLAK...
HOW LONG HAS IT BEEN, SENGOKU?
...
WAAH
KLAK...
KLAK...
WAAH

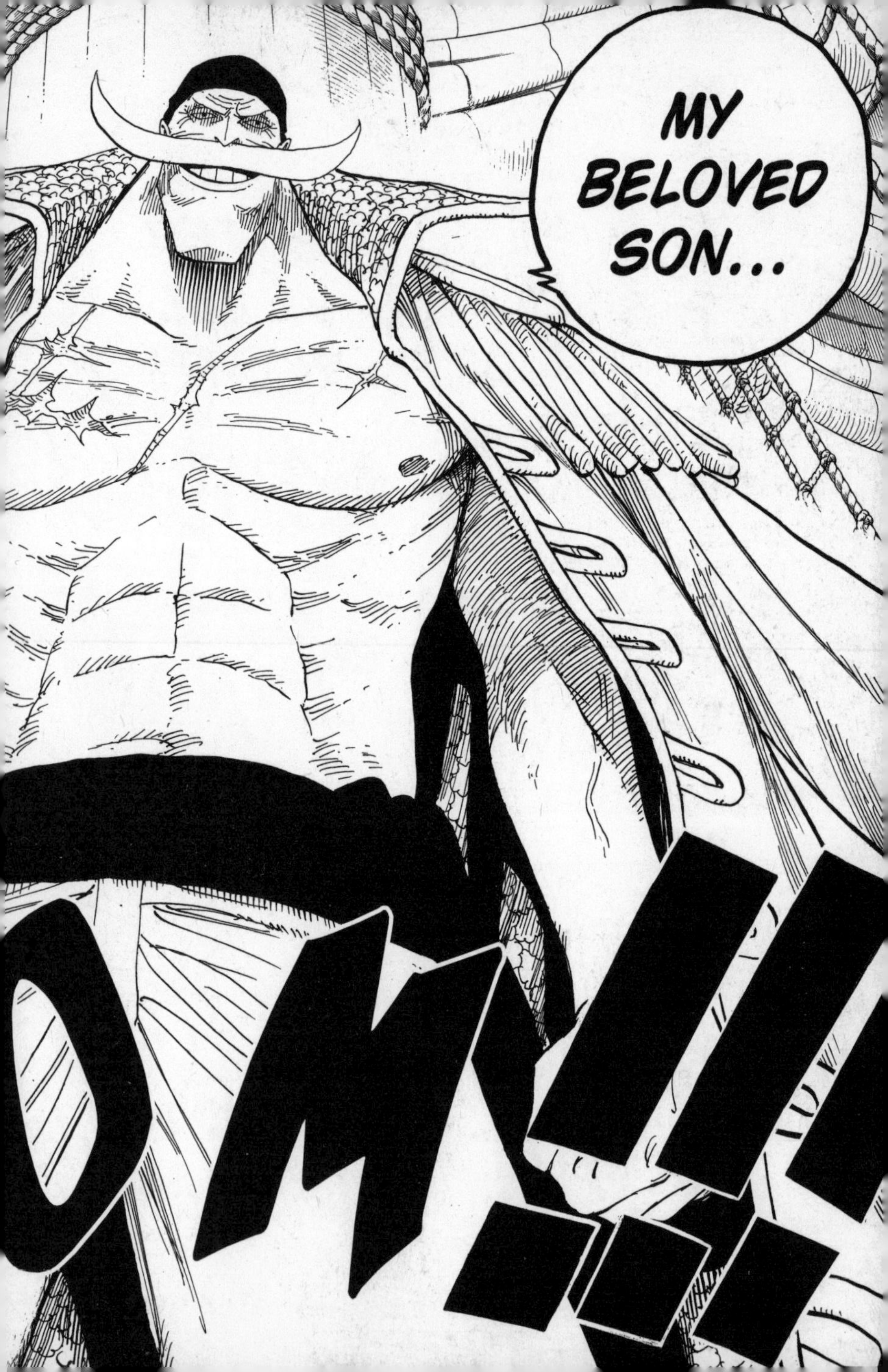
MY BELOVED SON...

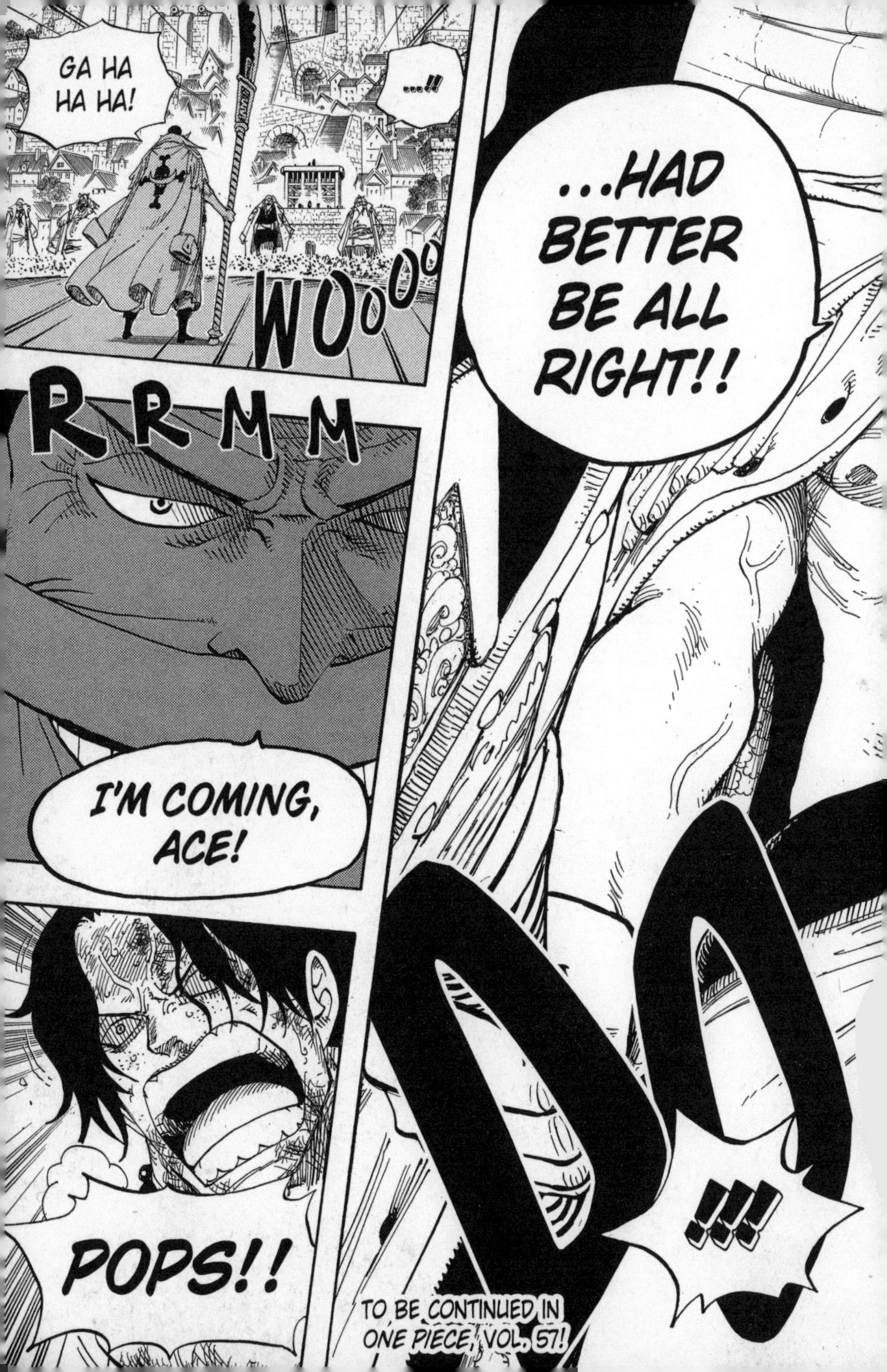
...HAD BETTER BE ALL RIGHT!!
!!!
...!!
GA HA HA HA!
WOOOOO
RRMM
I'M COMING, ACE!
POPS!!

TO BE CONTINUED IN ONE PIECE, VOL. 57!

COMING NEXT VOLUME:

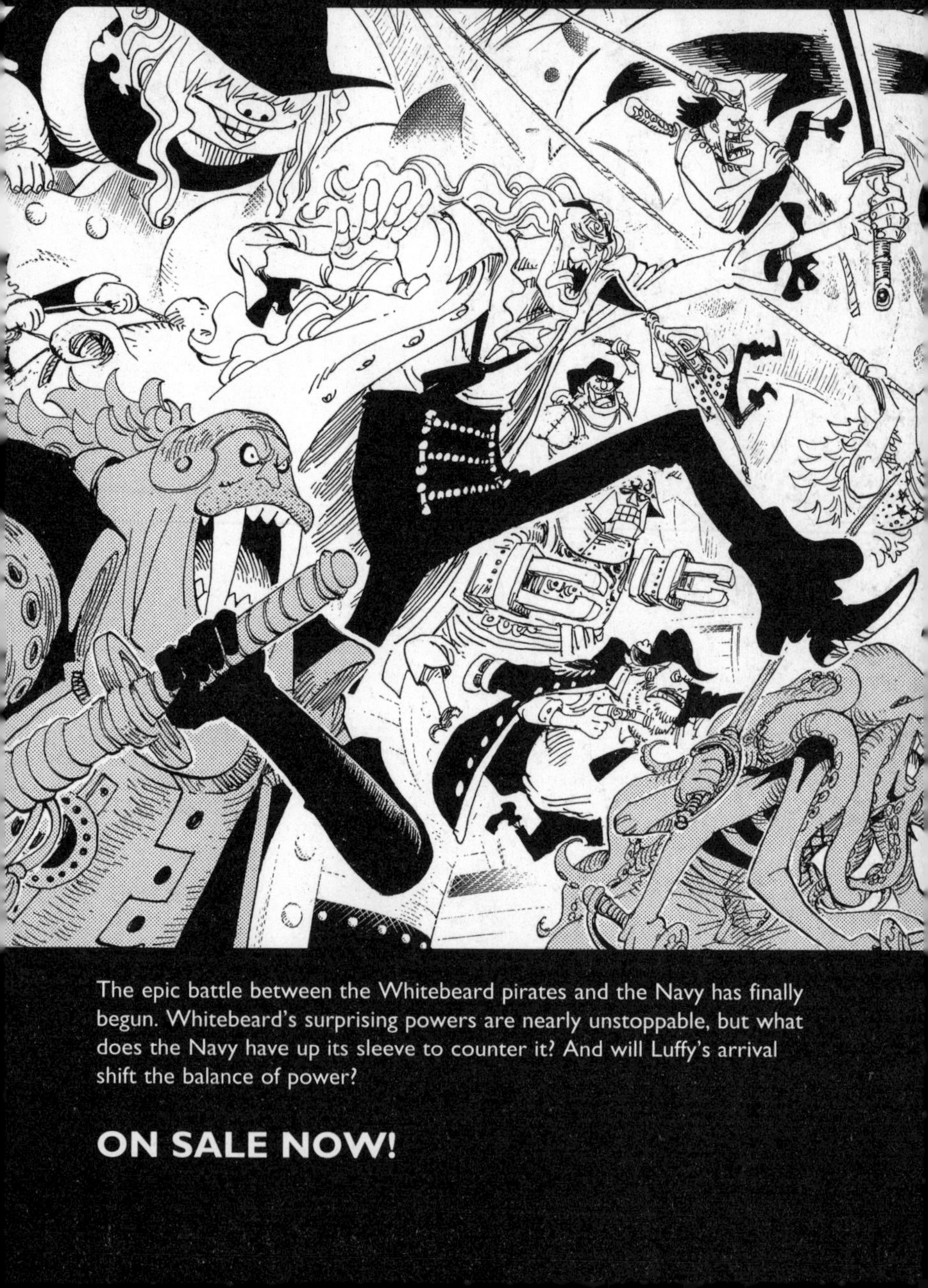

The epic battle between the Whitebeard pirates and the Navy has finally begun. Whitebeard's surprising powers are nearly unstoppable, but what does the Navy have up its sleeve to counter it? And will Luffy's arrival shift the balance of power?

ON SALE NOW!

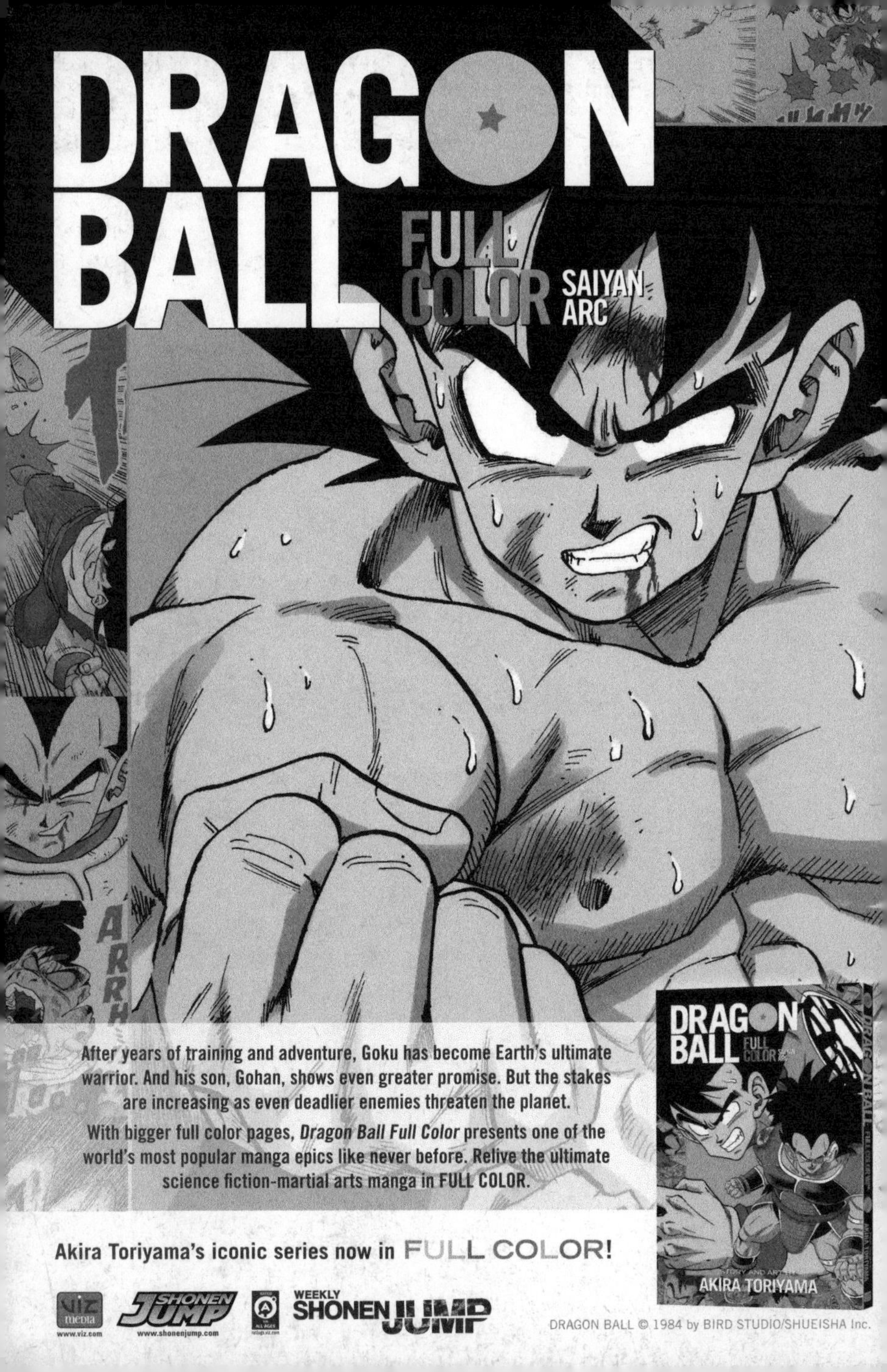
DRAGON BALL FULL COLOR SAIYAN ARC
ARRH
After years of training and adventure, Goku has become Earth's ultimate warrior. And his son, Gohan, shows even greater promise. But the stakes are increasing as even deadlier enemies threaten the planet.
With bigger full color pages, *Dragon Ball Full Color* presents one of the world's most popular manga epics like never before. Relive the ultimate science fiction-martial arts manga in FULL COLOR.
DRAGON BALL FULL COLOR SAIYAN ARC
AKIRA TORIYAMA
Akira Toriyama's iconic series now in FULL COLOR!
viz media
www.viz.com
SHONEN JUMP
www.shonenjump.com
WEEKLY SHONEN JUMP
DRAGON BALL © 1984 by BIRD STUDIO/SHUEISHA Inc.

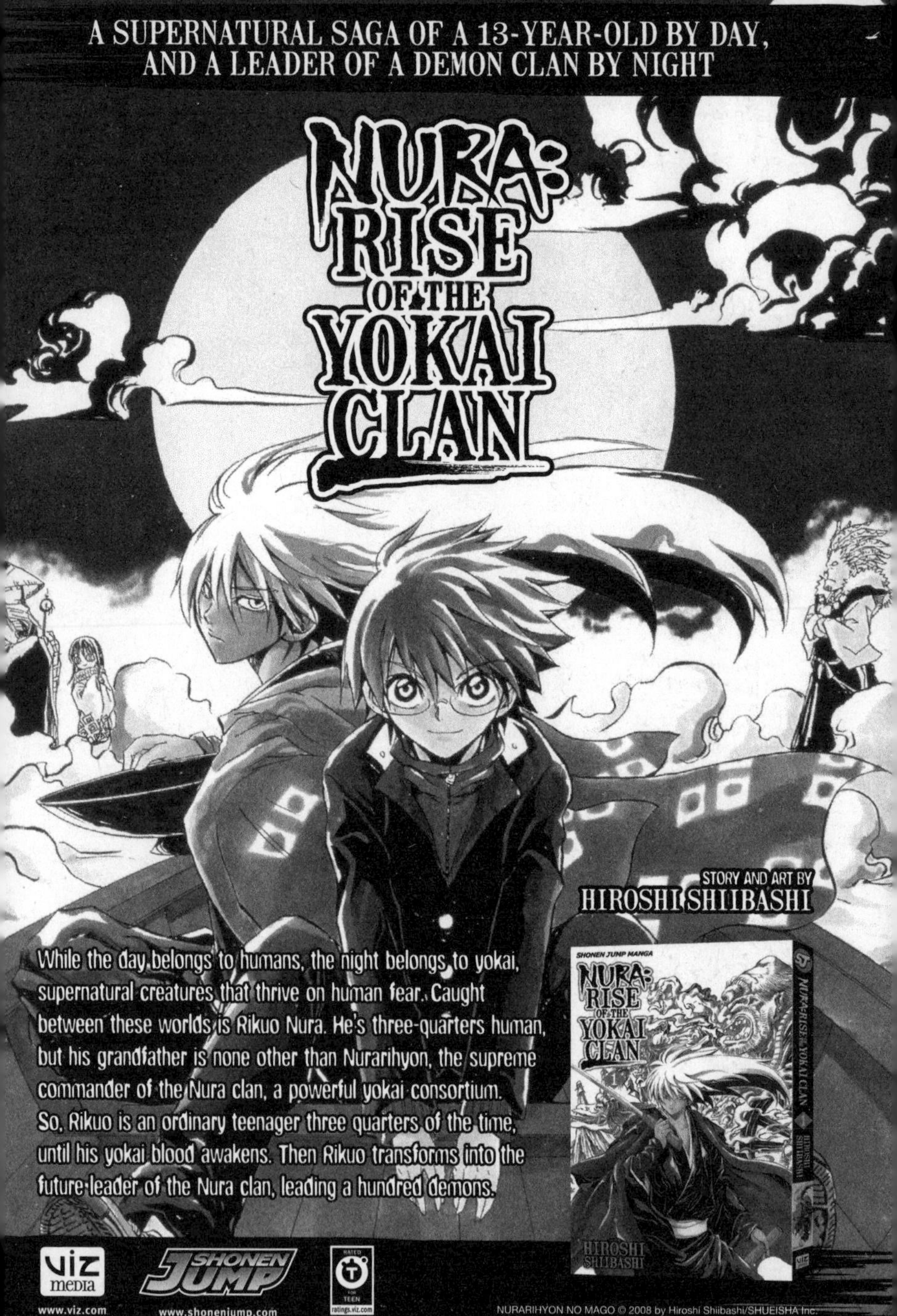
A SUPERNATURAL SAGA OF A 13-YEAR-OLD BY DAY, AND A LEADER OF A DEMON CLAN BY NIGHT
NURA: RISE OF THE YOKAI CLAN
STORY AND ART BY
HIROSHI SHIIBASHI
While the day belongs to humans, the night belongs to yokai, supernatural creatures that thrive on human fear. Caught between these worlds is Rikuo Nura. He's three-quarters human, but his grandfather is none other than Nurarihyon, the supreme commander of the Nura clan, a powerful yokai consortium. So, Rikuo is an ordinary teenager three quarters of the time, until his yokai blood awakens. Then Rikuo transforms into the future leader of the Nura clan, leading a hundred demons.
SHONEN JUMP MANGA
NURA: RISE OF THE YOKAI CLAN
HIROSHI SHIIBASHI
viz media
www.viz.com
SHONEN JUMP
www.shonenjump.com
RATED T FOR TEEN
ratings.viz.com
NURARIHYON NO MAGO © 2008 by Hiroshi Shiibashi/SHUEISHA Inc.